Who's Who in Tudor England

Who's Who in Tudor England

being the fourth volume in the
Who's Who in British History series

C. R. N. ROUTH
(Revised by PETER HOLMES)

Series Editor:
GEOFFREY TREASURE

SHEPHEARD-WALWYN

© 1990 C. R. N. Routh
All rights reserved
First published as *Who's Who in History* Vol. II
by Basil Blackwell, 1964

Revised and enlarged edition first published 1990
by Shepheard-Walwyn (Publishers) Ltd
Suite 34, 26 Charing Cross Road, London WC2H 0DH

British Library Cataloguing in Publication Data

Routh, C. R. N.
  Who's Who in Tudor England. (Who's Who in British
  History series)
  1. England, 1485-1603] Biographies] Collections
  I. Title   II. Series
  942.05'092'2

  ISBN 0-85683-093-3 *cased*
  0 85683-119-0 *limp*

Typesetting by Alacrity Phototypesetters, Banwell Castle,
Weston-super-Mare, Avon.

Printed in Great Britain by BPCC Wheatons Ltd., Exeter

CONTENTS

GENERAL INTRODUCTION

The original volumes in the series *Who's Who in History* were well received by readers who responded favourably to the claim of the late C. R. N. Routh, general editor of the series, that there was a need for a work of reference which should present the latest findings of scholarship in the form of short biographical essays. Published by Basil Blackwell in five volumes, the series covered British history from the earliest times to 1837. It was designed to please several kinds of reader: the 'general reader', the browser who might find it hard to resist the temptation to go from one character to another, and, of course, the student of all ages. Each author sought in his own way to convey more than the bare facts of his subject's life, to place him in the context of his age and to evoke what was distinctive in his character and achievement. At the same time, by using a broadly chronological rather than alphabetical sequence, and by grouping together similar classes of people, each volume provided a portrait of the age. Presenting history in biographical form, it complemented the conventional textbook.

Since the publication of the first volumes of the series in the early sixties the continuing work of research has brought new facts to light and has led to some important revaluations. In particular the late mediaeval period, a hitherto somewhat neglected field, has been thoroughly studied. There has also been intense controversy about certain aspects of Tudor and Stuart history. There is plainly a need for fuller treatment of the mediaeval period than was allowed for in the original series, in which the late W. O. Hassall's volume covered the years 55 B.C. to 1485 A.D. The time seems also to be ripe for a reassessment of some Tudor and Stuart figures. Meanwhile the continued requests of teachers and students for the series to be reprinted encourages the authors of the new series to think that there will be a warm response to a fuller and more comprehensive *Who's Who* which will eventually include the nineteenth and early twentieth centuries. They are therefore grateful to Shepheard-Walwyn for the opportunity to present the new, enlarged *Who's Who*.

Following Volume I, devoted to the Roman and Anglo-Saxon period, two further books cover the Middle Ages. The Tudor volume, by the late C. R. Routh, has been extensively revised by Dr. Peter Holmes. Peter Hill and I have revised for re-publication our own volumes on the Stuart and Georgian periods. Between Edward I's conquest of Wales and the Act of Union which joined England and Scotland in 1707, the authors' prime concern has been England, with Scotsmen and Irishmen figuring only if they happened in any way to be prominent in English history. In the eighteenth century Scotsmen come into the picture, in the nineteenth Irishmen, in their own right, as inhabitants of Great Britain. It is hoped that full justice will be done to Scotsmen and Irishmen – and indeed to some early Welshmen – in subsequent volumes devoted to the history of those countries. When the series is complete, we believe that it will provide a comprehensive work of reference which will stand the test of time. At a time when so much historical writing is necessarily becoming more technical, more abstract, or simply more specialised, when textbooks seem so often to have little room to spare for the men and women who are the life and soul of the past, there is a place for a history of our country which is composed of the lives of those who helped make it what it was, and is. In contributing to this history the authors can be said to have taken heed of the stern warning of Trevor Roper's inaugural lecture at Oxford in 1957 against 'the removal of humane studies into a specialisation so remote that they cease to have that lay interest which is their sole ultimate justification'.

The hard pressed examinee often needs an essay which puts an important life into perspective. From necessarily brief accounts he may learn valuable lessons in proportion, concision and relevance. We hope that he will be tempted to find out more and so have added, wherever possible, the titles of books for further reading. Mindful of his needs, we have not however confined our attention to those who have left their mark on church and state. The man who invented the umbrella, the archbishop who shot a gamekeeper, a successful highwayman and an unsuccessful admiral find their place among the great and good. Nor have we eschewed anecdote or turned a blind eye to folly or foible: it is not the authors' view that history which is instructive cannot also be entertaining.

With the development of a secure and civilised society, the range of characters becomes richer, their achievements more diverse. Besides the soldiers, politicians and churchmen who dominate the mediaeval scene there are merchants, inventors, industrialists; more scholars, lawyers, artists; explorers and colonial pioneers. More is known about more people and the task of selection becomes ever harder. Throughout, whether looking at the mediaeval warrior, the Elizabethan seaman, the Stuart radical or the eighteenth century entrepreneur, the authors have been guided by the criterion of excellence. To record the achievements of those few who have had the chance to excel and who have left a name behind them is not to denigrate the unremarkable or unremarked for whom there was no opportunity to shine or chronicler at hand to describe what they made or did. It is not to deny that a Neville or a Pelham might have died obscure if he had not been born to high estate. It is to offer, for the instruction and inspiration of a generation which has been led too often to believe that individuals count for little in the face of the forces which shape economy and society, the conviction that a country is as remarkable as the individuals of which it is composed. In these pages there will be found examples of heroism, genius, and altruism; of self-seeking and squalor. There will be little that is ordinary. It is therefore the hope of the authors that there will be little that is dull.

GEOFFREY TREASURE
Harrow

PREFACE TO THE SECOND EDITION

The task I was invited to perform was to bring the late Mr Routh's text up to date. This has involved a major revision of the entries for the principal characters: kings, queens, and their ministers. I have also done my best to check all the other entries for errors, and to alter them in the light of the progress of historical research in the quarter century since the first edition was written. Needless to say, there will be biographers whose work I have omitted to consult, but I hope they are not many. I have brought the short bibliographies up to date as far as possible. Large parts of the book remain unaltered, however, and while these parts contain nothing with which I disagree strongly, they cannot, of course, reflect my own opinions.

P. J. HOLMES
September 1989

PREFACE TO THE FIRST EDITION

The second volume of *Who's Who in History* * covers the years 1485 to 1603 and deals with England and Wales. These years form one of the great creative periods in English history, comparable, for example, with the nineteenth century. Both experienced a tremendous revolution: in the Tudor age an ecclesiastical and doctrinal revolution, the Industrial Revolution in the Victorian age: both saw the British People travelling to the ends of their known world in search of wealth and trade: in both there was a great flowering of English literature: to each a woman on the throne bequeathed her name. The problem has been to know whom to include and whom to omit in this selection of Tudor biographies. Although the size of the book has been considerably increased beyond the original intention, space could not be found for all the men and women who

x

might be thought to have strong claims to be included. Very reluctantly, in order to avoid scrappy biographies, I have left out all Scottish and Irish characters, the printers, the musicians, most of the writers and all the lesser statesmen or politicians. It may be possible to bring all these omissions together in another volume later on.

I wish specially to thank the Librarian and his staff of the Public Library at Stratford-on-Avon for their unfailing help, courtesy and co-operation. They have spared no trouble to meet my incessant and often baffling demand for books. No doubt there are many other towns as well catered for as Stratford-on-Avon: I have not met them.

Above all I must thank Professor Joel Hurstfield and Mr. Christopher Morris for their great kindness in reading this book in typescript. Their time and scholarship has been put at my disposal most generously and their conscientious reading and penetrating criticisms have saved me from innumerable errors. What errors remain are mine and not theirs. I am grateful also to Mr. William Baring Pemberton for reading the page-proofs.

Finally, it is a very great pleasure to me to put on record how much I have appreciated the unfailing patience, courtesy and friendship of Mr. J. A. Cutforth.

C. R. N. ROUTH
1964

* Basil Blackwell, 1964.

LIST OF ILLUSTRATIONS

The author and publisher wish to express their grateful thanks to the owners of the portraits listed below for permission to reproduce them in this book. Unless otherwise stated they are from the collection of the National Portrait Gallery in London.

TABLE I.—TUDOR AND STUART SUCCESSION

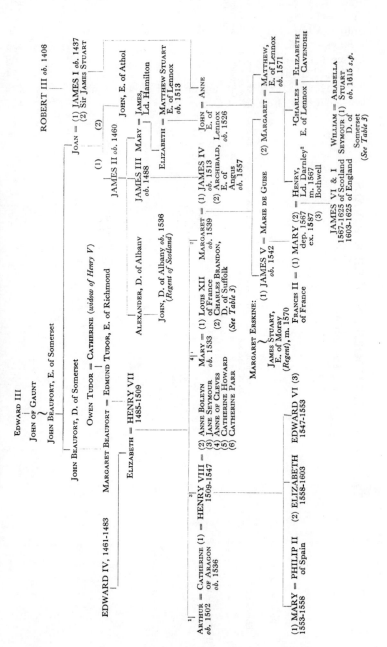

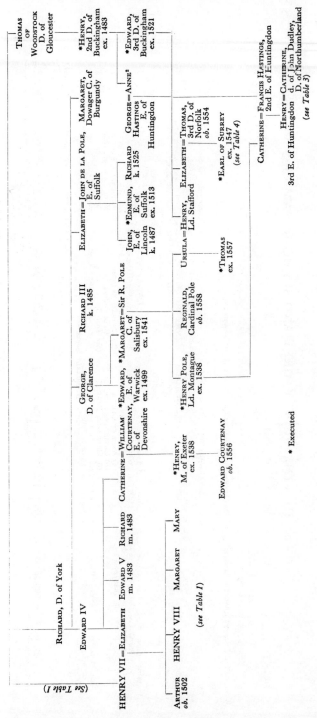

TABLE II.—THE TUDORS AND THEIR RIVALS

TABLE III.—THE DUDLEY, GREY AND SEYMOUR FAMILIES

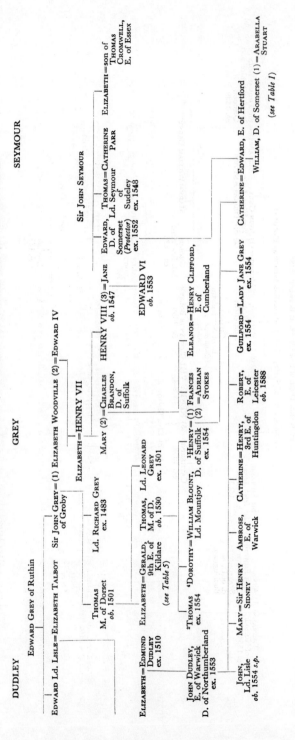

TABLE IV.—THE HOWARD FAMILY AND DACRE FAMILY

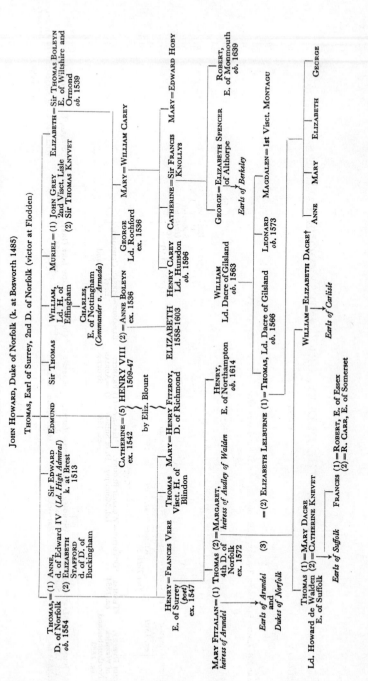

WHO'S WHO IN TUDOR ENGLAND

MARGARET BEAUFORT (1443–1509), Countess of Richmond, the mother of Henry VII, was the daughter and heiress of John Beaufort, Duke of Somerset and through him was descended from John of Gaunt, son of Edward III. She was contracted to marry while still a child John de la Pole, but the marriage was dissolved. Her next husband was Edmund Tudor and she wed him at the age of twelve (1455), then buried him and bore his son, the future King of England, all before she was fourteen. She went on to marry Henry Stafford and finally Lord Stanley, probably in 1473.

It is not too much to claim that she placed her son on the throne of England. She certainly gave him his claim to the throne, for through his father he had none. She played little part in his early education, but was in a position to help him flee abroad to safety in 1471, when the victory of Edward IV over the Lancastrians, and more important the death of Henry VI and his son, put the young Henry Tudor's life in danger, for he was now the leading male representative of the Red Rose. In 1483, after Richard III had seized the throne, she plotted to overthrow him, encouraging the Duke of Buckingham to rise and sending to her son in exile, urging him to invade England. The plot failed, and she narrowly missed death at Richard's hands. In 1485, however, her plans bore fruit and what had been started two years before was finished when Henry VII won the battle of Bosworth. In the battle it was the support or neutrality of her husband's family (the Stanleys) which gave Henry victory. Henry's marriage soon after to Elizabeth of York, which joined the houses of York and Lancaster, was also her handiwork.

Henry VII recognized the services his mother had performed for him. When answering a request of hers, he wrote, 'I shall be glad to please you as your heart desire it, and I know well that I am as much bounden so to do, as any creature living for the great and singular motherly love and affection that it hath pleased you at all times to bear me.' Margaret's letters to him were equally affectionate: Henry was 'my own sweet and most dear king and all my worldly joy' and 'my good and precious prince, king, and only beloved son.' The

1

Lady Margaret Beaufort
(Artist: Unknown)

Spanish ambassador reported in 1498 that she was one of the most important advisers of the King, but we know little in detail of the work she did. The King allowed her to sign her name 'Margaret R.', apparently, as if she were a queen herself.

Polydore Vergil described Margaret as 'a most worthy woman

whom no one can extoll too much or too often for her sound sense and holiness of life.' Her chaplain was John Fisher. She was a great patron of the Arts, giving her support to John Skelton and to Bernard André, the blind poet laureate. She translated Thomas à Kempis into English and gave her support to William Caxton. She (with Fisher's help) did more for Cambridge University than anyone before or since, founding two colleges (Christ's and St John's), encouraging a protégé to found another and giving generously herself (Jesus), and helping a fourth considerably (Queens'). She endowed the Lady Margaret Professorships of Divinity at both universities. She visited Cambridge to supervise her work, having a suite of rooms above the Master's Lodge in Christ's College. Like many Catholics of her generation, she believed in an active, learned ministry for the Church, endowing a preachership at Cambridge with the condition that the priests appointed should give a dozen lectures during their terms of office in a number of rural parishes.

HENRY VII (1457–1509), was born in Pembroke Castle on 28 January 1457 and came to the throne of England in 1485. His mother was Margaret Beaufort and from her he derived his claim to the throne. His father was Edmund of Hadham, Earl of Richmond, the son of a Welshman named Owen ap Meredith ap Tudur who had the good fortune to marry Catherine of Valois, the widow of Henry V and a French princess. The Tudur (it was also spelt Tydier, Tidir, Tyther) gives us our Tudor, although it might just as well have been Meredith, and with more justice Beaufort. Henry was therefore part-Welsh, but also had English, French and Bavarian blood in his veins, and a lot more besides. He was Earl of Richmond from the moment of his birth, since his father had died a few months before. As a child, he was no more than a wealthy nobleman's son and had little hope of becoming king. His parentage and connections placed him on the Lancastrian side in politics and after the Yorkist victory in 1461 he was taken into the custody of Lord Herbert, who gained rights of wardship over him, saw to his education and probably planned for him to marry his own daughter, Maud. The see-saw of the Wars of the Roses led to a brief Lancastrian recovery in 1470–1, and Henry was taken in tow by his uncle, Jasper Tudor, Earl of Pembroke. When the Lancastrians were finally defeated in 1471, Jasper fled into exile with the young Henry, who was now a far more important person, since a series of deaths made him the chief Lancastrian claimant to the throne of England. Henry passed the next twelve years under the protection of the Duke of Brittany, although Edward IV, the Yorkist King, did what he could to have him returned. His chance to seize the throne came when in 1483 Edward IV died and Richard, Duke of Gloucester, was foolish enough to seize the throne and (all reputable historians agree) murder his nephews. It was fortunate for Henry that he was the right age to take advantage of this opportunity. His first attempt to invade England, in 1483, failed when his ships were dispersed by storms, although this again was probably fortunate since the uprising of the Duke of Buckingham, which he hoped to join, had already come to an unsuccessful end by then. Henry was now forced to leave his refuge in Brittany following this set-back, but was received in France (after all, his grand-mother had been a French princess) and was given money to raise an army by the French King. On 1 August 1485 he embarked from Honfleur and landed at Milford Haven with between three and four thousand men. He marched into England, but received little support as he did so. Richard III, a seasoned campaigner, should have defeated Henry at the Battle of Bosworth, but the treachery of Sir William Stanley (Henry's step-uncle) and the doubtful loyalty to Richard of Lord Stanley (Henry's step-father) was decisive. Richard III was killed on the battle-field and dragged naked behind a horse. The story that Richard's crown was found in a hawthorn tree seems to be untrue, although the Tudors did use the thorn-bush as one of their heraldic emblems.

Henry VII was the most successful of the Tudor monarchs. He may be said to have enjoyed certain advantages when he came to the throne. There was a considerable desire for peace among the people of England in 1485 and they were prepared to follow, to obey and honour a king who could bring an end to civil war. Richard III had been unpopular, especially in the South of England. The Yorkists had succeeded in killing off one another to such a degree that adult alternative candidates for the throne were few. On the Lancastrian side, there was only the Duke of Buckingham and he was a minor, whom Henry wisely entrusted to his mother, Margaret Beaufort. The machinery of government was largely intact, and under Edward IV (1461–70, 1471–83) it had enjoyed a period of recovery and even

Henry VII
(Artist: M. Sittow)

some degree of improvement. However, these advantages should not blind us to the grave problems Henry faced. His experience of government was nil: he brought with him from exile a devoted band of followers, but few real experts in the field of government. His claim to the throne was rather weak, since it rested on the marriage of John of Gaunt (his mother's great-grandfather) to Catherine Swynford, a marriage which while it had been legitimised by parliament in 1397 had subsequently been made valid only on the condition that no descendants should use it to claim the throne. The last four kings of England, however good their right to the throne, had all been deposed at one time or another, and three of them killed in the process. Henry's own victory at Bosworth showed the power of the nobility to make or break a king, and his exile in France and Brittany demonstrated how foreign powers might seek to exploit civil dissensions in England. It says a great deal for Henry's abilities that he was able to overcome these problems.

Henry's first great achievement was to bring the Wars of the Roses to an end and to establish the Tudor dynasty firmly on the throne of England. He married Elizabeth of York and she soon bore him an heir. This did much to unite the Yorkist and Lancastrian factions and to give a degree of confidence to the new regime. Threats to the security of his throne were countered with all the resources at Henry's disposal, and in the end both Simnel and Warbeck were defeated. Henry developed a sophisticated intelligence network which helped protect his position from the danger of Yorkist subversion. In 1502, a new threat emerged in the shape of Edmund de la Pole, Earl of Suffolk, no impostor, but a real representative of the White Rose party. Careful espionage, patient diplomacy, economic sanctions against those foreign powers who harboured Suffolk led eventually to his return to England and to custody in 1505. That Henry VII died in his bed and that he passed his kingdom on to an adult son, indeed to a succession of Tudors who ruled for a further century must count as one of his greatest achievements.

A patient, hard-working approach to the problems of administration helped bring peace to England. As everyone knows, Henry's *forte* was finance. A rich king was a strong king, one able to raise troops when necessary, to reward faithful service and to display his magnificence to his subjects and to visiting foreign dignitaries. Henry inherited a bankrupt treasury, even the Crown jewels were in pawn. He soon achieved solvency and died in the black, although with nothing near the £2 million surplus once said to have been left by him to his son. This success was based on a policy of low expenditure, and the avoidance of unnecessary foreign war, although Henry was no miser and would spend lavishly when it was needed. The administration of Crown finances was made more efficient. Like Edward IV before him, Henry by-passed the cumbersome Exchequer and used his Chamber to deal with money. He personally checked the accounts of the Chamber every day and employed auditors to act as a double check. Crown lands were more efficiently run under the Surveyors of Land Revenues and revenue from Customs grew with the expansion of trade, which Henry was keen to stimulate. Henry made profits from justice, by extracting fines and bonds for good behaviour and by selling pardons. His foreign policy earned him a French pension. He exploited to the full his feudal rights, especially wardship, appointing a Master of the Wards, and a Surveyor of the King's Prerogative to ensure that no nobles avoided their death duties. He taxed his subjects directly only when it was unavoidable, since taxation might easily provoke rebellion, as it did in 1489 in the North and more famously in 1497 in Cornwall. Taxation was normally granted by parliament, but the king also raised a benevolence and forced loan on the authority of his Great Council.

Henry was not a great reformer; he used the system of government he inherited, but used it to the best possible advantage. At the centre of government were the three great officers of state; the Lord Chancellor, the Lord Treasurer and the Lord Privy Seal. Henry appointed men of ability to these posts: like the other Tudors he had the knack of choosing the right man for the right job, and when he had made his choice, Henry supported him to the full. These men and the King worked through the Council, which met regularly as a law-court, a policy-making 'Cabinet' and as the centre of the whole administrative system of the country. Henry was the sort of king who worked personally even at the most mundane aspects of government and he was to be found presiding over all the important Council meetings, although the system could function without the King's presence when necessary. Good government depended on the King exercising what was called 'good-lordship', that is, working successfully with his chief subjects, the nobles and gentry. The trick was to make these men work with the King, in the King's interest, and not against it. Henry succeeded in large part in doing this, using a judicious blend of generosity and firmness. He created very few new nobles, allowing the number of peers to decline a little by natural wastage. He used the great magnates of the realm in government but saw to it that they did not work independently of him, and were balanced in Council by the presence of representatives of other classes, and of men more completely dependent on himself from lower down the social scale. He made it clear that no noblemen could consider themselves above the law, and he sought to limit their employment of retainers in what amounted to private armies. He pursued no vendettas against Yorkist grandees, and accepted their co-operation and support if it was genuine, seeking to bind up the wounds of civil war and to forget past injuries done to the House of Lancaster.

As the nobles were tamed and brought back to habits of loyalty, so the general level of order in the country improved, and the law was administered with a greater regard for justice. It would be wrong to exaggerate Henry's success here. The law was expensive, and its delays were proverbial, and in such circumstances the rich were placed at a great advantage. Moreover, the every-day exercise of justice lay in the hands of the gentry and chief merchants, who acted as largely unpaid Justices of the Peace, Sheriffs and commissioners of oyer and terminer in the shires and towns of England. They worked with the more substantial householders as constables and jurors. At both levels, justice could be corrupted and influenced by the rich and unscrupulous. The central law courts at Westminster and the royal justices who travelled out from Westminster on their assize circuits around the country were more directly under royal control and Henry used them to keep an eye on the rest of the system.

In foreign affairs, Henry's principal aim was to prevent foreign powers giving support to the Yorkists. This presented difficulties, since the Dowager Duchess Margaret of Burgundy was Edward IV's sister and enjoyed a privileged position in the Netherlands, from where she was able to give support to both Simnel and Warbeck. Much patient diplomatic work was expended to counter this threat. One way to strengthen his position at home was to make marriage alliances abroad and he was successful in arranging valuable matches for all his children. Another consideration which influenced his foreign policy was the desire to stimulate England's overseas trade. He made commercial treaties with France, Spain, Portugal, the Hanse cities, Denmark, Florence and the Netherlands. However, when interests of trade conflicted with his dynastic concerns, Henry made the economy suffer, twice placing an embargo on the Low Countries to persuade them to stop helping the Yorkists. Henry's instincts told him to avoid international war, and apart from the forces sent to Ireland in 1487 under Edgecombe and in 1494 under Poynings, he sent only one expeditionary contingent abroad. This was in 1492 and was intended to prevent the French King from absorbing Brittany completely into his sphere of influence. It failed to do this, but it gave Henry a little glory in the eyes of his people and was a financial success, enabling him both to tax his subjects and to win a French pension under the terms of the Treaty of Etaples (1492).

Henry was an impressive figure of a man: a little above average height, with a majestic presence and handsome, aquiline features. He was no Scrooge: he enjoyed hawking, hunting, books, architecture and music; pastimes on which he was prepared to spend money. Great court ceremonies with lavish displays, processions, banquets and jousts were almost as common in his reign as in his son's. Henry's later years were marred by tragedy: his eldest son died in 1502 and his wife's death followed in the next year. Henry became suspicious and his government became harsher, perhaps because he feared for the future now that there was only one male Tudor heir, who was still quite young. He consulted his subjects less in parliament and Great Council in these later years, and controlled the nobles more tightly by placing them under bonds for good behaviour in very many cases. The consequence was that when he died in 1509 after a number of years of illness, he was missed by few and cursed by many. This was unfair: he had brought an end to civil war, his government had been founded on three pillars — justice, prosperity and efficiency — and as Bacon said, 'What he minded, he compassed'.

R. L. Storey, *The Reign of Henry VII*, 1968.
S. B. Chrimes, *Henry VII*, 1972.
R. Lockyer, *Henry VII*, 1983.
A. Grant, *Henry VII*, 1985.
P. J. Holmes, 'The Great Council of Henry VII', *English Historical Review*, 1986.

ELIZABETH OF YORK (1465–1503), wife of Henry VII, was born at Westminster on 11 February 1465, and she died giving birth to a daughter on her birthday in 1503. She was the daughter of Edward IV and Elizabeth Wydeville (or Woodville). When she was five years old she was to have married George Neville, eldest son of John, Earl of Northumberland, later Marquess of Montagu, and Neville was created Duke of Bedford, but his father switched sides against the King, Bedford was deprived of all his titles and Elizabeth's betrothal was cancelled. In 1475 Edward planned to marry her to Louis, the French Dauphin, but Edward soon discovered that Louis had no intention of keeping his obligations and therefore the engagement was broken off. Bernard André, the blind poet laureate and historian, hints that Edward offered Elizabeth to Henry of Richmond, later Henry VII and her husband to be, but that Henry declined, suspecting that the offer was a trap to put him into the King's power.

Edward IV died in 1483. His Queen, suspicious of Richard of Gloucester, put herself with her younger son and her five daughters into sanctuary at Westminster. Elizabeth was at the time just eighteen. Elizabeth's mother now made a plan, together with Margaret Beaufort, to marry their two children, Henry and Elizabeth. On Christmas Day, 1483, at the cathedral of Rennes in Brittany, where he was in exile, Henry Tudor swore to marry Elizabeth as soon as he had secured the throne.

Richard III, of course, was determined to stop such a scheme being put into operation. He declared Elizabeth, his own niece, illegitimate and then when his own wife died in 1485 he proposed to marry the girl himself. Luckily, his advisers persuaded him to drop this strange notion. When Henry of Richmond landed at Milford Haven, Elizabeth was sent to safe keeping at Sheriff Hutton, near York, deep in the heart of Gloucester country. Henry's victory meant Elizabeth's release and her journey to London to meet the man she was to marry, a man she had not seen for fourteen years (if then). Henry delayed the wedding for a number of months, possibly because he wished to make it quite clear that he was King of England in his own right and not because he was marrying the heiress of Edward IV, but probably also for simple practical reasons. Parliament was impatient of the delay and before Christmas 1485 the Commons urged him to honour his pledge. So, on 18 January 1486, having acquired the necessary papal dispensation, the marriage was solemnized. Thus the two royal houses — York and Lancaster — were finally united.

Elizabeth is one of the least important, though not the least attractive, of the Queens of England. Little is known about her. What evidence there is suggests that the relations between Henry VII and his Queen were happy. There is a pathetic account in Leland's *Collectanea* of how Henry VII broke the news of Prince Arthur's death to his wife and how Elizabeth 'with comfortable words' said to him that 'my Lady his mother had never had no more children but him only, and that God ... had left him yet a fair prince, two fair princesses; and that God is where he was and we are both young enough'. She seems to have been beautiful, gentle, kind, generous to her relations, her servants and benefactors. Her income never covered her expenses. She was fond of dancing, of music, dicing, hunting, she kept greyhounds, and she may have been fond of archery — at any rate she bought arrows and broadheads, perhaps for hunting. It is well known that Henry VII personally signed the account book of the Treasurer of his Chamber; what is less well known is that Elizabeth signed her own accounts too. She is still commemorated as the model for the queen on our playing cards.

Elizabeth bore Henry eight children, of whom only four lived beyond infancy. When she died in 1503, the King was most upset; he 'privily departed to a solitary place, and then would no man should resort unto him' according to one account. He never married again, although he considered it, largely because of the diplomatic power it gave him.

H. Nicolas, *Privy purse expenses of Elizabeth of York*, 1830.

ARTHUR, PRINCE OF WALES (1486–1502), the eldest son of Henry VII and his wife, Elizabeth of York, was born on 20 September 1486, and died on 2 April 1502. Henry, in order to strengthen his claim to the throne, set the genealogists to work to trace his descent back to Cadwallader and the ancient British kings: he identified Winchester with Camelot, and therefore he sent his wife to Winchester to have her baby and the boy was named Arthur after King Arthur of the Round Table — one example of Henry's consciousness of being Welsh. He was christened in Winchester Cathedral, his godfathers being the Earl of Oxford, who arrived late for the ceremony, and the Earl of Derby. When he was three, he was made Prince of Wales. When he was five, he was made a Knight of the Garter, having been made a Knight of the Bath at his christening.

Henry saw to it that his son should have the best education which the revival of learning could provide. Arthur's first tutor was one John Rede, but later he was instructed by the blind poet laureate, Bernard André, who wrote an unfinished life of Henry VII, in which he asserted that by the age of fifteen Arthur was familiar with all the best Greek and Latin authors. Arthur was probably never a strong child and there is no evidence that he was ever an athlete like his younger brother, Henry, but it is possible that he may have shown some aptitude for archery.

In 1488, when Arthur was only two years old, negotiations had begun for his marriage to Catherine of Aragon. Ferdinand of Aragon was clearly not going to commit himself until he saw whether the Tudor dynasty was going to be securely settled on the throne, therefore he held back for some years; but after the execution of Perkin Warbeck and the Earl of Warwick in 1499 he agreed to the marriage. For two years the Prince of Wales from Ludlow Castle was writing letters in formal Latin and still more formal terms at the age of fourteen to a girl two years older than himself whom he had never seen. The letters are characterized rather by politeness than by passion. At last, in 1500, the terms of the marriage were settled at a meeting outside Calais.

The marriage took place in St. Paul's Cathedral on 14 November 1501. Arthur and Catherine then went to Ludlow and set up court there as Prince and Princess of Wales. They were thought, however, to be too young to cohabit. On 2 April 1502, Arthur suddenly died before the marriage was consummated. This fact was to have momentous results, not only for Catherine but for England and the Papacy, when Henry VIII, having married Catherine, later sought to have the marriage annulled by the Pope.

PERKIN WARBECK (c. 1474–1499), impostor and pretender to the throne, first appeared on the political stage in the autumn of 1491 at Cork in Ireland. It was claimed at first that he was the Earl of Warwick, then that he was an illegitimate son of Richard III and finally, and for the rest of his career as an impostor, that he was

Richard, Duke of York, the younger of the Princes in the Tower murdered by their uncle, Richard III. Henry VII immediately made great efforts to discover who this fraud was and eventually found that he was the son of a customs official from Tournai, a city in the Netherlands close to the French border. His name was Peter (or Perkin) Osbeck, sometimes spelt Werbecque, anglicised as Warbeck.

According to Warbeck's confession, made after he was captured, he assumed the role of Yorkist pretender largely by accident when acting as male model for a Breton merchant named Pregent Meno who called at Cork. The people of that town, impressed by his appearance, decked out in the imported finery of Meno, apparently took him for a nobleman and then began a rather Irish process of exaggeration. But this is surely too good to be true. There is some evidence that the French king, Charles VIII, who in 1491 was in conflict with Henry VII, was involved in the plot in some way before Warbeck arrived in Ireland. Warbeck's origins are also significant: Tournai was, for a time, the seat of the Duchess Margaret of Burgundy's court, and this fact suggests that the plot was hatched there, where Warbeck lived. A link with the Yorkist high command is provided by the fact that Warbeck was employed before 1491 as a servant of Sir Edward Brompton, a converted Portuguese Jew who had been a close adherent of the Yorkists and was made Governor of Guernsey by Edward IV.

Warbeck received little support in Ireland, perhaps understandably in view of Simnel's fate, and he went next to France. The war between Henry and Charles VIII, which broke out in 1492 ostensibly over Brittany, owed something to the presence of the Pretender in the French court. Following his invasion of France, Henry secured a peace treaty with France, signed at Etaples in 1492, under the terms of which Warbeck was expelled. He turned up next in the Netherlands, under the protection of the Duchess. Henry imposed an embargo on trade to the Low Countries to show his displeasure at this. In 1493, Warbeck appeared at the court of Maximilian Habsburg, head of the Holy Roman Empire, and was recognised as King Richard IV of England. Two years later, a conspiracy was revealed in England, implicating, among other important men, Sir William Stanley, the King's step-uncle. Stanley had been in communication with Warbeck and he was executed. In the same year (1495), Warbeck launched an abortive attack on the coast of Kent, at Deal, but his small force was easily repulsed. He attempted next to take Waterford in Ireland, but was sent packing by Sir Edward Poynings and so he fetched up finally in Scotland. James IV, who was at the time on bad terms with Henry, received him warmly and married him to a royal cousin, Lady Catherine Gordon. Henry was incensed at this recognition shown to the impostor and also at a raiding party which Warbeck accompanied a few miles over the border into Northern England, and he prepared to lead an expedition into Scotland (1496). The threat of war made James IV treat for peace, and Warbeck left, via Ireland, for Cornwall (1497). He hoped to raise a rebellion among the troublesome Cornish who had only recently risen in rebellion against the King's taxes. Indeed, he did receive some support and led a force eastward, besieging Exeter and Taunton, both with no success. Warbeck's forces melted away as the King's army approached, and he fled to sanctuary at Beaulieu Abbey. Henry had decided at the beginning of his reign (and the Pope had agreed) that sanctuary should not prevent arrest for treason, and Warbeck was captured. Henry spared his life, in an effort to make it appear that he had no fears of Warbeck, whereas, of course, the past six years of the reign had been dominated by the King's efforts to bring the Pretender down. For a year, Warbeck lived as a courtier, but when he tried to escape he was placed in the Tower. In 1499 a plot was revealed, perhaps as the result of the activities of royal *agents provocateurs*, which involved Warbeck and the Earl of Warwick in a conspiracy to escape the Tower. Warbeck was hanged and Warwick beheaded. As for Lady Catherine Gordon, she was treated generously by the Tudors and married a further three times, finally dying in 1537.

JOHN MORTON (1420?–1500), Archbishop of Canterbury and Cardinal, was born probably in 1420 at Milborne St. Andrew, near Bere Regis in Dorset. He was the son of Richard Morton, of a Nottingham family, and Elizabeth, daughter of Richard Turburville and Cecilia Beauchamp, being the eldest of five sons. He was educated at the Benedictine Abbey at Cerne, from which he went to Balliol, Oxford. He took up law, but he also took orders, and in 1446 he appears among the vice-chancellors of Oxford, known also as commissaries. He moved to London and practised as a lawyer principally in the Court of Arches, and became a Privy Councillor and Chancellor of the Duchy of Cornwall. From this moment he became a great pluralist and might almost be said to have collected offices and livings. All these appointments were ecclesiastical, but Morton's work was almost wholly legal or political, and there is little evidence that he resided in any of his livings.

During the Wars of the Roses Morton was mainly on the Lancastrian side, but he managed to keep in with the Yorkists when they were in the ascendant. He was present at the battle of Towton and at one point had to fight for his life: he was wrongly reported to have been taken prisoner (1461). He escaped to the north and sailed for Flanders, not to return to England for ten years. He was in 1461 attainted, convicted of treason and sentenced to lose all his possessions. While he was abroad he attended the Queen Margaret, first at Bruges and later at Louvain. He played a large part in reconciling Warwick and Clarence to the Lancastrians, and when they sailed for England (1470), Morton went with them, landing at Dartmouth on September 13th. He was present at the battle of Barnet (April 1471), after which he hurried to Weymouth to meet the Queen and her son, who were expected there. He took them to Cerne Abbey and thence to Beaulieu.

The battle of Tewkesbury put paid to Lancastrian hopes, and Morton now (1471) reconciled himself with the Yorkists. Edward IV evidently looked on Morton as a trustworthy and valuable servant; he reversed the attainder and in 1472 appointed him to be Master of the Rolls. In a short time Morton held many prebends and five archdeaconries. One sign of the King's confidence in Morton may be seen in the embassy which Edward entrusted to him to bring the Emperor and the King of Hungary into an alliance against the King of France, Louis XI (1474). The next year he was one of the negotiators of the Treaty of Picquigny where peace was made with Louis XI, and he received as his share of the spoils a pension of £2000 a year.

In 1478 he was appointed Bishop of Ely. On the day of his enthronement, after a night of prayer, Morton walked from Downham to Ely with his head uncovered, bare-footed and bare-legged, with his beads in his hand, saying his Paternosters. He now gave up the Mastership of the Rolls and to a great extent devoted himself to religious duties. He also became tutor to the Prince of Wales. At his palace in London he held reading parties both for young and promising scholars and also for men of learning, English and foreign: he set about reforming his diocese and he revived his connection with Oxford. When Edward IV died in 1483, Morton was one of his executors, but he refused to act on the grounds that he was not given large enough powers to act effectively.

When Richard of Gloucester began to scheme to seize the throne from his young nephew, Edward V, Morton was in a difficult and dangerous position. He was present at the council meeting at which Richard's plans began to make themselves known, a meeting made famous by Richard's reference to one of Morton's favourite hobbies, the growing of fruit:

> My Lord of Ely, when I was last at Holborn,
> I saw good strawberries in your garden there:
> I do beseech you send for some of them.
>
> (Richard III, iii, iv.)

That Morton at once went to order some did not save him from arrest: he was put into prison, but he was released on a petition from Oxford University on behalf of 'our dearest son' and allowed to reside with Buckingham at Brecknock Castle. Buckingham had already been forming his own plans against Richard, which he now divulged to Morton. Morton himself had almost certainly come to the conclusion that the hopes for the country rested now, not on Richard, but on Henry of Richmond. He approved of Buckingham's plans and he became the intermediary between Buckingham and Reginald Bray, and this brought him into touch with Margaret Beaufort, Countess of Richmond, mother of Henry Richmond, later Henry VII. It is possible that it was Morton who first implanted in Margaret Beaufort's mind the idea that her son should marry Elizabeth of York, daughter of Edward IV, and thus end the feud of the Roses. If this is true, it goes a long way to establishing Morton, rather against the factual evidence, as being a clear-sighted and honest man, who did his best in the most difficult times for his country. A rising was planned to take place in the west. Morton decided that he ought to be at Ely: it is possible that he distrusted the success of a purely local rising and wanted to be in the east of England to raise forces there. Buckingham was suspicious of allowing so important a personage to leave his side. Morton escaped

secretly by night and went to Ely. Shakespeare records for us Richard
III's feelings:

> Ely with Richmond troubles me more near
> Than Buckingham with his rash-levied strength.
>   (Richard III, iv, iii.)

Buckingham's rising failed, Henry of Richmond's expedition from
Brittany had to turn back, Buckingham was arrested and executed.
Morton had gone to Flanders and was there till after Bosworth,
except for a visit to Paris where he met Richard Fox, later Bishop of
Winchester, and won him over to Henry's side. Morton was able to
warn Henry that the Duke of Brittany meant to betray him to
Richard III and thus to advise him to fly into the realm of the King of
France.

In 1485 Henry Richmond invaded England and won the throne.
Morton came back; his attainder was again reversed; he was made a
Privy Councillor; in 1486 he was Chancellor and Archbishop of
Canterbury. From that point on until his death in 1500 Morton was,
under Henry VII, the most important and powerful man in the
kingdom. He was supreme, except for the King, in Church and State.
He now set himself to remedy the abuses in both, immorality in the
monasteries, over-mighty subjects in the state. He reformed clerical
abuses, even down to the form of dress: he ordered residence for
those with care of souls: bishops were to take trouble in selecting
clergymen. He set out on visitations (1490) to Lichfield, Coventry,
Bath and Wells, Winchester, Lincoln, Exeter. He petitioned the
Papacy to canonize Henry VI, in which he failed, and Anselm was
canonized instead. In 1493 Morton was made a Cardinal. His
position now was something like a foreshadow of Wolsey's position
later on: Morton was head of the Church as Primate, Cardinal and
Legate; he was chief administrator in the State as Chancellor of
England, especially in the law; he was Chancellor of Oxford University; he opened Parliament for the King and defended policy,
especially taxation, in speeches more like modern speeches than
those in the past; he received foreign embassies; he persuaded the
Pope to allow some modification in the laws governing sanctuary.

In the realm of finance there seems little doubt now that Morton's
position was extremely difficult. The King had to have money, and
left to himself Henry might have pursued a much more heavy-

handed and even tyrannical policy than he did: he was restrained by Bray and by Morton. 'Morton's Fork' or 'Crutch' has passed into history, but it looks as if he accepted all the unpopularity for financial measures which would have been worse but for him, in order to save the reputation of the King. And he had to bear the burden of unpopularity for the many 'benevolences' which were raised out of the nobility.

In one respect Morton was a herald of the future: he was an indefatigable builder. He repaired the palace at Canterbury; the Manor House at Lambeth, where the Gateway is his work; the episcopal residences at Maidstone, Aldington Park, Ford, Charing: his arms are on the tower at Wisbech: he built what is now the old part of Hatfield House: restored Rochester Bridge; put the splendid roof on to the nave of Bere Regis church. In addition he cut a great canal from Peterborough to Guyhirne near Wisbech, known as Morton's Leame, which brought the High Fen into cultivation amounting to 4,387 acres: this canal was 40 feet wide, 4 feet deep, with new outlets to the sea, and 40 miles in length. It lasted until 1725.

In legislation his most famous Act is that of 1495 to protect from the penalties of Treason those who act under a *de facto* King, in order to protect all who had supported or were serving Henry VII.

Bacon records of him that 'he was a wise man and an eloquent, but in his nature harsh and haughty, much accepted by the King, but envied by the nobility and hated of the people'. In that tribute there is nothing to persuade us that Morton was not a highly valuable statesman in harsh and difficult days. But Sir Thomas More, who as a boy was brought up in Morton's household, puts into the mouth of Hythlodaye in *Utopia* a more generous tribute: 'a man not more honourable for his authority than for his prudence and virtue ... In his speech he was fine, eloquent and pithy. In the law he had profound knowledge; in wit he was incomparable; and in memory wonderful excellent. These qualities, which in him were by nature singular, he by learning and use had made perfect. The King put much trust in his counsel: the weal public also in a manner leaned unto him.'

The general opinion nowadays is that Morton was not, and Sir Thomas More was, the author of *The History of Richard III*, both in the Latin and English versions. (Chambers, *Thomas More*, p. 55.)

Morton died on 15 September 1500, at Knowle in Kent.

T. Mozley, *Henry VII, Prince Arthur and Cardinal Morton*, intro. 1878.
R. I. Woodhouse, *Memoir of Morton*, 1895.
C. Harper-Bill, *Journal of Ecclesiastical History*, 1978.

RICHARD FOX (1447?–1528), Bishop of Winchester, Lord Privy Seal, was born between 1446 and 1448 at Ropesley in Lincolnshire, the son of yeoman stock. His early education is unknown, but he went to Oxford to Magdalen College where he studied law, then to Paris University where he took the degree of Doctor of Canon Law and was ordained. This close connection between the law and ordination was typical of the time and dictated Fox's future career.

While he was abroad in Paris he became secretary to Henry Tudor, Earl of Richmond, the future Henry VII of England. That he was already a known man is proved by Richard III's order prohibiting Fox from being appointed to the vicarage of Stepney, on the grounds that he was with 'that great rebel Henry ap Tuddor'. Fox obtained the living in 1485.

In that year he accompanied Henry on his invasion of England, was with him at Bosworth, and when Henry became King, Fox was made principal Secretary of State and Keeper of the Privy Seal: at the same time he was appointed to the see of Exeter. For the next thirty years Fox was the typical ecclesiastical statesman of the type of which Gardiner was probably to be the last. In 1491 Fox was translated to Bath and Wells, in 1494 to Durham (probably because it was valuable to Henry to have him resident on the ever-dangerous Scottish border), in 1501 to Winchester. He never attended to his ecclesiastical duties until his retirement from politics, but he appointed a suffragan to do the work. During this period Fox was concerned in negotiating all the main treaties; he had a major hand in the treaty with Scotland in 1487, in the treaty of Etaples (1492), in the *Intercursus Magnus* in 1496, in the marriage treaty of Margaret Tudor and James IV (1502), and in the abortive marriage treaty for Mary Tudor and Charles of Castile in 1508. His work also included such military exploits as organizing the harbour works at Calais, and the defence of Norham Castle when Perkin Warbeck was in Scotland (1497). He was also an executor for Henry VII's will.

When Henry died (1509), Fox was still in favour with Henry VIII, but the rise of Wolsey (about 1513) marks the end of Fox's pre-eminence. He was still used by the King and he went with Henry VIII to France in 1513 and was present at Thérouanne, but he was now a sick man, 'much hurt by the kick of his mule, and for some days he could neither sit nor stand', as the diarist John Taylor recorded. Fox disapproved of the new foreign policy and he found the campaign very distasteful. He wrote to Wolsey, who was just about to cross over to France, that unless he took with him a good supply of beer, he would have 'a cold stomach, little sleep, pale visage, and a thin belly', as he himself had.

In 1516 Fox resigned the Privy Seal and retired to look after the spiritual needs of his diocese. By 1518 he was seriously blind, yet he had ten more years to live. He seems genuinely to have regretted and even repented of his neglect of his bishoprics while he was 'meddling with worldly matters'. 'I have no little remorse in my conscience, thinking that if I did continual penance for it all the days of my life, though I shall live twenty years longer than I may do, I could not yet make sufficient recompence therefor.' He died on 5 October 1528.

Fox may be remembered principally for his founding and building of Corpus Christi College, Oxford, but he was also a benefactor of other colleges both at Oxford and Cambridge. The screen and chantry which he built at Winchester display his well-known device of a pelican. He was also a Humanist and had contacts with Erasmus when that scholar visited England.

G. H. Blore, 'Richard Fox, Bishop of Winchester, 1501–1528', *The Record of the Friends of Winchester Cathedral*, 1947.

E. C. Batten, *Fox's Register for Bath and Wells*, 1889.

P. S. and H. M. Allen, *Letters of Richard Fox*, 1929.

LAMBERT SIMNEL (1475?–1525), impostor, was the son of Thomas Simnel of Oxford, variously described as a joiner, an organ builder, a shoemaker or a baker.

Polydore Vergil records that Simnel was a 'comely youth and well-favoured, not without some extraordinary dignity and grace of aspect'. An Oxford priest, Richard Symonds, conceived the idea of setting up Simnel as Richard, Duke of York, the younger of the two princes murdered in the Tower. Later, Symonds decided it would be better to pass Simnel off as the Earl of Warwick, son of 'false, fleeting perjured Clarence', and hence nephew to Edward IV. This was a more difficult task because the Earl of Warwick was alive and in the Tower of London. It seems likely that Symonds was acting from the beginning with the support of the Yorkist leaders, and it may be that the plot is indicative of Yorkist sympathies in Oxford University, 'the home of lost causes'.

Simnel was sent to Ireland early in 1487 where the Yorkists were strong and where his alleged father (the Duke of Clarence) had been born. The Earl of Kildare, the uncrowned king of Ireland, welcomed him and he was crowned King in Dublin Cathedral, taking the title Edward VI and using as a crown a circlet of gold filched from a statue of the Virgin Mary. By now a full-scale plot against Henry VII was taking shape: Margaret, Dowager-Duchess of Burgundy, sister of Edward IV and implacable enemy of Henry VII, sent 2000 mercenaries under Martin Schwartz to Ireland, where they were joined by the Earl of Lincoln (a genuine nephew of Edward IV) and Lord Lovell, a Yorkist noble who had led a rebellion against the King the previous year.

To meet the emergency, Henry VII had called a Great Council in February and had paraded the real Earl of Warwick in London in an attempt to show that Simnel was an impostor. He then marched out from London, unclear at first whether to expect an attack from the Netherlands, where Margaret was, or from Ireland.

Simnel's forces crossed from Ireland and landed at Furness (Lancs.) on 4 June 1487, marching across the Pennines and down the Fosse Way. They met the King's army at Stoke, a village near Newark and after a battle of three hours the King was victorious. This was the last battle of the Wars of the Roses. Schwarz was killed, as was Lincoln. Lovell escaped but then disappeared, perhaps drowned fording the River Trent in his armour, perhaps starved to death when hiding from his pursuers in the walled-up cellar of his house at Minster Lovell. Most authorities claim that Symonds was also taken prisoner at Stoke, but Cardinal Morton's register (in Lambeth Library) makes it clear that he was committed to prison in February 1487 and hence did not even go to Ireland with Simnel. Symonds apparently stayed a prisoner for the rest of his life. It seems likely that if Simnel had succeeded in defeating Henry — as well he might — the Earl of Lincoln would have been the chief beneficiary and have made himself king.

Henry VII behaved with much politic leniency towards the young and gentle Simnel. He turned him into his scullion, and Simnel later rose to be his falconer. When the Earl of Kildare and a number of Irish nobles visited Henry a few years later, Henry had Simnel serve them wine after a feast, an experience which brought a momentary pause to the jollity of the occasion, but which was soon passed off as a good joke. Later, Simnel was transferred to the household of Sir Thomas Lovell, where he died in 1525.

Polydore Vergil, *Anglica Historia.*
D. Scott Daniell, *The Boy They Made King*, 1959.

SIR RICHARD EMPSON (*c.*1450–1510), was born in about 1450 or a little before, and rose to be one of Henry VII's chief ministers. He was described by John Stow as the son of a 'sieve-maker', or basket-maker of Towcester, but his father, Peter Empson, was a man of considerable local importance who could afford to have his son trained as a lawyer. All Henry VII's chief advisers among the laity were of gentle birth, and it seems probable that Empson was too.

Richard Empson soon had a busy legal practice, especially in the Midlands, and was appointed a Justice of the Peace. In 1478 he was made Attorney-General in the Duchy of Lancaster, an office which he lost on the accession of Richard III, but recovered after Bosworth. Empson was therefore typical of many royal servants who staffed Henry VII's administration in that he had gained experience under the Yorkists. He was a Member of Parliament on several occasions in Henry VII's reign and in 1491 was chosen Speaker of the Commons, a position showing he had royal favour.

Empson came to prominence in the later years of Henry's reign. In 1505 he was finally made Chancellor of the Duchy of Lancaster, but his most important work was as royal debt-collector and associate of Edmund Dudley. The two men worked closely on a rather mysterious body known as the 'Council learned in the law', a sort of committee of the royal council which met from at least 1495 and which saw that the King's monies were collected. From about 1502, it seems clear that Henry's government of England became stricter and that the burdens imposed on the rich especially grew. Bonds for good behaviour were placed on many of the upper classes, and they suffered severe financial penalties if they stepped out of line. In consequence, when the King died, there was something of a reaction. The young Henry VIII, anxious to make himself popular at the beginning of his reign had Empson and Dudley arrested the day after his accession. All the pent-up hostility to the old King's way of doing things was directed against these two unfortunate ministers. The main case against them seems to have been that they enforced the law and legal agreements too strictly. So, trumped up accusations of treason were used against them and on 17 August 1510 Empson was executed. He and Dudley were, therefore, the first victims of Henry VIII's cruelty. It is worth noting that Empson himself was placed under a bond in 1504 to prevent him persecuting an unfortunate royal chaplain who had written satirical verses against him. This would seem to indicate that any harshness in Henry VII's reign, if such there was, came eventually from the King and not his ministers, and that it was inflicted in the interests of justice and good order. Empson's latest biographer concludes his study thus: 'It was perhaps the driving force of his life to make the laws of England profitable for his monarch'. By medieval standards such an aim was not dishonourable.

M. R. Horowitz, *Bulletin Institute Historical Research*, 1982.

EDMUND DUDLEY (1462?–1510), minister of Henry VII, was born probably in 1462. Bacon says he was 'of a good family', being descended from a baronial family called Sutton. He was trained in the law and rose rapidly in the favour of Henry VII. He was a royal councillor from early in the reign and in 1506 was appointed President of the Council, an unusual post giving him, it seems, a dignity at council meetings equal to that usually held by the Lord Chancellor.

That he was high in the esteem of Henry VII is shown by his appointment in 1504 as Speaker of the House of Commons, a post at that time within the gift of the Crown. The Speaker's job was to keep the Commons under control and to bring it round to the tasks the King required it to perform. As a matter of fact, the Commons in

1504 were rather troublesome, so perhaps Dudley even then was not very popular.

Dudley was at the height of his power in the last years of Henry's reign, working in conjunction with Richard Empson. On the 'Council learned in the law', these two royal servants worked hard to ensure that the King received what he was owed. They exploited, in particular, the King's feudal rights and the profits to be made from the law. Part of this policy was financial, part had to do with maintaining order. Through the use of bonds and recognizances, Dudley — working for the King — bound many of the upper classes to be obedient to the law. At the same time, Dudley made himself and his family rich.

As Henry VII grew older, resentment developed towards this harsh and avaricious policy and when the old King died, a reaction immediately set in. Dudley and Empson were arrested on the day following the accession of Henry VIII, who wished to impress his subjects at the very beginning of his reign with a sense of how different his policies would be from his father's. Dudley was accused of treason, on the grounds that he had armed his friends and supporters when news came that Henry VII was dying. This was a perfectly natural thing to do in what was still a fairly lawless society, and certainly the accusations of treason were false. Nevertheless, that Dudley had been an instrument of Henry VII's harshness (even perhaps injustice) in the last years of his reign is proved by the recent discovery of Dudley's 'Petition', addressed to the executors of Henry VII's will and giving details of specific cases where men were unfairly treated and deserving of compensation out of the King's estate. While in prison, Dudley also wrote *The Tree of the Commonwealth*, a sanctimonious and largely conventional discussion of the nature of kingship, which contained some veiled criticism of Henry VII's methods of government.

Dudley was executed on 17 August 1510. He was the father of John, Duke of Northumberland and Protector under Edward VI, and the grandfather of Robert, Earl of Leicester, Elizabeth's favourite.

The Tree of the Commonwealth, ed. D. M. Brodie, 1948.
D. M. Brodie, *Transactions Royal Historical Society*, 1932.
C. J. Harrison, *English Historical Review*, 1972.

HENRY VIII (1491-1547), was born at Greenwich on 28 June 1491: he died at Westminster at midnight on 28 January 1547. He was the second son of Henry VII and Elizabeth of York, and became King in 1509.

Like all the Tudors he was given an excellent education, and like all the Tudors he made the most of it. Lord Herbert of Cherbury in his *Life of Henry VIII* records that 'his education was accurate, being destined (as a credible author affirms) to the Archbishopric of Canterbury, during the life of his elder brother Prince Arthur; that prudent king his father choosing this as the most cheap and glorious way for bestowing of a younger son', but he does not cite the authority for this improbable statement. All the same, Henry proved himself more than once a far from contemptible theologian: he could speak French, Italian and Spanish, and he was, of course, proficient in Latin. His book against Luther (1521) was almost wholly his own work. He was also passionately devoted to music, and the Venetian ambassadors have left it on record that he practised the lute, organ and harpsichord (probably the virginals) 'day and night'. He also, according to these Italians, 'acquitted himself divinely' as a dancer. Physically he was above average height, enormously strong and of great courage. He excelled in all athletic sports: nobody outdid him in jousting: he drew the best long-bow of his age and he could defeat the tallest archers in his own guard. He was an accomplished player of tennis and he was a strenuous rider to hounds, able to tire out eight or ten horses in the course of a day's hunting, mounting one after the other as they were exhausted. He had a love for finery and display, he was generous (but sometimes mean-spirited), handsome, hot-tempered and the idol of the country. His morals were neither better nor worse than those of Charles V, infinitely better than those of Francis I, Charles II or Louis XIV. Such was the paragon who ascended the throne in 1509. The portrait was to change during the next thirty-eight years.

Henry VIII and his ministers. The greatest problem facing the historian who studies Henry VIII is to know whether the achievements of his reign are to be ascribed to him or to his ministers, especially Thomas Wolsey who dominated the years 1515 to 1529 and Thomas Cromwell who held sway from 1532 to 1540. The king certainly had no great taste for day-to-day administrative tasks of the sort which had appealed to his father, and he found writing 'both tedious and painful'. He was not exactly a lazy man, but he considered the detailed business of government to be beneath his dignity, preferring to play in the main a ceremonial role. In this he was like most other rulers of his day: it was Henry VII who had been unusual. Nevertheless, Henry VIII was in this, as in all things, unpredictable, and pricked perhaps by conscience or out of a desire to be fully in control, he was capable at times of taking a great and detailed interest in affairs. There was no doubt where power ultimately lay, as is shown by the events of 1540, when Cromwell was executed, and of 1529, when Wolsey fell. There can be no question that the final decision to go to war or to dissolve the monasteries, for example, was the King's. What is less easy to say is how far policy was developed in consultation with the King, and at what level in the decision-making process he became involved. In the end, the fact that Henry chose two brilliant men, in their different ways, to serve him says a good deal for his political skill. It should also be remembered that the government of England survived the fall of both great ministers, and that for sixteen years Henry ruled without either Cromwell or Wolsey at the helm. It may be that recent historians have tended to undervalue the part Henry played, perhaps because the written records present a picture in which administration, the field where the minister worked, looms larger than politics, where the King was active.

Henry VIII's foreign policy. For Henry this was the most important area. He was determined at the beginning of his reign to make a mark for himself in European politics, and he seems to have developed alone, and against the advice of his father's old councillors, a policy which led to what Henry at least regarded as a considerable degree of success. The aim was to fight the ancient enemy, France, and after some delay war broke out in 1512. The following year, Henry led a large invasion force across the Channel, which captured two French towns, Tournai and Thérouanne. These two places were held by the English for the next five years. Henry was not a great military leader and took no real risks on the battlefield, but this invasion of France was largely popular in England, although there were to be complaints later at the expense involved in acquiring what some cynics regarded as 'ungracious dogholes'. While Henry was campaigning in France, a major victory had been

Henry VIII
(Artist: Hans Holbein)

won at Flodden (1513) against the Scots, who had responded to the call of the Auld Alliance and invaded England. Peace with France was made in 1514 and continued for eight years despite a period of hostility when Francis I came to the throne. In 1520 these improved relations seemed to be at their height when the two Kings of England and France met outside Calais on the Field of Cloth of Gold, a very luxurious camp-site, where a few days were passed in sports and feasting. However, these celebrations concealed preparations for another war which lasted from 1522 to 1525, with England again in alliance with Spain and the Empire, now joined together in the person of Charles V. This war resulted in no gain, but considerable expense, which, together with the desertion of his Allies, forced Henry to make peace in 1525. For the next seventeen years England was at peace, at first because of a shortage of money, later because internal affairs, especially the Reformation were the all-consuming concern. The danger now came from Charles V, who might seek to avenge his aunt, Catherine of Aragon, or chastise Henry in the name of the Church. To counteract this danger, allies were sought in France and among the German princes. At the end of the reign Henry returned to his old warlike ways, pleased to recover the friendship of Charles V and with monastic money burning a hole in his pocket. In 1542 war with France and Scotland began. A great victory was won over the Scots at Solway Moss (1543) and further devastation wrought in Scotland in subsequent years, though the only effect of it seems to be that it strengthened Scottish determination to remain independent. There was greater success in France, and in 1544 Henry captured Boulogne, which was held to the end of the reign.

Henry VIII and the succession (see also under biographies of his wives). Every schoolboy knows that Henry had six wives, but the usual deduction that Henry was therefore a lascivious Bluebeard is wide of the historical truth, for it leaves out of account what for a hundred years was the nightmare for all the Tudors, the problem of the succession, the provision of a male heir to the throne. Everyone agreed that a woman on the throne was unthinkable. If the Princess Mary were to succeed, whom could she marry without bringing the realm in danger, danger from abroad, if she married a foreigner, danger from a second Wars of the Roses, if she married at home? By 1524 Catherine of Aragon, whom Henry married in 1509, was forty years old and it was clear that she would have no more children. She had borne Henry seven children, including four sons, but only Mary survived. Henry began to search for other means to provide a male heir. In 1525 he brought out of retirement his illegitimate son, Henry Fitzroy, and showered honours on him, probably with a view to nominating him as his heir. He even contemplated for a moment marrying him to Mary, half-sister to Fitzroy. But Henry himself was only thirty-four years old and he had fallen in love with Anne Boleyn. But it was essential that their children should be legitimate in order to provide an indisputably legal male heir to the throne. That his love for Anne was genuine is proved by the series of love letters which he wrote to her in his own hand. He married her in 1533. By 1536 she had given the King only one daughter, Elizabeth. In that year Catherine of Aragon died. Henry was already casting eyes on Jane Seymour. When Anne's second child was still-born (1536), the problem of the succession was no nearer a solution. The execution of Anne followed inevitably.

Jane Seymour gave Henry the son that he wanted (1537), but in doing so Jane herself died. The boy was delicate, and who could be sure that he would survive? Left to his own inclinations, it is possible that Henry would not have married again. But when in 1538 Thomas Cromwell wanted a Protestant alliance with Cleves, the King showed no liking for Cromwell's policy or for his proposal, but he reluctantly agreed. When Anne of Cleves arrived in England (1539), he showed even less liking for the lady, and within six months the marriage was dissolved.

Meantime Bishop Gardiner had brought to court Catherine Howard, whom he intended to set up as a Catholic rival to the German Protestant queen, Anne of Cleves. Anne had helped in no way to solve the problem of the succession, and now Parliament petitioned Henry to marry again and thus to strengthen the line of succession. He married Catherine Howard (July 1540), but in November 1541, much to the sorrow of the King, the story of her many indiscretions and misdemeanours was revealed and she was executed, in February 1542, before she had borne any children to Henry.

In 1543 Henry married again and for the last time. His last wife was Catherine Parr, who survived him by less than two years. There were no children by this marriage.

Henry VIII and the Annulment. On 11 June 1509, a few months after he succeeded to the throne, Henry married Catherine of Aragon. She had already been married to Henry's elder brother, Arthur, who died in 1502. This former marriage put Catherine within the forbidden degrees of relationship with Henry. The canon law was based on Leviticus, xx, 21, 'If a man shall take his brother's wife, it is an unclean thing ... they shall be childless'. To get over this canonical prohibition a dispensation was sought and obtained from Pope Julius II. When by 1524 Catherine had given Henry no male heir, Henry began to meditate upon Leviticus xx. 21 and to doubt the validity of his marriage, for only one child had survived out of seven. This happened to coincide with Henry's falling in love with Anne Boleyn, but in fact from the very first doubts had been expressed on the validity of the marriage, even by Pope Julius himself. An egoist like Henry must always have his own way; he is not capable of listening to argument. For argument Henry substituted his conscience, and his conscience was of the kind which always convinced him that what he wanted must be right. What Henry wanted was an undisputed male heir and Anne Boleyn: he could only obtain both by being rid of Catherine: hence the divorce or annulment of the marriage was indispensable: Henry turned to Wolsey to obtain it for him. Wolsey was in a dilemma: if he got the divorce, he would put into power his arch-enemies, the anti-clerical Boleyns; if he failed to get the divorce, Henry would rid himself of Wolsey, and might break with Rome.

On 17 May 1527, Wolsey collusively summoned Henry before him to explain why he had married his brother's widow. On 31 May Henry told Catherine that they were living in sin and must separate. He then set about trying to convince the clergy, but Fisher, Bishop of Rochester, would have none of it, although most of the clergy professed themselves to be convinced. Suddenly the news came that Charles V's troops had sacked Rome and Pope Clement VII was in the hands of Catherine's nephew. For two years the question of the divorce came to depend on foreign policy and on the success or failure of the French armies against Charles V. In 1528 the French King, Francis I, was having it all his own way, and the Pope felt sufficiently independent of Charles to send Campeggio to England to try the case with Wolsey and to pronounce sentence. The two Cardinals opened their court on 31 May 1529. Three weeks later, before any decision could be arrived at, Charles had destroyed the French army at Landriano (21 June), Clement and Charles made peace at Barcelona (29 June) and Charles and Francis at Cambrai (5 August). Campeggio adjourned the court to 1 October. It never met again. Clement revoked the case to Rome. The fall of Wolsey followed inevitably.

Having failed to obtain the divorce by cooperating with Rome, Henry now made up his mind to put pressure on Rome. In November he called Parliament in order to use its anti-clericalism to force the Pope's hand. He intended also to subject the Church completely to his own authority. He began to take the opinions of the universities of Europe on the question of the divorce, a suggestion first made by Cranmer (August 1529). He followed this up by threatening to appeal to General Council. His policy was a failure, yet throughout 1530 and 1531 Henry continued to try to obtain Papal sanction for the divorce and Papal approval for his marriage to Anne Boleyn.

Between 1532 and 1534 a series of measures was passed which brought about the Reformation in England and the breach with Rome. On 25 January 1533, Henry secretly married Anne Boleyn. The Act of Appeals (March 1533) forbade any appeals from the Archbishops' courts to Rome in cases involving wills or marriages. The divorce could now be legally settled in England. In the previous January Cranmer had been appointed Archbishop of Canterbury. He opened his court on 10 May 1533, and on 23 May he declared Henry's marriage with Catherine void and his marriage with Anne valid. On 1 June Anne was crowned and on 7 September her daughter Elizabeth was born. On 23 March 1534, the Pope at long last declared in favour of Catherine, but it was too late for any effect in England. Henry had outfaced Pope and Emperor, he had got his own way, but he was no nearer solving the problem of a male heir.

Henry VIII, the Royal Supremacy and the Reformation. The need to annul his marriage to Catherine of Aragon was the match which fired the powder, beginning the Reformation in England. The word Reformation in Henry VIII's reign covers the abolition of some abuses in the Church, the transferring of the government of the Church from the authority of Rome into the hands of King and Parliament, transferring ecclesiastical property to the Crown, and severing all political and financial relations between the Church in England and the Papacy. Apart from this, Henry did not alter the doctrine of the Church very significantly.

There was anti-clericalism among the laity, as had been shown in 1515 by the cases of Hunne and Standish. Henry determined in 1529 to use this anti-clericalism to strengthen his own position at the expense of the Church and to secure Papal consent to the Divorce. It is open to question, however, whether this anti-clericalism was as widely and popularly held as some historians have alleged. Certainly, however, it was exploited by Henry and his advisers. As soon as Parliament met in 1529, a group of Acts was passed which reformed some of the abuses in the Church. Two Acts limited the charges which the clergy could make in administering wills and as a mortuary fee; another tried to stop pluralism, the holding of more than one benefice at a time. It would be wrong to suppose that these measures permanently removed these abuses.

The attack on the clergy was also made on a wider front. Wolsey had been brought low by using the old statute of Praemunire (1393) which forbade the introduction into England of any papal letters and the exercise of jurisdiction by the clergy to the prejudice of the King. In 1530 this Act was turned against the whole clergy for having recognised Wolsey's legatine authority, despite the fact that the King himself had also recognised it. The clergy surrendered rather than lose its corporate property. The province of Canterbury bought its pardon for £100,000, York for close on £19,000, though not all of this money was in the end actually paid. They were compelled to recognise Henry as 'sole protector and also sole head of the Church of England', but insisted on adding the clause which diluted this fulsome title, 'so far as the law of Christ allows' (1531). 'Infinite clamours' continued in Parliament against the Church, and in 1532 the Commons presented to Henry its *Supplication against the Ordinaries*, which complained against the Church's right to independent legislation and of many abuses in the ecclesiastical courts. Henry sent the petition on to Convocation, the clergy appealed to him for protection against the laity, and Henry thus appeared to become the mediator between the two sides. He demanded from the clergy their assent to the reform of ecclesiastical law, the surrender of the right to make laws independently of Parliament and their recognition that all existing canons must be approved by the Crown. The clergy surrendered, this time more fully than in 1531, in what is known as the 'Submission of the Clergy', and in doing so the Church accepted the King in place of the Pope as its supreme legislator.

These complicated procedures in the years 1529–32 had not decisively broken with Rome. It seems likely that in these years — especially at first — the King was not following a clear or consistent line of policy, and had not yet fully accepted the idea of a schism until in 1532 Thomas Cromwell emerged as the King's chief adviser. It was Cromwell who achieved the Breach with Rome by a series of Acts of Parliament passed in the years 1532–35, initiated when Henry had finally given up all hope of a papal annulment to his marriage, and had decided to marry Anne Boleyn. In 1532 an Act was made forbidding the payment to Rome of annates, the first year's income of the high-ranking clergy. Henry postponed enforcing the Act for a year — a last hint to the Pope of what he might expect if he did not grant the divorce. The Pope ignored the hint and the Act was enforced in 1533. The Act in restraint of appeals (1533) was perhaps the greatest of the Reformation statutes; it laid down that in all cases dealing with wills, marriages, tithes and similar 'spiritual' matters, the final appeal should not be to Rome, but should be settled in England. This meant that the divorce could now be legally settled in England and need no longer wait upon the Pope's pleasure. This also meant that the supply line for finance from England to Rome was irreparably cut. The Act further maintained in clear terms that 'this realm of England is an empire... governed by one Supreme Head and King'. The royal supremacy was now legally and indisputably established, and papal authority in England was wholly eliminated. The submission of the clergy was embodied in an Act in 1534, by which the clergy also lost the right of finally deciding ecclesiastical cases in the archiepiscopal courts; appeals were now allowed from these courts to the King in Chancery. In the same year, the Act of Supremacy legalized all Henry's claims, laid down that the King 'is and ought to be Supreme Head of the Church of England', and gave him power to carry out visitations, which until now had been within the competence of the Church. The way to the dissolution of the monasteries was now clear.

Henry VIII and the Church of England. After the breach with Rome the Catholic Church *in* England became the Church *of* England, the Royal Supremacy replaced the Papacy, Henry replaced the Pope — but he never claimed full priestly or spiritual powers, he never claimed the right to celebrate the mass or to ordain priests. Short of this Henry was supreme: he controlled legislation and administration, he defined doctrine and he regulated ritual. Back in 1521 Henry had attacked Luther in his book *Assertio Septem Sacramentorum*, for which he had received from Pope Leo X the title of *Fidei Defensor*. He was no more ready after breaking away from the Papacy to embrace Lutheran doctrine. There was an inconsistency and variability after 1535 in Henry's religious policy, as he responded to the conflicting advice of the factions which surrounded him, and to the stimulus of foreign and domestic pressure. This inconsistency was apparent in the definitions of the doctrine of the Church of England which were issued in these years.

In July 1536 there appeared the *Ten Articles*, which were largely orthodox, although they failed to mention four of the seven Catholic sacraments. In August 1536 Cromwell issued a series of religious injunctions enforcing the *Ten Articles* and also attacking pilgrimages and the veneration of relics. The Pilgrimage of Grace later in the same year persuaded Henry that a clearer and even more conservative definition of doctrine was required. Hence in 1537 there was issued *The Institution of a Christian Man*, commonly known as *The Bishops' Book* because it was issued without the royal emendations Henry had suggested, and consequently did not have full royal approval. There was little in it of which a Catholic then or now could disapprove. Thus it failed to please the reforming party, and by the mere fact that it was new it disturbed the ordinary Englishman. In 1538 an official version of the Bible was published, and by further injunctions of 1539 it was ordered to be placed in every parish church.

Henry's conservative instincts and the pressure of those of his advisers who favoured the old religion led to the passage in 1539 of the Act of Six Articles or 'whip with six strings', which laid down severe penalties, including death, for speaking against six Catholic doctrines. Henry yearned for the unity which had preceded the onset of schism. In 1540 he executed both Catholics and Protestants, which demonstrates well his rather confused wish for unity. Henry came to think that the unrestricted reading of Scripture was dangerous, and in 1543 an Act was passed condemning all 'craftye, false and untrue' translations of the Bible, including that by Tyndale, and the reading of the Bible in the official version was restricted to the upper classes. On 29 May 1543 was published *The Necessary Doctrine and Erudition of a Christian Man*, commonly known as the *King's Book*, because on this occasion it did have royal approval. It was again a rather orthodox statement of views based on the earlier *Bishops' Book*.

Henry was no bigot. In 1543 he married Catherine Parr, who had Protestant tendencies, and he unswervingly supported his Archbishop, Cranmer, who was much more 'modern' in his theology than the King. Three times, in 1543, 1544 and 1545, Henry by his personal intervention saved Cranmer from charges of heresy. And it was Henry who ordered an English Litany, which Cranmer translated and which is still the basis for what is used by the Church of England (1544). In his last years, the more radical or Protestant of Henry's councillors were gradually growing more powerful, which prepared the way for the religious changes of the next reign. It is possible that if Henry had lived longer, his reign and not his son's would have seen an English Prayer Book and the dissolution of the chantries.

Henry had none of the rock-like faith of his daughter, Mary, but he had a conventional affection for the Catholic Church in which he had been brought up. In days when religion and politics were very much the same thing Henry had also a highly developed flair for politics. It was the combination of flair and affection which allowed him to carry through the Reformation without the civil wars which religious change brought in other countries.

Henry VIII and Wales. Under Henry VIII, Wales was most thoroughly reorganised, thanks largely to the efforts of Thomas Cromwell. The changes began with the execution in 1531 of the dominant figure in Welsh affairs, Rhys ap Gruffydd. The President of the Council in the Marches at the time was Voysey, Bishop of Exeter, but he was an ineffective ruler and it became clear that an entirely new policy was necessary for Wales, where law and order had ceased to exist. It was also necessary to secure Welsh support for the revolution in church and state which had been carried out between 1529 and 1536 in the Reformation Parliament. It was

Thomas Cromwell who recognized that action in Wales was essential. In 1534 Voysey was succeeded by Rowland Lee, who was sent to Wales in order to restore good government. A series of Acts was passed to re-establish order: one aimed at preventing felons from crossing the Severn to, or from, South Wales and the Forest of Dean; another inflicted a year's imprisonment on any person who assaulted those who tried to arrest him; a third Act tried to ensure that jurors would convict guilty defendants; a fourth prohibited the carrying of arms when attending Courts and gave full power to officers of an English shire to arrest and indict any person who was accused of murder or felony in a neighbouring Marcher lordship. The general authority of the Lord Marchers was still recognized, but in 1535 an Act was made to bring the administration of the Welsh shires into line with that of the English shires. It also entrusted local government to Welshmen, of which Rowland Lee did not approve. In 1536 the Act of Union was passed, by which Welshmen became citizens of the new kingdom of England and Wales, English methods of law and administration were extended to Wales and the English system of shires and hundreds became the basis of local government. Wales was represented in Parliament, and English became the official language. Monmouthshire became an English shire. The many adjustments made in the following half dozen years were summed up in detail in the Act of 1543, which completely assimilated Wales to England. If Tudor policy was antagonistic to Welsh nationalism, it did at least provide the Welsh with security, law and order.

Henry VIII and the Navy. Henry VII had been concerned mainly with securing his position at home and avoiding foreign entanglements, and therefore no great fleets were necessary for him. He had, however, been responsible for a certain amount of naval reorganisation, and the great *Mary Rose* was laid down at the end of his reign. With the accession of his son, this policy developed further, since Henry VIII wanted to play a leading part in foreign affairs. The King of France, Francis I, adopted an aggressive naval policy by moving his fleets from the Mediterranean to the Channel and by beginning to build more ships. The union of Brittany with the French crown gave France Channel ports and a race of seamen. The union of Spain, the Netherlands and the Empire under Charles V created a danger to England from Spanish ships, and the existence of a Scottish navy to back the Franco-Scottish alliance was a further threat to England. It was obviously sound policy for Henry to strengthen his fleet, and Henry had much personal interest in ships and in sailing.

Henry VIII inherited from his father 7 ships. By the end of 1512, in three and a half years, 17 new vessels had been added to the navy either by construction or by purchase. By 1546 the navy numbered 85 vessels (excluding 13 row-barges), of which Henry had built 46, purchased 26 and obtained 13 as naval prizes. At his death in 1547 the navy consisted of 53 ships with a total tonnage of 11,268, carrying 7,780 men and 2,087 guns. The best-known ship is the *Henry Grâce à Dieu*.

Henry's achievement was considerable. He built the largest and most powerful navy in the world, he revolutionized its armament — the moment is marked when the curtall, a heavy gun of 3,000 lbs., hitherto used only as a siege-piece on land, was transferred to ships: the *Sovereign* was rebuilt in 1509 and given four. He improved its fighting and sailing qualities and he himself invented or adapted a type of ship suitable for the narrow seas. He enlarged the existing dockyard at Portsmouth and made two new ones at Woolwich and Deptford, and he also built forts for the defence of the coast. Henry may well be called the founder of the Royal Navy. It remains true, however, that this great Henrician navy was seldom used, and the best-remembered maritime incident of the reign is perhaps fittingly the entirely accidental — and avoidable — loss of the *Mary Rose* with all hands in 1545.

Henry VIII and the coinage. The sixteenth century saw a revolution in prices, and this made existing methods of public finance totally inadequate to meet the needs of government. Like their colleagues all over Europe, Tudor financiers were faced with inflation on a very large scale, the result in part of the increased silver mining in Austria, and from the 1540s of the growing flood of silver from the Spanish New World, but mainly of a rising population and of heavy government expenditure on war. In 1526 Henry VIII and Wolsey *devalued* the coinage — *i.e.* they increased the amount of money in circulation by reducing the weight of the silver coins. This was a sensible and reputable operation, because all it did was to bring the English coinage into a proper relationship with the continental coins.

In 1542, when Henry was virtually his own minister in every sphere, in order to meet his financial difficulties, which arose from his wars and other extravagances, he embarked on a policy which he kept up until his death in 1547, of *debasing* the coinage — *i.e.* he put more alloy into each silver coin, thereby altering the weight and adulterating the fineness of the silver coinage (the proportion of metal to alloy) to such a degree that he reduced the value of the silver coin to one sixth of what it had been in the time of Henry VII. The silver thus left over could be recoined at an enormous profit — about £500,000. This of course only increased inflation and drove up prices. Henry thus left severe economic problems to his successors, but it should in fairness be added that there was in his day no science of taxation and Parliament would not vote enough money to cover the needs of modern government when the value of money was falling.

Henry VIII: summary. No other English King is better known or more quickly recognized in his portraits than Henry VIII. The gigantic figure with the broad shoulders, no doubt a little exaggerated by the fashion in dress at the time, the feathered cap set slightly atilt, the strong legs set wide apart, planted firmly, even arrogantly, on the ground, the general air of commanding self-confidence, make Henry VIII easily identifiable and give an immediate key to his character. This is indeed a regal figure. A closer inspection, especially in the later portraits, raises some doubts: that small and narrow mouth, those piggy eyes suggest meanness and even cruelty. Henry was as much a Renaissance prince as was ever Francis I or Lorenzo Il Magnifico. He could be affable, affectionate, as he was at one time to Sir Thomas More; generous, as he was to Reginald Pole before their quarrel or to Wolsey after his fall, and always to Cranmer. He was highly intelligent and highly talented; he loved books and games, pictures and music, fine clothes and rich jewellery, as his portraits prove. He could also be completely selfish, mean and treacherous, as he was to Robert Aske and the rebels in the Pilgrimage of Grace: ruthless, as he was to the clergy in 1530; relentless, as he was to Sir Thomas More and John Fisher in 1535, although it is fair to add that there is some evidence that he disliked and regretted the execution. If Henry is to be judged by the constancy of morals, his character will not stand up to much cross-examination. If he is to be judged by the standards of his own times, he must be recognized as a great and to a large extent a successful king. The splendid young man who came to the throne in 1509, by 1547 had become a revolting, swollen mass of putrifying flesh, too heavy for his legs to bear and suffering agonies from an ulcerous leg as he was wheeled in a chair from place to place. Yet he was still (and even more so) his old self, arrogant, self-centred, merciless, still full of affection for his last wife, still popular with his people, even while they dreaded him.

Too often his foreign policy was vitiated by his natural bellicosity and by his desire to play a leading and active part on the Continent. This is especially true of his warlike policy in the last decade of his reign and of his most unwise treatment of Scotland. But he lived in dangerous times, and by his realism, his capacity for seeing things as they really were, by his invincible courage and by his genius for ruling, he triumphantly rode out every storm and kept his kingdom free from foreign invasion and from the civil wars which beset continental countries.

At home Henry showed greater judgment. Nothing is more remarkable than the way in which he made Parliament into his ally. It is difficult to say now how far Parliament was 'packed'. What is certain is that Henry knew exactly how to 'manage' the House of Commons, both through the Lords and through the able servants of the Crown who sat in the Lower House. He had an uncanny understanding of the feelings of the Commons, so that the relations between the Crown and Parliament were on the whole very satisfactory. Always Henry remained the supreme authority, and to him Parliament was only a support for the Royal Supremacy, but that did not prevent him from declaring that 'WE be informed by our judges that we at no time stand so highly in our estate royal as in the time of parliament'. His daughter Elizabeth inherited her father's wisdom and popularity.

Henry left many problems to his successor — religious, economic and social, but his achievements were outstanding and invaluable. He made the English people aware of themselves: he gave them the English Bible: he built and manned for them the finest navy in the world: he implanted in them a respect for government and an affection for the Crown as head of that government: he guided a great politico-religious revolution along conservative lines so that for the most part he carried the nation with him — as Somerset and Northumberland in the next reign failed to do. He had none of the spiritual strength which marks out Sir Thomas More in glaring contrast, but in an age when material dangers threatened even the survival of the state, and when only strong government could have provided salvation, Henry provided what was needed courageously, ruthlessly and effectively.

G. R. Elton, *Henry VIII*, H. A. pamphlet GS 51.
A. F. Pollard, *Henry VIII*, 1919.
C. Morris, *The Tudors*, 1955.
J. J. Scarisbrick, *Henry VIII*, 1968.
L. B. Smith, *Henry VIII: the Mask of Royalty*, 1971.
J. Ridley, *Henry VIII*, 1984.
D. Starkey, *The reign of Henry VIII*, 1985.

CATHERINE OF ARAGON (1485–1536), first wife of Henry VIII, was the youngest child of Ferdinand of Aragon and Isabella of Castile. Spain was the rising country in Europe: in search of powerful allies, Henry VII sought a marriage alliance with one of the Spanish royal family. In 1489 at the treaty of Medina del Campo Arthur, Prince of Wales, (aged 3), was promised to Catherine (aged 4). Not until 1501 did Catherine arrive in England and see Arthur. The marriage took place at St. Paul's on 14 November 1501. Arthur was now 14, his wife nearly 16. They went to live together in Wales, but they were thought to be too young for cohabitation. On 2 April 1502, Arthur died: the marriage had never been consummated. At the age of 16 Catherine was a widow and remained so for the next seven years. Those seven years were a foretaste of what was to come later on.

Henry VII refused to allow her to return to Spain, and negotiations were at once begun to marry her to his second son, Henry, in 1503. Before the plan was completed, Henry's wife died and he suggested that he should marry his daughter-in-law. This may have been merely a move in the diplomatic game; if so, it was successful. Isabella was so shocked that the marriage with Prince Henry was agreed to quickly. It was not to take place until he had reached his fourteenth birthday, which would be in 1505. So valuable a pawn did Henry VII find an unmarried Catherine in the business of international diplomacy that he refused to allow the marriage to take place, and it was not till after his death and Henry VIII's accession that the wedding took place (1509). For seven years Catherine's father left his daughter in England penniless and in debt, while Henry VII refused to finance her. She was wretchedly attended, scarcely ever allowed to see her future husband, and falling ever deeper into debt. During these years she shewed herself to be a diplomat of a very high order, all the time working to maintain the Anglo-Spanish alliance with a shrewdness and skill not belonging to the official Spanish ambassadors. On 11 June 1509, she and Henry VIII were married, and both were crowned on 24 June.

From 1509 to about 1525 Henry and Catherine led a happily married life. The King was not always faithful, but she was a devoted and wise wife, who could shut her eyes to momentary lapses, while Henry treated her with affection and courtesy.

But in the sixteenth century a Queen was expected to provide male heirs to the throne. Between 1510 and 1518 Catherine bore six children, of whom only one survived, a girl, the Princess Mary. These disappointments may have weakened Henry's affection: the perfidious behaviour of his father-in-law, Ferdinand, weakened his desire for a Spanish alliance: his conscience began to wonder why the children died: a male heir to the throne was a necessity: incidentally, also, Henry had become infatuated with Anne Boleyn. For five more years, from 1526 to 1531, Henry and Catherine remained together on friendly, but deteriorating, terms. On 14 July 1531, Henry slipped away from Windsor without saying goodbye and never saw Catherine again. From that moment her life became more and more wretched. She was commanded to abandon the use of the word queen; she refused. Continual pressure was brought to bear on her to acknowledge that her marriage with Henry had been illegal from the start; she refused. She was assailed to accept the Act of Supremacy and to take the oath; she refused. She was moved from house to house; her daughter was forbidden to visit her. Her household was whittled away, her income reduced, the furniture removed, until she lived virtually in one room. And all the time she was in deadly fear of poison. She could get no help from her nephew, Charles V, the Emperor. For five years she warned the Pope that unless he pronounced in her favour on the question of marriage, the English church would break from Rome. Clement VII took no notice. At last on 23 March 1534, he gave his verdict that the marriage was valid. It was too late. Anne Boleyn had been declared Queen by Parliament and the breach with Rome was complete.

Catherine was a woman of great intellectual ability. She was a strong supporter of the New Learning and of the Classical Revival — Erasmus found her scholarship more impressive than Henry VIII's. She was a shrewd diplomatist and a most formidable debater — as Henry VIII found to his cost. But she was much more than that — she was a heroine. In all her later troubles she had only one friend, Chapuys, the Imperial Ambassador. She relied on him, and he did all he could for her. But she relied on her religious faith much more. She never deviated from the line she adopted at the start. She declared she was Henry's legal wife and always had been, and she would never admit she was not. She was Henry's loving wife and she seems to have retained some affection for him even to the end. In her last letter to him she said, 'Lastly, I make this vow, that mine eyes desire you above all things'. She was Henry's loyal subject, she would obey him in everything, except that she would not disobey God and her conscience. Thomas Cromwell said of her that 'Nature wronged the Queen in not making her a man. But for her sex she would have surpassed all the heroes of history'. The people of England loved her and demonstrated their affection on every possible occasion.

Catherine died on 7 January 1536. Polydore Vergil records that her last letter (quoted above) brought tears to the eyes of Henry VIII. Chapuys — admittedly a hostile witness — records that the King, dressed from top to toe in yellow with a white feather in his cap, gave a ball at Greenwich and went about among the revellers with the Princess Elizabeth in his arms, crying out, 'God be praised, the old harridan is dead'.

G. Mattingley, *Catherine of Aragon*, 1942.

ANNE BOLEYN (1501?–1536), second wife of Henry VIII and mother of Elizabeth I, was born perhaps in 1501 or perhaps in 1507 and died on the scaffold on Friday 19 May 1536. She was the second daughter of Sir Thomas Boleyn, afterwards Earl of Wiltshire and Ormond. Like all Henry VIII's wives, she was descended from Edward I. Some of her early years were spent in France, and possibly

Anne Boleyn
(Artist: Unknown)

the Netherlands, but by 1522 she was home and living at the Court
of Henry VIII. She had many admirers, although she seems not to
have been very beautiful and had an incipient sixth finger on the left
hand, which led her enemies to talk of her as a witch. She was,

however, witty, vivacious and adept at the courtly accomplishments. She was on the point of marrying Lord Henry Percy, heir to
the earldom of Northumberland, but by the King's command
Wolsey put an end to this proposed marriage. It is not known for
certain at what point Henry fell in love with Anne. He had already
had Anne's sister, Mary, as his mistress. It was not until 1527 that he
began seriously to contemplate divorcing his wife, Catherine of
Aragon. By 1528 Anne was living at Greenwich with the King, and
by 1531 she was openly going about with him, to the fury and
detestation of the English people. At Easter 1533 it became known
that Henry and Anne had been married on 25 January. Anne had
already been for some months pregnant. It was vital to all Henry's
hopes for a male successor to the throne that the child should be
legitimate; therefore Archbishop Cranmer pronounced the marriage
with Catherine of Aragon to be null and void and that Anne was the
King's lawful wife. But already Henry's passion was cooling, and he
was complaining of her arrogant behaviour. On 7 September 1533,
Anne gave birth to a daughter, the future Elizabeth I. The King's
disappointment was tremendous. Probably by 1534 he was in love
with Jane Seymour. On 7 January 1536, Catherine of Aragon died.
Only one thing could have saved Anne — the birth of a male heir.
On 29 January she was delivered of a son: it was still-born. On 2
May she was arrested, and on 19 May 1536 she was executed on
charges of adultery with four men, including her own brother —
charges which have never satisfactorily been proved to be true. She
fell victim in part to a struggle in Henry's court between rival
political factions, who sought to gain power over the King through
his wives. Decapitation by the sword was the method of execution
chosen, and an executioner had to be brought over from France
specially for the occasion, since there was no-one in England capable
of performing this task. Anne spent the last night before her
execution in the same room in the Tower of London as she had
occupied the night before her coronation.

Anne occupies an important place in English history since in some
senses she was responsible for the Break with Rome and hence for the
English Reformation. She was not an entirely passive participant in
these great events: her religious views were modern and she
patronised those who shared such inclinations; her steadfast refusal
to give in to the King's advances until she was married may have

strengthened Henry's resolve to divorce Catherine; and she wielded for a while considerable political influence, which she used to advance her family and friends. All that in the end could not save her from the block.

E. W. Ives, *Anne Boleyn*, 1986.
H. Paget, *Bulletin Institute of Historical Research*, 1981.
M. Dowling, *Journal of Ecclesiastical History*, 1984.

JANE SEYMOUR (1509?–1537), Henry VIII's third wife, was born probably in 1509 and died on 24 October 1537. She was the eldest of eight children born to Sir John Seymour of Wolf Hall, Savernake, Wiltshire, and his wife, Margaret, daughter of Sir John Wentworth, who claimed distant relationship with the royal family. She was the sister of Edward Seymour, later Duke of Somerset and Protector in the reign of Jane's son, Edward VI, and of Sir Thomas Seymour, Lord High Admiral, who was executed in 1549 by the reluctant command of his brother.

Little is known for certain of Jane's life, especially of her early life. Before Catherine of Aragon ceased to be Queen, she was one of her ladies-in-waiting, and after Anne Boleyn married Henry VIII, she was in the service of the new Queen. Probably it was in 1534 that Henry fell in love with her, and from that moment he paid much attention to her, to the fury of Anne Boleyn. Jane behaved with the greatest discretion and propriety, refusing all the King's advances until he was able to marry her. While the trial of Anne was pending, Jane lived with her brother and his wife, and Henry undertook to see her only in the presence of her friends. Two days before Anne's execution Cranmer declared his marriage with Anne null and void and on the day of execution (19 May) he issued a dispensation for Henry to marry Jane without publication of banns. They were married on 30 May 1536.

Her married life lasted a little more than a year. During that time she was able to reconcile Henry with his daughter, Mary, and to win golden opinions from all who came in contact with her. She seems to have had no sympathy with the Reformation: Luther called her 'an enemy of the gospel'; Cardinal Pole declared that she was 'full of goodness'. It is said that during the Pilgrimage of Grace she pleaded with Henry to restore the monasteries, but that he warned her not to

Jane Seymour
(Artist: After Hans Holbein)

meddle in affairs of state, if she wanted to avoid Anne Boleyn's fate. On 12 October 1537, she gave birth to a son, Edward, later Edward VI, but she herself died on 24 October.

Jane Seymour appears to have been the best loved of Henry's wives. He went into mourning for her, which he did for none of his other wives, and he ordered that his own body should be buried beside hers in St. George's Chapel, Windsor. Owing to her frail health she was never crowned Queen.

ANNE OF CLEVES (1515–1557), Henry VIII's fourth wife, was the daughter of John, Duke of Cleves: she was born on 22 September 1515, and died on 16 July 1557. Plain, ungraceful, ill-educated, this unfortunate German woman appeared for a moment

Anne of Cleves
(Artist: J. Houlbraken, after Hans Holbein)

on the chess-board of European politics, a pawn in the foreign policy of Thomas Cromwell. In 1538 the Emperor Charles V and Francis I of France were drawing together, a league had been made against the Turks, and it looked to Pope Paul III and to Cardinal Pole as if the time was ripe for an attack on the King of England. Cleves, situated on the lower Rhine, was strategically a threat to the Emperor. The then Duke of Cleves, William, was not himself a Lutheran, but he was allied with Lutherans and was as much an Erastian as was Henry VIII. Cromwell, therefore, proposed a marriage between Henry and Duke William's sister, Anne. Politically there might be something to be said for the policy: but no one could have been less suitable to wed the English King than Anne, who could speak no language but her own, had no manners and could neither sing nor play any instrument. Henry was averse to the match from the first, but he was deluded by a flattering portrait of Anne painted by Holbein.

Anne arrived in England on 27 December 1539. Henry took an immediate dislike to her: 'Is there no remedy, then,' said the king, 'but that I must needs put my neck in the yoke?' They were married on 6 January; in the morning Henry said to Cromwell, 'My lord, if it were not to satisfy the world and my realm, I would not do that which I must do this day for none earthly thing.' The marriage was soon seen to be unnecessary, for the French King and the Emperor were falling out once more. Cromwell's policy was utterly discredited, he was arrested and executed (June 1540). On 9 July Convocation declared the marriage null and void. Anne was set aside and pensioned off with lands to the value of £3,000. She accepted her fate calmly and lived out the rest of her life quietly in England. If in private Henry called her the 'Flanders mare', in public he treated her with courtesy and consideration, and when she had to give up the title of Queen, she was accorded that of the King's 'sister'.

CATHERINE HOWARD (*d.* 1542), fifth wife of Henry VIII, was the daughter of Lord Edmund Howard, a younger son of the second Duke of Norfolk. The date of her birth is unknown: she was executed on 13 February 1542, possibly in her nineteenth year. Largely owing to the poverty of her father she had a bad upbringing and was much neglected as a child, and when her father married a second time, Catherine went to live with her grandmother, the old Duchess [Agnes] of Norfolk. Very soon the girl's irresponsible and volatile character revealed itself. She allowed a musician named Mannock (or Manox) to treat her with much familiarity, probably in 1536. A more serious affair occurred between her and Francis Dereham, who was related to Catherine. The two became engaged and called each other husband and wife, although the engagement was hidden from the outside world. According to the views of the times, such an engagement would invalidate any other marriage in the future. When Catherine went to Court, the intimacy between them was ended, and Dereham went off to Ireland. He returned before she married Henry VIII and heard that she was engaged to marry a cousin of hers, Thomas Culpepper, a report which Catherine denied to Dereham.

In 1540 Henry VIII married Anne of Cleves, but from the first sight of her he hated the marriage. There is little doubt that he was soon attracted to Catherine Howard, and as little doubt that Bishop Gardiner hoped to set her up as a Catholic rival to the Queen. On 9 July 1540 Anne was set aside and on 28 July Henry married Catherine privately at Oatlands. In July 1541 Henry and Catherine went on a progress to the north of England. They arrived at Pontefract in August and stayed there until the beginning of September. It was here that Catherine, with the help of Lady Rochford, had several meetings with Thomas Culpepper, and she also appointed Francis Dereham as her secretary. In November the royal party was back at Hampton Court.

On All Saints' Day the King gave thanks to God for the good life he led and hoped to lead with his new Queen, 'after sundry troubles of mind which had happened to him by marriages'. The next day Cranmer revealed to Henry the story of his Queen's indiscretions. An investigation was ordered by the King, who was deeply unhappy at the news. The principal witness against Catherine was Dereham, who confessed to having often lain with her before she became Queen. Catherine herself denied all the charges until denial was no longer possible. No proof was forthcoming of adultery after her marriage to the King. Torture was employed to wring further evidence from Dereham and Culpepper: probably a charge of adultery was not provable, only assumable with some degree of certainty in the case of Culpepper, who denied it to the end. Lady Rochford was arrested and went out of her mind. Legal and constitutional considerations prolonged the proceedings. Ultimately a 'pitiful confession' was made by Catherine, and she and Lady Rochford were executed on the same spot as had been Anne Boleyn.

Lacey Baldwin Smith, *A Tudor Tragedy*, 1961.

CATHERINE PARR (1512–1548), Henry VIII's sixth and last wife, was born in 1512 and died on 7 September 1548. She was the daughter of Sir Thomas Parr, Controller of the Household to Henry VIII. Her father died in 1517, and Catherine was brought up by her mother, who was 22 years old at the time of her husband's death. Her education was careful and thorough and she became an accomplished scholar in Greek and Latin and modern languages.

When she was 12 years old an offer of marriage was made for her for Lord Scrope's son, but the offer was declined as not fulfilling the conditions laid down in her father's will. At some unknown date later she married Edward Borough, of whom nothing is known. Her second husband was John Neville, Lord Latimer, who had already been twice married and had two children by his second wife. He took some part in the Pilgrimage of Grace, but he escaped punishment and was held in favour by the King. He died in 1542 or 1543, and Catherine was at once sought in marriage by Sir Thomas Seymour, brother of Jane Seymour. She intended to marry him, but she was 'overruled by a higher power', which was in fact Henry VIII, whom she married on 12 July 1543. Catherine was physically a small woman, but she had character, spirit and much shrewdness, besides great kindness of heart. She managed Henry more successfully than any other of his wives: it was probably she who persuaded him to restore to Mary and Elizabeth the rank of Princess, which had been taken away from them as being bastards: she interceded for the victims of the persecution under the Six Articles: and she took much interest in the education of Elizabeth and of Edward, her step-children. For three months in 1544, while Henry was abroad invading France, she was Regent of England.

Henry's temper in his last years was very unreliable, for he was irritated by religious dissensions and in constant pain from an ulcer on his leg. Catherine nursed him and sometimes discussed religious questions with him. Once she differed from him. 'A good hearing it is', Henry said, 'when women become such clerks; and a thing much to my comfort to come in mine old days to be taught by my wife.' It is said that a charge of heresy was brought against her and was signed by the King without her knowledge. But she got to know of it and fell ill with anxiety. Henry sent his doctors to her and also visited her himself. When she recovered she went to see the king and explained that she had only meant 'to minister talk' and not to assert opinions of her own. 'Is it even so, sweetheart? Then perfect friends we are now again', said Henry. But the next day she was walking with him in the garden at Hampton Court when the Lord Chancellor arrived with forty of the King's Guards to arrest her. Henry took the Chancellor aside, and all that Catherine could hear was 'Knave! beast! and fool!' Catherine interceded for the Chancellor, if he had done anything wrong. 'Ah poor soul!' said Henry, 'thou little knowest, Kate, how ill he deserveth this at thy hands. On my word, sweetheart, he hath been to thee a very knave.'

Henry VIII died on 28 January 1547. At once Sir Thomas Seymour, who had lately been created Baron Seymour of Sudeley, asked Catherine to marry him. Their engagement is certain, and Seymour passed several nights with her at Chelsea. Royal assent had not been yet asked for: when it was, the Protector was hostile to the marriage, but Edward VI in the end took Seymour's part and the Protector became reconciled to the event. On 30 August 1548 Catherine gave birth to a girl, but she died on 7 September from puerperal fever. Catherine lies buried in the chapel at Sudeley Castle.

Jean Plaidy, *The Sixth Wife*, 1953.

MARY TUDOR (1496-1533), Queen of France, Duchess of Suffolk, grandmother of Lady Jane Grey, was born probably early in March 1496, and she died in 1533. She was the second daughter of Henry VII and Elizabeth of York, and therefore sister of Henry VIII. In 1508 she was betrothed to Charles of Castile, afterwards the Emperor Charles V. In 1509 her father died and her brother succeeded as Henry VIII. In 1514 arrangements were all but completed for her marriage to Charles, but the Emperor Maximilian I, Charles's grandfather, played false and the marriage never took place.

Henry VIII was not the man to lie down under such an insult. Swiftly and secretly he made peace with France and compelled his sister, who was eighteen years old, to marry Louis XII of France, an enfeebled and sickly old man of fifty-two. Mary was much in love with Charles Brandon, Duke of Suffolk, and she only agreed to marry Louis XII on condition that, were he to die, she should be free to marry whom she would. Her marriage with the French King lasted only eight months, for Louis died on 1 January 1515. Left alone in France, Mary was in a perilous position. To save herself from being compelled to make another political marriage either by Francis I or by Henry VIII, she persuaded Suffolk (who had pledged his word to Henry not to marry Mary without his consent) to marry her secretly in Paris, probably in the last week of February 1515. Henry was furious, not because he disliked the marriage, but because Suffolk had broken his word and the marriage was made without Henry's consent, and he was only placated by a present of £24,000 and 200,000 French crowns and all the plate, jewels and rich clothing which had formed part of Mary's dowry.

The marriage was generally unpopular in England, and therefore the Duke and Duchess retired into private life in Norfolk. During a short visit to London in 1516 Mary gave birth to a son. A year later she entertained Catherine of Aragon on her way to Walsingham (March 1517). In July she was at court, whence she moved to Hatfield, where she stayed in order to have her second baby, Frances, who became the mother of Lady Jane Grey. The King's anger over the marriage was short-lived: he had a deep affection for his sister Mary, much more than he had for his other sister, Margaret, the Queen of Scotland, and Mary was frequently at court. Her health was never strong, and she was from time to time seriously ill, but was able to meet her one-time affianced husband, Charles V, when he visited England in 1520; she was able also to accompany Henry VIII to the Field of Cloth of Gold, during which a treaty was made with Francis I which restored a great part of her dowry.

When Henry entered on his divorce from Catherine of Aragon, Mary was strongly on the side of the Queen, largely because she could not tolerate seeing Anne Boleyn, once one of her ladies-in-waiting, raised to the position of Queen above herself, who had once been a Queen.

The rest of her life is historically unimportant. She died on 24 June 1533 at Westhorpe in Suffolk and was buried in the abbey of Bury St. Edmunds. That monastery was dissolved in 1538, and the coffin was moved into St. Mary's church. It was opened in 1784 and Horace Walpole and the Duchess of Portland took away some locks of Mary's hair.

Mary Tudor was an exceptionally beautiful woman, not only physically but also in character. Her beauty of face was known throughout Europe: she never lost the deep feelings which Henry had for her: she won the hearts of all France by her devoted treatment of Louis XII. Her family life with Suffolk was one of untarnished happiness. Like all the Tudors she loved music and was an accomplished musician. She had a gay nature and a light step for dancing, she adored beautiful clothes and enjoyed to the full the fun and pageantry of the life into which she was born. She had also strength and courage to tell her formidable brother just how far he could go, and to fight for what she thought to be due to the meanest of her servants. No wonder that Mary Tudor has gone down in history and in modern literature as the most romantic of a hard-bitten family.

M. A. E. Green, *Lives of the Princesses of England*, Vol. 5: an admirable essay.
M. C. Brown, *Mary Tudor, Queen of France*, 1911.
Beatrice White, *Royal Nonesuch*.
J. Gainey. *The Princess of the 'Mary Rose'*, 1986.

MARGARET TUDOR (1489–1541), Queen of Scotland, was the eldest daughter of Henry VII and Elizabeth of York. She was born on 29 November 1489, and she died on 18 October 1541. She was two years older than Henry VIII. She was not so well educated as the rest of the Tudors, but she could write, though only what she called 'an evil hand', and she could play on the lute and the clavichord. In 1495 Henry VII tried to arrange a marriage for Margaret with James IV of Scotland, in the hopes of thus cutting off Scottish support for Perkin Warbeck. This attempt failed, but after long negotiations the marriage was finally arranged in 1502, the espousals took place in 1503. Margaret left England for Scotland on 27 June 1503; she arrived at Edinburgh on 7 August and the marriage took place on the following day.

After her marriage to the Scottish king, Margaret ceases to play a major part in English history, but on the death of James IV at

Flodden Field in 1513 Margaret became the Regent of Scotland and the rest of her life is bound up with the history of Scotland.

She married twice more. First to Archibald, sixth Earl of Angus, from which marriage there descended Lord Darnley, the unfortunate husband of Mary, Queen of Scots. After him, Margaret Tudor finally married Henry, Lord Methven. Her main importance in English history is as the grand-mother of Mary, Queen of Scots, and hence as the great-grand-mother of James VI of Scotland, who became James I of England by virtue of his descent, through Margaret, from Henry VII.

HENRY FITZROY, DUKE OF RICHMOND (1519–1536), was the natural son of Henry VIII by his mistress Elizabeth Blount, a lady-in-waiting to Catherine of Aragon. His birthplace was the manor of Blackmore in Essex 'reported to have been one of Henry VIII's Houses of Pleasure and disguised under the name of Jericho. So that when this lascivious Prince had a mind to be lost in the embraces of his courtesans, the cant word amongst the courtiers was, that he was gone to Jericho'. (Morant, *Hist. of Essex*, ii, 57.) He was given the best possible education under Richard Croke, a famous Greek scholar, and John Palsgrave, author of the first French grammar in the English language. The King's affection for him was deep and lasting: he called him 'my worldly jewel'. The boy showed great aptitude at his books and he was much 'inclined to all manner of virtuous and honourable inclinations as any babes living' (Palsgrave to Elizabeth Blount). He developed into a fine horseman and was also a good musician, like all the Tudors. He had beautiful handwriting in a clear Italian hand.

When he was six years old he suddenly blazed into the public notice. On 15 June 1525, he was created Duke of Richmond — the title may be significant, for it was that held by Henry VII before he was King. He had already a week before been made a Knight of the Garter. Other offices were showered upon him, including that of Lord High Admiral. He became also Lord-Lieutenant of Ireland and Warden of the Cinque Ports, and it was thought that Henry intended to make him King of Ireland. All this at six years old. The favour shown to him and the magnificence of his household contrasted glaringly with the treatment meted out to the Princess Mary, who was three years older. Catherine of Aragon watched with anxiety, and she had reason, for undoubtedly already the King was seriously disturbed by his failure to obtain a male heir from Catherine. That he had it in mind to advance his son even to the throne is suggested by the fact that two years before the divorce is said to have occurred to Henry, he was considering with the council to entail the succession on his illegitimate son, Henry Fitzroy.

Several proposals were made for marrying Fitzroy to a foreign princess, but in 1533 he married Mary Howard, daughter of the third Duke of Norfolk by his second marriage and the sister of the Earl of Surrey, the poet. He was present at the execution of Anne Boleyn in May 1536, but on 22 July he died, not without rumours that he had been poisoned by Anne Boleyn and her brother, Lord Rochford. He lies buried in St. Michael's church, Framlingham.

J. G. Nichols, *Camden Misc.*, Vol. 3, 1854.

WILLIAM WARHAM (1450?–1532), Archbishop of Canterbury, came of a Hampshire family and was educated at Winchester and at New College, Oxford, where he became a Fellow in 1475, a post which he held for thirteen years. He directed the school of Civil (Roman) Law in the university until he left Oxford in 1488 to practise as an advocate in London in the ecclesiastical Court of Arches. By 1490 he was one of the most considerable lawyers in the country, and in that year he travelled to Rome on business for the Bishop of Ely. In 1491 he was in Antwerp settling a dispute with the merchants of the Hanse: in 1493 he was again in Flanders, with Sir Edward Poynings, on an embassy to persuade the Dowager Duchess of Burgundy to abandon Perkin Warbeck. Although the mission failed, it is said that Warham's speech was an immense success. On 21 September 1493, Warham was ordained as sub-deacon at the age of forty-five and he now received many preferments. In 1494 he was made Master of the Rolls, in 1496 he negotiated the marriage of Arthur, Prince of Wales, with Catherine of Aragon, and from now onwards he was used in many important diplomatic cases by Henry VII, who trusted him completely. In 1502 he was consecrated Bishop of London, and in 1504 he became Archbishop of Canterbury and Lord Chancellor. The year 1506 saw him Chancellor of Oxford, and two years later he set about reforming some of the abuses in the Court of Audience. In 1509, he crowned Henry VIII

William Warham
(Artist: After Hans Holbein)

and Catherine of Aragon and was appointed by the Pope to present to Henry the Golden Rose.

The first part, the happiest and the most successful, of Warham's life was now finished. The accession of Henry VIII and the arrival of Wolsey marked the beginning of a new age in England. New men and new methods, new policies also, were now to destroy the position of trust which Warham had enjoyed under Henry VII. By the time Wolsey became a Cardinal in 1515 Warham's position both as a statesman and as Archbishop was growing increasingly difficult. In that year Warham resigned from the Chancellorship and he retired almost completely from the Council. For a while he still appeared on state occasions — in 1520 he was present at the Field of Cloth of Gold — but in ecclesiastical matters he represented an old and out-worn system. In 1512 he had quarrelled with Fox, Bishop of Winchester, over alleged encroachments by Canterbury on the jurisdictions of the suffragans. In 1523 he was to quarrel with the encroachments which Wolsey was making on the rights of Canterbury. And indeed Wolsey was totally ruthless and unreasonable. No doubt Warham was a stiff and upright man, who stood rigidly upon the old order, but Wolsey humiliated the Archbishop in every sort of way. After 1515 no cross was carried in front of the Archbishop, even in his own diocese. At the ceremony when Wolsey received his Cardinal's hat, Warham had to play a minor part, and the arrival of Campeggio further diminished his importance. It is difficult to say what were the real relations between Warham and Wolsey. In his letters Warham is always protesting how much he values Wolsey's kindnesses to him, but the language smacks strongly of the sycophantic style of the times. On the other hand, when Warham was once ill, Wolsey offered him quarters at Hampton Court.

There is no difficulty in judging the relations between Warham and the King. Once the divorce had been mooted and as soon as the Reformation Parliament met in 1529, Warham disliked most of Henry's policy. He declined to give a decision on the question of the validity of Henry's marriage: he was appointed one of the counsel for the Queen, but Catherine had the lowest opinion of Warham's efforts on her behalf. Warham watched the development of the attacks on the Church with consternation. It was he who suggested the addition to the title of Supreme Head of the Church at the time of the Pardon of the Clergy (1531). So far, Warham had not proved himself to be a very brave defender of the Church: he had agreed to too many damaging compromises. He was an old man now: he had shirked advising Catherine on the plea that *Ira principis mors est*. But now at the last moment he roused himself to make a valiant stand. In February 1532 he gave notice at his last appearance in the House of Lords that he would in the next session move the repeal of all the statutes passed against the Church since the beginning of that Parliament. Henry's answer was to threaten Warham with a writ of *praemunire*. The Archbishop saw clearly enough that a dangerous fate might now await him. The general weakness of the Church in its resistance to Henry was symbolised when after much debate Convocation accepted the Submission of the Clergy (1532), by which the Church in England surrendered its legislative independence to the King. Broken in health and too ill to leave his bed, he began to dictate the speech which he would make in the House of Lords: 'I intend to do only that I am bound to do by mine oath that I made at the time of my profession.' He refused to admit a royal claim which had brought about the martyrdom of Thomas Becket, 'which is the best death that can be . . . I think it better for me to suffer the same, than in my conscience to confess this article to be praemunire for which St. Thomas died'. Warham was always a better speaker of words than doer of actions. It was merciful that he should have died before any action was needed, on 23 August 1532.

Erasmus, whom Warham had more than once helped with generous gifts of money, has left a literary portrait of his friend in his *Ecclesiastes*. He tells us that Warham would give 'sumptuous entertainments, often to as many as two hundred guests, he himself ate frugal meals and hardly tasted wine: he never prolonged the dinner above an hour, but yet was a most genial host: he never hunted or played at dice, but his chief recreation was reading'. His income was very large, but he spent £30,000 on repairs and building of new houses, so that when he died he was so poor that there was hardly enough money to pay for his funeral.

The fine portrait by Holbein at Lambeth, and perhaps even more the beautiful drawing for that portrait which is in the collection of drawings at Windsor, give a vivid picture of the Archbishop in old age.

Hook, *Lives of the Archbishops of Canterbury*, New Series, Vol. 1, 1868.

THOMAS WOLSEY (*c*.1473–1530), Cardinal-Archbishop of York, Lord Chancellor and Henry VIII's chief minister from 1515 to 1529, was born about 1473 and died in 1530. Rumour held it that he was the son of a butcher in Ipswich: Cavendish, his gentleman-usher and eventual biographer, says that he was 'an honest poor man's son'. He went up to Magdalen, Oxford, where he became famous as the 'boy-bachelor' who took his B.A. degree at the age of fifteen. He became a fellow of his college, was ordained priest in 1498 and became bursar of the college in 1499, an office which he was compelled to resign allegedly for applying moneys to the completion of Magdalen Tower without the sanction of the college authorities. He became chaplain to Archbishop Deane of Canterbury and on his death chaplain to Sir Richard Nanfan, the Deputy of Calais. Nanfan died in 1507, but he had recommended Wolsey to Henry VII, whose chaplain he now became. Two years later Henry died and probably owing to the influence of the Lady Margaret Beaufort, who had small opinion of Wolsey, it was some months before Henry VIII gave him any office (1509).

1512 marks the first moment when Wolsey took a major part in deciding governmental policy. He supported the war against France to aid Pope Julius II. The expedition of 1513 was the work of Wolsey, who took into his own hands the entire organization of the war. He was triumphantly successful, and the campaign which brought to the English armies the victories at Thérouanne and Tournai and at the battle of the Spurs convinced Henry that Wolsey was indispensable.

As he rose in royal service, so Wolsey amassed offices in church and state. He became Dean of Lincoln in 1509, of Hereford in 1512, Bishop of Tournai in 1513, Bishop of Lincoln in 1514, the see of which he relinquished on becoming Archbishop of York in the same year. In 1515 Pope Leo X made him a Cardinal and in 1515, when Warham resigned from the Chancellorship, Wolsey was made Lord Chancellor in his place. In 1518 he achieved his great ambition when he was created *legatus à latere*. He also possessed at various times the Abbey of St. Albans, the richest abbey in England: the Bishopric of Bath and Wells (1518), exchanged for that of Durham (1524), exchanged for that of Winchester (1529), the richest see in England. Between 1515 and 1529 Wolsey, although he was always ultimately dependent on the will of the King, was to all intents and purposes the chief minister of England. He governed the state through the chancellorship, the church through his legateship. In these fourteen years he became one of the most powerful men England has ever known. At the height of his power he received £35,000 a year (perhaps equal to a quarter of the royal income) and he conducted himself with a pomp and pride which galled the nobility. He built Hampton Court Palace, and travelled accompanied by literally hundreds of his servants.

Wolsey has suffered badly at the hands of historians who have taken at face value the criticism of those who wrote immediately after his fall from power or who were the Great Cardinal's enemies. If he was rich, it is only fair to say that as a churchman he created no great dynasty at the nation's expense (unlike the Cecils and Howards, for example) and that he enriched himself largely at the cost of the Church in the true medieval fashion of a royal minister. He also spent lavishly in the royal service, financing his diplomatic missions out of his own pocket. He built, but he also gave Hampton Court to the King. It was not in the sixteenth century expected that a great royal servant should conduct his affairs with more than a pretence of modesty, especially when he went to meet foreigners. If Wolsey was 'vulgar', at least he had the excuse of his birth, which others — like Henry himself — could not plead.

Wolsey's great interest, like that of his King, was in foreign affairs. Here he has been badly misunderstood. It used to be claimed that he used English foreign policy to serve the interests of the Papacy, at first to achieve his legateship, then to make himself Pope. This view has now been demolished by detailed research, which has shown that Wolsey himself never actively sought to be Pope, although Henry VIII himself toyed with the idea. If English foreign policy did follow the papal line it was due in part to the simple fact that both England and the Papacy were anti-French during most of this period. The governing factor in the foreign policy of England while Wolsey held sway was Henry VIII's desire for glory and honour, which Wolsey sought to implement as best he might. If this policy failed, or was expensive, the fault lay not with Wolsey but with the King. It has been argued that Wolsey in fact used his talents to restrain the King's appetite for war. This was partly to save money, but also because Wolsey had accepted the pacifist case argued by the humanists like Colet and Erasmus. Such a view of Wolsey as a peace-monger has been criticised in its turn, but there would seem to be something in it, if we accept that this was as much Henry's policy perhaps as Wolsey's, and that on occasion the rhetoric of peace provided a good smokescreen for warlike pre-

Cardinal Wolsey
(Artist: Unknown)

parations (as in 1520). Wolsey was able to develop such a peace policy — if such it was — in the years between 1514 and 1522. The summit of his achievement here was reached in 1518 when the great Peace of London was signed by twenty-four nations: a treaty of universal, perpetual peace, which placed London at the centre of the diplomatic world. Of course, the peace lasted only for a few months, and Wolsey's pride and egotism shines through the whole episode. As the Venetian ambassador said: 'Nothing pleases him more than to be called the arbiter of the affairs of Christendom.' Nevertheless, such great international treaties also redounded greatly to the credit and glory of the King. In the end, peace could not last for ever, since Wolsey must serve the King and if the King wanted war, Wolsey had to serve him loyally: he sighed as a peace-maker, but obeyed as a careerist.

In his government of England, in his domestic policy, Wolsey continued the policy of Henry VII. He was not a great innovator in the field of administration like Thomas Cromwell, but worked with the materials already at hand. He maintained firm control over the nobility; punishing those who stepped out of line with a strong hand. The execution of the Duke of Buckingham in 1521 on a charge of treason was a measure taken very much in the tradition of the first Tudor, to defend the dynasty from possible threats — however remote — of subversion, and to frighten the rest of the nobility into obedience. This hardly made Wolsey popular with the upper-classes, but it was clearly the best policy for the monarch and nation as a whole. Wolsey was likewise unpopular with parliament, perhaps for rather similar reasons. Between 1515 and 1529, parliament met only once (in 1523) and on that occasion some of its members were critical of foreign policy. This, it has been argued, was a demonstration of opposition to a policy of war organised by Wolsey himself in order to persuade the King to make peace. But there seems to be little real evidence to support such a view, and it seems likely that parliament in 1523 was as much opposed to Wolsey as to war. Wolsey's failure to call parliament frequently contrasts markedly with the great use made at other times in Henry VIII's reign of that institution, but it is very similar to the attitude to parliament of Henry VII and Edward IV.

Wolsey taxed heavily during his reign, but this was largely to satisfy the needs of royal foreign policy. Between 1513 and 1527 England paid the King £413,000 in taxes and £250,000 in forced loans. This compares with taxation in the years 1485-1497 of only £258,000. These figures show Wolsey's considerable success as a tax-collector. Wolsey also ordered a major new assessment of the nation's wealth and military resources in 1522 in order to tax more fairly, and on this he based his demands for 'loans' in 1522 and 1523. Wolsey's attempts to gain money to pay for Henry's wars finally came unstuck in 1525 when his request for an 'Amicable Grant' met with flat refusal in the country and the threat of a rebellion. Faced with this crisis Henry VIII called a Great Council and announced his intention to excuse payment of the grant, pardoning those who had already opposed the tax and in effect blaming Wolsey for the whole episode. This illustrates another way in which Wolsey was useful to the King: as a scapegoat in case anything went wrong.

Wolsey may have been unpopular with the people as a result of taxation, but he sought to protect the commons from the more greedy of the 'caterpillars of the commonwealth', the enclosers of land. He instituted a great commission in 1517 to enquire into enclosure, and followed this up with over 260 prosecutions in Chancery. He continued to show an interest in this great social problem by issuing proclamations in 1526, 1528 and 1529 against enclosure. It is reasonable to doubt how much success these policies had in the long term, but anything which protected the peasantry from the pressure of 'market forces', even slightly, must have been welcome relief in what one historian sees as an 'Age of Plunder'.

Wolsey was an enthusiastic and able judge. As Chancellor, he presided in Chancery and played a dominant role in the court of the council in star chamber and in the court of requests. To all these courts he encouraged men to come with their suits, speeding up the process of justice and seeking to protect the weak from the mighty. He can in some ways be seen as the founder of the court of Star Chamber; at least he transformed it into an institution of state with fixed rules of procedure. Wolsey used his legal power to threaten the unruly upper-classes: as he put it, 'to learn them the law of the Star Chamber'. He boasted to the King in 1518 that 'for your realm our Lord be thanked it was never in such peace nor tranquillity. For all this summer I have heard neither of riot, felony nor forcible entry, but that your laws be in every place indifferently ministered without leaning of any manner'.

Wolsey was head of the church of England as legate. He established a degree of independence from Rome in this capacity which paved the way perhaps for the royal supremacy established in 1534. He practised little ecclesiastical reform, although there was some, especially of the friars. He projected a major reorganisation of small

monasteries and the creation of thirteen new sees but failed to bring
this to pass. His greatest work as a church-man was to found a new
college at Oxford, Cardinal College, later called Christ Church,
endowed by dissolving a number of small abbeys. He also founded a
new school in his home town, Ipswich, although Henry VIII
destroyed it when Wolsey fell.

Wolsey lost the King's favour when he failed in the years 1527–
1529 to secure an annulment of Henry's marriage to Catherine of
Aragon. While it may be true that he disliked the idea that the King
should divorce the Queen, he nevertheless threw himself into the
project with gusto. In the end what defeated him was the power of
Charles V in Italy and the Pope's consequent inability to grant the
divorce. On 24 June 1529, he lamented that, 'the Pope has refused
all the concessions which, relying on him, I had promised the King
... and that will be my ruin'.

Having failed to win for Henry the divorce, Wolsey was no longer
of any use to Henry. Between August and October 1529 it was clear
that Wolsey was rapidly losing favour. On 9 October he was
indicted for Praemunire. On 18 October he gave up the great seal.
On the 22 October he confessed his guilt. The King had for fourteen
years given Wolsey his unstinted confidence and now at his fall
Henry dealt generously with him. When the new Parliament on
3 November launched a grand attack on Wolsey and arraigned him
on forty-four charges, Henry refused to take any action and saved
him from being imprisoned. Wolsey was allowed to retain some of
his benefices and property and to retire to his archbishopric of York.
It is a comment on Wolsey's views of an ecclesiastic's duties that he
had never visited York since he was appointed archbishop fifteen
years before. Nor did he in fact ever reach York. He moved northwards at a snail's pace and got no farther than Cawood. During this
time he entered into most indiscreet correspondence with Rome, and
this became known to the government. Wolsey had taken with him
on his journey northwards six hundred horsemen in his train,
intending to make his enthronement at York a splendid spectacle.
The government was determined to prevent him. On Friday
4 November 1530, he was arrested and ordered to London. On the
24th at Leicester he died.

Wolsey had served Henry VIII well and was shabbily treated by
him, as so many others were. His former protégé, Sir Thomas More,

denounced him in parliament as 'the great wether', or ewe, who had infected the rest of the flock with disease and who was now turned out by the shepherd. Only Thomas Cromwell, to his great credit, stood by his old master, defending him in parliament and working to save his Oxford college. In the end, any comparison between Cromwell and Wolsey inevitably redounds to the credit of the former. Wolsey worked with the enthusiasm and drive of ten men, but he was flawed in many ways. By his ostentatious flaunting of wealth and power, he exposed the clergy as a whole to dangerous attack and contributed to the fall of the medieval church. He left few lasting monuments to his work. He was the last of the great ecclesiastical statesmen who had flourished in the Middle Ages and he had been content to work in a system which had long existed unreformed. In this capacity he may be held to have served his master and his country tolerably well, and to have continued to build on the stability and peace first established in 1485.

G. Cavendish, *Life and death of Cardinal Wolsey*, ed. Sylvester, 1959.
A.F. Pollard, *Wolsey*, 1919.
D.S. Chambers, *Bulletin Institute Historical Research* 1965.
P. Gwyn, *Historical Journal* 1980.

POLYDORE VERGIL (*c.*1470–1555), historian, was born at Urbino in Italy about 1470 and died there in 1555. He was educated at two universities, Padua and Bologna; he was for a time secretary to Guidobaldo, Duke of Urbino; and he was ordained at some date before 1496. His relation, Adriano Castelli, Cardinal of Corneto, became the official collector of Peter's Pence under Henry VII and was given the bishopric of Hereford. In 1502 Polydore came to England and joined Adriano: most of his life was thenceforward spent in England. He received the living of Church Langston in Leicestershire (1503), a prebend in Lincoln Cathedral and in Hereford Cathedral (1507); he was appointed archdeacon of Wells (1508) and was given the prebend of Oxgate in St. Paul's (1513), all owing to the influence of Adriano. In 1504 he was prosecuted for illegal speculation in foreign currency. In 1510 he secured a Papal bull for the foundation of St. John's College, Cambridge. In 1514 he went to Rome to try to get a Cardinal's hat for Wolsey. On his return he was put in the Tower by Wolsey with Adriano, whom Wolsey blamed for his initial failure (1515), but when Wolsey was made Cardinal that year, Polydore was released a few months later. The rest of his life was devoted to writing. He signed the denial of Papal supremacy, he accepted the Articles of 1536 and communion in both kinds in 1547. In 1553 he returned to Italy and died at Urbino in 1555.

In his own day Polydore's fame rested on his *De Inventoribus Rerum*, which was published in Venice in 1499. This book was written in three months and described the 'first begetters' of all human activities, e.g. the origin of the gods, language, religion, etc. In 1521 he greatly enlarged the book and dealt with the origins of Christianity, but because he traced some ceremonies back to pagan superstitions, the book was put on the Index. He had earlier written a small book, *Proverbiorum Libellus*, which brought about a quarrel with Erasmus. In 1525 Polydore edited the works of Gildas.

Today Polydore is chiefly remembered for his *Anglica Historia*. In 1506 Henry VII (or more probably Richard Fox, Bishop of Winchester) had suggested to him that he should write a history of England. The first printed edition appeared in 1534, a folio with illustrations by Holbein. The book was written in Latin and covered the history of England down to 1537. Down to 1450 the history is not much more than a compilation based on the old classical texts, such as Caesar, Polybius, Livy, Tacitus, etc., and on mediaeval histories such as Gildas and Bede, and on chroniclers such as William of Newburgh, William of Malmesbury, Geoffrey of Monmouth, etc. He also drew on manuscript sources, so that his book is in some respects a work of research. From 1450 down to 1537 Vergil's book becomes increasingly valuable as an original source, especially for the reign of Henry VII. His avowed purpose was two-fold: to tell the truth and to justify the rise of the Tudor family. On the whole Polydore was an accurate historian, but now and again he allows his passions to colour his writing — for example, in Book xxvii, where his hatred for Wolsey undermines his respect for the truth.

Vergil was an exponent of the new methods of writing history: he tested his authorities and he based his judgements on rational commonsense. He was a bold writer and he did not hesitate to criticize some English customs, traditions and institutions, such as the universities, the monasteries, the lawyers, for which he incurred much odium.

> Maro and Polydore bore Vergil's name;
> One reaps a poet's, one a liar's fame.

He was even accused of destroying his original sources. He hated and deplored the growing nationalism, especially in France, which was causing such suffering to his own country of Italy through the Italian wars of Charles VIII and Louis XII.

Denys Hay, *Polydore Vergil, Renaissance Historian and Man of Letters*, (1952).

Polydore Vergil, *Anglica Historia*, A.D. *1485-1537*. Ed. D. Hay, Camden Society, Vol. LXXIV, 1950.

GEORGE CAVENDISH (1499?-1562?), gentleman-usher to Cardinal Wolsey and author of *The Life and Death of Cardinal Wolsey*, was the son of Thomas Cavendish and Alice Smyth, both of well-to-do families in Suffolk. Thomas held the office of Clerk of the Pipe under Henry VII and Henry VIII, an office connected with the Exchequer, and it is probable that it was through his father's official position that George was introduced into the service of Wolsey. Little is known for certain about his early life, but he was at Cambridge in 1510, when he was about 11 years old, and he came down without a degree.

He was twice married: first, to a member of the wealthy Spring family of Lavenham, and secondly in the early 1520s to Margery Kemp, a niece by marriage of Sir Thomas More, a connection which was later to cause him some embarrassment when he was writing his life of Wolsey.

Cavendish was in Wolsey's service by 1522. His duties were to 'attend personally upon my lord', to act as his messenger or courier on important occasions, such as when Wolsey was paying a visit abroad, to look after the Cardinal's household and to organize his magnificent entertainments.

On Wolsey's fall in 1529 Cavendish did not desert him, but continued to work for him. On the Cardinal's death in 1530 he retired from public life to his home in Suffolk. Here he carried out a few duties in local affairs, but the chief work on which he was engaged, and the one on which his claim to be remembered is based, was the writing of *The Life and Death of Cardinal Wolsey*. The book was begun probably in 1554 and completed probably in 1558. It is impossible now to know how much he used previous chroniclers, such as Hall, but it is certain that his book is essentially a record of his own experience and his own first-hand knowledge of Wolsey. His book contains some errors of fact and errors in the sequence of events, probably due to mere forgetfulness. Curiously, he tells us little of Wolsey's private life, but on the whole he succeeds in convincing us that he himself was both honest and accurate as a historian. One curious point is that, although he was married to Sir Thomas More's niece and must have known More intimately, he never mentions him in his book. Both were orthodox Catholics, but More was extremely hostile to Wolsey, and it looks as if Cavendish wanted to avoid giving offence by attacking More's views as set out in the biographies which were then beginning to appear. As a literary work the *Life* is a masterpiece, for Cavendish had a real genius for writing: his narrative is lively, colourful and always interesting. Its historical value is proved by the fact that no later writer on Wolsey has been able to do without Cavendish's *Life and Death*, which gives us an admiring, sympathetic, but not adulatory portrait of the Cardinal.

The Life and Death of Cardinal Wolsey, by G. Cavendish, ed. by R. S. Sylvester for the Early English Text Society, 1959.

SIR RALPH SADLER [the usual spelling is nowadays SADLEIR, but Sir Ralph himself usually dropped the 'i': the form SADLEYER is also found] (1507–1587), diplomatist and statesman, was born in 1507 and died in 1587. His father was a steward or minor official in the service of the Marquis of Dorset and of Sir Edward Belknap. While still young, Ralph was taken into the household of Thomas Cromwell, later Henry VIII's great minister and Earl of Essex. Probably in 1536 Sadler was made a gentleman of the King's privy chamber, and he at once made so good an impression on the King that Henry VIII sent him in 1537 on a most delicate and important mission to Scotland, to try to find out how much truth there was in the complaints made by his sister, Margaret, the Queen-Dowager, against her third husband, Lord Methven, and to investigate the relations between the King of Scotland and the French. He succeeded in helping Margaret, and after a visit to James V, who was in France, he improved Anglo-Scottish relations. Until his death, Sadler was to be the foremost expert in English political life on the Scots.

So pleased was Henry VIII with Sadler's work that in 1540 he sent him again to Scotland to try to separate the King from the advice and policies of Cardinal Beaton, who was wedded to a Franco-Scottish alliance. Sadler was to advise James V to take to himself the wealth of the Scottish church, as Henry had done in England. The mission was a failure, but Sadler had done his best. Henry was so satisfied with Sadler's work that in 1540 he made him one of his two secretaries. He was also knighted and made a privy councillor and he entered parliament as Member for Hertford (1541).

After the battle of Solway Moss, which was immediately followed by the death of James V, Sadler was sent to Scotland again. He was specially charged to arrange a marriage alliance between the new Queen, the baby Mary, and Henry's son, Edward, Prince of Wales, in order to prevent any recovery of influence by the Cardinal Beaton, who had been imprisoned by the Protestant regent, Arran. The treaty was made, one clause of which provided that the Queen should be brought up in Scotland under the care of 'an honourable knight and lady of England'. Henry proposed that Sadler and his wife should undertake this charge, but Sadler succeeded in avoiding this task. Party feelings broke out again in Scotland, and at one point Sadler's house in Edinburgh was besieged by the mob, and he narrowly escaped death from a musket bullet as he was walking in the garden. Sadler retired to Tantallon Castle (1543), an episode which Sir Walter Scott commemorated in *Marmion*, Canto V. Sadler soon returned to England, but all his work was undone when war between England and Scotland broke out (1543). Sadler accompanied the Earl of Hertford on his campaign as treasurer to the army, an office which he filled again in the 1545 campaign.

Owing to his frequent absences on diplomatic missions, Sadler was not able to carry out his duties as Secretary of State and he was replaced by Paget (1543), but he himself was given the post of Master of the Great Wardrobe. When Henry died in 1547, he left Sadler a legacy of 200 gold marks and appointed him a member of the council to which the government of the country was entrusted during Edward VI's minority. When Somerset set out for the Pinkie campaign (1547), Sadler again went with him as High Treasurer of the Army. After the battle, in recognition of his outstanding services during the fighting, Sadler was raised to the rank of Knight-banneret, a dignity which Holinshed calls 'above a knight and next to a baron'. Sadler was present when Bishop Gardiner was arrested (1548) and he was also with the force which put down Ket's rebellion (1549). During Mary's reign Sadler remained in retirement at his home at Standon, near Ware in Hertfordshire.

In Elizabeth's reign Sadler, as a sound Protestant, became one of Cecil's most trusted servants. He was sent once more to Scotland with secret orders to arrange an alliance with the Protestant party. When hostilities broke out at Leith, he was at the camp and had a chief share in making the treaty of Leith (1560). In 1568 he was appointed Chancellor of the Duchy of Lancaster, a highly lucrative office. When Mary, Queen of Scots, fled to England, Sadler, very much against his will, was one of the commissioners appointed to meet the Scotch commissioners to deal with the problem of the Scots' Queen. He it was who made the *precis* of the Casket Letters for Cecil. He it was also who was sent to arrest the Duke of Norfolk at the time of the Rising of the Northern Earls. And Sadler it was who twice found himself warder over the Queen of Scots, at Sheffield in 1572 and at Wingfield in 1584. He hated these appointments and never ceased applying for release, but before it came he had had to transfer the Queen from Wingfield to Tutbury. He was relieved in 1585. The next year, after the Babington Plot, Sadler was one of the commission which condemned Mary to death.

Sadler was a man of much importance in his own day. He was loyal, courageous and shrewd; his abilities were indeed greater than the offices which he held suggest. Everybody trusted him and he was well rewarded by the sovereigns whom he served. When he died on 30 March 1587, he was said to be the richest commoner in England. He had sat in eight parliaments; he was a privy councillor under three sovereigns for close on fifty years; he knew more about Scotland than any other Englishman; he was a brave soldier; he was also 'a most exquisite writer' (Lloyd, *State of Worthies*), and his state papers are now invaluable historical sources. He was a little man, devoted to field sports, especially to hawking. He was married and had three sons and four daughters.

The State Papers and Letters of Sir Ralph Sadler, ed. by A. Clifford, with a memoir by Sir Walter Scott, 1809.

T. U. Sadleir, *A Brief Memoir of the Rt. Hon. Sir Ralph Sadleir*, 1907.

A. J. Slavin, *Politics and profit*, 1966.

RICHARD HUNNE (*d.* 1514) was a well-to-do merchant tailor in London, a freeman of the city and a liveryman of the Merchant Taylors Company. Sir Thomas More called him 'a fair dealer among his neighbours', and approved of his 'worldly conversation', but he also wrote that he was 'high minded and set on the glory of a victory'. He calculated that Hunne was 'well worth a thousand marks'. It has been asserted that Hunne was in trouble for heresy before 1514, but this is certainly untrue.

In 1511 Hunne had a baby out 'at nurse' in Whitechapel: the child died when five weeks old and was buried by the priest of St. Mary Matfellon, Whitechapel. The priest demanded the child's bearing-sheet (or christening robe) as a burial fee, but Hunne refused to pay. The priest, Thomas Dryffeld, sued Hunne in the consistory court and won his case. Hunne thereupon sued Dryffeld in the King's Bench under the statute of Praemunire, which limited the jurisdiction of church courts. It is doubtful whether Hunne had a case under this act. The ecclesiastical authorities then arrested Hunne. His house was searched and some forbidden books were found with marginal comments. He was examined by FitzJames, Bishop of London and he made a qualified admission of heresy, but refused to withdraw the action of Praemunire. He was therefore sent to the Lollards' Tower at St. Paul's. Hunne was an important man, and the ecclesiastical authorities were considerably embarrassed. Two days later Hunne was found hanged in his own silk girdle with clear indications that he had been strangled and had his neck broken before he was hanged. Was it murder or suicide? Anti-clerical London was convinced that it was murder by the ecclesiastical authorities. The coroners' inquest heard the evidence, which included a confession by Charles Joseph (extracted by 'pain and durance'), one of the servants of Dr. Horsey, the Bishop of London's Chancellor, and the body in the Lollards' Tower was inspected. A verdict of wilful murder was returned against Horsey and two of his servants. Professor Elton asks the very sensible question: why should Horsey and Joseph murder Hunne?

Since there seems to be no answer to this, it seems likely that Hunne died accidentally in a scuffle, which the gaolers then tried to conceal. Horsey was shut up in FitzJames' palace, and FitzJames wrote to ask Wolsey to intercede for him. In the meantime FitzJames had been proceeding against the corpse of Hunne, which was exhumed and burnt as that of a heretic on 20 December 1514. A consequence of this was that his children lost their right to their inheritance. On 3 March 1515, a bill was introduced into parliament to restore all Hunne's property to his children, which was violently opposed by FitzJames as tending to discredit the ecclesiastical court. Horsey and his colleagues were prevented by the church authorities from being brought to trial.

Hunne's case exacerbated the quarrel between the laity and the clergy, between the ecclesiastical and the civil courts. It perhaps played some part in preparing the way for the Breach with Rome. It should be stressed, however, that while London and the merchant class were anti-clerical — as this case shows — there is evidence that such views were not common in the rest of the country. Moreover, the dust settled fairly rapidly on the Hunne affair, and it was in very different circumstances in the 1530s that England broke with the Pope.

A. Ogle, *The tragedy of the Lollards' Tower*, 1949.
G.R. Elton, *Reform and reformation*, 1977.
C. Haigh, *History*, 1983.
R. Wunderli, *Journal of Ecclesiastical History*, 1982.

HENRY STANDISH (*d.* 1535), Bishop of St. Asaph, died in 1535; the date of his birth is unknown. Very little is known of his early life except that he studied at both Oxford and Cambridge. He became warden of the Franciscan house, Greyfriars, in London. Somehow he won the favour of Henry VIII and became a frequent preacher at Court. In 1515 he suddenly leaped into fame as the most popular man in London.

The arrest of Dr. Horsey, the Bishop of London's Chancellor, on a charge of murdering Richard Hunne put the Bishop and the ecclesiastics in a difficult position. If Horsey were brought to trial, he would almost certainly be found guilty. It was of paramount importance to prevent his being tried. FitzJames, the Bishop, very rashly determined to try to save him by confusing the issue. Parliament was just about to assemble and would be very anti-clerical. The Bishop appointed Richard Kidderminster, Abbot of Winchcombe, to preach at St. Paul's, and he instructed him to defend the thesis that no cleric could be cited in any secular court. The sermon raised violent passions; it was criticized in Parliament, where the Commons were engaged in trying to re-enact a temporary law of 1512 which subjected criminous clerks in minor orders to the secular courts. An appeal was made to the King, who agreed to a debate at Blackfriars at which he would be present (10 March 1515). Henry Standish defended the secular view with much success. The City of London showed its gratitude by repaving the church of the Greyfriars. Standish was summoned before Convocation and he appealed to the King for protection. A second debate at Blackfriars was held, in the presence of Henry VIII, where Standish again defended his point of view. The judges asserted that in citing Standish before them, Convocation was guilty of Praemunire.

A final meeting was held at Baynard's Castle at which the King arranged a compromise; charges against both Standish and Horsey were dropped; the King's dominance over the church in England was asserted and the parliamentary attack on clerical privileges was withdrawn.

Standish was soon rewarded by the King with the bishopric of St Asaph (1518). He remained popular at court and was employed on several less important diplomatic missions, although Wolsey blocked his promotion in the church. At one point he quarrelled with Erasmus, of whose translation of the New Testament he disapproved. He was one of Catherine of Aragon's counsellors in the matter of the divorce, but she never trusted him, not unnaturally thinking that he was really on the King's side. He took part in the coronation of Anne Boleyn and he was one of the three bishops who consecrated Cranmer Archbishop of Canterbury. He died on 9 June 1535, at an advanced but unknown age.

A. F. Pollard, *Wolsey*, 1929.
H. Maynard Smith, *Pre-Reformation England*, 1938.

THOMAS CROMWELL [usually **CRUMWELL** in his own day] (1485?–1540), chief minister to Henry VIII from 1533 to

1540, was born probably in 1485 at Putney, the son of a smith and fuller.

The details of his early life are much disputed and most of the amusing stories told of him on his travels are apocryphal. He was probably very badly brought up and he himself once told Cranmer 'I was a ruffian in my young days'. At some point he quarrelled with his father and went abroad. Perhaps he took part in the Italian wars; certainly he became a merchant and traded with Antwerp; as certainly he acquired legal knowledge and became an attorney. He had also learned some foreign languages while he was on the Continent. He was back in England in 1512, and in 1520 he entered the service of Cardinal Wolsey, to whom he is likely to have recommended himself by his legal knowledge, his command of foreign languages and his experience as a man of business. He was employed by Wolsey especially in the destruction of some of the smaller monasteries, in which work his ruthless methods caused him to be much hated.

On Wolsey's fall from power in 1529 Cromwell did not desert his master, as did Stephen Gardiner: he continued to serve him and he spoke in opposition to the Bill of Attainder in the House of Commons. But he used Wolsey's affairs to bring himself to the notice of the King. In November 1529 he entered Parliament with the expressed approval of the King. He spoke in support of the government's policy in the anti-clerical debates (1529), entered the King's service and was sworn of the council in 1530. His rise was not, as is often said, sudden and dramatic. He won the King's confidence by his exceptional administrative ability, displayed in a variety of offices which he gradually accumulated between 1532 and 1536. In 1532 he became Master of the King's Jewels, then Clerk of the Hanaper (1532), Chancellor of the Exchequer (1533), principal Secretary (1534), Master of the Rolls (1534), Lord Privy Seal (1536). The turning point in his career was 1532, when he became the King's closest adviser in the crucial matter of the divorce. The first three offices were relatively minor offices, all connected with finance, which set up Cromwell as a finance minister. The other three offices were more important and gave him control of the whole bureaucratic machine. By 1536 he had an assured but by no means large income, an official house in which to live as Master of the Rolls, great prestige as Lord Privy Seal, and the complete confidence

EARL OF ESSEX.

Thomas Cromwell, 1st Earl of Essex
(Artist: After Hans Holbein)

of the King. From 1533 to 1540 he was the King's most powerful minister, but he was always dependent on the support of the King.

The best modern view of Cromwell is that set out by Professor G. R. Elton in his *The Tudor Revolution in Government*. Briefly, he argues that from the fall of Wolsey (1529) to 1533 Henry VIII had no consistent policy: in 1533 Cromwell appears on the scene with a ready-made plan for the divorce of Catherine of Aragon, the subjection of the clergy, the establishment of the Royal Supremacy, the breach with Rome and the attack on ecclesiastical property. Further, he regards Cromwell as having carried out a complete revolution from mediaeval, personal and household government to a modern system of bureaucratic departments which functioned independently of the monarch. This view is challenged by Professor Wernham in *The E.H.R.,* January, 1956. Dr. Elton holds that 'Cromwell not Henry, was really the government'. Professor Wernham holds that it was 'the minister and not Henry who did as he was told'.

There can be no doubt that Cromwell played a leading part in the great questions of the Divorce and the Breach with Rome. He was in large part responsible for implementing the policy which gave Henry what he wanted; freedom from Catherine of Aragon and control over the church in England. Cromwell drafted the great legislative programme by which this was accomplished, steered it through parliament and then enforced these measures in the face of stiff opposition. In the attack on the monasteries, he as Vicar-General and Vicegerent in Spirituals (1535), was the leading spirit. He began with a statistical survey of church property, the *Valor Ecclesiasticus*, the first survey of ecclesiastical wealth since 1291 and still the most up-to-date in 1836. The next step was to make a rapid and highly prejudiced Visitation of the monasteries, to gather ammunition with which to attack the abbeys. By an Act of 1536 the smaller religious houses (those worth under £200 per annum) were dissolved. Whether it was at this stage planned to dissolve all the monasteries is open to question. By 1538, pressure was being applied to the larger abbeys to surrender voluntarily to the Crown, and in 1539 an Act swept them all away. By 1540 all the monastic land was in the hands of the King, administered through Cromwell's new creation, the Court of Augmentations.

Cromwell was a man blessed with many talents and he made good use of them. He was a first class administrator and much of his work lasted. The Court of Delegates remained the supreme ecclesiastical court until it was superseded by the Judicial Committee of the Privy Council in 1832. The six new bishoprics established by Cromwell were the first to be created since the time of Henry II and the last until the reign of Queen Victoria. The parish registers, which are still maintained and which have proved a most valuable source of information to the historian, were first made compulsory under Cromwell.

The Tudor state was very thoroughly reorganized under Cromwell's direction. He separated the royal Council finally from the Court of Star Chamber, thus creating the Privy Council. He created new courts of revenue to supervise the newly increased income of the Crown. Cromwell reorganized the government of Ireland, of the North of England and of Wales and even Calais. The Council in the North and the Council in the Marches of Wales were re-created under his guidance. He removed medieval franchises and liberties (1536) and abolished sanctuary once and for all (1540). He was responsible for the police work connected with the enforcement of the Henrician Reformation, and directed a mild but effective 'Reign of Terror' in the interests of public order. He developed a social policy with the help of a number of enthusiastic 'social engineers', which involved a new approach to poverty, an effort to control inflation, enclosure, and a drive to encourage the cloth industry.

It was impossible that such an efficient and such a ruthless monopolizer of power should be popular. Cromwell had steadily concentrated into his own hands the administration of the whole realm — lay administration through the offices enumerated above, ecclesiastical through the office of Vicar-General. In religion Cromwell was by conviction neither old-fashioned Catholic like Norfolk or Gardiner, nor new-fangled Protestant like Cranmer. He once told some Lutheran envoys that 'as the world now stood he would believe even as his master the king believed', which might be taken to mean 'as the king might at any moment believe'. On the whole his sympathies lay with the Protestants. After the Royal Supremacy was established, Cromwell had to deal with two parties: one which wanted a Catholic church without the Pope, and another which wanted a reformed church. Cromwell's ecclesiastical policy was intimately bound up with foreign policy. Broadly speaking, when France and the Empire were at loggerheads, there was no danger to England from the Continent: when these two countries showed signs of coming together, Cromwell tended to look to an alliance with the German Lutheran states. The King disliked close alliances, especially a Protestant alliance, and Henry was always a better judge of the international situation than was Cromwell.

Norfolk and Gardiner were representative of the conservative point of view and they were always opposed to Cromwell (who had ejected them from office) on personal grounds and on grounds of policy and religion. They could hope for the King's support. The struggle between the two sides was long and bitter. In the early months of 1539 it looked as if Cromwell was beaten. By midsummer he had apparently wholly recovered the lost ground. In 1540 he made a fatal mistake by forcing the King into an alliance with Cleves and into a marriage with Anne of Cleves. Henry hated the alliance and disliked the lady. Norfolk set up at Court his niece, Catherine Howard, as a rival to Anne in the King's affections. Cromwell could not get rid of Anne for Henry without installing in her place the nominee of his rivals, the Howards. (Wolsey had been in a similar quandary over Anne Boleyn). His fall seemed certain, yet on 17 April he was made Earl of Essex and Great Chamberlain of England. On 23 May he suddenly arrested one of the conservative leaders, Sampson, Bishop of Chichester. On 10 June as suddenly he himself was arrested. An Act of Attainder was rapidly passed and Cromwell was sent to the Tower, where he was kept until 23 July — presumably in order to provide the necessary evidence for the separation from Anne of Cleves. On that day he was executed with barbarous inefficiency.

The reasons for Cromwell's fall have been minutely investigated, but no satisfying explanation has yet been found which covers his sudden arrest following so quickly on his being created Earl of Essex. One element which has not been dealt with in what has been said above is Cromwell's support for the further development of the Reformation; it is significant that Cromwell's overthrow was accompanied by the execution for heresy of a number of the more radical preachers of London, including Robert Barnes. The conservative faction at court was able to play successfully on the King's fear of heresy and to argue that until Cromwell was removed dangerous religious opinions would continue to flourish.

Cromwell was a successful innovator, a destroyer, but also a builder. He was not crueller than most people of his own day; he seems not to have been vindictive, rather to have been devoid of passion. He has frequently been called a disciple of Machiavelli and is said to have read *Il Principe*, but it is doubtful whether his policies owed much to the direct influence of Machiavelli. Rather, he wished to create an efficient state, independent of foreign interference and centralised in such a way that the King's power was not limited by feudal survivals. But the King should rule with parliament, and Cromwell's greatest legacy was probably to give the English parliament a permanent position in the constitution by the repeated and frequent use he made of it to bring about the Breach with Rome and the creation of his new, reformed polity.

R.B. Merriman, *Life and letters of Cromwell*, 1902.
A.G. Dickens, *Thomas Cromwell*, 1959.
G.R. Elton, *Reform and Reformation*, 1977 (which summarizes the work of Elton in this field, where he is the great expert).
S. Brigden, *Historical Journal*, 1981.

JOHN COLET (1466/67–1519), Dean of St. Paul's, founder of St. Paul's School, was born in London in either 1466 or 1467. He was the son of Sir Henry Colet of the Mercers' Company, who was twice Lord Mayor of London, and his wife, Christian Knyvet of Ashwellthorpe in Norfolk, who had connections with the Grey de Ruthyn family and with the Stafford (Buckingham) family, so that John came of an extremely wealthy and distinguished family. Christian bore her husband eleven sons and eleven daughters, but only John survived infancy, and his mother survived both her husband and her son. The Colets lived in the country outside London at Stepney, a house and neighbourhood for which they all had much affection and where Christian continued to live after the death of her husband in 1505 and her son in 1519.

John was probably educated at the well-known school of St. Anthony in Threadneedle Street, where were also educated Sir Thomas More, Nicholas Heath (later Archbishop of York) and John Whitgift, Elizabeth's Archbishop of Canterbury, her 'little black husband'. In 1483 he went up to Oxford, almost certainly to Magdalen College. He took his M.A. in 1490 and then he travelled abroad into Italy, and on his way home at Paris he first heard the name of Erasmus, with whom he was later to form a lifelong friendship. He was back in England in 1496 and he had made up his mind to be ordained. He was ordained deacon in 1497 and priest in 1498; the next year Erasmus arrived in Oxford and their long friendship began. According to the custom of the time John was provided with a number of wealthy benefices, but far fewer than such a well-connected young man might have expected.

Between the years 1496 and 1505 Colet was at Oxford and gained an immense reputation for the lectures which he gave, first of all on the Epistle to the Romans. There can be no doubt that Colet owed a good deal to the studies in Platonism of Marsilio Ficino and Pico della Mirandola, and also to the writings of Plotinus. But his lectures broke new ground in the style and methods which he adopted. He abandoned the traditional style of taking the Scriptures sentence by sentence, word by word, the allegorical interpretation and the belief in verbal inspiration. Instead, he expounded the meaning of St. Paul's writing as a whole; he illustrated his lectures with comments on the life of St. Paul and his personal character; and he made many references to the historical conditions in which the Epistles were written. Colet was in fact working a revolution in teaching the Scriptures, and doctors and abbots were to be found at his lectures armed with notebooks.

About the same time, Colet was much influenced by and lectured on the alleged writings of Dionysius the Areopagite. The Reader in Divinity at Magdalen was the great scholar Grocyn, who came to the conclusion that these writings were not the work of Dionysius. It is a proof of Colet's intellectual honesty that he at last accepted Grocyn's view. Colet was always concerned as a scholar with arriving at the truth.

In 1504 Colet was made a D.D. and for a few years he held the very valuable benefice of St. Dunstan and All Saints, Stepney.

In that year Colet was appointed Dean of St. Paul's and he held this post until his death in 1519. His time at St. Paul's was marked by his attempts to reform the Chapter and by his frequent sermons in the cathedral. The first made him very unpopular with the cathedral clergy. They resented the simplicity of Colet's life, the plain dress which he wore and the simple style of living which he adopted, and still more the attacks which he directed upon the abuses which he found in the church at large and in the London clergy in particular. His sermons took the form of a series of lectures preached from the pulpit on the New Testament, often delivered in English, and he also invited outside divines to preach in the cathedral. It was his firm belief that the abuses in the church existed because men were not concerned with holiness, that holiness could only be attained by an understanding of the Scriptures, and to attain to that it was necessary for the Scriptures to be expounded rationally.

On the death of his father Colet became a very wealthy man. He made up his mind to devote the whole of that wealth to the cause of education. By 1509 he was planning to found a new school, to be known as St. Paul's. By 1510 the building was finished, and in 1518 Colet framed the statutes for the government of the school. His ideas were unorthodox — for example, he placed the management of the school not under the clergy, but under the Mercers' Company. Already some of Colet's sermons had seemed to the Bishop of London, FitzJames, to be more than unorthodox and to lay him open to a charge of heresy, and in 1510 Colet was charged with heresy, for having preached against the worship of images and the large revenues of the bishops. Warham, the Archbishop of Canterbury, dismissed the charges as frivolous, but this did not put an end to the persecution which FitzJames kept up against Colet. As a result Colet grew weary of life at St. Paul's and he was planning to retire to the Carthusians at Sheen. He actually built a house there for himself, but in 1518 he had three attacks of the sweating sickness which so enfeebled him that on 16 September 1519, he died.

Today Colet is remembered principally as the founder of what has grown into a great English public school. In his own day he was remarkable, not only for his scholarship, but also for the originality of his methods in preaching. His courage in attacking what he felt to be wrong was invincible; in 1512 he preached the opening sermon at the meeting of Convocation and took the chance of inveighing against the worldliness of the church in England. In 1512 and again in 1513 he was commanded to preach before Henry VIII, who was about to go to war against France; Colet openly denounced war in front of the King. Henry bore him no grudge, asked him to meet him at Greenwich and had an amicable talk with him, only in the end asking Colet to explain more clearly his views, in case his sermons might have undermined the courage of the soldiers whom Henry was about to lead to war. Erasmus records that after Colet had left Henry turned to his courtiers and said: 'Let every man have his own doctor; and everyone follow his liking; but this is the doctor for me.'

It is difficult to say how far Colet would have supported the Reformation in England. It is not possible to know now whether he would have taken the oath of supremacy or would have taken sides with More and Fisher and lost his head. There was a practical side to Colet's saintliness which put him further on the side of reform than, for example, Fisher would have approved. There is an amusing and lively account written by Erasmus of a pilgrimage which he and Colet made to Canterbury, in which he records the irritation, disrespect and finally the angry rudeness with which Colet treated the ridiculous relics which were shown to the visitors. It is typical of him that when he was drawing up the statutes for his new school he inserted permission for the Mercers' Company to alter them when it seemed good to them to do so. In his last will there is a charming phrase in which he begs the boys of his school to 'lift up their little white hands' for him. It is notable that in that will Colet made no reference to the Virgin Mary and the saints, and that he left no money to provide masses for his soul.

The beautiful drawing of Colet made by Holbein cannot have been made from life, since Holbein did not come to England until 1525. It is almost certainly made from the sculpture on Colet's monument which was later destroyed in the Great Fire of London.

F. Seebohm, *Oxford Reformers*, 1887.
J. H. Lupton, *Life of Colet*, 1887.
S. Jayne, *John Colet and Marsilio Ficino*, 1963.
L. Miles, *John Colet and the Platonic Tradition*, 1962.

WILLIAM GROCYN (1446–1519), 'the patriarch of English learning' (Hallam, *Lit. of Mod. Europe*, i, 386), the first man to introduce literature into England and to profess it publicly at Oxford, was born in 1446 (not 1442, as is often said). It is pretty certain that his father was a copyholder at Colerne, near Bath, where William was born (not at Bristol, as is frequently asserted). The boy went to Winchester in 1463; he went on to New College in 1465 and was admitted as a full Fellow in 1467.

A biography of Grocyn must inevitably consist mostly of a list of his offices and the dates when he acquired them. For example, he resigned his Fellowship in 1481 on being preferred to the living of Newton Longueville near Bletchley in Buckinghamshire. In the same year he became Reader in Divinity to Magdalen College and he took a distinguished part in a disputation before Richard III and Bishop Waynflete in 1483. He resigned the Readership in 1488.

In 1488 he left Oxford and travelled to Italy to learn Greek from those Greeks who had settled in Italy. He had already learned the rudiments of the Greek language in England from Vitelli, who had been appointed as Praelector of New College not later than 1475. Grocyn met the great classical scholars, Poliziano and Chalcondyles, and from them perfected his knowledge in the Greek tongue and literature.

Vitelli left England for Paris in 1489. The way was clear for Grocyn when he reappeared in Oxford in 1491. He now rented rooms in Exeter College until 1493. In that year he resigned from Newton Longueville and devoted his time to daily lectures in public in Greek. His reputation grew and when Erasmus arrived in England on his first visit in 1499, he quickly made friends with Grocyn and his circle, which included More, Colet and Linacre. His admiration for Grocyn was almost unbounded. He wrote that Grocyn held 'the first place among the many learned men of Britain'. 'Who can help admiring the unbounded range of his scholastic knowledge?'

It is not known when Grocyn finally left Oxford. In 1496 he was appointed to the living of St. Lawrence, Jewry, but the probability is that he did not reside. Perhaps the appointment of his friend Colet to the deanery of St. Paul's in 1505 brought Grocyn to London, for after that date he was frequently there and often preached in St. Paul's at the invitation of Colet. One proof of Grocyn's scholarship and critical mind is that he had studied the supposed writings of Dionysius the Areopagite and had come to the conclusion that they were spurious, a decision which modern scholarship has confirmed. Colet had accepted the writings, but he was at last persuaded by Grocyn to the right view.

How close and intimate was this circle of friends may be seen from a letter written by Sir Thomas More in 1504 to Colet: 'Grocyn is in your absence, as you know, the master of my life, Linacre the director of my studies, Lily the dear companion of my affairs.'

Grocyn was a considerable pluralist and at one time held as many as four preferments. Probably the reason was that while at New College he had acted as tutor to Warham, and when Warham became Archbishop he was generous in giving preferments to

Grocyn. These livings brought in a very large income, and Grocyn grew to be a wealthy man. He was also a very generous man and hospitable. In 1514 Erasmus wrote, 'I do not see what arrangements can be made for my residing here (in London) with anyone except with Grocyn, and certainly there is no one I should more like to live with, but I am ashamed to live at his expense, especially since I can make no return, and he is so kind that he will allow no payment from me ... his extreme scrupulousness quite affected me. Give my heartiest salutations to Dr. Grocyn, the patron and preceptor of us all'.

Grocyn died in 1519, after being struck with paralysis. He is a somewhat shadowy figure, but he seems to have been a man of dry humour, simple, plain-speaking. Lily wrote of him that 'he lived content with a little, charming people by his exquisite urbanity, though his manner of speaking was simple and almost rustic'. Erasmus suggested that Grocyn was impatient of blunders, and that he 'greatly despised the divine genius of Plato in his laudations of Aristotle'. He left all his great wealth to Linacre to be used 'for the weal of my soul ... and all Christian souls as it shall please him.' It happens that a list of Grocyn's books has been discovered at Merton College, written in Linacre's handwriting, together with an account of his expenses. Linacre fulfilled the wishes of Grocyn by relieving the poor and by purchasing books at Louvain to be distributed among Oxford scholars, and he gave 'Master Lily' forty shillings to buy Greek books to give away.

Montagu Burrows, article in *Collectanea* II, 1890, pp. 332–80.

THOMAS LINACRE (1460?–1524), physician and classical scholar, was born probably in 1460 and died in 1524. Nothing is known for certain about his family origins or his early life. About 1480 he went to Oxford, but to which college is not known. He became a Fellow of All Souls in 1484. It is possible that he learned the elements of Greek from the Italian scholar Vitelli, who was then at Oxford, and that he attended lectures given by Grocyn, with whom he became an intimate friend.

Perhaps Linacre obtained his earliest education from William de Selling, Prior of Canterbury, who may have been his uncle. We know for certain that Linacre accompanied Selling when the latter travelled to Rome in 1485 as Henry VII's ambassador. Probably they parted company at Bologna and Linacre attached himself to the great Italian classical scholar, Poliziano, and went with him to Florence. Linacre at once attracted attention by his quick and intelligent mind. He shared his studies with Lorenzo de Medici's two sons, one of whom later became Pope Leo X and did not forget this early friendship.

At some unknown date Linacre visited Rome, where he met the classical scholar, Hermolaus Barbarus, and it is more than probable that it was Barbarus who first turned Linacre's attention to the study of medicine. It may have been Barbarus also who gave Linacre his accurate and critical knowledge of Aristotle.

In 1495 Linacre was in Venice where he lived with Aldus Manutius, the founder of the Aldine Press and the greatest of the Italian printers. Aldus was devoted to Greek scholarship, especially to Aristotle rather than to Plato. He published the first volume of the Aldine edition of the works of Aristotle in 1495: the third volume appeared in 1497 with a tribute in the preface to the scholarship of Linacre. Aldus paid a further tribute to him when he published in 1497 Linacre's translation of Proclus's work *de Sphera*.

Linacre was at Padua, the most famous university in Europe for medicine, late in 1495. On 30 August 1496, he took his M.D. at Padua and Richard Pace has recorded the vivid impression which Linacre made on his examiners by his learning and his quickness. The next year he set out for England and on his way he visited at Vicenza the greatest of the Italian medical scholars, Leonicenus, who was the author of the first treatise on syphilis, the new disease which was beginning to attack Europe.

The precise date of Linacre's return to Oxford is not known, but after he was back, on the strength of his degree in medicine at Padua, he was given an M.D. at Oxford. He soon established a high reputation as a lecturer on medical subjects, and he probably also lectured on Greek subjects, especially on Aristotle. From Linacre Thomas More learned Greek; Erasmus owed much to his friendship and inspiration; and Colet was one of his closest friends until an unfortunate quarrel over a Latin grammar which Linacre wrote for Colet's new school of St. Paul's. It is not improbable that Linacre spent a time at Cambridge, according to Dr. Caius (the refounder of Gonville Hall under the name of Gonville and Caius College), and the fact that Linacre founded a lectureship at Cambridge suggests that he had some reason for remembering that university.

In 1500 or 1501 Linacre became tutor to Prince Arthur, but the prince died in 1502, so that Linacre's post was a short-lived one. In 1509 he was appointed physician to Henry VIII at a salary of £50 a year. This entailed his leaving Oxford and living almost exclusively in London, where he soon acquired a large and distinguished practice as a doctor: his patients included Wolsey, Warham, Fox, Colet, More, Erasmus and many others.

It is probable that Linacre was ordained deacon in 1511, but he was not admitted priest until 1520. Even before 1511 he was receiving many ecclesiastical benefices, and after 1520 he was given many more. He never resided in them: it was a common thing to present these livings to distinguished men who then sold them to clergy who were willing to pay for a living. Thus Linacre built up a considerable fortune which later he decided to use for the public advantage. About 1520 Linacre gave up his medical practice so as to have more time for literary work. Sir John Cheke tells a story that late in life Linacre took up the New Testament for the first time in his life and on reading the Sermon on the Mount exclaimed, as he threw the book away, 'either this is not the Gospel or we are not Christians'.

In 1523 he was appointed tutor to the Princess Mary, when she was five years old. But he died on 20 October 1524, and was buried in the old cathedral of St. Paul's. He died of the stone, the medical name for which was *calculus*. Linacre was a noted grammarian, and it is likely that it was Linacre whom Browning had in mind when he wrote his *Grammarian's Funeral*:

> 'Back to his book then; deeper dropped his head;
> Calculus racked him.'

Although Linacre was a priest, although he was a very considerable classical scholar with great interest in Latin grammar, he cannot be called typical of the Oxford humanists who were his contemporaries, for his chief interest was not in theology but in medicine. His principal claim to fame lies in the immense amount he did to further medical knowledge in the sixteenth century by translating several of the medical works of Galen out of Greek into Latin, thereby making them more widely understandable, and to make possible further advances in medical knowledge by his founding the College of Physicians in 1518, and by the foundation of two lectureships in medicine at Oxford and one at Cambridge. In his own day it was as a classical scholar that he was revered by such men as Erasmus. His most important contribution to scholarship was his treatise *De Emendata Structura Latini Sermonis*, published in the year of his death, 1524, printed by Richard Pynson.

The Queen owns a portrait which is said to be of Linacre and to have been painted by Quentin Matsys.

R. Weiss, *Humanism during the Fifteenth Century in England.*
J. N. Johnson, *Life of Linacre,* 1835.
J. F. Fulton, *New England Journal of Medicine,* 1934.
W. Osler, *Linacre Memorial Lecture,* 1908.
R. J. Mitchell, *English Historical Review,* 1935.

DESIDERIUS ERASMUS (1466?–1536), the greatest of all the Humanists, the man who restored the Latin language to Western Europe: his name occurs so often in the biographies of the English Humanists that a sketch of him may justifiably be included in this volume. He was born probably in 1466, at Rotterdam and he died at Basle on 12 July 1536. He was an illegitimate son of Roger Gerhard, a monk. He was christened Erasmus, the Greek form of the German Gerhard, and he himself took the additional name of Desiderius, the Latin form of Erasmus, in 1496. All three words mean 'longed-for'. He first used the full form of Desiderius Erasmus Roterdamus in 1506. Much against his will he took monastic vows in 1488; he was ordained in 1492. His first visit to England took place in 1499, when he came with one of his pupils, Charles Blount, the young Lord Mountjoy. He stayed there for rather less than a year, some of which time he spent at Oxford. It was there that he met the English Humanists, especially Colet, and it was Colet who first influenced Erasmus to make theological study the chief purpose of his life. He soon recognized that he would have to learn Greek. He became also a friend of Sir Thomas More. He seems to have approved of England and especially of the charming English girls who accompanied all handshakes with a kiss. Unfortunately he was misinformed by More about the laws governing the export of currency, with the result that when he left England he had all his money confiscated by the customs officials at Dover (1500).

In the autumn of 1505 Erasmus again visited England and at once renewed his old friendships with Mountjoy, Colet and More, and became intimate also with Fox, Bishop of Winchester, Fisher of Rochester and Warham, Archbishop of Canterbury. He also was promised ecclesiastical preferment by Henry VII, which did not materialize. In 1506 he left for Italy.

Erasmus's third visit was a longer one, lasting from 1509 to 1514, and during this time he gave lectures on divinity and Greek at Cambridge, residing at Queens'. Warham proved a generous and helpful patron and gave him a prebend in Kent. Many countries in Europe were now vying to attract Erasmus to live among them. Gradually Cambridge began to pall; the plague appeared; Erasmus suffered from kidney-trouble, which he attributed to English beer. By 1514 he had made up his mind to leave England. He paid three more very short visits to England, but he never again lived there.

It was in 1509 that Erasmus composed his most popular work, *The Praise of Folly (Moriae Encomium*: the title is a play upon the name of Sir Thomas More). The book was in fact a satire on contemporary society in which Erasmus singled out the ecclesiastical hierarchy for his most bitter and scathing attacks. The book went through seven editions in a few months and twenty-seven in a few years. Written originally in Latin, (illustrated by Holbein), it was translated into most European languages. Two other books had enormous success — the *Adages* of 1500, a collection of ancient thoughts and proverbial sayings and witticisms, with Erasmus's comments on them, and the *Colloquies* of 1516, of which twenty-four thousand copies were sold in a few months, a book of wonderful humour, wit, sarcasm and criticism, containing his account of his visit to Canterbury and Walsingham and his views on the superstitions he found there. In the course of his life he produced a stream of editions of various works by the classical authors — Cato, Cicero, Aristotle, Demosthenes, Josephus, a Greek text with Latin translation of the New Testament, Latin translations of Euripides, Isocrates and Xenophon; and he translated the works of the early Fathers of the Church — Hilary, Jerome, Cyprian, Ambrose and Augustine. The quality of his Latin prose was said by his contemporaries to be superior to that of Cicero himself.

Erasmus was essentially an international figure, having no fixed home of his own, moving restlessly from town to town, from country to country, happy in none, happiest perhaps in England. He was a small man, thin, frail and timid, not being made, as he himself said, for martyrdom. He was querulous and ready to take offence, he was always cadging money, in his early years having none of his own; he was a martyr to the stone and he had so weak a stomach that the smell of fish would make him ill for days. If we judge him by his letters, we must form a very poor opinion of him. But he must have had a genius for friendship, otherwise such men as Colet and More and Linacre and Warham could never have held him in such affection as they did. The greatest scholar and theologian of his time, he was looked upon as the outstanding figure in Europe. He played a leading part in reviving Greek learning to supersede Latin: and he more than anybody else succeeded in getting scholarship applied to Scripture and the Fathers, as if they were classical texts. The Catholic Church looked to him to champion the old faith; the leaders of the Reformation expected him to take their side. It was an unenviable and impossible position. Erasmus was no hero and no leader. What he was, was a man who believed implicitly in Liberty of thought, in Charity as 'the greatest of God's commandments', and in solving problems by the use of reason and moderation.

Preserved Smith: *Erasmus*, 1923.
J. Huizinga, *Erasmus of Rotterdam*, Phaidon, 1952.
F. M. Nichols, *The Epistles of Erasmus*, 3 vols., 1901–18.
H. R. Trevor-Roper, *Historical Essays*, 1957, pp. 35–60.
R. H. Bainton, *Erasmus of Christendom*, 1970.

JOHN FISHER (1469–1535), Bishop of Rochester, martyr, was born in 1469 at Beverley in Yorkshire, the son of Robert Fisher, a well-to-do mercer. (A papal dispensation of 1491 states that Fisher was then in his twenty-second year, which settles the date of his birth. The date given in the *D.N.B.* is wrong by ten years.) He was educated at the collegiate church attached to the Minster: about 1483 he went to Cambridge to Michaelhouse, at the approximate age of 13 to 14: he took the preliminary degree in grammar in 1483, his B.A. in 1488, his M.A. in 1491, in which year he was elected a Fellow of Michaelhouse. In 1494 he became a Proctor and in 1497, at the age of twenty-eight, he was elected Master of the college. He became a D.D. in 1501, in which year he was made Vice-Chancellor of the University. From 1504 to 1514 he was annually made Chancellor, and in 1514 he was elected Chancellor for his lifetime. In 1504 he was appointed to the bishopric of Rochester, the smallest and poorest diocese in England, and he was never translated to any more lucrative see.

The turning-point in his life was when he became (probably in 1500 or 1501) one of the chaplains to the Lady Margaret Beaufort, mother of Henry VII. They became the firmest of friends; Fisher was soon advanced to be her confessor, and it was this intimacy between them which resulted in Fisher's advising her on her plans for endowing professorships of divinity at Oxford and Cambridge and for building the two new colleges of Christ's and St. John's at Cambridge. Fisher preached the funeral oration on the death of Henry VII and a few months later he delivered the funeral speech on the Lady Margaret with his deeply felt eulogy of his best friend (1509).

During the whole of his life Fisher remained a devoted friend to Cambridge University. He was the first Lady Margaret Reader at Cambridge, 1503: in 1505 he became President of Queens' College at the instigation of the Lady Margaret, but he resigned the post three years later. In 1525 he made an endowment at Christ's College, and it was he who persuaded the Lady Margaret to found a second college at Cambridge. He himself gave to St. John's £500 and nearly 1,500 acres out of the lands which she had given to him. He also bequeathed to this college his large and valuable library, but unfortunately the books were wilfully destroyed at the time of his execution. At the age of 48, under the influence of Erasmus, Fisher learned Greek, and at the age of 50 he was taught Hebrew by Robert Wakefield. When he drew up his statutes for St. John's College, he ensured that junior students should learn Greek and senior students Hebrew. He laid stress on the religious purpose of the college, especially on the duty of preaching and the study of theology. Indeed, Fisher's main purpose and hope was that these two colleges would prove a recruiting ground for future priests and raise the quality both of learning and also of preaching among the clergy in England, which he felt had fallen very low of recent years. Fisher was himself a noted and popular preacher, preaching in the vernacular

John Fisher
(Artist: After Hans Holbein)

and using a style and a diction which could be understood by everybody, however humble.

In an age which was much given to controversial writings Fisher was a man of his age. Being confronted with a Lutheran book which sought to prove that the claims of the Popes were false because St. Peter had never been at Rome, Fisher wrote a reply which was published in 1522. But the most notable passage in it is that in which he forthrightly attacks the scandalous behaviour of the Church in

Rome: 'Nowhere else is the life of Christians more contrary to Christ than in Rome, and that, too, even among the prelates of the Church'. Opposed as he was always to Luther and the Lutherans, he was yet clear-sighted enough to see and bold enough to denounce the vices of the Church at that time. When Wolsey ordered a public burning of heretical books at St. Paul's Cross, Fisher was appointed to preach the sermon, which took two hours to deliver. When Luther published his *Assertio* (1520), Fisher replied with his *Confutatio* (1523), a work of 200,000 words, which was written, as were all Fisher's controversial writings, in Latin. This book was filled with all Fisher's profound learning, but it makes much more dreary reading than does Sir Thomas More's *Dialogue against Heresies* which is enlivened with wit and humour. Fisher also wrote a *Defence of the Priesthood* and a *Defence of the King's Assertion* in reply to Luther's attacks on the Mass and on Henry VIII's book on the seven sacraments. Fisher always emphasized that the Scriptures by themselves are not enough: to understand them rightly they must be read in the light of interpretations made by the Early Fathers and of the teaching of the Church throughout the ages (1525). In this same year he wrote one more book, *De Veritate Corporis*, against the Lutheran, Oecolampadius of Basle. The book was much too long to be successful and the fact that it was written in Latin confined its circulation to the learned. At the same time Fisher was involved in the controversy over Robert Barnes.

It was not, however, only on religious matters that Fisher stood out against what he held to be wrong. In the Convocation of 1523 he had strongly withstood Wolsey's demand for a high tax on clerical incomes, and it is more than probable that this attitude had brought Fisher to the notice of Henry VIII in no very good light, so that the King was already prejudiced against him when Fisher found himself deeply and fatally involved in the matter of the King's divorce. Throughout the whole of this long business Fisher and Sir Thomas More are revealed as men of integrity, courage and determination. On the question whether the Pope had the power to grant a dispensation for a man to marry his deceased brother's wife, Fisher never wavered in asserting that the Pope had that power. He was equally steadfast in his opposition to the royal supremacy.

In 1528, Fisher was appointed to be one of the counsellors to Queen Catherine of Aragon and in the next year spoke boldly on the side of the Queen, asserting that the marriage could not be dissolved by any power, divine or human. The King was furious. It was largely owing to Fisher that the wording of the document drawn up in Convocation to purchase the King's pardon in 1531 was modified to include the phrase, 'as far as the law of God allows'. When in 1532 the clergy submitted to the King, Fisher also voiced his opposition, while Sir Thomas More gave up the Great Seal. Fisher's opposition to the Divorce and to the Breach with Rome became dangerous as Henry and Cranmer prepared to forge ahead with the matrimonial case at Dunstable, so Henry had Fisher restrained in the custody of Gardiner (April 1533), but in June, after Anne Boleyn had been crowned Queen, he was allowed to go to Rochester.

Just at this time Fisher most foolishly allowed himself to become embroiled in the episode of the Nun of Kent, Elizabeth Barton. The Act of Attainder (1534) included the name of Fisher, and he was found guilty of misprision of treason, the penalty for which was imprisonment at the King's pleasure and the forfeiture of all his goods. In the end Fisher was let off with a fine of £300, one year's revenue of his bishopric.

The first session of the 1534 parliament established the royal supremacy and settled the succession to the throne on the children of Henry and Anne Boleyn. It also enacted that an oath must be taken to accept and defend 'the whole effects and contents of this present Act', that is of the Succession Act. On 13 April 1534 Fisher was summoned to Lambeth to take the oath. He refused to do so and was given a few days to think the matter over. On 17 April he again refused and was sent to the Tower. Fisher, like More, refused to countenance any diminution in the supremacy of the Pope such as was implicit in the oath of succession, although both were willing to support the new succession itself. Both were attainted for misprision of treason and Fisher was deprived of his bishopric.

The passing of the Act of Treason in 1535 turned Fisher and More's refusal into treason, for by this Act a refusal to take the oath could be construed as an attempt to deprive the King of his title, which was treason. Many attempts were made to get Fisher to accept the oath, but all failed. Up to this point Fisher had made no direct declaration of his views: he had merely refused to take the oath. But on 7 May he was tricked by a messenger from Cromwell into believing that Henry was truly desirous of hearing his genuine views and the reasons for them, and he was given a solemn promise that no harm should come to him as the result of anything he said. Fisher therefore declared openly and fully his views and thereby he provided the government with the plainest evidence against him.

Even so it is possible that Henry would not have put Fisher to death, if at that moment the Pope had not made Fisher a Cardinal. This drove Henry to ungovernable rage and sealed Fisher's fate. On 17 June 1535 he was brought to trial and condemned to death for high treason, and the penalty was that he should be drawn on a hurdle to Tyburn and there be hanged, drawn and quartered. This penalty was remitted and he was allowed to be executed by beheading. The sentence was carried out on 22 June. Sir Thomas More was executed on 6 July.

When the news reached the Continent, Europe was horrified and bewildered. Both Fisher and More were men of international reputation, partly through their controversial writings, partly by the eulogies of them which Erasmus had spread abroad — More for his legal and theological learning, his piety, his wit and his happy family life: Fisher for his scholarship and holiness of life. Erasmus described them as 'the wisest and most saintly men England had'. The Pope wrote to Francis I of France of the 'innocence and holiness of' Fisher and 'of his learning, both famous and spread throughout the whole world, for the defence of the Catholic faith'. Many leaders in Europe had visited More, many called on Fisher at Rochester which lay on the main road from Dover to London, and among them Campeggio in 1518.

Fisher was the most conscientious bishop of his time. He looked after his diocese with pastoral care, investigating cases of heresy, always trying to raise the quality of the clergy, visiting the sick, giving alms which he could scarcely afford and entertaining visitors at his table, although his own personal standard of living was almost ascetic. There is no record of any heretic in the diocese of Rochester being sent to the stake, but Fisher maintained in his *Confutatio* that it was lawful to hand over relapsed heretics to the secular arm.

In his religious views and in his religious behaviour Fisher was essentially a mediaevalist — he kept a small closet where he would spend many hours in secret prayer and where he would scourge himself with whips. He was essentially also a spiritually-minded man. The portrait of him by Holbein (Plate 9) reveals a steady, calm and sympathetic man, gazing a little beyond this world: but the strong modelling of the face, the firm and broad nose, the square chin, the flexible line of the mouth combined with the firm set of the lips, all speak of conviction built upon faith. He stood as the representative of the old order: Henry VIII represented the new, modern world. In that world there was no room for both Henry and Fisher, just as in the new world of the United Provinces there was to be no room for both Maurice, Prince of Orange and Oldenbarne-feldt (1619). Old, tired, desperately ill, short of money, denied his books of devotions and writing materials, always cold and often hungry, Fisher endured his imprisonment in the Tower with unfailing courage and embraced death with cheerful calm. He and Sir Thomas More were canonized in St. Peter's, Rome, on 19 May 1935, as martyrs for the Catholic faith.

Bridgett, *Life of Blessed John Fisher*, 1888.
E.E. Reynolds, *Saint John Fisher*, 1955.
M. Maklem, *God have mercy*, 1967.

SIR THOMAS MORE (1478–1535), Lord Chancellor, was the son of the judge, Sir John More by his first wife, Agnes Graunger. After beginning his education at St. Anthony's school in Thread-needle Street, he was then put to live in the household of Archbishop Morton, who was also the Lord Chancellor. More would have been about twelve years old then and he spent two years in the Morton family, where he soon made a reputation for his intelligence, wit and liveliness. Years afterwards he paid a tribute to the Archbishop, for whom he always had much affection and respect, in his *Utopia*. About 1492 More went to Oxford, almost certainly to Canterbury College, later to be incorporated into Christ Church. Here he came under the influence of the New Learning, studying Greek and Latin and French, theology and music. After two years or less he returned to London to study law (1494); he became an intimate friend of Colet and in 1499 was first introduced to Erasmus, who became his lifelong bosom friend. He began his legal life at New Inn, but in 1496 he was transferred to Lincoln's Inn, where he had a rapidly successful career.

In 1499, however, More began to have doubts whether he ought to follow a legal career and ought not to become a priest. For some

Sir Thomas More
(Artist: After Hans Holbein)

four years he seriously examined this possibility and for a time lived in close touch with the brothers of the Charterhouse. In the end (1503) he abandoned the idea of an ecclesiastical life and turned with renewed energy to the study of law, in which he was quickly and brilliantly successful.

In 1504 he was elected to Parliament, but his constituency is not known. It is said that in this year 'as a beardless boy' he opposed and 'clean overthrew' the King's demands for a huge sum of money to cover the marriage of the Princess Margaret to the King of Scotland. Henry in fury revenged himself by keeping John More in the Tower until he paid a fine of £100. (Pollard in his *Wolsey* denies this story.) The next year (1505) More married Jane Colte and settled in London in Bucklersbury. During the next six years he lived a quiet and enjoyable life, rejoicing in his four children, dividing his leisure time between developing his home and literary pursuits. Twice Erasmus came to visit him: in 1508 More went to Paris and Louvain, but he returned convinced that Oxford and Cambridge were superior universities. In 1511 his wife died, and within a month he had married again, this time a widow, Alice Middleton, who had one daughter. Alice was seven years older than More and proved to be a capable housekeeper rather than a sympathetic wife. More now moved from Bucklersbury to Crosby Place in Bishopsgate Street, where he remained until he bought land in Chelsea and built for himself what was to become one of the famous houses of England.

All this time he had been proving himself a notable lawyer: he was made under-sheriff of London (1510) and he soon came into close relations with the new and young King Henry VIII, who professed for More much affection. More never allowed himself to be blinded by this and he never put much trust in the King's protestations. 'If my head should win him a castle in France, it should not fail to go.'

The year 1516 saw the publication of *Utopia*, a literary master-piece which, under the guise of representing an ideal society, was in fact a bitter attack on the political and social evils of the day.

In 1517, More became a royal councillor. He was an astute politician, who rose rapidly in royal favour, largely because of the King's personal friendship for him, but also because Wolsey trusted him. He acted as unofficial secretary to the King, and was rewarded with a knighthood in 1521 and the office of Chancellor of the Duchy of Lancaster in 1525. In 1521 he was called in by the King to help him in writing his book on the seven sacraments against Martin Luther. Later Henry was to accuse More of having 'villainously and traitorously' provoked him to write this book in defence of the

Papacy and thereby to put a sword in the Pope's hands to fight against himself. More replied that he had been 'a sorter out and placer of the principal matters' after the book was finished, 'wherein when I found the Pope's authority highly advanced, and with strong arguments mightily defended, I said unto his Grace "I must put your Highness in remembrance of one thing, and that is this. The Pope, as your Grace knoweth, is a prince as you are, and in league with all other Christian princes. It may hereafter so fall out that your Grace and he may vary upon some points of the league, whereupon may grow breach of amity and war between you both. I think it best therefore that that place be amended, and his authority more slenderly touched".' In 1523 More became Speaker of the House of Commons. Up to this point More had himself been in favour of reform, but he always envisaged the reform of the church as coming from within and he was utterly opposed to reform by revolution. For this reason he himself wrote a letter against Luther, and in 1528 he wrote his *Dialogue* against the English reformers, especially against Tyndale.

On the fall of Wolsey in 1529 More was appointed Lord Chancellor. He must be regarded as one of the greatest of Chancellors, both for the unassailable integrity with which he conducted his court, for the unequalled rapidity with which he discharged the cases, and for the great labour with which he applied himself to the job of providing justice. In the words of a recent student of More's career (Dr. J. A. Guy), 'It was as a judge, not a politician, that his reputation stands highest'. Part of More's drive against lawlessness and a part which suited his religious outlook was his encouragement of censorship of the press, and of the persecution of heretics. It has been charged against him that he was implacable against heretics and sent some of them to the stake. It is true that he was stern against seditious heretics, those who stirred up strife. To others, he was lenient and helpful, as he was to his future son-in-law, Roper.

More resigned the Chancellorship in 1532 because he found himself increasingly out of sympathy with the King's policy over the Divorce and towards the Church: the last straw was when the clergy were forced to subscribe the Submission in answer to Cromwell's Supplication of the Ordinaries. For the next two years he continued to write his pamphlets against heretics, in some of which he sank to the lowest depths of vulgar abuse and vindictive wit, especially against Tyndale. In 1533 he became for a short while embroiled in the episode of the Nun of Kent, Elizabeth Barton, and his name was included in the Bill of Attainder, but it was removed at the third reading. More himself said that his danger was only postponed, not removed, and when on 30 March 1534 a new Act of parliament required an oath to the succession of Anne Boleyn's children, More knew that his end was very near. He was willing to accept the altered succession, as a matter within the powers of parliament to deal with, but he refused to take the oath which also in effect repudiated the Papal supremacy. He sought to avoid execution by not making an open declaration of why he refused the oath, but was tricked by Sir Richard Rich into explaining his position. He was committed to the Tower in April 1534, charged with high treason and tried at Westminster on 1 July 1535. He was, of course, found guilty and was executed on Tower Hill on 6 July. Thomas More died protesting that he was 'the king's good servant but God's first'. As he had said to Thomas Cromwell before his trial, 'though I was a prisoner and condemned to perpetual prison yet I was not thereby discharged of mine obedience and allegiance upon the King's Highness'. He was canonized by Pope Pius IX in 1935.

Of More's execution it must be said that the law was strained to breaking point in order to secure a 'legal' conviction. Even so, it is possible on purely political grounds to make out a case on Henry's side. Henry was always a political realist and never a man of moral principle. The need for an indisputably legitimate heir to the throne, and a male heir at that, was paramount in his and in most people's view. More was a 'wise, righteous and brave man who went to his death for his conscience' (J. D. Mackie, *History*, June 1936). He was a first-class scholar, a man of the highest principles, a practising Christian, a faithful husband, a devoted father; his capacity for friendship, his wit, his hospitality, his kindness to servants, his love of music, his affection for animals (as his menagerie at Chelsea proves), his powers of conversation, made and still make him a great and good and lovable man. But More was also a saint, and like many other saints there was in him a hard core of granite, a fibre strong as steel, which made him a formidable opponent in controversy, a severe critic where he felt his principles to be outraged, and which gave his saintliness that almost fanatical desire for martyrdom which one sees in men like Southwell. It was not that he was impervious to the reasonable arguments of his friends and of his beloved daughter Meg: rather, he simply declined to listen to argument; one almost has the feeling that he feared he might lose the martyr's crown. It is claimed for him that he died in order to save the Papacy and the unity of Christendom. Yet there is a curious letter which he wrote to Cromwell when he was in prison in which he urges the King to pursue his idea of a General Council on the grounds that the present Pope might be deposed and a new Pope appointed with whom His Highness might be well content; 'never thought I the Pope above the General Council' (Eng. ed. of More's works, 1557, p. 1427). Perfection is not given to man, and More was not perfect. The shock which his execution caused throughout Europe is the measure of his status and reputation in his own day.

Roper & Harpsfield, *Lives of More*, Everyman ed.
R. W. Chambers, *Thomas More*, 1935.
Utopia, ed. E. Surtz & J. H. Hexter, 1965.
J. A. Guy, *The public career of Sir Thomas More*, 1980.
R. Marius, *Thomas More*, 1984.
A. Fox, *Thomas More*, 1982.

ROWLAND LEE or LEGH (*d.* 1543?), Bishop of Coventry and Lichfield and Lord President of the Council in the Marches of Wales, was the son of William Lee of Morpeth, Northumberland, and of Isabel Trollope of Thornley in Co. Durham. The date of his birth is unknown: he probably died in 1543. He first entered public life in 1528 under Wolsey. He shared with Stephen Gardiner and Thomas Cromwell in the suppressing of those monasteries whose wealth Wolsey required for his foundation of Cardinal College at Ipswich. After Wolsey died, Lee stuck to Cromwell, who put his son under Lee's charge, and he became one of the principal agents between the King and Cromwell and the clergy, and in the matter of the King's divorce; and for his many services he received frequent preferments. It is possible that it was Lee who secretly married Henry VIII and Anne Boleyn on 25 January 1533. His final reward was the Bishopric of Lichfield and Coventry, known in those days as Chester, on 10 January 1534. This appointment caused much offence to at least one person. Stephen Vaughan, a close friend of Cromwell's, wrote to him: 'You have lately holpen an earthly beast, a mole, and an enemy of all godly learning, into the office of his damnation, *a papist*, an Idolater, and a fleshly priest'. (Ellis, *Original Letters*, 3rd series, ii, 285.)

In May 1534 he was appointed President of the King's Council in the Marches of Wales with the object of restoring law and order, which had broken down under Voysey, Bishop of Exeter. He owed his appointment to Cromwell, who seems first to have recognized the need for a new and consistent policy in Wales. Lee proved himself a man of loyalty and of resolute energy, 'stowte of nature, readie-witted, roughe of speeche, not affable to any of the Walshrie, an extreme ponisher of offenders, desirous to gain credit with the Kinge and comendacon for his service'. (Gerrard to Walsingham.) There is some evidence, not above suspicion, that he hanged five thousand criminals.

When Henry VIII and Cromwell began to carry out a reorganization of government in Wales and introduced the shire system from England and appointed Welshmen as J.P.s, Lee opposed the policy, since he did not think Welshmen would be impartial in administering justice and he himself was not 'of that perfectness to know what shall chance in time coming'. We know little about the last three years of his Presidency and very little of interest about the last years of his life. He died at Shrewsbury probably on 28 January 1543, and is buried there in the church of St. Chad's.

J. F. Rees, *Tudor Policy in Wales*, Hist. Assoc. pamphlet, 1935.

THOMAS HOWARD, EARL OF SURREY, 2nd DUKE OF NORFOLK (1443–1524), soldier and statesman, was born in 1443 at Tendring Hall in Stoke-by-Nayland: he died at Framlingham in 1524. His father was Sir John Howard, later 1st Duke of Norfolk, who was killed at the battle of Bosworth (1485), and his mother was Catherine, daughter of Lord de Moleyns. He was educated at Thetford Grammar School. His father was a firm supporter of Edward IV and it was as a Yorkist that Thomas first made his name. He held a number of household appointments under King Edward: first as a henchman and then as esquire to the body. At some point, probably in the late 1460s, he went with a number of other English knights to serve Charles the Bold of Burgundy in his wars with France.

When war broke out between Edward IV and Warwick the King-Maker (1469), and Edward had to go into exile, Howard was prevented from accompanying him by a surprise attack of Lancastrian ships which compelled Howard to take sanctuary in Colchester. On the return of Edward to England, Howard broke sanctuary, joined the Yorkist leader and fought for him at Barnet (1471), where he was wounded.

In 1472 Howard married a rich heiress, Elizabeth, daughter of Sir Frederick Tilney of Ashwell Thorpe in Norfolk and widow of Humphrey Bourchier (son of Lord Berners) who was killed at Barnet. In 1475 he accompanied Edward IV to France and was present at his meeting with Louis XI at Picquigny. On his return to England he went to live at Ashwell Thorpe as a country gentleman and became sheriff for Norfolk and Suffolk (1477–8). On 18 January 1478 he was knighted by the King at the marriage of the infant Richard, Duke of York, to Lady Anne Mowbray, only child of the 4th Duke of Norfolk who died in 1476. Anne died before the marriage was consummated, and thereby the direct line of the Mowbrays became extinct; Sir John Howard was next of kin, but did not inherit the lands because Edward IV had assigned them to his son, the Duke of York.

Thomas Howard and his father, Sir John, gave their enthusiastic support to the usurpation of Richard III and were very richly rewarded as a result. It has been suggested that the Howards were responsible, on Richard's orders, for the death of the Princes in the Tower. Among the rewards for service to Richard III given to the House of Howard were the Mowbray titles and lands; the Duke of York being conveniently dead (in the Tower). Sir John Howard became Duke of Norfolk and his son, Thomas, became Earl of Surrey: the family holds these titles to this day.

It might also be said that from this moment Surrey became the prototype of those Tudor statesmen who later accepted the royal supremacy and adhered loyally to the person and the policy of whoever sat on the English throne. Surrey had supported the Yorkist cause in the person of Edward IV: he supported Yorkist Richard III and he fought on his side at Bosworth Field. He then accepted the Lancastrian Tudors. At Bosworth his father was killed and he himself was badly wounded and was taken prisoner.

Henry VII, desperately in need of money, seized all the Norfolk

Thomas Howard, Earl of Surrey, 2nd Duke of Norfolk
(Artist: Unknown)

estates and on 7 November 1485, the dead Norfolk and the living Surrey were attainted, but Surrey's life was spared. After Henry had married the Yorkist Elizabeth, Surrey accepted the Tudor right to the throne, and when the Earl of Lincoln raised rebellion against

Henry VII, Surrey refused to profit by it and declined the offer of the Lieutenant of the Tower of a chance to escape. He was not, however, released from prison until 1489 when the attainder was reversed and Surrey was given back some part of his estates, for Henry saw the value of such a man.

The first use which the King made of him was to send him in 1489 to put down a serious rising in Yorkshire, which he did successfully and humanely. As a reward he was created Lieutenant-General of the North and deputy to the young Prince Arthur as Warden of the Eastern, Middle and Western Marches towards Scotland. He put down another rising at Pontefract (1492) and by obtaining pardon from the King for all the rebels he won the affection of the people as well as the confidence of the King.

Surrey's principal duty now was to watch the Scottish border, which was being threatened by James IV and Perkin Warbeck. In 1497 he compelled James to abandon the siege of Norham Castle and to retreat home again. Surrey pursued him and took Ayrton Castle, but he himself had to withdraw owing to bad weather. In 1501 he was made Lord High Treasurer and a Privy Councillor. The King again shewed his confidence in Surrey by sending him to arrange a marriage between the Princess Margaret and James IV of Scotland. Two years later (1503) Surrey escorted the Princess to Scotland and on 8 August he gave the bride away on behalf of Henry VII.

In 1497 Surrey's wife died: the same year he married Agnes Tilney, a cousin of his first wife, Elizabeth Tilney. In 1507 he was in Antwerp negotiating a marriage between Princess Mary and Charles of Castile, afterwards the Emperor Charles V, which never took place. Henry VII now made Surrey an executor of his will.

When Henry VIII came to the throne in 1509, Surrey was sixty-six years old. His age, his experience, his reputation for disinterested loyalty and — to a young man like Henry — most especially his military reputation, all marked out Surrey as the chief member of the Privy Council. He still had fifteen years to live. Those years were embittered by his long duel with Wolsey, whose social origins he despised and whose policy he wholly distrusted. He lost that duel in the sense that he never acquired a commanding position in the Council over policy: that fell to Wolsey. In another sense he won his fight in so far that Henry paid no attention to Wolsey's great efforts to poison the King's mind against his rival. To the end Henry seemed to preserve his respect and liking for this loyal servant. Those years were sweetened by Surrey's tremendous military victory over James IV at Flodden in 1513, when Surrey was seventy years old. As a reward, on 1 February 1514, Surrey was created Duke of Norfolk. He was given twenty-six manors in Norfolk and Suffolk which brought him an income of £40 p.a., and he was given an augmentation of his heraldic arms which included a part of the royal arms of Scotland.

In an age which set great store by name, fame and glory, Norfolk found himself frequently called upon to fulfil functions and duties which much irked, and even deeply wounded, his sensitive nature. He was hotly opposed to Wolsey's policy of marrying the King's sister, Mary, to Louis XII of France, yet it fell to him to conduct the Princess to France for the wedding. More personally distasteful and humiliating, he found himself compelled to conduct Wolsey from the high altar to the West door of Westminster Abbey, when Wolsey was formally invested with the Cardinal's hat. In 1517 Norfolk was called on to put down the rising of the London apprentices, which he did with all his old skill. In 1520 Henry VIII went to France to the Field of Cloth of Gold and he left Norfolk in charge of his kingdom, a high enough honour and responsibility for any man. But a more terrible duty followed. In 1521 he was appointed Lord High Steward to preside over the trial of Edward, Duke of Buckingham, on a charge of high treason. Buckingham was Norfolk's oldest friend, father of the wife of Norfolk's eldest son. It is incredible to us of the twentieth century that Norfolk should have been appointed, that Norfolk should have agreed to serve; the more incredible when we remember that in the sixteenth century treason trials had only a foregone conclusion. 'With tears streaming down his face Norfolk passed sentence of death on a man with whose sentiments he entirely agreed, but had his reward in a grant of manors from Buckingham's forfeitures.' (D.N.B.)

Norfolk never after this made more than an occasional appearance at Court. His last appearance was in 1523, 'when he had a short and apparently affectionate conversation with the King'. (House of Howard, i, 109). He died on 21 May 1524, in his eightieth year, at his historic castle of Framlingham. He was buried at Thetford Priory, where an elaborate monument was erected over his tomb, on which was engraved a long biographical history, largely the work of his own hand, which remains a chief source of information about the details of his life. At the dissolution of the monasteries the tomb disappeared, but the inscription has been preserved. The bones of the Duke were translated to the Howard Chapel at Lambeth. Norfolk's second wife, Agnes Tilney, survived him for more than twenty years and she greatly damaged the Howard family by her lax guardianship of Catherine Howard, the fifth wife of Henry VIII. She was buried beside her husband at Lambeth.

Thomas Howard, second Duke of Norfolk, was first and foremost a soldier. He was a modest man and a humane man in an age when humaneness and modesty were fast disappearing. Henry VIII had a good deal of respect for him; the English people as a whole admired and even loved him. Polydore Vergil summed up the general opinion '*vir prudentia, gravitate et constantia summa,*' (a man of the utmost wisdom, solid worth and loyalty).

M. J. Tucker, *The life of Thomas Howard*, 1964.

ROBERT ASKE (*d.* 1537), leader of the Pilgrimage of Grace, was born about the beginning of the century. Little is known of his early life. He was in the service of the Earl of Northumberland and in 1527 he was admitted to Gray's Inn. He became a lawyer with 'great businesses' in London and he was clearly a gifted orator. His personal appearance was exceedingly plain and he could boast of only one eye. He was a man of considerable physical strength, who could spend day after day in the saddle with little time for food or sleep. He was also a man of absolute integrity and uncommon courage, but was too trustful of others for the treacherous times in which he lived.

The Pilgrimage of Grace began at Louth in Lincolnshire, (October 1536), where a rising took place against the suppression of the monasteries. Other motives added fuel to the fire, but the rising was quickly put down. At once another and much more serious rising broke out in Yorkshire. It was of this rising that Aske became the leader. It was a conservative and in no way a revolutionary rising in a backward area of England which resented the rise of 'new men' like Thomas Cromwell, the suppression of the religious houses, taxation and some of the ecclesiastical changes. The King promised a pardon to all and an inquiry into their grievances. On Henry's personal invitation Aske went to London to discuss the grievances. Henry sent him back home with assurances which were held to be enough to satisfy the rebels. Aske was able to settle another rising, under Sir Francis Bigod, for which loyal work he received the personal thanks of the King. But Henry was only biding his time. By May 1537 Aske was in prison in London. He was tried and sentenced to be hanged, drawn and quartered. Henry was determined that all the prisoners should be executed in their own counties. Aske was sent north to Yorkshire and was executed within the city of York. He had begged the King that he might be hanged until he was dead before being disembowelled. Henry granted this favour.

M. H. and R. Dodds, *The Pilgrimage of Grace*, 1915.
K. Pickthorn, *Early Tudor Government: Henry VIII*, 1934.
H. F. M. Prescott, *The Man on a Donkey*, 1952.

THOMAS, LORD DARCY (1467–1537), Statesman and rebel, a leader of the Pilgrimage of Grace, was the son of Sir William Darcy and his wife Euphemia, daughter of Sir John Langton. In 1488 he succeeded to the ancient family lands in Lincolnshire and Yorkshire, the family home being Templehurst. He was twice married, first to Sir Richard Tempest's daughter Dousabella, who was the mother of his four sons; secondly to Edith, widow of Lord Neville and mother of the young Earl of Westmorland, the steward of whose lands Darcy became in 1505. In that same year he was raised to the peerage. His family lands, his new title, and especially the new connection by marriage with the great northern family of Nevilles, greatly strengthened his position and prestige in the north. Between 1488 and 1511 he received many appointments in the north and on the border, such as the Captain of Berwick and the Warden of the East Marches. He was second only in importance to the Earl of Northumberland.

In 1511 Darcy, at his own request, was given command of a force of English archers which Ferdinand of Aragon had asked Henry VIII to supply for the invasion of France. Five companies of 250 men each sailed from Plymouth in May and arrived at Cadiz on 1 June. Unfortunately the English troops were quarrelsome and ill-disciplined, and Ferdinand soon got rid of them — they were only in

Spain for a little more than a fortnight. The journey home was long and stormy, and Darcy had to spend much money on victualling his men and paying their wages. He complained bitterly to Wolsey later, but the Spanish ambassador dealt with him very liberally and appeased his anger.

In 1513 Darcy accompanied Henry VIII on his French campaign and was present at the battle of Thérouanne, where he had some accident which caused a rupture from which he suffered for the rest of his life. On returning home from the war he was once more employed in governing the borders. In 1529 he did not scruple to prepare the indictment against his friend Wolsey which led to the fall of the minister. At first he was on the King's side in the matter of the divorce and he appeared as a witness at the Queen's trial. But it is likely that he was beginning to see whither Henry was tending. In 1532, in reply to a speech by the Duke of Norfolk, Darcy boldly supported the view that such causes as divorce were spiritual causes and ought to be settled by the Papacy. For the next three years Darcy was kept in London and not allowed to go home to the north. He was unemployed and he began to hate the growing despotism of the Cromwellian policy.

By 1534 he was hand in glove with Lord Hussey, and the two of them began to plot with Chapuys, the Imperial ambassador, for the Emperor Charles V to invade England and rid the country of a tyranny which was destroying the Church. He told Chapuys that if only he could get home to the north he would prepare for a general rising. At last he was allowed to go and he was at Templehurst by 13 November 1535.

It was in October 1536 that the first outbreak of the Pilgrimage of Grace occurred in Lincolnshire. It soon spread into Yorkshire. Only Pontefract Castle seemed capable of holding out against the insurgents, and Darcy was in command there. The castle was in disrepair and short of supplies. Darcy cannot be blamed for this, since he had been detained in London for three years. The rising was mainly caused by the suppression of the monasteries, of which Darcy strongly disapproved. It was aimed not against the King but against Cromwell, and Darcy sympathized with the view that the minister and not the King was responsible. In other words, all his instincts made him favourable to the rebels. He hesitated to join them only because he detested the thought that he would be branded as a traitor. At 7 o'clock in the morning of Saturday, 21 October he surrendered the castle to Robert Aske and took the Pilgrims' oath.

It has been suggested by Professor G. R. Elton that Darcy's part in the Pilgrimage of Grace was deeper, that he and Lord Hussey helped stir up the rebellion and that his claims to have been forced to join the rebels were insincere. Certainly many aspects of the Pilgrimage make it appear less than spontaneous, and Darcy had every motive to lead such a movement.

When Henry sent his representatives to deal with the situation, they were instructed to offer Darcy a safe conduct to London or a pardon, if he would submit. Darcy wrote a letter to Henry to explain his conduct. The King then sent him a pardon, but on 6 January 1537, he summoned Darcy to London. Darcy pleaded that he was too ill to go. Meantime the Pilgrimage of Grace was ended, but immediately another rising under Sir Francis Bigod took place. Darcy and Aske were able to deal with that, for which services they were sent the thanks of the King. But soon after Darcy was arrested, taken to London, charged with treason and condemned to be hanged, drawn and quartered (15 May 1537). The sentence was commuted to one of beheading, and Darcy was beheaded on Tower Hill on 30 June.

M. H. and R. Dodds, *The Pilgrimage of Grace,* 1915.
K. Pickthorn, *Early Tudor Government: Henry VIII,* 1934.
G. R. Elton, *Reform and Reformation,* 1977.

ELIZABETH BARTON (1506–1534), the Nun of Kent, or Holy Maid of Kent, was born in 1506 and was hanged at Tyburn on 20 April 1534. She was a domestic servant in the family of Thomas Cobb at Aldington, in Kent. In 1525 she fell ill, perhaps of epilepsy. She fell into trances and cried out with 'marvellous holiness in rebuke of sin and vice', making prophecies on occasion. It was a feature of mediaeval Catholicism that it produced such young female mystics. The Holy Maid of Ipswich was a contemporary of Barton's, although so also was the Holy Maid of Leominster, a proved impostor.

An enquiry was held into Barton's trances under the chairmanship of Dr. Edward Bocking, an official of Christ Church, Canterbury, and an Oxford divine of blameless reputation. He concluded that hers was a genuine case of religious ecstacy. Further miracles followed, and by 1526 she was recognised by Warham, Archbishop of Canterbury, Sir Thomas More, Wolsey and even the King himself. Under Bocking's direction she entered the nunnery of St. Sepulchre at Canterbury. Bocking became her spiritual adviser, or according to later hostile reports, the author of her continued imposture.

When it was known that Henry VIII was planning to divorce his wife and to marry Anne Boleyn, the Nun of Kent began to inveigh against the King and to prophesy that, if he married Anne, he would die 'a villain's death' within a month and should no longer be 'king of this realm'. This brought her into further contact with the opponents of the Divorce, notably Bishop Fisher of Rochester. The King himself met her and heard her prophecies on three occcasions. Henry of course, took no notice of these prophecies and married Anne. He was not dead in six months. The Nun announced that Henry, like Saul, was no longer King in the eyes of God and that his subjects were freed from their allegiance. The Nun, Bocking, Richard Masters (her parish priest) and six others were arrested. She was brought to admit that she was a fraud. In January 1534, an Act of Attainder was brought in against them, and both More and Fisher were included in it. Proceedings against these two were dropped. On 20 April Elizabeth Barton, Bocking and the other accomplices were hanged.

It would be wrong to doubt the seriousness of the Nun of Kent's challenge to Henry VIII. After her arrest, Henry called an assembly of his nobles, prelates, judges and councillors, in November 1533, to debate her case for three days. It was the importance of the threat she posed to his proceedings at this crucial stage in his affairs which made the King take the drastic step of having her executed merely for the words she spoke against him: an unusual, though not unprecedented, interpretation of the meaning of treason. The Maid's connections with the Marchioness of Exeter, mother of Henry's male heir presumptive (as it were) were also no doubt worrying to the King. Whether she was a genuine mystic or not, and how far she was manipulated by others, or whether she acted on her own initiative are questions which cannot easily be settled. Every modern history book dismisses her as an impostor and the puppet of Bocking and Fisher. But there may be another side to the story. Perhaps we might understand Elizabeth Barton better if we considered her case along with that of another mystic maid, Joan of Orleans, a near contemporary of hers and another recipient of English justice.

A. Neame, *The Holy Maid of Kent*, 1971.

THOMAS BILNEY (1495?-1531), martyr, was born probably in 1495 and died at the stake in 1531. His family name was derived from the Norfolk village of Bilney. While still very young he went up to Trinity Hall, Cambridge, in order to study law, and he did in fact take a degree in law. But by temperament he was much more religiously than legally minded. From his own account he was for some time unhappy and went through a spiritual conflict, but when Erasmus's version of the New Testament in Latin, not Greek, appeared, Bilney bought a copy 'and at first reading (as I well remember) I chanced upon this sentence of St. Paul (O most sweet and comfortable sentence to my soul!) in I Tim. i: "It is a true saying and worthy of all men to be embraced that Christ Jesus came into the world to save sinners, of whom I am the chief and principal". Immediately I seemed unto myself inwardly to feel a marvellous comfort and quietness, insomuch as my bruised bones leaped for joy.' In 1519 he was ordained priest.

Bilney was one of the group of Cambridge men who gathered at the White Horse to discuss the New Learning and from that to go on to religious disputes, hence the White Horse came to be known as 'Little Germany'. He became friends with such men as Hugh Latimer (whom he took as his Confessor), Robert Barnes (whom he converted), Matthew Parker, to be later Archbishop of Canterbury. Everybody loved 'little Bilney', so small, so modest, so friendly, and he became almost the leader of the Cambridge reformers.

Whereas many of his friends became gradually more and more heretical, Bilney remained orthodox on all the main doctrines of the Catholic Church, so orthodox that it is a misnomer to call him a Protestant martyr. Bilney was not without some eccentricities. He detested music: 'coming from the Church where singing was he would lament to his scholars the curiosity of their dainty singing which he called rather mockery with God than otherwise': and when Dr. Thirleby, at that time a scholar with rooms below Bilney's (later he was the first and only Bishop of Westminster), began to play upon his recorder, Bilney 'would resort straight to prayer'. Luther would not have approved of this hatred of music.

Bilney's sermons provoked a great deal of opposition because he stressed the direct access of the individual to God without the need for pilgrimage or the intercession of saints, and he came to be looked on, quite unfairly, even if naturally, as a Lutheran. In 1526 Wolsey himself examined Bilney at Cambridge. He seems to have exacted from him an oath that he did not hold and would not propagate Lutheran doctrines. But the next year (1527) Bilney preached a series of sermons in London denouncing the idolatry of saints and complaining of the idolatry of the Christian Church, but for which the Jews would have been converted. Inevitably he was had up before a panel of bishops presided over by Cuthbert Tunstal, Bishop of London. Bilney was in the most perilous position, for as the law stood he had recanted before Wolsey in 1526; now he was facing a charge of being a relapsed heretic, for which the only penalty was to be burned at the stake. Tunstal behaved with the most Christian patience and gentleness, obviously wholly anxious to save Bilney. He suspended the trial to give Bilney a chance to think again in private: Bilney refused to recant. On the fourth day Tunstal convicted him of heresy, rather on the accusations of his opponents than on his own answers, but he postponed sentence till the next day, when he again implored Bilney to consult his friends, and gave him till the afternoon to decide. Bilney refused to recant, Tunstal gave him two more days in which to consult his friends. On the seventh day of the trial Bilney recanted. He was sentenced to carry a faggot at St. Paul's, to refrain from saying Mass publicly and from preaching until he was given permission to do so. He was also to remain in prison until he was set free by Wolsey.

Bilney returned to Cambridge a broken man, tortured by the memory of his recantation. Latimer has recorded that so inconsolable was Bilney that his friends dared not leave him alone. At last he made up his mind. One night he left Cambridge, telling his friends that he was going 'up to Jerusalem'. He went to Norwich, where his unpopularity was greatest. He preached in the open fields and gave a copy of Tyndale's *New Testament* to the 'anchoress of Norwich', probably Dame Agnes Edrygge. Reluctantly the Bishop of Norwich ordered Bilney's arrest. What else could he do? Bilney was tried as a relapsed heretic and was burned at the stake.

A controversy sprang up after his death over whether he had at the last moment made a complete recantation. So nearly completely was he orthodox, that any statement he made would look like a recantation. The whole problem is examined in *The Recantation of Thomas Bilney* by E. G. Rupp, *London Quarterley*, April 1942. It is unlikely that any convincing answer can be produced now. When all is said and done, the orthodox 'little Bilney' lit as long-lasting a candle in England as did the reformers Latimer and Ridley.

One immediate effect of his execution was to encourage anti-clerical feeling and to create the right parliamentary climate for the document known as the Supplication against the Ordinaries to be agreed upon by the House of Commons (1532).

E. G. Rupp. *The English Protestant Tradition*, 1949.
J. F. Davis, *Historical Journal*, 1981.

JOHN FRITH (1503–1533), Protestant martyr, was born in 1503 at Westerham in Kent and he was burned at the stake in 1533. He was the son of an innkeeper; he went to school at Eton College and to Queens' and then to King's College, Cambridge. There was another Etonian at King's, Edward Fox, the great friend of Stephen Gardiner, which may be the reason for Frith's becoming Gardiner's pupil — a fact which was to have tragic consequences later. Perhaps this clever and scholarly young man frequented the White Horse Tavern, taken there by Gardiner and Fox. What Frith there imbibed became for him the truth, for which he suffered partly at the hands of Gardiner, who even so did his best to save his pupil.

Frith was well known for his personal beauty and for his wit and friendliness. He was also a young man of great abilities and a fine scholar. It is just possible that he may have met Tyndale at Cambridge. He took his degree in 1525 and the next year he was transferred to the new foundation at Oxford, Cardinal College — in itself a tribute to his scholarship, for Wolsey was on the look-out only for the best in the New Learning. But these young men from Cambridge were already infected with heresy. Frith was arrested and put into prison, whence he was rescued by Wolsey, who forbad him to go more than ten miles from Oxford. Frith disobeyed and went abroad (1528) to Antwerp, or possibly to Marburg. He was certainly in close touch with Tyndale, but it is untrue that he helped

Tyndale in the translation of the New Testament, for that book was published two years before Frith went abroad. It is possible that he helped in the revision of the 1534 edition, which was published after his death.

Henry VIII was very anxious to help Frith and to save him from heresy. Cromwell wrote to his close friend, Stephen Vaughan, who was trying to persuade Tyndale to return to England, that the King heard good reports of Frith's learning and lamented that he should use it in furthering the 'venomous and pestiferous works, erroneous and seditious opinions of the said Tyndale'. Henry hoped that Frith was not 'so far yet inrooted' in such evil doctrines and he wished Vaughan to try to persuade Frith to return to England. But Frith would not renounce his opinions.

In 1530 he came back to England, but he was arrested in Reading and put in the stocks, from which he was rescued by the local schoolmaster.

Probably he went abroad again and returned in 1532, to be arrested in Essex and put into the Tower, on what charge is not known. In the Tower he was well treated and was even allowed to go out to dine with friends. While he was in prison he formulated his religious views on paper, exactly what Tyndale had begged him not to do. His views on transubstantiation were highly heretical.

After five months in the Tower Frith was brought up in front of a commission of bishops, presided over by Cranmer, all of whom were only anxious to save Frith — Cranmer interviewed him alone 'three or four times to persuade him to leave that imagination'. It is possible even that Cranmer arranged for him to have a chance to escape abroad, but Frith would not take it. Gardiner, his old tutor, also did his best, but all to no avail. Frith refused to recant anything and revealed himself as undoubtedly a heretic by the standards of the times. He was condemned and was handed over to the secular arm to be burned.

He was burned at Smithfield on 4 July 1533, bound back to back with a young tailor's apprentice, Andrew Hewet, at the same stake. Dr. Cooke, a London parson, told the people, while Frith was burning, that it was as wrong to pray for the heretics as it was to pray for a dog. 'The Lord forgive thee' were Frith's last words. His doctrine of the Sacrament is that now adopted in the Book of Common Prayer.

M. L. Loane, *Pioneers of the Reformation in England*, 1964.

JOHN FOREST (1470/74–1538), martyr, was born in 1470 (perhaps 1474) and died in 1538. He became a friar Observant at Greenwich. Henry VIII greatly respected these friars, which may be the reason why Forest was appointed Confessor to Catherine of Aragon. When Wolsey determined to visit the house at Greenwich, the friars strongly opposed him, but Forest persuaded them to agree. After Henry began his search for a divorce from Catherine, the Provincial, Peto, preached a bold sermon in the presence of Henry forthrightly denouncing the divorce. As a result, Forest was made Provincial in Peto's place. No doubt Henry expected that Forest would take his side, but instead Forest began to preach quite as strongly as Peto against the divorce. In 1533 he was dismissed and put into prison. In October 1534 the Greenwich Observants were dispersed and it would be about this time that Forest made some sort of submission. Hall says that Forest at his later trial stated that 'he took the oath with his outward man, but his inward man was never consented thereunto'. Latimer gave a more respectable version: 'Laws must be obeyed and civil ordinances I will follow outwardly, but my heart in religion is free to think as I will.'

For about two years Forest was free from prison, but he went about exhorting people to stand firm in the old forms of religion and he produced a book *De Auctoritate Ecclesiae et Pontificis Maximi* in which he vehemently attacked the claim that the King could be head of the Church in spiritual matters. In 1538 he was arrested on a charge, not of treason, but of heresy. Under examination Forest's courage gave way and he made a full submission. When the recantation was brought to him, he recovered his nerve and refused to accept it. He was handed over to the secular arm to be burned as a relapsed and obstinate heretic.

Forest was burned at Smithfield on 22 May 1538. Care was taken to make the scene specially memorable. Cromwell, Lords of the Council, the Lord Mayor and many other important personages were present. Latimer made a long speech urging Forest to recant. Forest's answer was, 'I will die. Do your worst upon me. Seven years ago you durst not for your life have preached such words as these; and now, if an angel from heaven should come down and teach me any other doctrine than that I learned as a child, I would not believe him. Take me; cut me in pieces, joint from joint. Burn, hang, do what you will, I will be true henceforth to my faith.'

In a chapel in Llan Dderfel in Wales there had been a wooden figure of an ancient Welsh saint, Dderfel Gadern, which had for long been a lucrative shrine for the parish. Cromwell had ordered this image to be sent to London to be destroyed. One of its alleged attributes was that it could destroy a forest by fire. The image was now broken up and was used as faggots with which to burn Forest. Over the pyre was slung a kind of bed made of chains. In this bed Forest was laid and was slung above the flames to be slowly roasted to death.

Froude, *History of England.*
H. Maynard Smith, *Henry VIII and the Reformation,* 1948.

JOHN LAMBERT [his real name was Nicholson, but he took the name of Lambert, on his own showing for fear the bishops might murder him] (*d.* 1538), martyr, was born at some unknown date in Norwich and was burned at the stake at Smithfield in November 1538. Educated at Cambridge, he became a Fellow of Queens' College in 1521. It is said that Thomas Bilney converted him to Protestantism, but Bilney was never really a Protestant. Lambert, who frequented the White Horse in Cambridge, was ordained priest and had for a time a living in Norfolk, but he was in some trouble through reading forbidden books. The Merchant Adventurers then sent him to be their chaplain in the English House at Antwerp. In 1529 Sir Thomas More and Bishop Tunstal passed through Antwerp and no doubt heard about the Protestant propaganda which Lambert was carrying on. This may well be the reason why More, when he became Lord Chancellor, had Lambert sent back to England (1532).

Lambert was summoned to Lambeth and was confronted with forty-five articles which he answered with great skill and learning. Archbishop Warham saved him and kept him at his own house at Otford. Warham died in August 1532, and Lambert was free. He took up teaching Latin and Greek to children, resigned his priesthood and thought of marrying; he also entered the Grocers' Company. But Lambert was a man who simply could not avoid controversy. He was soon in trouble. In 1535 he was arraigned before Cranmer and Latimer on a charge of denouncing the worship of saints. Latimer was said to be 'most extreme against him', but Lambert won his point that it was not necessary to eternal salvation to pray for the intercession of the saints and therefore it could not be heresy to abstain. But he would not learn: freed from prison on Friday, he was there on Saturday trying to reopen the whole discussion: as a result he was put into prison for a very short time.

Freed again, again Lambert asked for trouble. When Bishop Taylor of Lincoln, almost a Lutheran, preached a sermon on the Real Presence with some of which Lambert did not agree, Lambert was there at the foot of the pulpit and tried to start a dispute there and then. Taylor refused to listen and told Lambert to put his criticisms into writing. Lambert did this and produced a point of view very near to that of the Swiss reformer, Zwingli. At this moment Robert Barnes was sitting on a commission charged with the duty of extirpating these 'Sacramentaries'. Taylor sent Lambert's paper to Barnes, who passed it on to Cranmer. Lambert was summoned to appear before Cranmer: very rashly he appealed from Cranmer to the Supreme Head of the Church, Henry VIII himself.

Henry was at this moment anxious to prove to the world that, although he had repudiated the Papacy, he had not repudiated the Catholic faith. What more convincing way than by personally presiding over the trial of an alleged heretic? The trial took place and Henry presided. The trial was not an edifying spectacle. Only the bishops behaved decorously. The King magnificently dominated the scene, but the occasion and perhaps the too similar characters of King and defendant combined to bring out the worst side of Henry's bullying character. Lambert kept his end up for some time, but after standing for five hours he was too weary to make any answers at all. The conclusion was inevitable. To Henry's question, 'Do you believe that in the Sacrament of the Altar is the Body of Christ?', Lambert infuriated the King by replying, 'St. Augustine ...': 'I do not want to know what St. Augustine says. What do you believe?' Lambert answered, 'I deny that it is the Body of Christ.' There was no answer to that except the flames of Smithfield.

H. Maynard Smith, *Henry VIII and the Reformation*, 1948.
A. G. Dickens, *The Reformation in England*, 1964.

ROBERT BARNES (1495–1540), Protestant martyr, was born
at Lynn in Norfolk in 1495 and was burned at the stake in 1540.
Very early in life he became an Augustinian friar and joined the
Austin Friars at Cambridge. Soon after he went abroad to study at
Louvain, and on his return he was made Prior of the Austin house.
Barnes's enthusiasm for learning soon turned his house into a centre
of classical reading and learning. It is most probable that he met
Erasmus, but there is no evidence that he did so. One of his pupils
was Miles Coverdale. In 1523 he took his D.D. and he became much
interested in theological questions, partly as a result of coming under
the influence of Bilney, who claimed to have converted Barnes. Soon
Bilney, Barnes and Latimer were the leading members of that group
of 'modernists' who met at the White Horse in Cambridge and
discussed the views of Luther.

Barnes first fell foul of the Cambridge authorities over a sermon
he preached on Christmas Eve 1525 in which he attacked with much
amusing scurrility the litigiousness of the age. The charge brought
against Barnes was that he had preached the doctrine of the
Anabaptists that lawsuits were unlawful between Christians. In
fact, he had never said this. His error lay in his never realizing that,
the law of England being what it was, he had put himself into a
perilous position. He was examined in Cambridge, but his case was
remitted to Wolsey in London.

Thanks to the friendly help of Gardiner and of Fox (the Master of
the Wards), Barnes was given a private interview with Wolsey.
Wolsey did all he could to save Barnes from the effects of the law.
Barnes was unhelpful and Wolsey at last warned him that if he
persisted in his attitude 'then you must burn' (February 1526).

At his own request Barnes was next formally tried by panel under
the Bishop of Bath. Barnes was argumentative and tedious. On being
at last told that he must either recant or burn, he recanted and
abjured all the articles preferred against him, none of which (it is fair
to add) had the remotest connection with the main doctrines of the
Catholic Church. A wiser man than Barnes would have spotted this.
He was commanded to make his recantation in public. Barnes has
left a vivid account of the ceremony, but one is justified in thinking
that he was more concerned with the sense of the ridiculous than of
the shame. Gardiner once described Barnes as 'a trim, minion friar
Augustine, one of a merry scoffing wit, friarlike, and as a good

fellow in company well loved of many'. A later historian has written of him 'he was the man who called for drinks'. (Cooper, *Athenæ* i, 215). But Barnes was also a conceited, vain man, one who overrated his own abilities and who loved to stand in the limelight. The sixteenth century was not an age in which it was safe to stand in the limelight. It may redound to Barnes's credit that he was ready to be burned for his convictions: it does not necessarily follow that those convictions were worth burning for, or that he need ever have burned for them, had he been a wiser and no less honest man.

After the trial Barnes was not allowed to return to Cambridge: he was put into house-arrest in London, but he was left free to work and to teach. He was not a staid enough man to take clear stock of his position. He now sold copies of Tyndale's *New Testament*, a forbidden book, and it is likely that he behaved in other indiscreet ways. Barnes was now sent to close confinement at Northampton. There his friends advised him to leave feigned evidence of suicide, which he did, and while the authorities dragged the river, Barnes escaped overseas to Wittenberg (1528). He had now put himself into the position of a relapsed heretic.

At Wittenberg he was welcomed by the German reforming theologians and he lived in the same house at Martin Luther. Here, under the name of Antonius Amarius or Anglus, he wrote his *Articles of the Christian Church*, published in German in 1531, which provided full evidence that he was a heretic. (See Rupp, *The English Protestant Tradition*, pp. 39–40.) His *Supplication unto the most gracious prynce Henry VIII* appeared in the same year (1531) and a copy was sent to Henry. Henry and Cromwell at this time were in need of Protestant help against the Papacy and sent for Barnes to come to England under a safe conduct. Barnes paid a short visit to England.

However, Barnes did not succeed in making any agreement between Henry and the Lutherans of Germany. Sir Thomas More, the Lord Chancellor, would have put him in prison: 'Barnes but for the King's safe-conduct should have standen in peril to be burned and his books'. In 1534, after another spell on the Continent, Barnes returned to England, and was able to live safely in royal favour for the next five years, despite his advanced views.

In 1535 Barnes dedicated his *History of the Popes* to Henry VIII in the hopes of obtaining some preferment, but all he got was a Welsh prebend worth £18 a year, although he had been employed by Henry and Cromwell on diplomatic missions to Germany. About this time Barnes took to saying the Mass and *Te Deum* in English, but he strenuously opposed the Anabaptists and the Sacramentaries, those who denied transubstantiation. He was put on to a commission to 'extirpate Sacramentaries' and in the course of this work he delated John Lambert to Cranmer, with the result that Lambert was burned at Smithfield.

In 1539 Barnes was sent to Germany to negotiate the marriage with Anne of Cleves: his success cannot have made him any more popular with Henry. In the Catholic reaction of 1540 Barnes soon found himself in serious trouble. He preached a sermon at St. Paul's in which he scurrilously attacked Bishop Gardiner for some criticisms Gardiner had made against the friars. Gardiner complained to the King, an examination was ordered and Barnes abjectly broke down. Gardiner behaved generously and offered Barnes a pension and to have him to live with him in his own house for instruction. Barnes signed a very mildy worded recantation and was ordered to preach again in London. He did so and Gardiner was present. Barnes preached such an ambiguous sermon that the Lord Mayor asked Gardiner if he should not commit Barnes to prison. Barnes was sent to the Tower; he was condemned by an Act of Attainder without trial and he was burned at the stake on 30 July, 1540.

Luther said of him: 'He was deceived by a hope; always he hoped that at long last his King would become a good man'.

W. Clebsch, *England's Earliest Protestants,* 1964.
E. G. Rupp, *The English Protestant Tradition,* 1949.
M. L. Loane, *Prisoners of the Reformation,* 1964.

WILLIAM BARLOW (*d.* 1569), Bishop, was one of four sons of John Barlow, who was a member of the Essex-Hertfordshire branch of the family and who was implicated in the rebellion of Perkin Warbeck. There was also a sister, Elizabeth, who became a lady-in-waiting to Margaret Tudor, wife of James IV of Scotland. Professor Rupp has shown in his *The English Protestant Tradition* that the articles in the D.N.B. and other dictionaries 'conflate the careers of two, three and possibly four persons besides being embellished with details proper to the career of his brothers John and Roger'. There are errors also in the 1958 edition of the *Oxford Dictionary of the Christian Church,* the *Dictionary of English Church History,* and in H. Maynard Smith's *Henry VIII and the Reformation.* The following account is written subject to any correction which future research may make necessary.

There is no evidence for the date of William Barlow's birth: none that he was ever at Oxford or Cambridge, and none that he was ever consecrated a bishop, probably because the Canterbury Register was carelessly kept. There is no doubt that he held a series of preferments as Canon or Prior, including Prior of Bromehill in Norfolk (1525). This house was dissolved in 1528 and the endowments transferred to Wolsey's new college at Ipswich. Probably Barlow was compensated with employment in Wolsey's household: he was sent to Italy in 1528 on the matter of the King's divorce. in 1534 he became Prior of the Canons Regular at Haverfordwest, a post which he owed to the patronage of Anne Boleyn. By this time Barlow was a strong reformer and he fell foul of the clergy in the district, who maltreated his servants and threatened him with persecution. Barlow wrote to Cromwell bewailing the blindness and ignorance of the Welsh clergy, saying that 'no diocese is so without hope of reformation'. He was transferred from Haverfordwest to Bisham, but in 1535–6 he was sent by Cromwell on an embassy to the court of James IV, no doubt because his sister was lady-in-waiting to the Queen.

Perhaps as a reward for his service he was made Bishop of St. Asaph's (1535), but he was almost at once translated to St. David's (1536) and probably never even visited St. Asaph's. At St. David's he at once fell out with the canons, who delated him to Rowland Lee, the Lord President of the Marches of Wales, for having preached against purgatory and confession and for claiming that when two or three persons, even 'cobblers and weavers were in company, and elected, in the name of God, that there was the true Church of God'. Barlow became impatient with one of his 'chaunters' and had him put into prison. He then refused to pay the fine which Rowland Lee imposed on him. At last Barlow tried to remove his cathedral seat away from St. David's to Caermarthen. But Barlow was genuinely interested in the education of his people and he obtained the grant of the endowments from some suppressed houses to found Christ's College, Brecon.

In 1548 under Edward VI Barlow attracted the favourable attention of Protector Somerset by a sermon against images. As a reward he was translated from St. David's to Bath and Wells. On the accession of Mary, Barlow resigned his see and fled the country to Germany. When Elizabeth came to the throne, he returned and assisted in the consecration of Matthew Parker as Archbishop of Canterbury. He was made Bishop of Chichester in 1559 and a prebend of Westminster. He died in 1569 and was buried at Chichester.

William Barlow was not the author of the *Burial of the Mass* or of the *Lutheran Factions*. These two pieces of vituperative propaganda were the work of Jerome Barlow, who had no connection with William. William was the translator of part of the Apocrypha for the *Bishops' Bible*, a new translation commanded by Matthew Parker and published in 1568, which remained the official version until the Authorised Version of 1611. Barlow was a typical Erastian bishop of his time on the reforming side, violent in his opinions, unwise often in his treatment of opponents, (as in Wales), and sometimes lacking in seriousness. Cranmer once said of him that 'Brother Barlow has spoken the truth, but in half an hour he will teach the world to believe that it was in jest'. One unique achievement he may claim, that he married his five daughters to five Anglican bishops.

E. G. Rupp, *The English Protestant Tradition*, 1949.
L. B. Smith, *Tudor Prelates and Politics*, 1953.

WILLIAM TYNDALE [the family also used the surname of Hutchyns] (1491/92/95–1536), translator of the Bible, was born almost certainly at Slimbridge in Gloucestershire, where is now established the Wildfowl Trust. It is possible that he was born on the west side of the Severn in Monmouthshire: certainly he was not born at North Nibley, where his monument now stands. The date of his birth is also uncertain, perhaps 1491, 1492, 1495. He was put to death at Vilvorde in the Netherlands in 1536. We know little of his early life and next to nothing of his family, which may possibly have tended towards Lollardy. Tyndale went to Magdalen Hall (later to be Hertford College), Oxford, in 1508 or 1510, under the name of Hychyns. He took his B.A. degree in 1512, his M.A. in 1515, and in 1518 he migrated probably to Cambridge to learn Greek, perhaps because Croke, the greatest teacher in Europe, had just returned to

Cambridge and Tyndale wanted to read the New Testament in the original Greek. In 1522 he is found in the service of Sir John Walsh at Little Sodbury in Gloucestershire, probably as tutor to his children. He stayed there about two years and left at his own request. He had quarrelled with the local clergy and the visitors at Sir John's table, where he tactlessly aired his modern theological views, so much so, that he was arraigned before the Vicar-General of Gloucester as a dangerous heretic. (The Bishop of Gloucester was an Italian absentee, Giulio de'Medici, later Pope Clement VII.)

Tyndale was cleared of the charge of heresy, but it was better for all that he should leave the district. Sir John recommended him to Sir Henry Guildford who introduced him to Tunstal, Bishop of London. Tyndale had made up his mind that he must translate the New Testament into English as an antidote to the sickness from which he believed the Church to be suffering. 'If God spare my life, ere many years I will cause a boy that driveth the plough shall know more of the scriptures than thou dost.' His plan now was to become chaplain to the Bishop of London, to live in his palace and there to translate the New Testament. But Tyndale was wholly unqualified for the post of chaplain and Tunstal told him that he had four chaplains already and had no room for any more.

Tyndale now fell in with a Gloucestershire man named Poyntz, a relation of Sir John Walsh, who arranged for him to preach at St. Dunstan-in-the-West. Here he became acquainted with a rich cloth merchant, Henry Monmouth, who had him to live with him for the next six months. Tyndale soon grew weary of London: he was disgusted with the London 'praters', despised the pageantry of the Church and was outraged by the magnificence of Wolsey. He made up his mind to go abroad, as 'there was no room in My Lord of London's house to translate the New Testament; but also that there was no place to do it in all England'.

It was while he was in London that Tyndale was first influenced by Lutheran ideas and it was here that he met and became friends with the future martyr, John Frith. When, therefore, he went abroad, he was already infected with heretical opinions. He set out with the intent to find some town where he could in peace translate the New Testament from the original Greek into vernacular English. The town he selected was Hamburg. Since he was destitute of money, somebody must have financed him. It must surely have been the Merchant Adventurers in London, of whom Henry Monmouth was one. They had agencies at Antwerp and Calais and were closely connected with Hamburg and Lübeck merchants in London. These wealthy merchants were much interested in Lutheranism, were strongly anti-clerical and hoped for a Lutheran reformation in England, partly in order to get rid of ecclesiastical laws which hampered their trade. They saw in Tyndale the right man for their purpose. They sent him to Germany where he could translate and have printed the New Testament in English, which they would arrange to smuggle into England.

At Hamburg Tyndale went to the house of a Protestant widow, Margaret von Emmersen, whose nephew was about to go to Wittenberg. Tyndale went with him, or as Sir Thomas More put it, 'gat him to Luther straight'. On 27 May 1524, there matriculated at the university a certain Gulielmus Daltin, who was in fact William Tyndale with the syllables reversed. He was probably the first Englishman to arrive at Wittenberg. He remained there from May to December 1524, when he returned to Hamburg to pick up a sum of money which had been sent to him by Henry Monmouth. In January 1525 he was back in Wittenberg, where he met a 'plausible but penniless' scoundrel named Roye, an apostate English friar, who now became Tyndale's amanuensis. In six weeks Tyndale's translation of the New Testament from Greek into English was copied out and the two of them went to Cologne to get the book printed (August 1525). Peter Quentel, a Catholic printer, was ready to print the book for the English market: a contract was made for a quarto volume with references, marginal notes and a prologue. It was a dangerous undertaking: Roye talked too much and the municipal authorities forbad any further printing. Only a fragment, less than half of the quarto as far as it had gone, is to-day in the British Museum, which is all that has survived of the gospels of St. Matthew and St. Mark which Quentel had printed before the work was stopped.

In September 1525 Tyndale and Roye went to Worms and started their work all over again. So rapidly did they work that the new complete version, printed by Schoeffer, in octavo, not quarto, was on sale in London early in March 1526. This edition was a plain text without glosses, references or prologue: the book was thus the less controversial, smaller and easier to smuggle, and cheaper to sell.

From 1526 to 1529 Tyndale was probably in Antwerp, where the Merchant Adverturers were strongly established, communications with England were easy and heretics escaping from persecution could foregather. In 1530 he went to Hamburg and on the way he was shipwrecked off the coast of Holland and lost all the manuscripts of his translation of the Old Testament. Once again he had to start afresh, this time helped by Miles Coverdale. In 1530, hearing of the death of Wolsey, which made Antwerp a safer place, Tyndale returned thither and his translation of the Pentateuch from the original Hebrew text — Tyndale had taught himself Hebrew in two years — was issued from Hochstraten's press, although the imprint is of Lufft at Marburg. Unfortunately Tyndale rashly and unnecessarily added glosses to the text which laid him and his book open to the charge of heresy and alienated all orthodox people, especially the English bishops.

When the New Testament was distributed in 1528, Sir Thomas More wrote as a counterblast his *Dialogue Concerning Heresies and Matters of Religion,* a statement of Catholic doctrine running to some 170,000 words. Tyndale replied in 1530 in his *Answer unto Sir Thomas More's Dialogue.* This was an able piece of criticism, but it was spoiled by its intense bitterness and grossly unfair personal attacks on More. Unhappily More replied with his wearisome *Confutation* in which he sank to unaccustomed scurrility and abuse. 'This contest of Tyndale and More was the classic controversy of the English reformation. No other discussion was carried on between men of such pre-eminence and ability and with such clear apprehension of the points at issue. To More's assertion of the paramount authority of the church Tyndale replied by appealing to scripture, with an ultimate resort to individual judgment' *(D.N.B.)*

During this period Tyndale published four other works of importance. In 1528 there appeared *The Wicked Mammon,* a work which owed almost everything to Luther, and *The Obedience of a Christian Man,* again largely inspired by Luther, being a defence of despotic government and an attack on personal freedom. It is difficult not to feel that Tyndale allowed himself to be overwhelmed by Protestant influences, difficult to believe that these two books represent his real views and feelings. His *Practice of Prelates* (1530) was both a forthright attack on the Papacy and also on Wolsey and the divorce proceedings. Before this last book reached England, Cromwell had read the *Christian Obedience*, with the views of which both he and Henry VIII agreed so strongly that they tried to persuade Tyndale to return to England. The negotiations, which were carried out by Cromwell's friend, Stephen Vaughan, failed and Henry was so infuriated by one answer that Tyndale sent him that he tried to have Tyndale kidnapped (1531). Tyndale therefore left Antwerp for two years: when he returned in 1533 he went to live in the 'English House', a building set aside by the local authorities for the Merchant Adventurers in England.

Tyndale was now very near the end of his life. A handsome, unprincipled young man turned up in Antwerp and made friends with Tyndale. This was Henry Phillips, the son of a wealthy landowner in Dorset. Probably because he was desperately in need of money and hoped to recoup his fortunes by serving Charles V against the Protestants, Phillips, by means of the lowest forms of treachery, caused Tyndale to be arrested in Antwerp (1535). Tyndale was imprisoned in the state prison of Vilvorde, where he remained for eighteen months. In September Thomas Cromwell tried to get lenient treatment for him, but to no avail. In 1536 Tyndale was brought to trial, degraded from his ecclesiastical orders as a heretic and condemned to death. He was executed on 6 October 1536, being strangled before his body was given to the flames to be burnt. At the stake he is said to have cried out, 'Lord, open the King of England's eyes'. Years before he had written, 'If they shall burn me, they shall do no other thing than I look for'.

Tyndale ought to be looked upon as one of the great heroes in English history. He described himself as being 'evil favoured in this world and without grace in the sight of men'; it is true also that he was apt to attribute to his opponents the lowest motives, although they were honourable men like Sir Thomas More. But his life was one of 'utter disappointment and struggle — persecuted in one city, fleeing to another' (Chambers). Only a man of the toughest fibre and the most invincible faith could have achieved what Tyndale achieved. Fundamentally, he was a simple and reasonable man, never a very good judge of character (or he would never have taken up with Roye or been taken in by Phillips), a very remarkable linguist and a wonderful writer of English prose. He died a martyr and he had his reward, in the most ironical manner. Those who had persecuted him as a heretic for translating the New Testament at last came to the conclusion that an authorized version of the Bible must be made available to the people. In 1538 Henry VIII commanded that Matthew's Bible should be placed in every parish church. This book was a composite work 'truly and purely translated by Thomas Matthew'. Matthew was in fact Rogers, the first victim of the Marian persecutions. But who had made most of the translations? Part of the Old Testament was the work of Miles Coverdale: part of the Apocrypha was translated by Rogers; the Pentateuch, the Book of Jonah, almost certainly Joshua to II Chronicles, and the whole of the New Testament were the work of Tyndale. When the compilers of the Authorized Version in James I's reign came to do their work, it was to Tyndale that they turned, so that our Authorized Version today is mainly the work of Tyndale. Has any other one man given as great a gift to his own country, and as the centuries go by, to millions beyond his own country? Tyndale's Bible laid the foundations of the English literary language and his words and phrases have become part and parcel of the everyday speech of Englishmen.

Tyndale's Works: Parker Society.
J. F. Mozley, *William Tyndale*, 1937.
W. E. Campbell, *Erasmus, Tyndale and More*, 1949.
H. Maynard Smith, *Henry VIII and the Reformation*, 1948.
R. W. Chambers, *Man's Unconquerable Mind*, 1939.
C. Morris: *Political Thought in England, Tyndale to Hooker*, 1953.
J. H. Maclehose, *The Burnished Sword*, 1956.
C. H. Williams, *William Tyndale*, 1969.

MILES COVERDALE (1488?-1568), first translator of the entire Bible into English, Bishop of Exeter, was born in Yorkshire — hence perhaps his name, Cover-Dale, in Richmond — almost certainly in 1488. It is as well here to make plain that exact details of Coverdale's life, especially in the early years, are a matter of conjecture. He went to Cambridge, studied theology, was ordained priest and (1514) entered the convent of the Austin Friars at Cambridge. Coverdale was never a very strong character, was too apt to fall under the influence of the immediately stronger character than himself. He fell under the influence of Robert Barnes, Prior of the Austin Friars, and as a result frequented the White Horse tavern to discuss modern theological problems. Barnes must have been pretty well what we should call 'left wing' in theological matters,

for he was summoned to London on charges of heresy and Coverdale
went with him to help him prepare his defence. In London he made
the acquaintance of Thomas Cromwell — it is now pretty certain
that he did not make the acquaintance of Sir Thomas More — and
the two became good friends. This must have been about 1526,
before Cromwell was of any importance in politics, but when he was
of importance in the City. The next year Coverdale got a grant from
the government, presumably through Cromwell, to buy books for
his theological studies. The next year (1528) Coverdale apostasized
from his order, became a secular priest and took to preaching heretical views — that the Sacrament was only a *remembrance* of Our
Lord's death: that auricular confession should be avoided: that
worship should not be made to images. He had become a complete
heretic. Thomas Cromwell, who was a careerist, if ever there was
one, abandoned Coverdale as an unsafe man.

It seems fairly certain that Coverdale was out of the country from
1528 to 1534. Probably he went to Antwerp and there met Tyndale,
and went with him to Hamburg, where he helped in the translation
of the Pentateuch. In 1534 he seems to have been in Antwerp and to
have joined Jacob van Meteren, a well-known Protestant printer of
the time. Van Meteren paid Coverdale to translate the Bible into
English, possibly because he had already heard that Cromwell in
England was ready to back such a translation.

Certain it is that the Convocation of Canterbury petitioned in
1534 that a translated version of the Bible should be put into every
parish church. It is not improbable that Cromwell turned to his old
friend, Coverdale, to provide such a book. More than that cannot be
said. What is known is that a complete translation of the Bible was
introduced into England. It was not printed in Antwerp, as that was
too dangerous: it was probably printed in Cologne. There was in
England a law against the sale of foreign books, and therefore an
English colophon was inserted: in 1536 Nycholson printed a new
frontispiece with the words 'faithfully and fully translated into
English' instead of the original 'translated out of Douche (German)
and Latyn'. The first issue contained a dedication to Henry VIII and
included the words 'your dearest wife ... Queen Anne', but in no
time the new Queen was Jane Seymour and the word Anne was
changed to Jane, in some copies by pen.

Coverdale was anxious to commend his book to Henry, and he

wrote in his dedication words which strongly upheld the royal authority. For this reason, having the divorce in mind, he translated Deuteronomy xxv, 5, as 'her kynsman' and not as 'her husband's brother shall go in unto her'. Coverdale's reading is still the alternative reading in the Authorized Version.

Coverdale was not the fine linguist that Tyndale had been, nor did he pretend he was. His translation of the Bible was not made from original sources, as had been Tyndale's, but he used (as he said) 'five interpreters' in German and Latin. He also used Tyndale, but he was not the purist for strict accuracy that Tyndale was. Coverdale often chose a more dramatic word; he would add a word to improve the music of his prose; he would paraphrase the source, if he thought a paraphrase would make the meaning clearer. His translation of the Psalms is very far from accurate, but it is the version we use today in our Psalter and it is by far the best for singing. It is to be noted that Coverdale was more extreme in his Protestant views than was Tyndale, but he was a much wiser man and avoided the glosses and comments which Tyndale had added to his translation, thereby laying himself open to charges of heresy.

In 1539 Coverdale came to England to help complete the work he had undertaken at the request of Thomas Cromwell on the Great Bible. Cromwell was executed the following year, and a period of reaction set in. Coverdale consequently went abroad again. In 1543 an Act of Parliament was passed which prohibited the lower classes from reading the Bible.

For a few years Coverdale lived at Tübingen, where he took a doctorate in divinity. In 1543 he was schoolmaster and pastor at Bergzabern. In the meantime he had defied Henry VIII's Six Articles and married Elizabeth Macheson. On the death of Henry he came back to England (it is possible that he was in England before Henry died). In 1548 he was staying at Windsor Castle, when Cranmer was there, preparing his First Book of Common Prayer. He had been appointed almoner to Queen Catherine Parr, but she died soon after her marriage to Lord Seymour, and Coverdale preached the funeral sermon (1548). He was an excellent and popular preacher, and in 1551 he was appointed to the see of Exeter in the place of Bishop Voysey, who had reached the age of nearly 90. He took an active part in all the reforms of Edward VI's reign, but on the accession of Mary he was deprived of his bishopric, on the grounds of his marriage, and he went abroad. The King of Denmark, at the suggestion of Coverdale's wife's brother-in-law (who rejoiced in the name of Maccabaeus McAlpine), invited him to go to Denmark, and he was given a free pass to leave England with two servants — one was said to be his wife — and to take his baggage unsearched. For a time he preached to the English refugees at Wesel, and then, on the invitation of the citizens, he returned to his old work at Bergzabern. In 1558 he was at Geneva and is said to have had a hand in the production of the Geneva Bible.

In 1559 he returned to England. He did not resume his bishopric, but he took part in the consecration of Parker as Archbishop of Canterbury, clad in a black gown, for his increasing Protestantism did not allow him now to wear vestments. In 1563 he refused the offer of the see of Llandaff and he began to pay little attention to the Act of Uniformity. Nobody seemed to mind until 1566, and then he resigned his living of St. Magnus near London Bridge rather than conform. He continued to preach and he always drew large congregations. He died in February 1568 and was buried in St. Bartholomew's: when this church was pulled down in 1840, Coverdale's remains were translated to St. Magnus.

Coverdale was never as great a man as Tyndale. He was neither such a fine scholar nor such a good linguist: his literary style was more ornate than Tyndale's, but perhaps more musical. But he was essentially a good man, a good Christian and a most conscientious priest and bishop.

J. F. Mozley, *Coverdale and his Bibles*, 1953.

ANNE ASKEW (1521-1546), Protestant martyr, came of an old Lincolnshire family, being the second daughter of Sir William Askew (or Ayscough) of Stallingborough, near Grimsby. She was very well educated and gave much of her time to studying the Bible and to disputing with the clergy of Lincoln Cathedral. Her sister was betrothed to one Thomas Kyme of Kelsey, but she died before the marriage could take place, whereupon Anne's father compelled her to marry Kyme, which she did much against her will. She had two children, but the marriage proved unhappy and Kyme turned her out of the house, to her great content.

In 1545 she was charged with heresy on account of her views on the Sacrament. Bonner did his level best to save her, and she was in the end acquitted for want of witnesses against her. Soon afterwards she was summoned before the Council at Greenwich: she refused to make any recantation and was put to the rack, because it was thought that she was being secretly encouraged by important people whose names she might reveal under torture. She herself recorded that Lord Chancellor Wriothesley and the Solicitor-General, Rich, turned the screws with their own hands.

What these two gentlemen were after was evidence which might be used against the Queen, Catherine Parr, a holder of advanced religious views, or at least evidence against some of the ladies of the court who were thought to be associates of Anne Askew's. The arrest of Anne was part of a campaign waged by the conservatives in the royal court in an effort to gain ascendancy over the reforming faction of which Catherine Parr was a supporter. The Queen, however, survived, but Anne did not.

In 1546 she was charged again with heresy along with Dr. Shaxton, formerly Bishop of Salisbury, and two others. Shaxton recanted, Anne would not, and she and the others were burned at Smithfield on 16 July 1546. So crippled was she from the rack that she had to be carried to the stake in a chair. Shaxton was appointed to preach the sermon before the fires were lighted, and at the last moment Wriothesley offered Anne a pardon if she would recant. She again refused and went to the fire with the utmost composure and resolution. Her sufferings were shortened by bags of gunpowder which were hung round her body.

C. Wriothesley's *Chronicle*, Camden Society.
Foxe, *Book of Martyrs*.

JOAN BOCHER (*d.* 1550), often known as Joan of Kent, Anabaptist martyr, died in 1550; the date of her birth is unknown. Her background was among the Lollards of Essex. She first came into prominence as a 'great dispenser of Tyndale's New Testament' in about 1540 to the ladies of Henry VIII's court. She was a friend of Anne Askew, who was burned for heresy in 1546. In 1543 she had been examined by Cranmer, but she was released, according to the Catholics in Canterbury, with Cranmer's connivance. In 1549 the Council was informed by the Justices of the Peace in Kent that Joan

was at work again, spreading extraordinary opinions which the
Justices could not well understand. One thing was certain, that she
was an Anabaptist. It seemed that she was spreading abroad that
Christ had not taken flesh of the Virgin, but had 'miraculously
passed through the Virgin as through a glass' (Burnet's *Records*, v.
246–7). This was clearly heresy, but unfortunately the Acts against
heresy had just been repealed and the Justices did not know what
action ought to be taken. The Council gave orders for Joan to be
arrested. She was examined and behaved defiantly before the
Commission. All attempts to get her to recant failed, and she was
excommunicated. There was no statutory power now to burn
heretics, but heresy could not be tolerated. Happily the Lord
Chancellor discovered that heretics had been burned in England
before any law against them had been passed (1401). Joan was
condemned to be burned, unless she recanted. The government did
all they could to persuade her to recant, and her execution was
postponed for more than a year, perhaps because *de heretico
comburendo* had been repealed, and Somerset was a tolerant man
(May 1549 to May 1550). Every day for a week Cranmer and Ridley
visited her to argue with her, but their efforts all failed. Joan was
defiant and abusive and she was at last burned on 2 May. She
interrupted the sermon preached before her execution with screams
and curses, so that the general opinion was that it would have been
better to send her to Bedlam than to the stake. There is not the least
evidence for the story that Edward VI viewed her execution with
horror and only agreed to sign the warrant very reluctantly.

Burnet, *History of the Reformation*, Vol. 5, pp. 246–9.
Pollard, *England under Protector Somerset*, 1900.
J. Davis, *Journal of Ecclesiastical History*, 1982.

EDWARD VI (1537–1553) was born at Hampton Court on
12 October 1537, and died on 6 July 1553, in his sixteenth year. He
became King of England in 1547. He was the third child and only
legitimate son of Henry VIII; his mother was Henry's third wife,
Jane Seymour. Archbishop Cranmer was one of his godfathers. His
mother died on 24 October and the heir to the throne, 'His Majesty's
most noble jewel', was brought up 'among the women' with every
kind of precaution to ensure his good health. The traditional view

Edward VI
(Artist: Unknown)

has been that Edward was all his short life a frail and unhealthy child, but a recent biography of him (H. W. Chapman, *The Last Tudor King*) reveals him as a normally strong and healthy boy until the last three years of his life, fond of athletic exercises. When peace was made with Scotland in 1543, one of the terms was that Edward, who was less than six years old, should marry Mary, Queen of Scots, who was not yet seven months old.

At the age of six Edward was placed under his first tutor, Dr. Cox. A year later Sir John Cheke was brought from Cambridge to help in the boy's education, and Sir Anthony Cooke and Roger Ascham also shared in the teaching. Edward proved himself an apt pupil, thanks largely to the enlightened methods of Cheke, who soon became wholly responsible for Edward's education and for whom Edward developed great affection, the only person on whose behalf he is known ever to have shewn any emotion. He quickly became proficient in Latin, Greek, and French; it is possible that he also spoke Italian, and he had the Tudor love for music and much interest in astronomy. Many boys of his own age and standing shared their education and recreations with him, on terms of equality, of whom his favourite was Barnaby Fitzpatrick, the son of Lord Ossory, and with him he continued to correspond all his short life.

Henry VIII died on 28 January 1547. The new King was 9 years old. Henry had nominated a Council of Regency, of which the chief members were Edward's uncle, Edward Seymour, Earl of Hertford, later Duke of Somerset, and John Dudley, Viscount Lisle, later Earl of Warwick and Duke of Northumberland. The history of Edward's reign is rather the story of the struggle for power between these two councillors than of the acts of King Edward VI. But the young King was not the priggish, tiresomely precocious and unimportant child which historians have painted. As a result of his own nature — he was not for nothing a Tudor and the son of Henry VIII — and his intensive education he matured quickly, too quickly. He soon revealed the Tudor capacity for bearing himself with dignity in public and for winning the affection of the people. Under Somerset the public appearances were frequent, long and exhausting, and the boy-king lived under too great pressure. He himself was intensely interested in religion and theology: he would listen to interminable sermons, making notes on them and discussing them afterwards. He became as fanatical for Protestantism as his half-sister, Mary, was for Roman Catholicism, and he strongly supported the doctrinal reformation which Cranmer, Somerset and Northumberland carried through and forced on the nation.

On the fall of Somerset and the victory of Warwick Edward was even more hardly pressed. Northumberland (as Warwick became) deliberately used the emotions and ambitions of the King to further his own selfish ends. Under the strain the boy's physical health gave way. 'Forced into the mould of a saviour and a genius, while being treated as a catspaw, he died in the process: probably because of it.' (Chapman, *ib.*) In April 1552, he was attacked by measles and perhaps smallpox at the same time, but by May he had recovered. In September he was visited by Girolamo Cardana, the famous physician and astrologer from Milan, who has left a vivid picture of Edward's powers of argument, and who cast the King's horoscope — wrongly.

In January 1553, Edward was again ill, this time with consumption from which he never recovered. He was well enough to take seriously Ridley's frequent sermons on the poverty of the people. He discussed the problem with Ridley, sent for the Lord Mayor and finally handed over to the Corporation of London Bridewell Palace, which became Christ's Hospital, as 'a place of correction for the idle and vagabond', which later became an orphanage. St. Thomas's was to be rebuilt and endowed, and Grey Friars was to be used for poor relief.

By June the King's condition was beyond hope. He was now persuaded by Northumberland to agree to altering the succession, to cut out his two step-sisters, Mary and Elizabeth, in favour of Northumberland's daughter-in-law, Lady Jane Grey, and on 14 June the law officers were summoned to witness the King's 'devise'. On 6 July Edward died. The news of his death was suppressed until 10 July to give Northumberland time to complete his plans. The body was neither embalmed nor coffined during the nine hectic days before Mary ascended the throne on the failure of Northumberland's plot. It was not until 8 August that Edward was buried in Westminster Abbey.

The accounts left to us by foreign ambassadors of their audiences with the King leave no doubt that Edward was a highly intelligent youth; they prove also that he had a mind of his own, strength of character to insist on his own way, and even at that early age diplomatic skill, as in his dealings with the Emperor Charles V recounted by himself in his diary. Some of the state papers which he himself drew up, such as his memoranda for the Parliament of 1552 in twelve 'bills' for a reorganization of the government, with their many divisions and sub-divisions, suggest that had he lived, he might have become an able administrator. But the intensity and the narrowness of his religious views suggest also that, if that had happened, the Church of England might well have been a very different thing from what it became under Queen Elizabeth, and much less well adapted to the genius of the English people.

H. W. Chapman, *The Last Tudor King,* 1958.
S. T. Bindoff, 'A Kingdom at Stake', *History Today,* September, 1953.
C. Morris, *The Tudors,* 1955.
W. K. Jordan, *Edward VI: the young king,* 1968.
W. K. Jordan, *Edward VI: the threshold of power,* 1970.

EDWARD SEYMOUR, 1st EARL OF HERTFORD, DUKE OF SOMERSET (1506?–1552), Protector, was born probably in 1506. He was executed on Tower Hill on 22 January 1552. He was the brother of Jane Seymour, Henry VIII's third wife. He led the normal life of a sixteenth-century courtier who had secured the good opinion of the King, holding various minor offices and amassing a very large number of estates, steadily advancing in the peerage, but for some time having little influence in politics. On the fall of Thomas Cromwell, Hertford (as he became in 1537) continued to rise in the King's favour. In 1542 he became Lord High Admiral, but he relinquished the post almost at once. In March 1544, he was in command of the force sent to Scotland which pillaged Edinburgh, and in 1545 and 1546 he saw further military service in France, where he won a brilliant military success over de Briez at Boulogne in 1545. Signs of his increasing importance were his appointment in 1544 as Lieutenant of the Kingdom during the King's absence in France and his diplomatic missions to the Emperor Charles V.

The jealousies between Hertford and the powerful Howard family (Norfolk and his son Surrey) came to a head in 1546. It is not possible to say that the dramatic fall of the Howards in January 1547 was Hertford's work, but when on 28 January the King died,

Hertford was by far the most important man in the kingdom. He succeeded in keeping the news of Henry's death secret until he had got possession of Edward VI; then the news was published, but the most inconvenient clauses of Henry's will were suppressed. In spite of some opposition in the Council, Hertford was made Protector, and on 16 February he became Duke of Somerset. For the next two years he exercised virtually royal authority. In one prayer used by him he speaks of himself as 'caused by Providence to rule', and he even wrote to the King of France as 'brother'.

The great historian of the early part of this century, A. F. Pollard, saw Somerset as the 'Good Duke', a big-hearted liberal in his government of England, whose aim was to help the poor commons and to advance the Protestant cause. According to Pollard, Somerset was too good for his age and his efforts to please the people led instead to rebellion in 1549, as a result of which he was overthrown by the unscrupulous Earl of Northumberland and the hard-nosed realists of the Council. Such an interpretation of Somerset has been emphatically rejected by Dr M. L. Bush in a recent study. Bush argues that the key to Somerset's policy is to be found in his desire to conquer Scotland, a goal he pursued with 'obsessive stubbornness'.

When Henry VIII died, the problem of Scotland, in which Somerset had been deeply involved already, was unresolved. The Protector decided, like a good soldier, to finish the job. He won the battle of Pinkie (September 1547), and then decided to conquer the Scots completely by establishing a series of fortresses to hold the country in a state of military occupation. He did so out of no idealistic desire for the union of the two countries, although he did plan to marry Edward VI to the infant Queen of Scots, Mary, to complete the English conquest. It turned out that he could not achieve his aim: England did not have the money to build and man the strongholds he contemplated. In the end, the Scots remained independent and sent their Queen to safe keeping in France, where she was betrothed to the Dauphin. While he fought Scotland, the French predictably enough attacked him in the rear. Somerset was forced to surrender Boulogne (1548).

To pay for the Scottish campaigns, heavy taxation was imposed on the people, the money gained from the dissolution of the chantries was squandered, and the currency was debased still further. The results were inflation and social discontent. In response to the complaints of the people, Somerset sought to regain popularity by supporting the reforming efforts of John Hales, one of the so-called 'commonwealth men'. Hales was responsible for setting up a commission in 1548 to enforce legislation against enclosure, and for the passage of Acts of Parliament to prevent enclosure and to relieve the poor. Somerset encouraged Hales so that the people would blame their ills not on government policy but on sheep-farming. It was as a result of this desire for support and popularity rather than for any really genuine liberalism that Somerset repealed the Treason Act of 1534 and the Act of Six Articles of 1539. Somerset's disastrous foreign policy also helped to determine the pace of his religious policy. He was a committed Protestant, but found it necessary to proceed slowly with the religious changes he favoured because of the need to keep on friendly terms with Charles V while he fought the French. At the beginning of the reign, therefore, all that was done was to allow communion in both kinds (1547) and to bring an end to traditional Catholic ceremonies like using palms on Palm Sunday, ashes on Ash Wednesday and to have the beautiful wall-paintings in the churches of England obliterated with lime (1548). By 1549, when his foreign policy had failed, he allowed the publication of an English prayer book, known as the Book of Common Prayer because unlike the Latin missals it was to be used commonly all over England, not in different forms in different dioceses. This was to be enforced by the Act of Uniformity, imposing a uniform service everywhere.

On the whole, Somerset carried the Council with him in his policies. He issued many proclamations in his brief reign, but this does not show a dictatorial spirit, merely that his period in office was a time of crisis, when urgent measures were often needed. However, in 1549 there occurred a series of rebellions which convinced many of the other councillors that Somerset was more trouble than he was worth. His position had already been shaken when he sent his own brother, Thomas Seymour, to the block. The revolts of 1549 were centred mainly on Norfolk and Cornwall, although there was trouble in many other parts of the country. Government policy, religious, fiscal and military, played its part in the causes of those uprisings. Somerset could not deal immediately with the rebels, largely because he needed all his troops for the Scottish wars and also because it was good policy in such circumstances to play for time, in the expectation that the rebels would soon get tired of rebellion and disperse. In the end, action was taken and the rebels were brutally supressed. The entire council now turned against Somerset, both the more conservative councillors like Arundel and Southampton and the radicals like Warwick. In October 1549 he was dismissed from his offices and imprisoned. It was not thought wise, however, to execute him immediately, and he was released and lived on until January 1552, when Northumberland felt secure enough to have him tried and executed.

Somerset was a failure: he did not conquer Scotland, and what had seemed a strong position as Lord Protector in 1547 had completely disappeared two years later. He misused his position, enriching himself and his supporters, and demolishing part of St. Paul's Cathedral to build Somerset House, his great London mansion. But it could have been worse. A monarchy is at its weakest when the ruler is a minor, and Somerset at least protected his nephew's life: he was no Richard of Gloucester. Nor, of course, was he a Duke of Northumberland; he did not seek to subvert the succession. He was careful to begin the political education of his charge, and to prepare him for the burdens of kingship which awaited him. It must say something of Somerset that while he held sway there were no religious executions in England, and also that, however muddle-headed he was as a politician, there were some poor people who did regard him as a 'Good Duke'.

M. L. Bush, *The Government Policy of Protector Somerset*, 1975.

JOHN DUDLEY, EARL OF WARWICK, DUKE OF NORTH-UMBERLAND (1504–1553), soldier, sailor, statesman, was the son of that Edmund Dudley, Henry VII's financial minister, who was executed by Henry VIII, and Elizabeth Grey, daughter of Edward Grey, Viscount Lisle. In 1512 Edmund Dudley's attainder was repealed and John Dudley was restored in blood when he was about eleven years old.

Dudley soon made a name for himself at court by his physical courage and his daring and skilful horsemanship both in tourney and in military exercises. In 1523 he was knighted by the Duke of Suffolk, in whose army he was serving at Calais. During the next fifteen years he received many minor appointments and in 1538 he became deputy governor of Calais. In 1542 he was created Lord Lisle and was also made Lord High Admiral for life. He was with the Earl of Hertford (later Protector Somerset) when he ravaged the low-lands of Scotland and burned Edinburgh to the ground (1544); he became a Privy Councillor in 1543; he led the assault on Boulogne in 1544 and was governor of Boulogne from 1544 to 1545. In 1546 he was made Earl of Warwick and the next year he was one of the executors of Henry VIII's will and a member of the commission which Henry provided to govern during the minority of his son, Edward VI. Warwick, however, readily agreed to Somerset's mono-polizing all the power as Protector (1547).

The next two years greatly increased Warwick's fame and repu-tation. He resigned the office of Lord Admiral, which went to Somerset's brother, Thomas Seymour. When Somerset invaded Scotland in 1547, Warwick was Lord-Lieutenant of the army which won the battle of Pinkie, largely through Warwick's military genius. He next became President of the Council in the Marches of Wales (1548–50): he served again in Scotland (1549): and he crushed Ket's rebellion at Dussindale outside Norwich (1549).

As his fame and reputation mounted, so mounted also his greed and ambition. On 13 October 1549, Somerset was driven from office and put in the Tower, leaving Warwick supreme in the Council. He seized most of the principal offices of state and in 1551 he became Duke of Northumberland. Somerset was now accused of plotting against Northumberland's life; he was tried, condemned and executed (1552).

Northumberland ruled England from late 1549 until the death of King Edward in the summer of 1553. He has been seen as a cruel tyrant, intent only on gaining power and wealth. To quote from a contemporary pamphlet, *The Epistle of Poor Pratte*: 'Keep that close which thou hast: the world is dangerous. The great devell Dudley ruleth: (duke I should have said); well, let that pass, seeing it is owte, but I trust he shall not longe'. Recent research has led to another picture altogether of Northumberland being drawn. As a man he is described by Professor Elton as 'hesitant, apprehensive, tearful'. While he no doubt enriched himself and his friends, he did so on a less lavish scale than Somerset had. He was content with the title of Lord President of the Council, not the more fulsome Lord Protector of his predecessor, and he ruled very much with the consent of all his colleagues in government.

As a politician, Northumberland emerges from recent revisionist accounts of his reign as something of a modest success. He saw the sense of making peace with France and Scotland by the Treaty of Boulogne (1550) and the Treaty of Angers (1551). This then enabled him to begin to restore the coinage which the debasement of the previous regime had almost destroyed. The most serious reform of the financial system of the country took shape under Northumberland when a commission of enquiry was appointed under Sir Walter Mildmay in 1552. In the field of local government, the office of Lord Lieutenant became established under Northumberland's rule. For better or for worse, significant strides were made towards Protestantism. Northumberland's religious beliefs are themselves open to some question: he came to power with the support of the 'conservative' group in the Council, but after a few months, the influence of the reformers is evident in his actions. The Prayer Book of 1552, enforced by the Act of Uniformity of the same year, contained the most thoroughly Protestant liturgy of the Tudor period. Cranmer was able to develop a scheme for the reform of canon law under Northumberland and to publish in 1553 the Forty-Two Articles, on which the Thirty-Nine Articles (which used to contain the doctrine of the Church of England) are based.

Under Northumberland, the young Edward VI was gradually brought more into the political field, and his education made more practical, since he was allowed to attend Council meetings and wrote compositions on matters of state. Early in 1553 the King fell ill, of what was to be his fatal illness. Northumberland decided to alter the succession in favour of his own family. He persuaded Edward to make a will in which he cut out his sisters Mary and Elizabeth and left the crown to Lady Jane Grey, daughter of the Duke of Suffolk and wife of Northumberland's son, Guilford Dudley. The Council was coerced into agreeing and Northumberland saw himself as sole ruler on behalf of his daughter-in-law, a young girl who was horrified at the prospect of being Queen.

The plot failed. Edward died on 6 July and Lady Jane Grey was proclaimed Queen, but Northumberland failed to get hold of the person of the Princess Mary, the legitimate Queen. The whole country sided with Mary, and ultimately Northumberland himself had to declare for her. He was arrested, taken to the Tower on 23 July and on 18 August he was tried for high treason and condemned; and on the 22nd he was executed on Tower Hill, asserting on the scaffold that he was and always had been a Catholic. He lies buried near the high altar in St. Peter's within the Tower, between Anne Boleyn and Catherine Howard and near to Protector Somerset, whom he hounded to death.

Clearly, Northumberland's reputation for statesmanship is severely dented by the fiasco which he superintended in Edward's last weeks. It has been suggested by Professor W. K. Jordan that the plot to alter the succession originated in Edward VI's own mind, but it is best to accept that the blame must be Northumberland's. It was a desperate scheme, which was dangerous to the Tudor dynasty and to civil peace. Northumberland probably acted out of fear rather than ambition and in the end even he did not work with much enthusiasm or resolution to prevent Mary's accession; consequently, he failed and paid the price.

B. L. Beer, *Northumberland*, 1973.
D. E. Hoak in J. Loach & R. Tittler, *The mid-Tudor Polity*, 1980.

LADY JANE GREY [more accurately, but less familiarly, **LADY JANE DUDLEY**] (1537–1554), 'the Nine Days' Queen', was born at Bradgate Old Manor in Leicestershire early in October 1537, and she died on Tower Hill on 12 February 1554, in her seventeenth year. She was the eldest surviving daughter of Henry Grey, Marquis of Dorset and later Duke of Suffolk, and his wife Frances, daughter of Charles Brandon, Duke of Suffolk, and Mary Tudor, sister of Henry VIII, the widow of Louis XII of France. Jane was thus cousin to Edward VI, to the Princess Mary and the Princess Elizabeth. Were Edward VI to die without issue, were Mary and Elizabeth to do the same or to be in any way debarred from the succession; then Jane Grey by Henry VIII's Will stood in the line to succeed to the throne. From this one fact and from the unscrupulous use made of it by ambitious and unprincipled politicians arose the misery of Jane's life and the tragedy of her death.

When she was nine years old Jane entered the service of Queen Catherine Parr, and she was much at court up to the death of the Queen in 1548. After Henry VIII's death in 1547 Catherine married

Lady Jane Grey
(Artist: Attributed to Master John)

Thomas Seymour, Lord Sudeley, brother of Protector Somerset. This unprincipled schemer purchased the wardship of Jane Grey from her father, assuring him that he would marry her to the King, Edward VI. But Protector Somerset was planning to marry the King to his own daughter (another Jane), and to marry his own son, the Earl of Hertford, to Lady Jane Grey. Already she was a pawn in the political game, but her life in the household of Thomas Seymour was perhaps the happiest that she knew: she had much affection for him, who treated her with a good deal of kindness. The fall of Thomas Seymour and his execution in 1549 meant that Jane had to return to her own family at Bradgate: she was never again to know any happiness.

One reason for her unhappiness was the extreme severity of her parents. Jane was a girl of unusual beauty both in her personal appearance and also in her mind and character — gentle, amenable, highly intelligent and a very apt pupil. Her parents are said to have been more severe 'than needed to so sweet a temper' (Fuller), and Jane herself told Roger Ascham that she had to endure 'pinches, nips and bobs'. Ascham found her sitting indoors at her books while the rest of the household were out hunting. 'I wis', said Jane, 'all their sport is but a shadow to the pleasure that I find in Plato.' Her education was liberal and she responded eagerly to the teaching of her tutor, John Aylmer, who entered the Dorset household after Edward VI came to the throne, probably in 1549 when Jane was twelve years old. Aylmer (he became Bishop of London in Elizabeth's reign) was in touch with the German and Swiss reformers, so that it was doubtless through him that Jane corresponded with Bullinger, chief pastor at Zurich, and his pupil, Ulmer or Abulmis. Ulmer came to Bradgate in 1550 and spent his vacations from Oxford there, when he gave Jane and her sister lessons in Latin and Greek. By the time she was fourteen Jane was proficient in both those languages, and it is possible that she also knew some Italian and French, but that she also added the Hebrew, Chaldean and Arabian tongues is mere flattery. Her immense reputation abroad as a scholar went far beyond her deserts. It is probable that the Protestant reformers on the Continent were only too anxious to keep in with and to magnify the abilities of the girl who might one day be Queen of England.

In 1551 Jane's father became Duke of Suffolk and she made her first appearance at the court of Edward VI. This was followed by a visit to the Princess Mary which lasted for nearly a month. Suffolk saw that the King's days were numbered and he took care to be on good terms with the heir to the throne.

The fall of Somerset put the political power into the hands of John Dudley, Duke of Northumberland. His purpose was to alter the succession and to secure the throne for his son, Guilford Dudley. He therefore first married his son to Lady Jane Grey — almost certainly against her will, for she wanted to marry the Earl of Hertford, but she was coerced into marrying Guilford Dudley by her ambitious father, who even used physical violence upon his daughter. The marriage took place on 21 May 1553, in the Dudleys' London house. Jane was then compelled to live with her husband's family, and so cordially did she come to detest her father-in-law that she fell seriously ill; she herself was convinced she had been poisoned, but in fact she suffered a nervous breakdown.

Northumberland's second purpose was to persuade the King before he died to cut out both the Princess Mary and the Princess Elizabeth from the succession and to leave the throne in his will to Lady Jane Dudley. This he succeeded in doing. Edward died on 6 July 1553, but news of his death was not published until 8 July. The next day Jane was informed by the Council that she was now Queen. She fainted at the news, but it cannot have come as a complete surprise to her, for some time earlier the Duchess of Northumberland had blurted out the possibility to her, and she records that when she came into the Council the Lords 'began to make me complimentary speeches, bending the knee before me, their example being followed by several noble ladies, all of which ceremony made me blush. My distress was still further increased when my mother and my mother-in-law entered and paid me the same homage.'

For nine days, from Sunday, 9 July, to Wednesday, 19 July, Lady Jane Dudley was Queen. During this time she resided in the Tower. She signed a few documents, perhaps six in all, she dined once in state, she received the Regalia, she made one or two appointments, and she resolutely refused the request of her husband and the violent demand of her mother-in-law that Guilford Dudley should be made King. It was a parody of Tudor monarchy. The whole country favoured the Princess Mary. By Tuesday the 18th Jane's cause (it was in reality Northumberland's cause) was all but lost; on the next day Mary triumphed, and Jane was no longer Queen.

Mary herself wished to save the life of Lady Jane Dudley, and it is probable that she would have done so, but Jane's father, the Duke of Suffolk, weakly took part in Wyatt's Rebellion and this sealed her fate and that of her wholly innocent husband. Both were executed on 12 February 1554, Guilford first outside the Tower, because he was not of royal blood: then Jane, being of royal blood, within the precincts of the Tower. On her way to the block she met the headless body of her husband being brought back into the Tower for burial.

It is easy to be sentimental and romantic over the fate of such a pathetic figure as Lady Jane Grey. But it has to be remembered that she was a staunch Protestant and that, had she lived, she might well have been used by the Protestant party in an attempt to be rid of Catholic Mary and to re-establish the Protestant religion of Edward VI. Lady Jane was thus a potential danger: it is possible to justify her execution on purely political grounds.

J. G. Nichols, *The Chronicle of Queen Jane and Two Years of Queen Mary*, Camden Society, 1850.
H. W. Chapman, *Lady Jane Grey*, 1962.

ROBERT KET or KETT (*d.* 1549), rebel, was put to death in 1549; the date of his birth is unknown. He came from an old Norman family (the name appears down the years as Le Chat, Cat, Kett, Ket, Knight), one branch of which had settled at Wymondham in Norfolk. Robert and his brother William were well-to-do tradesmen who were also landowners. Robert held the manor of Wymondham from John Dudley, Earl of Warwick, the man who in August 1549 came to suppress the rising which now goes by Ket's name. It was only by an accident that Ket became its leader.

On 20 June 1549, a small riot took place in south Norfolk, when the men of Attleborough, Eccles and Wilby threw down the fences with which the lord of the manor of Beckhall in Wilby had recently enclosed part of the common land over which these men had grazing rights. Trouble was also brewing further south, but it was not until 6–8 July that all these men joined hands in a series of attacks on the hedges in various manors. Robert Ket had a long-standing feud with John Flowerdew, a lawyer who had become a landowner. After the Dissolution of the Monasteries the splendid priory church of Wymondham had been bought from the Crown by the inhabitants. Flowerdew, who lived in the neighbourhood, stripped the lead off the roofs and carried away the bells. The Kets resented this. When in July Flowerdew's closes had been thrown down, he bribed the rioters to go and do the same to Robert Ket. On 9 or 10 July Robert Ket led the rioters back in a reprisal on Flowerdew's fences, and thus by accident he became the leader of the insurgents, and he was joined by his brother William.

Ket marched on Norwich, throwing down hedges as he went. On being refused admission into the city, Ket moved to Mousehold Heath, where he and his men encamped for the next six weeks. He soon had 16,000 men under his command. Good order was maintained, law-courts were established and chaplains said prayers every morning, using the new Book of Common Prayer.

On 21 July Ket rejected the Government's offer of a pardon, on the grounds that 'Kings were wont to pardon wicked persons, not innocent and just men'. Ket now seized Norwich. William Parr, Marquess of Northampton, was sent with 1,400 men to recover the city, which he did without opposition. But on 1 August Ket attacked and after a grim struggle he secured the place. Becoming now more ambitious, he tried to capture Yarmouth, but he failed.

On 23 August the Earl of Warwick arrived at Norwich, where he was joined by Lord Willoughby of Parham. Their joint forces amounted to about 10,000 men, some of them German troops. The offer of a pardon to all but Robert Ket was rejected. On the 24th Warwick got into Norwich. On the 25th the rebels left their camp, since their lines of communication were cut. On the 27th Warwick saw his chance and launching his troops at the rebels he utterly destroyed them. The Kets fled, but were soon captured. Robert was hanged in chains from Norwich Castle, William from Wymondham steeple.

Religion had played little part in the rebellion: Norfolk was a county largely in favour of Reform and hence unlikely to rise against Somerset's religious policy. However, complaints against the clergy form a part of the demands formulated by the rebels on Mousehold Heath, and the religious turmoil of Edward VI's reign perhaps stirred the peasants up to political enthusiasm as well. Agrarian grievances, such as enclosure, engrossing, rackrenting and the eviction of tenants, combined with the great distress of 1549, played a major part in driving the peasantry to rebellion. The Tudor system worked well so long as there was sound government, both centrally and locally. Somerset was not providing sound central government; his policies added to the burden on the poor commons, by increasing taxation and causing inflation through debasement. In Norfolk, local government had broken down with the sudden fall of the Howard family in 1546, and by 1549 no county was worse governed than Norfolk. Ket and his followers expected the central government of the 'Good Duke' to back them up in teaching the local landlords a lesson. The principal effect, however, of Ket's Rebellion and of the other uprisings which occurred in other parts of the country in 1549 was to bring about the fall of Protector Somerset, the man to whom the rebels appealed for help.

S. T. Bindoff, *Ket's Rebellion*, Historical Association pamphlet, 1949.
J. Cornwall, *Revolt of the Peasantry, 1549*, 1977.
S. K. Land, *Ket's Rebellion*, 1977.

JOHN HALES or HAYLES (*d.* 1571), author, was born in Kent, the son of Thomas Hales of Hales Place in Halden, Kent. He never went to the university, but he knew Greek, Latin, French and German. At some time he became lame through an accident and he was often known as 'club-foot Hales'. When the monasteries were dissolved, Hales obtained large grants of land in Coventry, but he converted St. John's Hospital into a free school, the first to be established in Edward VI's reign. For the use of the scholars in this school Hales wrote a Latin grammar, *Introductiones ad grammaticam*, partly in Latin and partly in English.

In 1538, Hales was a groom of the King's chamber, a position he achieved through his connection with Thomas Cromwell, his patron. He was closely associated also with Ralph Sadler, for whom he worked as his deputy in the Hanaper (a department of the Chancery) and then as co-Clerk of the Hanaper with Sadler. Through Sadler's influence he was made a Justice of the Peace in Middlesex and Warwickshire in 1547. In that year he was elected Member of Parliament for Preston in Lancashire.

In 1548 Hales came to public prominence. He was already known as an opponent of enclosures, and in this year he became a member of Somerset's commission to enquire into the progress of enclosures in the Midlands since 1489. He was indeed Somerset's right-hand man in the whole campaign against enclosures. In parliament, Hales tried to put his social ideas into practice through three bills: one for the rebuilding of decayed houses, one for maintaining tillage, a third against the regrating and forestalling of markets. All three failed. Hales was also very active over the Subsidy Act of 1548. This Act, the equivalent of our Finance Act today, contained a radical proposal, to put a tax on sheep and cloth. The immediate object was to allow the government to abolish the very unpopular custom of purveyance, by which the Crown purchased supplies from its subjects at low prices and on long credit. The new tax was to compensate the Crown for its loss of purveyance. Hales believed that the great expansion of the cloth trade and the growth of sheep farming was ruining the economy of the nation by diverting too much of its output into a single channel and he proposed to attack the evil by the method of taxation, 'an early essay in the use of taxation as an instrument of economic planning'. His plan was accepted by the Protector and also by Parliament, perhaps by the latter because the tax might prove easy to evade.

Hales was so closely associated with Somerset that he soon fell foul of Northumberland after Somerset had fallen from power. In 1551 he left the country and went to Germany, following a spell in the Tower of London. The death of Northumberland brought no relief for Hales, since the accession of Mary was to him, as a Protestant, anathema; in consequence he remained abroad, prominent among the Marian exiles. In 1558 he returned to England, but in 1564 he was in disgrace with Elizabeth for having supported the marriage of the young Earl of Hertford to Catherine Grey and for having written that, if the Queen should die and leave no heir, the Crown should go to the Suffolk family. He was put in the Fleet Prison, but was soon released through the help of Burghley. Hales died on December 28th 1571.

It is almost certain that Hales was not the author of *A Discourse of the Commonweal of this Realm of England*, written in 1549 and published in 1581; it is sometimes attributed to him, but is now generally seen as the work of Sir Thomas Smith.

S. T. Bindoff, *Tudor England*, 1950.
A. J. Slavin, *Bulletin Institute of Historical Research*, 1965.

JOHN KNOX (1512?-1572), Scottish Protestant reformer and historian, was born not earlier than 1512 and not later than 1515. He was ordained priest in April 1536: he was an Apostolic Notary from 1540 to 1543: he may have been a clerk in Cardinal Beaton's employ in 1545, but probably was not. He came under the influence of Wishart, the first Protestant martyr in Scotland, and his 'acceptable doctrine' and was then accounted an 'apostate priest'. He was saved from Wishart's fate of burning by Wishart's good advice, 'Nay, return to your bairns and God bless you. One is sufficient for a sacrifice.' He was in daily danger of arrest and eventually took refuge in the castle of St. Andrew's, which was held by the murderers of Cardinal Beaton. When that fell, Knox was sent by its French captors to the French galleys (1547-9). On his release he went to England, where the Protestant reformation under Edward VI was in full swing. He became a licensed preacher at Berwick and then at Newcastle. Here he became acquainted with Mrs. Elizabeth Bowes, wife of the captain of Norham Castle, and here he courted her daughter, Marjory, whom he married probably in 1553. But in 1550 he was up in front of Tunstal, Bishop of Durham, to explain his doctrine. Tunstal was a conservative in religion: Knox represented the most advanced side of the Reformation. To him and to Northumberland the Book of Common Prayer of 1549 did not go far enough. In 1552 Knox was appointed one of the six chaplains to Edward VI. He was all but offered the see of Rochester, but he quarrelled with Northumberland and was twice arraigned before the Privy Council. He could have had the living of All Hallows in London, but he refused it. That he had influence in ecclesiastical matters is proved by his success in getting the Black Rubric added to the Second Prayer Book of Edward VI, which laid down that to receive the Communion kneeling did not imply adoration.

Knox disliked Northumberland and he also saw that the Duke's days were numbered. On the accession of Mary, Knox (1554) went overseas.

He was one of the leading 'Marian exiles', engaging in an unseemly quarrel with Richard Cox and his followers over the form of service to use. Knox wanted a more extreme Prayer Book even than that of 1552; Cox was content to obey the Edwardian Act of Uniformity. Knox and his supporters withdrew to Geneva, where they drew increasing inspiration from the doctrines and practices of John Calvin, the great religious dictator of that city. Knox contributed to the attack on Mary Tudor by publishing in 1558 his most famous work: *The First Blast of the Trumpet against the Monstrous Regiment of Women*. In this book he claimed to prove from scripture, from classical authorities and from reason itself that women had no right to rule over men. Unfortunately for Knox, when Mary died within a few months of the printing of his pamphlet, she was succeeded by another woman, Elizabeth. The Scottish reformer was not, therefore, welcome even in Protestant England, and in consequence returned to Scotland, to become the major formative influence in the Reformation there, where we must leave him.

J. Ridley, *John Knox*, 1968.

MARY I (1516–1558), who became Queen of England in 1553, was the third child of Henry VIII and Catherine of Aragon and the only one to survive infancy. For the first years of her life she was given into the charge of the Countess of Salisbury.

For the first twelve years of her life she was Henry's 'pearl of his kingdom'. To begin with, Catherine supervised her education, entrusting it to Linacre and commissioning the great Spanish scholar, Vives, to recommend a curriculum. Mary was well educated, but showed little aptitude for learning, except perhaps in music. She mastered Latin and French, but never learned to write or to speak Spanish. Catherine was educating her, after all, to be an English princess.

Very early in life she became a pawn on the chess-board of international politics. In 1518 she was promised in marriage at the age of 2 to the newly-born Dauphin of France: that was broken off and she was promised to the 22-year-old Emperor, Charles V. Mary was then 6. Charles chose instead to marry Isabella of Portugal, whereupon Mary was offered to James IV of Scotland and then to Francis I of France, who was 32 in 1527.

In 1526 Mary was sent as Princess of Wales to Ludlow, where a

Mary I
(Artist: Hans Eworth)

court was established for her, her education provided for, and instructions were given to the Countess of Salisbury, mother of Reginald Pole, and to Mary's chamberlain, John Dudley (who later as Northumberland was to try to prevent her from succeeding to the throne) that the Princess was to have plenty of good food, clean linen, dancing and open air exercise. It is likely enough that these next two years were to be the happiest in Mary's life.

In 1528 the first suggestions of the divorce were mooted. From 1528 to 1530 Mary hardly ever saw her parents. In 1531 she was separated from her mother, she was forbidden to write to her, and she never saw Catherine of Aragon again. The next year began the unhappiest part of Mary's life. In 1532 Henry VIII spent on his daughter one-fifth in the whole year of what he spent in one day on Anne Boleyn. In 1533 Mary was deprived of her title of Princess of Wales: when in the same year Elizabeth was born to Anne Boleyn, Mary was declared a bastard and cut out of the succession to the throne by Act of Parliament. Her household was broken up, the Countess of Salisbury was sent away, and Mary was relegated into the new household set up for the new Princess Elizabeth.

The years 1534–6 were probably the most cruel time that Mary had to endure. Henry was determined to break what he called her 'Spanish pride' and force her to agree to the royal supremacy and her own bastardization. This became a major political problem for the King and his minister, Thomas Cromwell. In the end, after intense pressure had been applied, Mary gave in to her father, largely because of the death of Anne Boleyn in 1536, which Mary hoped might pave the way to better relations with Henry if first she submitted to him. So Mary capitulated to the demands Henry made upon her. She even acknowledged her own bastardy, that 'the marriage heretofore between his majesty and my mother . . . was by God's law and man's law incestuous and unlawful'. Mary is not to be blamed for this. One may guess how great a support Catherine had been, but she was dead now. Even Mary's cousin, Charles V, advised her to yield.

Mary's cup of sorrow was not yet quite full. Henry seemed very ready to restore Mary to his favour. The arrival on the scene of Jane Seymour brought her a good friend. And even Cromwell, always a swimmer with the tide, made her a present at the New Year. But there were still crosses to be borne. In 1540, her old tutor, Dr. Featherstone, and her mother's chaplain, Abell, were burnt at the stake. But worst of all was the wholesale attack made on the Pole family, so that among other sufferers Mary's best friend, the Countess of Salisbury, was executed.

That Henry's treatment of his daughter may have been only politic and even repugnant to him may be perhaps supported by his treatment of her after the execution of Anne Boleyn — which removed Mary's most bitter and dangerous enemy. It is said that Anne contemplated the murder of Mary by poison. At any rate from 1536 to 1547 Mary lived a life of ease and contentment, with apparently enough money to allow her to enjoy herself at the gaming tables and to indulge her love of giving presents to her relatives, friends, and especially her godchildren. (Madden, *Privy Purse Expenses of the Princess Mary, 1831.*)

In 1544, Mary was restored to the succession, after Edward, but before Elizabeth, by the Act of Succession and by Henry's Will. Between 1547, when her father died and 1553, when she ascended the throne, her difficulties continued. She had much affection for Edward VI, little liking for his religion. Her quarrels were mostly with the Council, not with Edward. The Council demanded conformity to the new Protestant religion. Mary stood up superbly, imperturbably and invincibly to all the attempts made to bring her to accept the new Protestant religion. By the time Edward died, Mary had conceded nothing and maintained her own position intact, without falling out herself with Edward VI, although after 1551 she did forgo the public celebration of the Mass, restricting herself to Catholic services in private.

In July 1553 Edward VI died and Northumberland made his desperate bid to substitute his daughter-in-law, Lady Jane Grey, in place of Mary as the new Queen. Mary was at Hunsdon when a message came from the Council telling her to visit her brother, who was very ill. On her way she was warned that the King was already dead. She rushed to her own house at Kenninghall in Norfolk, whence she wrote to the Council, promising a general pardon if she was proclaimed at once. Then she went with all the local supporters she could raise to Framlingham and there she proclaimed herself Queen. Her standard was hoisted over the Gatehouse and she announced that 'The Queen is not fled the realm, nor intendeth to do, as is most untruly surmised'. On 19 July, so swiftly did the nation react to her courage, she was proclaimed in London. On

3 August she entered London triumphantly as Queen, Northumberland having already been arrested at Cambridge. Her reign had begun and she had the whole nation at her feet.

Mary's reign, which lasted until 1558, has traditionally been interpreted as a failure, and while the latest generation of historians are prepared to modify this judgement to some extent, none has been brave enough to reject it completely.

Mary's marriage was in personal terms a disappointment, even a failure. The decision to marry her cousin, Philip, heir to Spain and Burgundy, can be defended on several counts. An alliance with the enemies of France suited English national feeling and it was by any standards a good match. Grave difficulties surrounded a marriage with an English noble, and though English xenophobia was aroused by the marriage to Philip II, this was less dangerous than the civil discord which could ensue from a domestic match. For Mary the wedding with Philip may have represented a return to her Catholic, Spanish roots, but most important she hoped to establish the succession as soon as possible by giving birth to a child, preferably of course a son. The marriage treaty with Philip (1554) was highly favourable to the English, since it would give to the future King of England born to Mary and Philip, possession of the Netherlands, even perhaps (if Philip had no further children) the whole Spanish empire. In the end, however, the marriage was fruitless and unpopular. Philip spent only two brief periods in England and there was to be no child, only a number of phantom pregnancies, which made Mary ridiculous, symbolizing her desperate desire for an heir, but underlining clearly her failure to bear one.

Mary's religious policy was at first something of a success. The restoration of religion as Henry VIII had left it at the end of his reign was in tune with the religious feelings of the majority of the nation, especially after the extremism of Edward VI's reign. In November 1554, Cardinal Pole arrived in England to reconcile the country to the Pope, but he accepted parliament's insistence that there should be no attempt to restore the property of the monasteries: in itself, a realistic acceptance of the facts of political life and one which does the regime credit. However, although well-intentioned, Pole had neither the time nor perhaps the energy to undertake a revival of English Catholicism in the spirit of Catholic Reform. The Counter-Reformation was visible in Mary's religious policy most clearly only in the persecution of heretics. All told, at least 274 were burnt at the stake in the years 1555–8. This was the fiercest bout of religious cruelty England ever witnessed and it had a profound and harmful effect on the Catholic cause which Mary so strongly supported. It failed to remove the canker of religious non-conformity, instead it strengthened Protestantism and gave to Roman Catholicism the stigma of tyranny and extremism, especially through the writings of John Foxe and of later historians, by which medium it became a long-lived, and not yet quite extinct, myth. The centre of the persecution was the capital itself, especially the Smithfield fires, and the diocese of London accounted for nearly half the total of those executed (112); this strengthened the Protestant cause in the most dangerous place. Catholicism was further weakened and heresy strengthened by the exile of about 800 Protestants in Mary's reign, who were allowed to escape to the Continent. Many of them found their way to Germany and Switzerland, where they strengthened their faith and made it purer by association with John Calvin and other Continental reformers. This gave to the English Protestant tradition a new and potentially dangerous twist.

Mary's third great failure was in foreign affairs. In 1557 she allowed herself to be drawn through the Spanish alliance into war with France. Of course, there was nothing very new or alarming in this; indeed, this was probably at first popular with the upper classes since it allowed them to rally round a patriotic cause and to sink their religious differences in the Queen's service. English forces acquitted themselves well at the Battle of St. Quentin, where the Spanish defeated the French. But the war was costly and led to heavy taxation, debts and popular discontent as the burdens on the poor commons increased. The great disaster came early in 1558, when a series of English blunders and a brilliant surprise attack by the Duke of Guise led to the loss of Calais, the last remnant of the great English empire in France.

In some less spectacular areas, Mary's reign scored some successes. Government ran smoothly enough under an effective Privy Council, and parliament in the main co-operated with Mary. The reform of the financial system projected under Northumberland was brought to completion and there was a general drive against corruption, for example in the administration of Crown Lands and in the Court of Wards under Sir Francis Englefield. The Customs were reformed when a new Book of Rates was issued in 1558. An important Militia Act was passed in 1558, the foundation for the Elizabethan and early Stuart armies, and national defences were built up. Exploration and trade were fostered and a charter granted which incorporated the Muscovy Company in 1555. A number of parliamentary acts tightened up in the field of public order and strengthened the hand of the Justices of the Peace.

Mary was the first female ruler England had had since Matilda in the twelfth century, and it is perhaps surprising that in such an age of male chauvinism she was not less successful than she was. She prepared the way for the more spacious days of her sister and both Mary's successes and failures helped give Elizabeth some advantages in 1558. It is difficult to pass final judgement on Mary; she had only five years of government and given more time she might have been able to build on some of her sound beginnings. As it was, her brief reign must on the evidence before us be accounted a failure, but by no means an unmitigated disaster.

D. M. Loades, *The Reign of Mary Tudor*, 1979.
R. Tittler, *The Reign of Mary I*, 1983.

EDMUND BONNER (1500?–1569), Bishop of London, was born probably in 1500 and died in 1569. There is more reason to believe that he was the lawful than the illegitimate son of Elizabeth Frodsham and Edmund Bonner of Hanley in Worcestershire. About 1512 he went to Broadgate Hall, Oxford, now Pembroke College. He became Bachelor of both Civil and Canon Law in 1519, was ordained about the same time and in 1525 became Doctor of Civil Law. In 1529 Wolsey appointed him as his chaplain, and Bonner was with him at Cawood when he was arrested. Between 1532 and 1543 Bonner was frequently employed by Henry VIII on diplomatic missions, especially to Pope Clement VII on the business of the divorce of Catherine of Aragon. During this period he received several minor ecclesiastical preferments, including the living of East Dereham, Norfolk, and the Archdeaconry of Leicester (1535). From 1537 to 1539 he was Prebend of St. Paul's, and in 1538 he superseded Gardiner, Bishop of Winchester, as ambassador in Paris. His behaviour in announcing his appointment greatly offended Gardiner, as did also his appointment to the see of Hereford in 1538, and the two men were never on good terms. Bonner could be arrogant and overbearing: he once used such language to Francis I that the King told him that only his own love for Bonner's master saved him from a hundred strokes with a halberd. Before Bonner could be consecrated to Hereford, he was translated to London (1539), where he was consecrated and enthroned in 1540.

As long as Henry VIII was on the throne Bonner accepted the Royal Supremacy and was able to be a loyal servant of the Crown. When the government went into the hands of Somerset and he insisted that during the King's minority the Royal Supremacy was vested in the Privy Council, Bonner could not accept that. He resisted the Visitation and Injunctions of 1547 and was sent to the Fleet prison for two months. In 1549 he was accused of being lax in enforcing the new Prayer Book and was ordered to preach at St. Paul's on points laid down for him, which included the Mass and the full powers of the King while still a minor. Bonner obeyed in every respect except one — he omitted the Royal Supremacy. After a lengthy examination he was deprived of his bishopric and sent to the Marshalsea, where he remained until the accession of Mary.

In September 1553 Bonner was restored to his see of London and became a leading figure in religious matters. The violent accusations brought against him by Foxe the martyrologist may be discounted. There is no doubt that Bonner was unpopular, especially in London, the centre of Protestantism, but that he enjoyed sending men and women to the fire is certainly untrue — indeed he was admonished by letter from Mary not to treat heretics as lightly as he had been doing. The number of burnings was appalling and inevitably so in his own diocese of London.

Altogether in London diocese, 113 suffered death. Bonner combined his enforcement of the laws against heresy with a strenuous campaign of re-education through sermons and catechizing, and with the careful supervision of his diocese to weed out corruption and immorality.

On the accession of Elizabeth, Bonner's position was impossible. For a while he retained his bishopric, but he would make no concession to the new policy. Even after the Act of Uniformity he still insisted on the old Use at St. Paul's, and not unnaturally he was again deprived of his see. He refused to take the oath under the Act of Supremacy, but by an ingenious piece of legal argument he saved himself from further trouble. He was left in peace in the Marshalsea, where he died in September 1569. He was buried in St. George's, Southwark.

Bonner is the clearest example of the conservative bishops of the English Reformation. In his youth he was a humanist and a reformer. He had seen Pope Clement VII at Bologna and had had the greatest contempt for him. Bonner and his friends were well aware of the need for reform and they accepted the breach with Rome and the Royal Supremacy as long as Henry VIII was King. In 1547 Bonner and the others changed their point of view and abandoned the ideals of their youth, because they saw that the Reformation was now a revolution. The great mistake he and they made was that they only realized too late that the Papacy was worth fighting for, even if the Pope was not; for the unity of Christendom could not be saved without the vital link of the Papacy.

First and foremost Bonner was a lawyer and he always saw the legal side of the Reformation as being at least as important as the spiritual. 'When anything is called into question, if ye dispute it, ye must see whether it be decent, lawful and expedient.' John Ponet told him 'thou ... allowest nothing to be well done (by whatsoever authority it be done) except it be lawful nor nothing to be lawful that is not agreeing to thy canon law.' Cranmer was even more outspoken: 'Well, my Lord, ye be too full of your law: I would wish you had less knowledge in that law and more knowledge in God's law and your duty.'

Bonner was a government official and he expected the individual to accept decisions made by the government. His defence of the Marian persecutions was 'in matters of state, individuals were not to be so much regarded as the whole body of the citizens'. It was this reliance on the rule of the majority in search of unity which caused the conservatives to compromise with their opinions and to comply with the Royal Supremacy. It was this which made Bonner so mistrustful of rash preachers who taught the 'zely (*i.e.* simple, ignorant) people' that individual judgement was of more value than the authority of the Church.

Experience came to his aid. He never really liked the use of the Bible in English and he not unnaturally attributed the rebellions and the economic troubles of the last years of Henry and the reign of Edward VI to the discontent caused by reading the Bible in English and by the idealism of men whom he looked on as fanatical idealists. He was ready to admit the benefits of an English Bible, but he could not agree with Sir Thomas More that a 'commodity ought not to be kept back for the harm that may come of it'.

It is difficult to tell how sincere Bonner was. He told Mary that 'fear compelled us to bear with the times, for otherwise there had been no way but one' — death. Was he speaking the truth? It was safer to admit compulsion through fear than acceptance through approval. On the other hand, in July 1547, when he first protested against the *Book of Homilies* and then changed his mind, he explained that he did so 'upon a better consideration of my duty of obedience and of the ill example which may ensue to others thereof', thinking that his resistance had been 'neither reasonable nor such as might well stand with the duty of a humble subject'. Within two years he was ready to go to prison for defying the state.

On the whole Bonner usually appears as a somewhat inhuman man. Yet there was another side to him. He deeply appreciated the arts and he had a collector's eye for the anatomy of the human body. He once sent a print from Paris to Lord Lisk: 'this present, which of late was imprinted here' is said to be a fine example of French art. 'The anatomy of the man is judged here to be exquisitely done. The anatomy of the woman pleaseth me not so much; howbeit, Mr. Beckinsall that is married and hath had but one child, telleth me that that is the figure of women in travail; to whose judgement, because I am ignorant, I leave the matter, thinking that he took consultation with some midwife touching his sentence.' Was Bonner perhaps more human than he makes out? Like Thomas Cromwell, Bonner was an ardent gardener and he used to send Cromwell seeds from 'Rome, Bobonye and parts of Lombardy'.

L. B. Smith, *Tudor Prelates and Politics*, 1953.
S. R. Maitland, *Essays on the Reformation*, xvii–xx.
G. Alexander, *History*, 1975, & *Bulletin Institute of Historical Research*, 1983.

STEPHEN GARDINER (1497?–1555), Bishop of Winchester and Lord Chancellor, was born probably in 1497 and died in 1555. The son of a cloth merchant, he went to Cambridge, where he distinguished himself in Greek and later in canon and civil law. In

1525 he was elected Master of Trinity Hall, a position which he held until his death (though he was ejected for a period under Edward VI). He attracted the attention of Wolsey and became a secretary and adviser of his, and hence effectively entered the royal service. In 1529 he became the King's secretary. For the rest of the reign he was largely employed in diplomatic missions abroad and in matters arising out of the divorce. Almost the entire time he enjoyed the King's confidence, so that Henry once said of him that when Gardiner was away, he felt he had lost his right hand. But once or twice, as notably over the spoliation of the monasteries, Henry detected in him 'a coloured doubleness', but Gardiner always returned to favour. He was extremely hostile to Catherine of Aragon and was King's counsel at the court which pronounced her marriage with Henry null and void, and Gardiner it was who, with the Bishop of London, carried the robes of Anne Boleyn at her coronation. In 1531 he became Bishop of Winchester. On 10 February 1535 he signed a declaration repudiating the Papal jurisdiction in England. In 1535 he followed this up by publishing his *De Vera Obedientia*, which was regarded as the ablest defence of the Royal Supremacy. It is said that he caused it to be spread among the Roman party that he had written the book under compulsion and in fear of death.

All this time his relations with Cromwell and Cranmer were steadily deteriorating. In 1539 there was issued the Act of the Six Articles, which involved the persecution of the Protestants. This was said to be mainly the work of Gardiner. Cranmer fought strongly against it, but in vain. On the fall in 1540 of Thomas Cromwell, Gardiner was elected Chancellor of Cambridge University, where he much disapproved of the growing Protestantism which he found there. At this time he launched an attack on Cranmer for heresy, but Henry VIII would listen to no accusations against the Archbishop, for Cranmer was the one servant whom Henry always entirely trusted. Gardiner disliked a good deal of Henry's treatment of the Church, but he was invaluable to the King as a proof to the outside world that the Church had not fallen away from the old faith. Cranmer was no less valuable in enforcing the Royal Supremacy.

In 1547 Henry died and Gardiner was not included in the Council of Regency. He was utterly opposed to the policy of Somerset and Cranmer, partly on principle and partly because violent changes were being enforced during the King's minority. For his opposition he was put in the Fleet, then released, then put in the Tower, where he remained for five years until the accession of Mary. In 1551 he had been deprived of his bishopric.

When Mary Tudor came to the throne, Gardiner was released, restored to Winchester and made Lord Chancellor. At her coronation it was he who put the crown on the Queen's head. He had much to explain away — De Vera Obedientia, his treatment of the Queen's mother, his support of Anne Boleyn, his repudiation of Papal jurisdiction. He had to undo much of his work in order to prove the Queen legitimate and to bring the country back to the Roman faith and Papal control. He was opposed to the Spanish marriage, suggesting instead that Mary should wed Edward Courtenay. However, he himself negotiated the marriage treaty with Philip II, in order to secure the best terms he could for his country. He seems to have reconciled himself quite quickly to the Spaniards, composing, it seems, a treatise for Philip II which uses a great deal of Machiavelli's writings to justify the Spanish take-over of England. Gardiner was certainly a crafty, unscrupulous politician, and historians have seldom praised him, but the story that he considered murdering the Princess Elizabeth is certainly untrue; even John Foxe, the originator of the tale, admitted that he had it on hearsay alone.

It is difficult to assess Gardiner's degree of responsibility for the burning of Protestants. The revival of the heresy laws was his work, and it was he who revived De Heretico Comburendo. He sat in judgement on Hooper and others who finally went to the stake. On the other hand, he tried to save their lives by persuading them to follow his own course. Certainly he tried to save Cranmer, and there were no burnings in his own diocese.

Gardiner has been abused almost as much as Cranmer — crafty, abject, vindictive, bloodthirsty, despicable, are adjectives which have been applied to him. Yet he remained in prison for five years rather than sacrifice his belief in Transubstantiation. There is no reason to think that he was not sincere. All men were inconsistent in the sixteenth century, and both Gardiner and Cranmer were Erastians — Gardiner a Roman Erastian, Cranmer a Protestant Erastian. Gardiner was first and foremost a lawyer and an administrator, a man of the world, ambitious, self-confident, clear-sighted, with a practical attitude towards the Church typical of his times. He loathed irregularity, lack of order and discipline; he was horrified by the laxness of the German Protestants, not less by the chaos which ensued in England after the Second Act of Uniformity. The Royal Supremacy could supply the discipline and the necessary control. Reunion with Rome under the Marian Supremacy would ensure order in the English Church. Cranmer was a spiritual man in days when to be spiritual was highly dangerous. Cranmer did not see the chaos in German Protestantism he saw only the value of German scholarship. Both he and Gardiner accepted the supremacy of the State; both had qualms of conscience. Both were driven back to solve their difficulties by their own personal opinions. Cranmer's was the crueller dilemma and the crueller fate. There was no love lost between the two. Gardiner had his reward in his own day: Cranmer's was delayed but is imperishable.

J. A. Muller, *Stephen Gardiner and the Tudor reaction*, 1926.
P. Donaldson, *Historical Journal*, 1980.

JOHN ROGERS (*c.* 1500–1555), first Protestant martyr in the Marian persecution, was the son of John Rogers of Deritend, in the parish of Aston, near Birmingham. He was educated at Pembroke Hall, Cambridge, where he took his B.A. in 1525, and in 1532 was appointed Rector of Holy Trinity in the City of London. He resigned this living in 1534 and became chaplain to the Company of the Merchant Adventurers in Antwerp. At that time he was an orthodox Catholic priest, but he now fell in with Tyndale and was soon converted to Protestantism. Before he was arrested in 1535, Tyndale handed over to Rogers his incompleted translation of the Old Testament. Tyndale was burned in October 1535; during 1536 Rogers devoted himself to completing the Old Testament by adding to it Miles Coverdale's renderings (published in 1535) of the untranslated books and of the Apocrypha, and Tyndale's own translation of the New Testament (published 1526). Rogers's only original contribution was the Song of Manasses in the Apocrypha which he found in a French Bible printed in 1535. Rogers was also responsible for the preface, the marginal notes (the first English commentary on the Bible), and a calendar and almanack and other additional matter. Rogers signed the title-page with the name 'Thomas Matthew' and the book came to be known as Matthew's

Bible. This was the book largely drawn upon for the Great Bible of 1539.

While at Antwerp Rogers married, probably in 1537, Adriana de Weyden: Weyden means 'meadows' and when in 1552 he naturalized his wife and children by a special act of parliament, the name was anglicized into Pratt from the Latin form 'prata'.

When Edward VI came to the throne, Rogers returned to England (1548). He was given three livings in London and in 1551 he was appointed to a prebend of St. Paul's by Nicholas Ridley and shortly afterwards became divinity lecturer at St. Paul's.

With his Protestant views Rogers naturally sympathized with Lady Jane Grey rather than with Mary Tudor. He preached two sermons for which he was had up before the Council, and in 1554 he was sent to Newgate. Here, in conjunction with Hooper, Bradford and others, he drew up a confession of faith of the most extreme Protestant type. He was again examined by Gardiner with much rudeness and even brutality and was condemned to death as a heretic. When he asked to be allowed to see his wife, he was refused, and it is said that he met her and his eleven children on the way to the stake. At the stake he was offered a pardon, if he would recant, but he refused and he was burned just outside the entrance to the church of St. Bartholomew in Smithfield. He was the first of the Protestant martyrs, and his example had a widespread effect in encouraging others. Ridley confessed that the news of Rogers' death had destroyed 'a lumpish heaviness' in his heart.

J.L. Chester, *Life of John Rogers*, London, 1861.
J.F. Mozley, *Coverdale and his Bibles*, 1953.
M.L. Loane, *Pioneers of the Reformation in England*, 1964.

THOMAS CRANMER (1489–1556), Archbishop of Canterbury, was born on 22 July 1489 and was burned at the stake on 21 March 1556. In his youth his education was severely scholastic, but he also became a courageous and skilled horseman. At the age of 14 he went to Cambridge, and after graduating he was elected in 1515 to a fellowship at Jesus College. When he married, he lost his fellowship, but his wife died within twelve months and Cranmer was re-elected. In 1529 the King's suit for a divorce from Catherine of Aragon had opened. Cranmer fell in with two of Henry's offi-

Thomas Cranmer
(Artist: G. Flicke)

cials, Gardiner and Fox, and threw out the suggestion that Henry
VIII ought to consult the divines at European universities. Henry
sent for Cranmer and commanded him to write a treatise on the
subject. He also arranged for him to live with the Earl of Wiltshire,

the father of Anne Boleyn, as his chaplain. Between 1530 and 1533 he was employed on diplomatic missions to Germany, during which time, although now a priest, he married a German woman. In 1533 he was recalled by Henry to succeed Warham as Archbishop of Canterbury. Cranmer did his best to avoid this office, but in the end he most reluctantly accepted. From that moment his troubles began.

On the secular side he found himself involved mainly in two problems, the ever present difficulty for the Tudors of providing a male heir to the throne, and the enforcing of the Royal Supremacy after the breach with Rome. On 23 May 1533, he declared the marriage of Henry with Catherine of Aragon null and void and on the 28th he declared Henry's marriage with Anne Boleyn legal (he did not himself marry them). In 1536 he pronounced that second marriage null and void, but he made efforts to save the life of the Queen, in which he failed. In 1540 he married Henry to Anne of Cleves and within six months arranged the separation. By 1535 the Breach with Rome was complete and the Royal Supremacy took the place of Papal headship of the Church in England. Sir Thomas More and Fisher, Bishop of Rochester, refused to acknowledge it. Cranmer did his best to persuade them to accept it, and when they persisted and were condemned to death, he did his best to plead for them with Henry, but again he failed.

On the religious side, he was occupied largely in making the church services intelligible to the congregations by gradually introducing the use of the English language in place of Latin. In 1538 injunctions were given by Cromwell for a Bible in English to be available in every parish church, and in 1539 the Great Bible, based on Matthew's Bible, was issued. In 1544 Henry authorized the use in English of Cranmer's Litany. But there was at this time a reaction against innovations in religion and there was passed in 1539 the Act of the Six Articles, which laid down severe penalties for any divergence from their demands. Cranmer fought strenuously against them, especially against the clause dealing with the marriage of clergy. He failed and was compelled to send his wife back to Germany. When in 1540 Thomas Cromwell fell from power, Cranmer pleaded courageously for his life, but again to no avail. When Henry died in 1547, Cranmer, much against his will, was nominated to the Council of Regency.

In Edward VI's reign the move towards Protestantism was

accelerated, but at first Cranmer went cautiously. He said Mass for Henry's soul and he withstood a bill for the suppressing of all colleges and chantries. But in 1549 was issued his First Prayer Book and the first Act of Uniformity. This was modified in 1552, when a second Prayer Book and a new Act of Uniformity appeared. In 1553 were issued the 42 Articles of Religion to which all the clergy were required to agree. In the reign of Edward VI, Cranmer was faced with a set of ruffians who were bent on despoiling the Church still further of its wealth. Cranmer withstood boldly this attack on church property, just as he boldly withstood Hooper's attempt to force Zwinglianism on the Church. Had Edward VI lived any longer, Cranmer would probably have failed, but he died just in time.

The accession of Mary Tudor was for Cranmer no solution to any problem. At the last moment, wholly against his will and only because the King on his death-bed virtually commanded him to do so, he had agreed to the substitution of Lady Jane Grey on the throne for Mary. There was no hope of mercy from Mary. Catherine of Aragon, Bishop Fisher and the Roman religion must be avenged. Cranmer was arrested for treason and condemned. For a time his life was spared, because what was required was a public recantation of his heresies. Until March 1554 he was in the Tower. He was brought out and at a disputation at Oxford he was commanded to recant. He refused and went back to prison. Alone and separated from all his friends and from all help and encouragement, he was examined and re-examined. He made four so-called recantations, of which none is a recantation, only a reaffirmation of his acceptance of the Royal Supremacy. For three more weeks he held out, then he collapsed and made two complete and ignominious recantations. This did not save his life. He was to be burned outside Balliol College. Before this he was set up in St. Mary's Church to recant publicly all his heresies. Instead he recanted his recantations, denied any belief in Transubstantiation and rejected the Pope and all his 'enormities'. It was, he said, his right hand that had offended and it should burn first. He was hurried to the stake and when the fire was lighted, he first thrust his right hand into the flames, crying 'this hand hath offended'; he met his death with a courage and patient endurance which filled all who saw him with admiration.

Cranmer's reputation has been grossly maligned by nineteenth-century historians. The strictures of Macaulay and Gasquet and Dixon are really irrelevant, because they see him only through nineteenth-century eyes and never against a sixteenth-century background. He is charged with being a timeserver, inconsistent, and a coward. There may have been a streak of timidity in him, yet timid men do not make good horsemen. It is necessary to remember that Cranmer was a scholar called to high office in days when toughness rather than scholarship was desirable. Further, he was an Erastian in days when everybody was Erastian. Gardiner was an Erastian under Henry VIII, and he had much difficulty in explaining away his book *De Vera Obedientia*, written in 1535, when he was restoring Papalism in 1553. Cranmer was perfectly consistent in his accepting the Royal Supremacy, whether it was exercised by Henry VIII or Edward VI or Mary. He was consistent in his dislike of the Papacy. Nor was he a coward in his daily life. 'He alone, as far as we know, tried to save the monks of Sion from the block; he alone interceded for Fisher and More; for Anne Boleyn and the Princess Mary, for Thomas Cromwell and Bishop Tunstall. He told Henry VIII that he had offended God, and Cromwell that the Court was setting an evil example. He maintained almost unaided a stubborn fight against the Act of the Six Articles, and resisted longer than any one else the Duke of Northumberland's plot.' (Pollard.)

Thomas Cranmer ought to be remembered with gratitude and admiration. If for a moment his courage failed, at the end he recovered and more than recovered it and he died heroically. He was the founder of the Anglican Protestant Church and he gave it a liturgy unsurpassed by any other. He worked to try to unite all the Protestant churches in Europe, and he was always searching for the truth.

A.F. Pollard, *Thomas Cranmer*, 1905.
F.E. Hutchinson, *Cranmer and the English Reformation*, 1951.
Thomas Cranmer: Three commemorative lectures in Lambeth Palace, 1956.
J. Ridley, *Thomas Cranmer*, 1962.

NICHOLAS RIDLEY (*c.*1503–1555), Bishop of London, martyr, was born at Willimotiswick Castle, South Tynedale, in Northumberland, in about 1503; he died on 16 October 1555. He was the second son of Christopher Ridley of Unthank Hall, Northumberland, and Ann Blenkinsop, having one brother, Hugh, and two sisters, Elizabeth and Alice. He was educated at Newcastle, but not at the Grammar School, which was not founded until 1525. He then went to Pembroke Hall, Cambridge. His uncle, Dr. Robert Ridley, was a Cambridge man, being a fine scholar who collaborated with Polydore Vergil and who taught Greek in the university, and he offered to pay Nicholas's expenses. Nicholas repaid his uncle's generosity by soon becoming an outstanding scholar in both Latin and Greek. He took his B.A. in 1522 and then turned to study Philosophy and Divinity. He was ordained probably early in 1524 and was offered a Fellowship at Oxford which he declined. In that year he was made a Fellow of Pembroke Hall and the next year (1525) he took his M.A.

Ridley was said to be a man of small stature, handsome, well built and clean-shaven. He was not a political priest like Wolsey or Gardiner, nor a saintly reformer like Bilney and Latimer: he was a scholar, an intellectual, living among books and disputations and preferring an academic life to any other. It was probably during this period that Ridley met and made friends with Cranmer. From 1527 to 1530 Ridley was abroad studying (again at his uncle's expense) at the Sorbonne in Paris (1527) and at Louvain for some six months in 1529. He was back in Cambridge in 1530.

In 1532 he was made chaplain to the University, a post which he held for four years together with that of Senior Proctor for part of the time. He resigned probably in 1537 when, having taken his B.D., he became private chaplain to Cranmer and left Cambridge to live at Cranmer's manor of Ford in Kent. It was almost certainly during this last period at Cambridge that Ridley changed from an orthodox Catholic into a Protestant. When in 1538 Cranmer presented him with the living of Herne, close to Ford, Ridley still believed in Transubstantiation and probably thought that auricular confession was beneficial and to be encouraged, but not essential to salvation, because he could find no scriptural authority for it.

The passing of the Act of the Six Articles changed the whole situation (1539). This was a conservative measure which put the brake on the trend towards Protestantism. The fall of Thomas Cromwell made the position of the Protestants extremely dangerous. Ridley was by that time the most able debater among the Protestants, even including Cranmer. In 1540 he was elected Master of Pembroke Hall, Cambridge, but he did not reside in the University, because he was helping Cranmer to bring about gradually the Protestant Reformation and this was not a moment when he could leave the Archbishop. Cranmer now appointed him to one of the prebendal stalls at Canterbury, but Ridley found life there far from pleasant, owing to the incessant quarrels between the Catholic and Protestant clergy, not only over religious matters, such as church services in English, but over petty questions such as the boundary between his garden and Dean Wotton's.

It was while he was at Herne that Ridley came to his decision on the question of Transubstantiation. He had certainly made up his mind by the end of 1546, although he made no public declaration until December 1548. When the Lutherans and the Zwinglians renewed their controversy in 1544, Ridley sat down to examine the whole question. He read Bertram of Corbie's treatise, which had been written in 840 for the Emperor Charles the Bald and which was published in 1532. That led him to examine the writings of the early Fathers. As a result he came to the conclusion that no change took place in the inward nature of the bread and wine after the prayer of consecration and that the flesh and blood of Christ were not corporeally present in the bread and wine: but he never denied the spiritual presence of Christ in the bread and wine. Ridley was now a heretic.

In October 1545 Ridley was made the Eighth Prebendary in the Cathedral Church at Westminster. On 4 September 1547 he was designated Bishop of Rochester and he was consecrated at St. Paul's on the 25th. He had also just been given the living of Soham in Cambridgeshire. When he became a Bishop, he was allowed to retain all his preferments and to hold them *in commendam*. He was also chaplain to Edward VI.

From now onwards throughout the reign of the Protestant Edward VI Ridley was engaged with Cranmer in carrying through the English Reformation. The first problem which confronted them was that of images. The more extreme Protestants in London took the law into their own hands and removed the images in St. Martin's Church in Ironmonger Lane. Cranmer decided to support this action. On Ash Wednesday, 23 February 1547, in a sermon preached before Edward VI Ridley dealt with the question. The line he took was that as far as he could see it was wrong for images to be displayed in the churches, but he was open to be persuaded that he was wrong in his opinion. He made a cautious and tentative suggestion that both images and holy water should be dispensed with.

The question of the Mass was a far more important and difficult matter and at this moment Cranmer and Ridley had no intention of allowing any attacks to be made on it. The success which the extremists had won over images led them to think they would be as successful, if they tried to force the government's hand over the Mass, which they now openly denounced as idolatry. In December 1547 Ridley preached at St. Paul's Cross and hotly attacked the fanatics. He did not indicate at all what was his own belief about the Real Presence, so that everybody assumed that he believed in it. Ridley was to be reminded of this sermon in 1554/5, when he was in prison and being tried for his life.

In November 1548 Cranmer produced the first draft of his Book of Common Prayer. There is no evidence that Ridley had any direct hand in the drafting, but it is reasonable to suppose that he was much consulted by Cranmer in its composition. It was clear that the Prayer Book struck at the very roots of Transubstantiation and therefore Cranmer and Ridley now came out into the open. A disputation was arranged in the House of Lords for 17 December and it lasted three days. Ridley was said to be at his very best and to have confounded the arguments of Heath and Day. It was just about this time that Ridley also spoke in favour of a bill to allow the clergy to marry.

During March and April 1549 Ridley was mostly in his diocese at Rochester, ensuring that the Book of Common Prayer was being accepted by everybody, but this work was interrupted by his being called on to deal with the ravings of Joan Bocher. He had been put on the commission of Visitors who were to ensure that the new religious policy was universally enforced in Cambridge. The Visitors arrived in Cambridge in May. Ridley found himself involved in a dispute over a proposal to suppress Clare Hall. Ridley firmly stood out against Protector Somerset, and Clare Hall was saved. In June he presided over three disputations between Catholics and Protestants on the subject of the Mass. This was an academic exercise in the Philosophy Schools involving no political action afterwards. At the end Ridley summed up and decided against the doctrine of Transubstantiation: even the Catholics admitted that his speech was a wonderful performance.

Bonner was deprived of his bishopric in October 1549; in the following February Ridley was appointed to the see of London, but he was not installed until 12 April when he himself was not there and he was installed by proxy. Ridley behaved with notable kindness to Bonner's family, allowing Bonner's mother and sister to reside in his palace at Fulham and frequently inviting them to dine with him, and treating Mistress Bonner with the utmost respect; he would seat her at the head of the table and would not allow her to move lower down, even when a member of the Council was at dinner.

London was a difficult see to administer, for it was the centre of the extreme Protestants and Anabaptists. Ridley was always a strict disciplinarian and he was determined to crush the extremists, and at the same time to see to it that the Reformation was enforced throughout his diocese.

The first problem he tackled was that of the altar — was there to be an altar for the communion service or a communion table? If a table, where was it to stand, at the east end or in the body of the church? Ridley had already in 1549 removed the altar in Rochester Cathedral and substituted for it a movable table which he placed for the time being in the position which the altar had occupied. In May 1550 he made a visitation of his new diocese of London which lasted for seven weeks. At the end of it not a single altar remained. During the visitation Ridley interviewed every vicar and curate in his diocese and insisted on each of them making a written submission to his Injunctions.

The second problem was that of vestments. John Hooper was about to be consecrated Bishop of Gloucester, but he refused to wear vestments. At that moment the wearing of vestments was prescribed by law, therefore Ridley strongly opposed Hooper and also the Council, which was inclined to give way. Ridley's line was that he himself did not care much for vestments, but he did not regard them as being of spiritual importance. On the other hand, the law said they must be worn and the law must be upheld. Hooper became defiant and unreasonable and at last he was put in the Fleet. A royal pardon was granted to Cranmer and Ridley if they consecrated Hooper without vestments. Ridley still stuck out, because he saw in Hooper's obstinate opposition a desire to place individual judgement above ecclesiastical authority; that could only create chaos, that sort of anarchy which was characteristic of the Anabaptists. In the end Ridley carried his point and Hooper was consecrated wearing vestments.

Meanwhile Ridley was employed in various ways: he was frequently examining and disputing with Gardiner, the deprived Bishop of Winchester who was in prison: he was a member of a commission which was sent to enquire into scandals at Eton College (1552): he met John à Lasco to discuss how best to solve the difficulties raised by the church services of the foreign Protestant exiles in London: he paid a visit to the Princess Mary and tried to persuade her to hear him preach, but he failed entirely (1552). In 1553 he preached before Edward VI a sermon on the poverty of the London poor, a sermon which did a great deal to move the King to reopen St. Thomas's Hospital, which had been suppressed for its wealth by Henry VIII, to found St. Bartholomew's and to grant the revenues of the Savoy to St. Thomas's.

The death of Edward VI and the accession of the Catholic Mary left Ridley in a perilous position. He had signed the will of Edward VI by which the succession to the throne was altered so as to cut out Mary and bring in Lady Jane Dudley as Queen. On July 16th, not the 9th, Ridley preached at St. Paul's Cross to a crowd which was wholeheartedly in favour of Mary. Ridley attacked Mary resolutely and called both her and Elizabeth bastards, an attack which Mary never forgot nor forgave. Northumberland's plot failed; Ridley went towards Framlingham to try to make his peace with the Queen, but she had him arrested before he got there and sent him to London to the Tower. He was deprived of his bishopric, and Bonner was reinstated. Wyatt's rebellion made things still more difficult for the Protestant prisoners, but what Mary wanted was for the Protestant leaders to make a public recantation. In 1554 Ridley, Latimer and Cranmer were sent to Oxford for a public disputation. At the close of a noisy and hostile session Ridley was declared a heretic and was excommunicated. Every effort was made to persuade him to recant, but Ridley stood firm. He spent his time in prison writing to his followers to encourage them to remain loyal to the Protestant cause: he wrote a series of treatises on various aspects of Protestantism which he smuggled out of prison and which were sent abroad and there printed and smuggled back into England for distribution. On

15 October he was formally degraded from the priesthood and handed over to the Mayor for execution. The next day, 16 October, he and Latimer were burned 'on the north side of the town in the ditch over against Balliol College'. Whereas Latimer died quickly and in little pain, Ridley's death was prolonged and agonizing. The fire had been badly laid and burned only slowly under the faggots, with the result that the flames did not reach the gunpowder which had been provided to hasten his death. Slowly the lower part of his body was burned away. Ridley screamed in agony 'I cannot burn. For God's sake let the fire come unto me'. He was not burning at all above his waist, his shirt was not even scorched. At last a soldier hauled a faggot away and let the flames rise: they reached the gunpowder and Ridley's pain was over.

If Bonner may be looked on as the outstanding example of the uncompromising conservative bishop; if Latimer stands for the plain, down-to-earth defender of what he felt to be right; if Hooper may be taken to represent the violent, irrational and extreme reformer; Ridley may well be taken as standing for everything which was best in the English Reformation. He was gentle by nature, devoid of rancour, kind to his opponents, firm in his opinions, bold in opposition, as good a scholar as Cranmer and less timid, a man of independent judgement and with an understanding of genuine statesmanship, of invincible faith and undaunted courage. The Anglican Reformation probably owes as much to Ridley as to any other single man.

J. G. Ridley, *Nicholas Ridley*, 1957.

HUGH LATIMER (1485?–1555), Bishop of Worcester, martyr, was born probably in 1485 at Thurcaston in Leicestershire. The clearest portrait of Latimer is to be obtained by allowing him to speak for himself. 'My father was a yeoman and had no lands of his own, only he had a farm of three or four pound by year at the uttermost and hereupon he tilled so much as kept half a dozen men. He had walk for a hundred sheep and my mother milked thirty kine. He was able and did find the king a harness with himself and his horse. I can remember that I buckled his harness when he went unto Blackheath field (1497). He kept me to school or else I had not been able to preach before the king's majesty now.' 'In my time my poor father was diligent to teach me how to shoot as to learn me any other thing. He taught me how to draw; how to lay my body in my bow, and not to draw with strength of arms as other nations do, but with strength of body.'

In 1506 Hugh was sent to Cambridge, where he was elected to a Fellowship at Clare Hall in 1510. In 1516 he took holy orders and in 1524 he became B.D. That Hugh was still a believer in the old religion is proved by the sermon he preached that day against the teaching of Melanchthon. One of his hearers was Thomas Bilney, who was so much struck by the sermon that he called on Latimer. 'Bilney was the instrument by which God called me to knowledge; for I was as obstinate a Papist as any was in England. Bilney heard me at that time and perceived that I was zealous without knowledge, and he came to me afterwards in my study and desired me for God's sake to hear his confession. I did so, and by his confession I learned more than before in many years. So from that time forward I began to smell the word of God and forsook the school-doctors and such fooleries.' The use of such words as 'smell' and 'fooleries' is typical of Latimer's racy and arresting English, touched sometimes with what we today might regard as coarseness.

In 1525, according to one story, Latimer preached in the university church and the Bishop of Ely was present. He suspected that Latimer had Lutheran tendencies and he inhibited him from preaching in the diocese. Latimer was also examined by Wolsey's chaplains, but he disowned all connection with Lutheranism and was given permission to preach throughout the kingdom. He was soon again in trouble on account of two sermons he preached 'on the card', in which he explained allegorically how men could win salvation by playing trumps. He had also given much offence by deprecating what he called 'voluntary works', such as pilgrimages, in comparison with works of faith, e.g. of mercy (1529). Nor was his popularity at all increased when it was known that he strongly favoured the King's side over the divorce of Catherine of Aragon. But he won the favour of Henry VIII when he denied the validity of the marriage before the committee which Gardiner took to Cambridge in 1530 to ascertain the opinion of the university divines. He was at once appointed to preach before the King (1530). As a reward he was given the living in Wiltshire of West Kington, to which he was instituted in 1531. A few months later he preached in a neighbouring parish and gave much offence by denouncing all the bishops and clergy in England as being, not shepherds entering by the door, but thieves whom there was not enough hemp in England to hang. In 1532 he was accused of preaching that the Virgin Mary was a sinner, of denouncing invocation of saints and denying purgatory and hell fire. The Bishop of Salisbury, in whose diocese West Kington lay, was Campeggio, an Italian and an absentee. After a delay of almost a year Latimer was cited to appear before the Bishop of London. At first he refused to sign the articles which were presented to him, but ultimately he made a complete submission. Foolishly he wrote a letter denying that he had confessed to any error of doctrine, only to indiscretion. For this he was compelled to admit to Convocation that he had erred in doctrine.

In 1533 he was again in trouble over a sermon he preached at Bristol, and he was inhibited by the Bishop of London. But he had good friends at Court and he regained the King's favour, so that he was commanded to preach before Henry on Wednesdays in Lent (1534), and in 1535 he was made Bishop of Worcester in direct succession to four consecutive absentee Italians. Perhaps he owed these favours to the support which he gave to the marriage of Anne Boleyn with Henry VIII.

From now onwards his preaching became more outspoken. In 1536 he denounced the luxury of the bishops, abbots and 'other strong thieves'. At a meeting of Convocation he asked the clergy what they had done to benefit the poor during the last seven years. They had burned a dead man (Tracy) and tried to burn a living one — meaning himself. More and more in his sermons he dwelt upon the poverty of the poor and the wealth of the rich. And he moved more and more towards Protestantism. It is to be noted that when the Pilgrimage of Grace broke out, the rebels repeatedly demanded that Latimer and Cranmer should be handed over to them.

In his diocese Latimer worked hard. He issued orders that every priest was to possess a whole Bible in English, or at any rate a New Testament: he commanded his clergy to pay first attention to preaching, to admit no one to the Communion who could not say the Lord's Prayer in English, and to instruct the children in their parishes to read English. He had a statue of the Virgin in Worcester Cathedral — 'our great Sibyl', as he called it — stripped of its jewels and ornaments, and was anxious for it to be burned: 'she herself with her old sister of Walsingham, her young sister of Ipswich, with their other two sisters of Doncaster and Penrice would make a jolly muster in Smithfield.'

In 1538 he was on a commission to examine John Forest, and at the execution he preached a sermon, or (as he put it either callously or in the Pauline sense of 'I speak as a fool') 'played the fool after my customable manner'. In the same year he sat on a commission to investigate the famous miracle of the 'Blood of Hailes' and found it to consist of a yellowish gum. When in 1539 there was passed the Act of the Six Articles, Latimer and Shaxton, Bishop of Salisbury, resigned their sees. For more than twelve months he was a prisoner in the house of Sampson, Bishop of Chichester. He was then released, but he was forbidden to preach in or to visit London, either university, or his late diocese. For the next six years his life becomes a blank: then in 1546 he was brought before the Council on a charge of having encouraged his friend Crome, who was in trouble over his preaching. Latimer was put in the Tower and remained there until he was released by the general pardon at the accession of Edward VI.

Latimer set to work at once. His servant said of him, 'then most of all he began to set forth his plough and to till the ground of the Lord and to sow the good corn of God's word . . . preaching for the most part two sermons every Sunday . . . For he being a sore bruised man and above three score and seven years of age took notwithstanding all these pains in preaching, and besides this every morning ordinarily winter and summer about two of the clock in the morning he was at his book most diligently.' He refused to go back to his bishopric, but he became the most notable of preachers. Of all his sermons the most famous is still that 'of the Plough', in which he attacked unpreaching and non-resident bishops, citing the devil as the best example of a diligent bishop: 'He is the most diligent preacher of all other; he is never out of his diocese; he is never from his cure; he is ever in his parish; the diligentest preacher in all the realm; he is ever at his plough'. In another course of sermons he took as his main subject the oppression of the poor by the rich, and included eulogies of Somerset's government. Latimer worked in concert with Hales and the 'commonwealth men' on behalf of the poor. Nothing could more vividly picture for us the effect Latimer's preaching had on his congregation than the entry in the churchwarden's accounts at St. Margaret's, Westminster, in 1549, one shilling and sixpence paid for 'mending divers pews that were broken when Dr. Latimer did preach'.

When Mary came to the throne Latimer was well aware of the danger in which he stood. On 4 September 1553 a summons against him was issued, but he was given six hours' notice beforehand to give him a chance to escape. He refused to take it. In March 1554 he, together with Ridley and Cranmer, was sent to Oxford to take part in a dispute on the doctrine of the Mass. He was condemned for heresy and was handed over to the secular arm to be burned. Ridley was at the same time condemned. On 16 October 1555 — after so long a delay — they were both led to execution in Oxford 'upon the north side of the town in the ditch over against Balliol College'. They were fastened to the stake with a chain round the middle of both. Bags of gunpowder were hung round their necks and the fire lighted. 'Be of good comfort, Master Ridley and play the man', said Latimer, 'we shall this day light such a candle, by God's grace, in England as I trust shall never be put out.' Latimer died quickly with little suffering.

Latimer was a man sincere, courageous and full of vitality. His manner was aggressive, his style of preaching extremely effective, his English racy, easily understood, arresting and prone to become even harsh. His mind was clear but not subtle: he saw things in black and white. Being supremely self-confident he was often rash in his decisions, bold but ill-advised in utterance. As a reformer he had no patience with conservative bishops who had been trained as lawyers in the canon law. He was perfectly right in thinking that these men, men like Bonner and Gardiner, would always see the lawyers' or legalistic side of the Reformation as at least equal with the doctrinal or spiritual. He could not tolerate their readiness to compromise and comply. On the other hand, he had no understanding at all of what was involved in government or diplomacy, which are based on compromise, and he misunderstood the nature of law, which aims not at prefection but at the enforcement of order.

It was impossible for such a mind to yield to the will of the majority in order to achieve unity, at the expense of his convictions. That is why he opposed *The Bishops' Book*, which he looked on as a temporary expedient to secure unity. In his refusal to believe in purgatory he was wholly logical: 'The founding of the monasteries argued purgatory to be; so the pulling down of them argueth it not to be. What uncharitableness and cruelness seemeth it to be to destroy monasteries, if purgatory be!' His denunciation of images, pilgrimages and other traditions was not merely iconoclastic. The reformer Hilsey said of him, 'I have perceived that his mind is much more against the abusing of things than against the things themselves.'

Latimer's attacks on enclosures and the new landed interest were not directed solely against their cupidity. He felt their actions to be immoral and irreligious. 'If ye bring it to pass that the yeomanry be not able to put their sons to school ... and that they be not able to marry their daughters to the avoiding of whoredom; I say ye pluck salvation from the people and utterly destroy the realm. For by yeomen's sons the faith of Christ is and hath been maintained chiefly.' Yet for all his preaching, he probably achieved more for Protestantism by the nobility of his death.

R. Demaus, *Hugh Latimer*, 1869, abridged edition 1935.
H. S. Darby, *Hugh Latimer*, 1953.
H. R. Trevor-Roper, *Historical Essays*, 1957, pp. 85–90.
A. Chester, *Hugh Latimer*, 1954.

JOHN HOOPER (*d.* 1555), Bishop of Gloucester and Worcester, martyr, was born late in the fifteenth century. Nothing is known of his life until in 1519 he took his B.A. degree at Oxford, and the name of his college is not known. It is probable that he was a Cistercian monk at Gloucester and it may have been then that he took Orders. When the monasteries were dissolved, Hooper went to London and became much impressed by the writings of Zwingli and Bullinger. He returned to Oxford in order to spread their reforming views, but when the Act of the Six Articles was passed (1539) he fled first of all to Paris, then he came back to England, but he soon fled again to Ireland and thence to Switzerland. In 1546 he married an Antwerp lady at Basle, and in the following March he went to Zurich, where he became intimate with Bullinger and corresponded with such reformers as Bucer and John à Lasco.

In 1549, when the Protestant reformation was being established, he came back to England and was made chaplain to Protector Somerset, and he now represented the more extreme views of

Protestantism. He was much more sympathetic with Zwingli than with Luther: he objected to the Lutheran doctrine of the Eucharist and held that 'the minister gives what is in his power — namely the bread and wine, and not the Body of Christ; nor is it exhibited by the minister and eaten by the communicant . . . to eat the Body of Christ is nothing else than to believe, as He Himself teaches in the sixth of John.'

Hooper's time was now given to preaching, usually twice a day, when he drew huge audiences: in engaging in disputes on such subjects as Predestination and divorce, which he held to be legal for both parties in cases of adultery; in denouncing Bonner; and in denouncing the new 1549 Prayer Book on the grounds that he objected to vestments and to the form of the oath by the saints. After the fall of Somerset, Hooper became chaplain to Northumberland, by whom he was completely deceived into looking on him as an honest and sincere man.

The controversy over vestments landed Hooper in great trouble and eventually in the Fleet. In 1550 he was appointed Bishop of Gloucester, but he declined to be consecrated wearing vestments. His obstinacy and unreasonableness at last angered even Northumberland, but if it had not been for Ridley, it is probable that the government would have given in to Hooper. Ridley stuck out against Hooper, and Hooper found himself in the Fleet. With good common sense, Hooper saw no advantage in remaining in prison unable to further the Protestant reformation. He therefore gave in and was consecrated Bishop of Gloucester (1551).

Hooper's record as a Bishop was entirely creditable. He preached three or four times a day and one wonders whether quality may not have suffered at the hands of quantity. He tried to organize his diocese on the model of Zurich, although in doing so he was running counter to the tide of Protestantism in England. He made a most illuminating visitation throughout his diocese, in which he discovered that out of 249 clergy 10 could not say the Lord's Prayer, 27 did not know who was its author, 30 could not tell where it was to be found.

In 1552 the sees of Gloucester and Worcester were amalgamated and Hooper was made Bishop of both. He met with more opposition to his methods in the new part of his diocese in Worcestershire than he had in Gloucestershire.

The accession of the Catholic Mary Tudor to the throne meant, of course, that Hooper would be one of the first Protestant Bishops to be attacked, in spite of the fact that he had opposed the attempt to put Lady Jane Grey on the throne. His imprisonment was specially severe: he was deprived of his bishopric, he was excommunicated for refusing to recant, he was degraded from his clerical orders and was handed over to the civil arm to be executed. It was thought politic to have him burned in his own diocese of Gloucester. There on 9 February 1555 he was put to death. Owing to a contrary wind which blew the flames away from him, Hooper suffered terribly, but he never flinched or (as far as is known) uttered a word. He had specially asked for a quick fire 'shortly to make an end'.

Hooper is on the whole the least attractive of the Protestant martyr Bishops. By his writings as much as by his preaching he did a tremendous amount to popularize the more extreme Protestant views. But he was personally, although of the highest moral character and generous to the poor, so austere, so stern and unbending, that he frightened away many who sought his help and whom he would have wished to help.

In his opinions he was uncompromising: he would never dream of compromising his faith in order to arrive at a temporary solution agreeable to all (L. B. Smith). To him the salvation of the individual soul was far more important than mere unity in church services or rule by the will of the majority (*ib.*). He was wholly impartial in his denunciations, for he castigated the enclosing landlords (men who 'hath enough given them from God, yet are not content therewithal') as severely as he attacked the common people (who 'live idle and will not labour'). He believed passionately in the beneficial effects of spreading knowledge of the Bible by giving it to all in the English language, just as he believed that the social discontents and riots were the direct result of ignorance of the divine law. He could never easily admit himself to be in the wrong, and like others who have absolute confidence in their own opinions, he was easily gulled by those who pretended to think as he did (*e.g.* Northumberland). In our own age of compromise it is difficult to be sympathetic with so uncompromising a character; but also in our own age, when persecution is rife outside our own boundaries, we can hardly not admire a Bishop who would today have as willingly gone to prison and 'brain-washing' as he went in his own day to the fire in Gloucester.

L. B. Smith, *Tudor Prelates and Politics*, 1953.
J. G. Ridley, *Nicholas Ridley*, 1957.

ROBERT FERRAR (*c.*1504–1555), Bishop of St. David's, martyr, was born probably not later than 1504, perhaps as early as 1502. He came of a Yorkshire family and was born at Ewood near Halifax, according to tradition for which no evidence exists. He was educated perhaps for a short time at Cambridge, certainly later at Oxford, where he became an Augustinian Canon. He then came under the influence of the Protestant Gerard, was involved in a charge of heresy and was compelled to recant (1528). He accompanied Bishop Barlow on a mission to Scotland, after which he became Prior of St. Oswald's, Nostell, near Pomfret.

When Edward VI came to the throne Ferrar became chaplain to Protector Somerset, who made him Bishop of St. David's (1548), the first appointment to be made by letters-patent without any election by the Chapter. Ferrar soon found himself in trouble with his Welsh diocese, where his predecessor, Barlow, had also had difficulties. The Chapter brought a series of ridiculous charges against him, including an accusation that he 'daily useth whistling to his child and says he understood his whistle when he was but three days old,' that he whistled to a 'seal-fish tumbling in Milford Haven', and that 'he useth bridle with white studs and snaffle, with Scottish stirrups, with spurs, a Scottish pad with a little staff of three-quarters long'. Unfortunately Somerset fell from power at this time and fifty-six charges were laid against Ferrar before the Privy Council and a commission was set up to examine 127 witnesses. Ferrar was in prison until the accession of Mary, when he was deprived of his bishopric, because he was a married priest (1554). The next year he was examined by Gardiner, who accused him of breaking his monastic vow by his marriage, to which Ferrar replied that his vow was to live chaste, not single. Gardiner sent him down to Carmarthen to be tried by Morgan, the man who had become Bishop of St. David's when Ferrar was deprived. At his trial Ferrar was required to subscribe to a list of articles which he refused to accept. He was condemned as a heretic and was burned on 30 March 1555, 'on the south side of the market Cross'. He told a looker-on that if he saw him 'once to stir in the pains of his burning, he should then give no credit to his docrine'. Ferrar's sufferings were intense, but he never flinched or moved until he was struck on the head by a man named Richard Gravell, to put him out of his agonies.

Ferrar was a simple, sincere and brave man, but he was no match for the greedy Welsh Chapter whose outrageous robberies he tried to end. Fuller says of him that he was 'not unlearned, but somewhat indiscreet or rather uncomplying, which procured him much trouble; so that he may be said, with St. Laurence, to be broiled on both sides, being persecuted both by Protestants and Papists'.

R. Bretton, 'Bishop Robert Ferrar' *Halifax Antiquarian Society*, 1934.

REGINALD POLE (1500–1558), Cardinal and Archbishop of Canterbury, was born in March 1500 and died on the night of 17 November 1558, aged 58 years. He was the son of Sir Richard Pole, who had married Margaret, Countess of Salisbury, the daughter of Edward VI's brother, George, Duke of Clarence. He was, therefore, one of the Yorkist claimants to the throne. (See genealogical tree, Table II). It was this relationship to the reigning King in England which made him so important in the eyes of foreign rulers. Henry VIII showed him considerable kindness and made generous grants of money towards the cost of his education at the Carthusian school at Sheen, at Magdalen College, Oxford, and at Padua University. In addition he made over to him ecclesiastical revenues to ensure him an income equal to his rank. At Oxford his teachers were Linacre and Latimer, in Italy the great scholars Longolius, Leonicus and Bembo. He also corresponded with Erasmus, met John á Lasco, the Polish reformer, and paid a visit to Rome. He proved himself a man of great intellectual qualities, brilliant in debate, and ultimately an admirable teacher, but he was never a learned theologian.

Pole was in Italy from 1521 to 1527. He was back in England by 1527 and was cordially welcomed by the King. But Pole disliked life at Court and retired to Sheen to pursue his studies. Pole was much opposed to the divorce from Catherine of Aragon which Henry was planning, and when the King sought his advice, he got leave to go abroad to Paris. But when he was there, Henry demanded that he should obtain the views of Paris University. Thanks to the influence

Reginald Pole
(Artist: Unknown)

of Francis I the opinion was favourable. Recalled to England, Pole was, on the death of Wolsey, strongly urged to accept either the bishopric of Winchester or the archbishopric of York. Henry was anxious to have him on his side in his quarrel with Rome, but Pole would not accept on those terms. In an interview with the King, Pole behaved tactlessly and violently, the King lost his temper and almost hit Pole, finally leaving him dissolved in tears. The quarrel was soon mended, and in 1532 Henry allowed him to go abroad to Avignon and then to Padua.

Up to 1536, the year in which Pole visited Rome and became a Cardinal, Henry made many attempts to win him over, for he recognized the danger to England which might come from a hostile Yorkist. But Henry's impatience and Pole's inflexibility always prevented a reconciliation, which was at last made impossible by the publication of Pole's *De Unitate Ecclesiae*, in which discretion was thrown to the winds and abuse was poured out on Henry. From that moment Pole revealed his inherent lack of political insight. He thought the Pilgrimage of Grace was symptomatic of all England; he was prepared to become a traitor to his own country and to urge France and Spain to invade England, and he advocated a commercial blockade of England.

Henry retaliated by executing Pole's brother and his mother, although he may have been justified in suspecting them of being directly involved with Pole in treasonable conspiracy. The King may even have tried to have Pole murdered, but it may be that Pole only imagined this. Henry took all possible steps to obstruct Pole's legatine missions; that is, his missions from the Pope to England and to foreign powers to depose Henry.

Foreigners also recognized the importance of Pole in the diplomatic world. His dynastic position became a reason for trying to arrange a marriage between him and Mary Tudor, and the Pope gave him a legateship to sustain English rebels with money. Nor did the Pope underrate the value of Pole's scholarship. From 1536, when he became a Cardinal, to 1549, when it looked as if Pole was likely to succeed Paul III as Pope, Pole's career was distinguished and he was probably happier than he was either before or after. Twice he presided over the Council of Trent and he was made Governor of the Patrimony of St. Peter, while he enjoyed the friendship of the most famous woman of Italy, Vittoria Colonna. But in truth he was losing ground. He belonged to the liberal Catholics, who hoped for reconciliation between Lutheranism and the Catholic Church, and when this party failed to secure control of the Church, and the more extreme party was successful at the Council of Trent, Pole's own influence began to wane. He bowed to the inevitable and accepted the Papal authority. He was not a strong enough man to oppose the policy of the papacy on principle and risk exile a second time. He had been exiled from England for denying the Royal Supremacy, he now accepted the Papal Supremacy. He was within an ace of being elected Pope on the death of Paul III; but although he was supported by the Imperial cardinals, that inevitably put the French cardinals against him, while the Italian cardinals wanted an Italian Pope.

On the accession of Mary Tudor it was only a question of time before Pole would return to England. He was appointed the new Archbishop of Canterbury. But his return for various reasons was delayed, and it was not until 20 November 1554 that he landed in England. He at once set about restoring England to the Catholic fold, reorganizing the Church and preventing the later succession of Elizabeth. Up to this moment he was still only in deacon's orders; on 20 March 1556 he was ordained priest and the next day, when Cranmer was burned, Pole as Archbishop celebrated Mass for the first time in his life. For two years the government of England was very largely in the hands of Pole, who busied himself both in religious and secular affairs. But although the ecclesiastical settlement of Henry was reversed by Act of Parliament and Pole enforced many reforms which he wanted, he failed in the end both in making England Roman Catholic and in keeping Elizabeth off the throne. He must accept his share of responsibility for the burnings. All his life he hated extreme measures, but he dared not oppose the persecutions. He died the same night as Queen Mary, with his work unfinished.

Reginald Pole was a sincere and single-minded man, a passionate believer in the Christian religion, a man of perfect integrity and unblemished morals. He had a genius for friendship and he was intimate with the best spirits in Italy, men like Contarini, Priuli and Sadoleto, women like Vittoria Colonna. But he was intransigent and inherently weak; he dreaded holding public office, and although he was able to speak his mind fearlessly and even violently, as he did to Pope Paul IV, he often shirked his clear duty, as he did when he failed to withstand the Marian persecutions. Yet he saw clearly the dangers inherent in the growing modern State and he took his stand courageously and consistently in defence of religion and the Church. It is his chief claim to be remembered that he also saw the need for reform in the Catholic Church, tried patiently to achieve reform and

by his example and work made the ultimate reforms of the Jesuits
the easier to achieve.

K.B. McFarlane: *Cardinal Pole*, 1924.
W. Schenk: *Reginald Pole, Cardinal of England*, 1950.
P. Hughes: *Rome and the Counter-Reformation in England*, 1940.
W.G. Zeeveld: *Foundations of Tudor Policy*, 1948.
D. Fenlon, *Heresy and obedience in Tridentine Italy*, 1972.
R.H. Pogson, *Historical Journal*, 1975.

JOHN PONET [variations in spelling are **POYNET, POINET**
and **PONNET** but he always used the form **PONET**] (1516–1556),
Bishop of Winchester, was born in Kent in 1516 (not 1514). Little is
known of his early life. He arrived in Cambridge at the Queens'
College about 1528, took his B.A., became a Fellow in 1532, M.A.
1535, Bursar 1537–9, Dean 1541–2. He was ordained in 1536 and
took his D.D. in 1547. At the time of his arrival at Queens' that
college was the most advanced in the University in its theological
opinions, but Ponet was a member of a group of young men who
were more distinguished for their humanistic interests than for
theological opinions. His friends included John Cheke, Roger
Ascham and William Cecil.

Ponet made good use of his time at Cambridge. He was a man
with considerable intellectual abilities, he had a mind which ranged
over many interests and he had great facility in learning languages.
'It was no sluggish attention which he gave to learning languages —
Latin, of course, Greek, Italian, and at last German' (Bale). He was
said to be an excellent mathematician and he was greatly interested
in astronomy. As bursar of Queens' he designed the complicated
sundial which is still in the front court there, and he gave a copy of it
to Henry VIII for Hampton Court. 'It shows not only the hour of the
day, but also the day of the month, the sign of the moon, the ebbing
and flowing of the sea, with divers other things as strange'. In
addition to all this he made a greater study of the Scriptures and of
the Church Fathers than any of his contemporaries with the ex-
ception of Cheke.

In about 1547 he became chaplain to Cranmer and he quickly
acquired much influence with the Archbishop. He was said to have

advised him 'in the hidden secrets of divine mysteries' and there is no doubt that Cranmer came to rely on Ponet more and more.

In 1549 Ponet wrote a tract defending the marriage of the clergy (Cranmer was a married man). On 23 February 1550 he was nominated to succeed Bonner as Bishop of London, but in March he was nominated to Rochester and he was consecrated in June. Within a year he was translated to Winchester in place of the deprived Gardiner. He was compelled to surrender the enormously wealthy revenues of that see and he received in exchange a fixed income of 2,000 marks a year.

At some point he seems to have been married to a butcher's wife at Nottingham while her husband was still alive. Machyn in his *Diary* records: 'The 27th day of July (1551) was the new Bishop of Winchester divorced from the butcher's wife with shame enough', and he was ordered to pay the butcher an annual pension as compensation. Ponet then married again, and when Mary Tudor came to the throne in 1553 he was deprived of his bishopric as a married priest. He took part in Wyatt's rebellion, and when he saw that it was a failure he fled overseas to Strasbourg.

Little is known of his life abroad. He became involved in a dispute with Dr. Martyn over the marriage of clergy (1556) and he also wrote in the same year his *Short Treatise of Politike Power*. He died in Strasbourg in 1556.

Ponet has acquired a bad reputation among historians. The *D.N.B.* calls him 'clever, but somewhat unscrupulous': Miss Garrett in her *Marian Exiles* writes that 'of John Ponet the man there is little good to be said: he was quarrelsome, avaricious, unscrupulous and a coward'. Later writers tend to take a more generous view of his character and a higher view of his importance. Probably he was rather above than below the average standards of his time in character and integrity. His literary style was pungent, his mind vigorous and even aggressive, but he had a generous spirit and much magnanimity of heart. He has been called 'the highest ranking English churchman in Germany' during his exile, in daily touch with the humanists like Cheke and Morison (Zeeveld). His *Short Treatise of Politike Power* was the 'most important contribution of the exiles to the history of English thought' (Zeeveld). 'He was laying down a principle which anticipated by almost a hundred years Milton's declaration of the individual's independence from the state' (*ib.*):

and the American John Adams calls him 'the theorist whose *Politike Power* contains all the essential principles of liberty which were afterwards dilated upon by Sidney and Locke'. Ponet's main thesis is that rulers, just as much as subjects, have the duties of Christians and of citizens to obey the laws of God, of Nature and of men. Their position is one of trust and it may be forfeited, for 'all laws do agree that men revoke their proxies and letters of attorney when it pleaseth them, much more when they see their proctors and attorneys abuse it' (C. Morris, *Political Thought in England: Tyndale to Hooker*, p. 152).

W. S. Hudson, *John Ponet, Advocate of Limited Monarchy*, 1942.
W. G. Zeeveld, *Foundations of Tudor Policy*, 1948.
J. W. Allen, *History of Political Thought in XVI Century*, ed. 1954.
C. Morris, *Political Thought in England: Tyndale to Hooker*, 1953.

ROGER ASCHAM (1515/16–1568), author, was born in 1515 or 1516. He was educated privately to begin with, as was the custom of the time, in the household of Humphrey Wingfield, where he learned not only English and the Classics, but also a love for sport, especially archery, which never deserted him. He went on to St. John's College, Cambridge, where he became so proficient in Greek that he taught the language to other students while still himself an undergraduate. He was sympathetic both to the New Learning and to ideas of religious reform. In 1538 he became a Reader in Greek at St. John's and he greatly influenced the development of the study of Greek in Cambridge. His handwriting was so beautiful that he was used by the University to write its official letters. In 1545 he published his *Toxophilus*, a treatise in the form of a dialogue, written in English, on the sport of archery. Three years later he became tutor to the Princess Elizabeth. He greatly admired her learning, but found the life cramping. He soon quarrelled with the steward and fell out with Elizabeth, and as a result he resigned his post. In 1550 he was appointed secretary to the English ambassador to Charles V and up to 1553 he resided abroad, at first at Augsburg and then wherever the imperial court stayed. Later he returned to England and became the Latin secretary to Queen Mary; he seemed as happy in the service of a Catholic monarch as he had been under a Protestant regime. On the accession of his former pupil, Elizabeth, he continued in his office of Latin secretary. He had married in 1554 and produced about seven or eight children. The last years of his life were devoted to writing his *Scholemaster*.

It may well be asked why a man whose life was so comparatively undistinguished and unsuccessful should be worth remembering today. The reason probably is that Ascham was not only a typical product of the age in which he lived, but he was also always something a little bit more than that, always a little bit ahead of his own times. Like many men in the sixteenth century, Ascham suffered from perpetual ill health; like many others he was always short of money and his life was one long struggle to keep going. Therefore he pestered his patrons for pensions and presents even more than was the habit of the time. He was a first class scholar, in days when learning and scholarship were fashionable, and he had all the irritability which so often marks the Renaissance scholars. But Ascham was more than a mere pedant and he deserves to be remembered specially by two classes of people. All who love and revere English prose literature should recall that Ascham, classical scholar though he was, fought for the use of the English language. In the introduction to *Toxophilus* he pleaded for the use of the 'Englyshe tonge' rather than the Greek or Latin, and while he was secretary to the English ambassador at Augsburg he wrote all his letters in English and not in Latin. The style of *Toxophilus* is itself a remarkably early example of pure English prose. But most especially all boys ought to honour Roger Ascham for the enlightened views he held on education. In his *Scholemaster*, published in 1570 after his death by his widow, he denounces the use of force in teaching and urges that the pupil should be attracted to learning by the gentle persuasion of his teacher. Those students who today follow gladly a classical education will there find set out clearly for the first time those methods of teaching Latin which have been generally adopted by succeeding generations of 'scholemasters'. Not least may Ascham be remembered as the man who pleaded (in *Toxophilus*) that sport should find an important place in any system of sound education.

E. M. Nugent: *The Thought and Culture of the English Renaissance*, 1956.
L. V. Ryan, *Roger Ascham*, 1963.

NICHOLAS UDALL (1505–1556), reformer, dramatist and schoolmaster was educated at Winchester and at Corpus Christi College, Oxford. While he was at Oxford he came strongly under the influence of the New Learning and in religion he favoured the Lutheran point of view. He came into prominence at Court at the coronation of Anne Boleyn, when he was author, or part author, of the pageants and masques which formed a large part of the celebrations and which laid the foundations for his reputation as a literary man.

In 1534 he was appointed Head Master of Eton, soon after he had published a book entitled *Flowers for Latin Spekynge, selected and gathered out of Terence, and the same translated into Englysshe*. It was the custom at Eton for some of the boys to act the plays of Terence and Plautus under the direction of the Head Master 'about the feast of St. Andrew', a custom very acceptable to Udall.

In 1541 his career as a schoolmaster came to an end — only temporarily, as it proved. A theft of silver images and other plate was committed by two of the scholars with the help of Udall's servant. Udall was examined on suspicion of having been aware of the theft, but although he appeared to be innocent of the theft, he confessed to being guilty of a moral offence with one of his pupils. He lost his mastership and was sent to the Marshalsea, but he was soon released and was once again in favour at Court, and he also received several church preferments.

In 1549 he was employed by the government to write the answer to the demands of the West Country rebels for the old religion to be restored. Udall's answer was a forceful and able reply to the Catholic arguments, and he defended with spirit the royal authority in matters of religion. On the accession of Mary, Udall was one of the few Protestants who were retained in favour and in employment, so much so that in 1554, in spite of his past record, he was made Master of Westminster School. This appointment is a proof of Mary's respect for learning and ability. He died in 1556 and was buried in St. Margaret's, Westminster.

The importance of Udall lies in the fact that he combined in himself activities as a moderate Reformer, as a humanist and as an able dramatist. Only one of his plays remains to us, *Ralph Roister Doister*, which is generally regarded as the first genuine comedy in English literature. It was written almost certainly in 1553–4 and therefore must have been intended for the boys of Westminster School and not of Eton College. The play has close affinities with Plautus and Terence, but Udall has succeeded in making the characters recognizably English. There is only one early copy of the play in existence and it is in College Library at Eton.

W.D. Cooper, Shakespeare Society's edition of *Ralph Roister Doister*.
Maxwell Lyte, *History of Eton College*, 1911.
Cambridge History of English Literature.

SIR JOHN CHEKE (1514–1557), tutor to Edward VI, scholar and Secretary of State, was the son of Peter Cheke, one of the esquirebedels of Cambridge University, and his wife Agnes Dufford, according to Roger Ascham 'a venerable woman'. He was educated at St. John's College, Cambridge, where he acquired a high reputation for his knowledge of the classical languages, especially Greek. While he was at St. John's he absorbed the doctrines of the Reformation and he probably had much influence on the development of William Cecil, later Lord Burghley, who married Cheke's sister. He was generally regarded as the leader of Greek studies, and in 1540 he became the first Regius Professor of Greek. He became embroiled in a dispute with Stephen Gardiner over the pronunciation of Greek and he was compelled to practise the view held by Gardiner: his own pronunciation was much like that usually adopted in modern England up to very recent times. In 1544 he became tutor to Prince Edward and devoted himself to educating that intelligent boy in the reading of the classical authors, and Cheke seems to have been one of the very few people of whom Edward VI was really fond. He also taught the Princess Elizabeth. About the same time Cheke was made a canon of what is now Christ Church, Oxford; when Henry VIII turned the college into a cathedral, Cheke was given a pension as compensation for the loss of his canonry.

With the accession of Edward VI Cheke's fortunes rose: the new King loaded him with gifts of land, including one grant in Suffolk which Strype described as 'no question a good pennyworth'. He was made Provost of King's in 1548 and was knighted in 1552. During Edward's reign Cheke was an ardent supporter of the Reformation and had a hand in some of the religious changes which marked that period. In 1553 he was made a third King's Secretary. On Edward's death Cheke accepted Lady Jane Grey as Queen. With the accession of Mary he went into exile in Italy and Germany, but Philip II had him kidnapped and brought back to England, probably because Cheke was the chief propagandist among the Marian exiles. Faced with the fear of being burned for heresy, Cheke recanted publicly and ignominiously, which he so much regretted that he fell ill and died on September 13th, 1557. He was one of the most learned men of his time and the author of innumerable books. His life was written by Strype in 1705.

C. H. Garrett, *The Marian Exiles*, 1938.
W. G. Zeeveld, *Foundations of Tudor Policy*, esp. pp. 244–5, 1948.

ELIZABETH I (1533–1603), daughter of Henry VIII and Anne Boleyn, who became Queen of England in 1558, was born at Greenwich on 7 September 1533, and died at Richmond on 24 March 1603, in her seventieth year. None of her predecessors had ever reached such an age. On 19 May 1536, when she was three years old, her mother was executed and she and her sister Mary were declared illegitimate, when Henry VIII married Jane Seymour. Henry married three times more: his last wife, Catherine Parr, proved herself an excellent step-mother to Elizabeth, taking much interest in her education and in that of Edward, Prince of Wales. Both children were above the average intelligence and were good friends. Elizabeth had some instruction from Edward's tutor, Cheke, more from the young William Grindal, who died in 1548, but the mainspring of inspiration in her education was undoubtedly Roger Ascham, who had the highest opinion of her abilities. Like all the Tudors, Elizabeth was fond of music and of dancing ('high and disposedly' in later years with Leicester), and she was also very proficient in Greek, Latin, French and Italian, and later she also learned Spanish. She knew, thanks to Ascham, something also about the writings of the early Church Fathers.

In 1547, soon after Edward VI had come to the throne, Protector Somerset's brother, Thomas Seymour, the Lord Admiral, a worthless and self-seeking adventurer, offered marriage to Elizabeth. She prudently declined on the grounds that she was too young. Seymour at once married Catherine Parr, with whom Elizabeth was living.

Seymour took advantage of this to carry on a vulgar form of romping with Elizabeth, which seriously offended Catherine. But she died within a year: at once Seymour renewed his plan to marry Elizabeth. As a result he lost his head for high treason and Elizabeth was in dire danger, but she skilfully extricated herself. Her cold comment, when she heard of the execution, was, 'this day died a man with much wit and very little judgment.'

Elizabeth had, of course, no part in Northumberland's plot to exclude Catholic Mary and herself from the throne, so that when Mary rode triumphantly into London as Queen, Elizabeth was at her side. But Mary knew her to be at heart a Protestant, and Elizabeth's position throughout the reign was uneasy and sometimes perilous. She refused to have anything to do with Wyatt's rebellion, but when that failed she was put in the Tower. When she arrived there, she sat down in the pouring rain and burst into tears, no doubt fearing that her fate was sealed. Wyatt, however, before his execution, publicly cleared Elizabeth of any hand in the plot and her examinations in front of the Council produced no evidence to justify her being put to death. She was left in the Tower for two months and released in April 1555. For the next two years she lived quietly, biding her time, sometimes at Court, always popular with the English people. On 17 November 1558, Mary died and the long reign of Elizabeth I began.

The new Queen was 25 years old. She had need of the highest form of statesmanship. England was at war with France, and Calais was lost. Her only ally was Spain, and little trust could be placed in Philip II. Trouble was threatening on the Scottish border. The exchequer was bankrupt, heavy debts were owing to the Antwerp bankers, the currency was debased and inflation was hitting all classes. The nation was split by religious differences: there was no Archbishop of Canterbury: nine bishoprics were vacant: the Marian persecutions had sickened the people of Roman Catholicism, yet the heir to the English throne was Mary Stuart, a Roman Catholic and more French than Scotch. The navy had decayed and there was no efficient army. Such was the new Queen's inheritance. Her first act was to appoint Sir William Cecil as her Principal Secretary of State and she thereby created the longest and perhaps the most successful partnership in government in English history. In the last analysis, however, most decisions of policy were the Queen's.

Elizabeth I
(Artist: By or after G. Gower)

The first thing was to make peace with France, which was done at Câteau Cambrésis, in March 1559. The next most urgent problem was that of religion.

Elizabeth's religious settlement was achieved with the help of parliament in 1559; it established the Church of England in some senses in the form in which it still exists. Two great Acts of Parliament were responsible. First, the Act of Supremacy, which made the Queen supreme governor of the Church, avoiding the more contentious 'Supreme Head' of her brother and father. Second, the Act of Uniformity, which enforced the use by ministers of an English Prayer Book based on a slightly modified version of the Second Prayer Book of Edward VI. This settlement failed to satisfy either the Catholics or the Puritans. The latter sought unsuccessfully throughout the rest of the reign to persuade the Queen to modify the measures taken in 1559 and make them more in tune with what they regarded as pure, reformed Christianity. It seems reasonable to accept that this moderate Protestant settlement fitted in with what Elizabeth herself personally preferred in religious matters. The parliamentary history of the Settlement of 1559 is rather obscure, but modern research (by Dr Norman L. Jones) has largely debunked the notion of Sir John Neale that Elizabeth was forced by a Puritan House of Commons to adopt a settlement of religion more Protestant than she herself wanted. By and large, it seems that she got what she wanted in 1559, and if the settlement was opposed in parliament it was by Catholic bishops in the Lords; most Protestants in 1559 were satisfied, although no doubt some hoped that in later years the Queen would develop and purify what had been defined at the beginning. Elizabeth was no bigot or persecutor, but she did insist on outward conformity to this settlement, at least after an initial period of adaptation when laxity was almost inevitable. This insistence on conformity and on protecting the settlement led her into a long battle with Catholics and Puritans, but a battle which in the end she largely won.

In foreign affairs Elizabeth, who was always her own foreign minister in the final decisions, had to watch three countries — France, Spain and Scotland. In 1558 Spain was her ally and Philip II offered her marriage. She declined: she was not going to repeat the mistake of Mary. She saw also that Philip could not afford to break with England while he was at war with France. The problem of

France was closely knit with that of Scotland. The *de jure* Queen of Scotland was Mary Stuart, but she was married to Francis of Valois, heir to the French throne. She was also heir to the English throne; she was already quartering the arms of England with those of Scotland and France, while her own kingdom of Scotland was being governed by the Regent, Marie de Guise, in the interests of France, and her Guise brothers in France were Mary's uncles. In 1559 Philip II of Spain married Elizabeth of Valois. At the same moment the King of France, Henri II, died and Mary became Queen of France as husband of Francis II.

The situation for Elizabeth was complex. The key lay in Scotland. There the Regent's French policy was most unpopular and Protestantism was spreading under the leadership of John Knox. The Protestant Lords of the Congregation were soon at war with the Regent. Clearly Elizabeth had to support the Lords. In 1560 she sent a fleet to stop French reinforcements reaching Scotland and she sent troops to expel the French from Leith. By the Treaty of Edinburgh (1560) she cleared Scotland of the French and left the Protestant Lords in command and in alliance with England, at least for a time.

Thus by 1560 Elizabeth had preserved friendship with Spain, isolated France and bolted the back door from Scotland into England.

To the average Englishman the burning question was that of Elizabeth's marriage. Of course, she must marry, in order to ensure the Protestant succession. But she must not marry a foreigner, as Mary had done so disastrously. Whom could she marry at home? To marry a foreigner was to alienate her people: to marry an Englishman was to stir up civil war. As soon as she came to the throne foreign princes were swarming round her for her hand — the King of Spain, the heir to the Swedish throne, two sons of the Hapsburg Emperor, the Scottish Earl of Arran. Elizabeth would have none of them. Later in her reign, when she wanted to gain time, she played with the idea of marrying the French King, Charles IX, then two of his brothers. In the end she died unmarried. We shall never know whether she wanted to be married, or whether the idea of marriage physically revolted her: whether she was capable or incapable of bearing children. The odds are heavily that she wanted to marry Robert Dudley, and was perfectly capable of having children, but she recognized that politically the marriage was impossible, and Robert was already married to Amy Robsart. Not to be married left her with a trump card for any trick: to use the card was to throw it away for ever. With marvellous dexterity she kept her wooers dangling at the end of a string; with equal dexterity she left the frequent petitions of her Parliaments to marry 'answered answerless'. And when Peter Wentworth in 1576 took her openly to task, she shut him up in the Tower. How important this question of marriage was may be seen from the panic in the country when in 1562 Elizabeth all but died of smallpox. She was saved by a young German doctor who happened to be present when all the other doctors had given her up for lost. He asked for a red blanket in which he wrapped the Queen and set her in front of the fire. In a short while the spots had come out and the Queen's life was saved. There is a tradition that the colour red is the only one which does not aggravate smallpox, and beds with red curtains are often called 'smallpox beds'. Such a bed exists at Charlecote Park, Warwickshire.

Francis II died in 1559, and in 1561 Mary Stuart returned to Scotland. During the next seven years, while Elizabeth was showering honours on Robert Dudley, visiting Cambridge (1564), where she made Latin speeches, visiting Oxford (1566), where she heard Edmund Campion disputing in Latin, while she was refusing Parliament's petitions to marry and to name her successor, and while she was behaving in the most miserly way to her Lord Deputy in Ireland, Sir Henry Sidney, Mary was ruining herself in Scotland. After her defeat at Carberry Hill (1567) she was shut up in Lochleven Castle, but escaped in 1568 and after losing another battle came to England to ask for Elizabeth's help. Elizabeth was in a difficult position: protocol and the laws of hospitality demanded that Elizabeth should listen sympathetically to Mary's requests for aid, but on the other hand, to support the Scottish Queen against her Protestant subjects seemed folly. Elizabeth's handling of Mary after her arrival in England showed the Queen of England's diplomatic skills to the full, although the course she followed was governed more by *realpolitik* than by generosity of spirit. Elizabeth in the end kept Mary prisoner in England permanently, although such a policy developed only gradually. At first Elizabeth's plan was to arrange a tribunal of enquiry to examine the points of dispute between Mary and her Scottish subjects. This tribunal met at York and then at Westminster and Hampton Court in the winter of 1568–9. It decided nothing, but served to bring to English attention the accusations of complicity in Darnley's murder levelled against Mary by her Scottish enemies. By keeping Mary a prisoner, Elizabeth strengthened her hand in Scotland, building up a strongly pro-English party of supporters among the Protestant adherents of the young James VI. The imprisonment of the Scottish Queen also removed from Elizabeth the embarrassing difficulty caused by the undecided succession: English Protestants were now less worried by this since their great enemy, the Catholic heir presumptive, was in safe custody. To have released Mary would have enabled her to go to France or even Spain, there to plot against the Elizabethan party in Scotland and against the Queen herself in England. The danger, of course, was that Mary in England would encourage Catholic conspiracy or stir up the nobility to disturb the state of the realm. This did happen, but on balance it was a price worth paying: Mary would have been far more dangerous at liberty.

The arrival of Mary, Queen of Scots, in England coincided with, and helped to provoke, a major crisis in Elizabeth's affairs. After Elizabeth had been on the throne for ten years those who were discontented with her many compromises became more active. There were those who had always disliked her religious settlement, the Catholics and the Puritans: the old families, such as the Howards, resented her government through the 'new men', such as Cecil: the Northern Catholic families detested her 'interference' with their old independence of the central government, families such as the Nevilles and the Percies. And in foreign affairs relations with Spain were deteriorating. Hawkins's slave-trading voyages had roused tempers on both sides; the expulsion from Spain of the English ambassador had infuriated Elizabeth: Elizabeth's seizure of the Spanish pay ships when they took refuge in English ports (1568) infuriated Philip. Alva retaliated by taking over all English property in the Netherlands, and Elizabeth retorted in like manner in England. It was in these circumstances that a proposal was made that Mary should marry the Duke of Norfolk. The plan was backed by the Northern Catholic Earls and it had the approval of Spain. Its purpose was to marry Mary to Norfolk, to substitute the Mary-Howard (Norfolk) faction for Cecil and his party, and to restore Catholicism, which would inevitably have led to the deposition of Elizabeth. The situation was extremely dangerous, and Cecil was almost in despair. This was one of the crises of the reign, but the Queen knew what was going on and warned Norfolk, who denied any share in the plot. The Northern Earls were thus let down and felt that they must rise at once or never at all. The rebellion was easily put down (1569) and there followed a fearful vengeance — some 450 insignificant rebels were hanged throughout the northern villages.

In 1570, immediately following the Rising, the Pope, Pius V, issued his bull of excommunication, *Regnans in excelsis*, by which Elizabeth's subjects were absolved of their allegiance and Catholic princes were encouraged to invade England. The bull came too late to be of much use to the Northern rebels, and the King of Spain was critical of the Pope for publishing it. What is far more surprising than that it was issued in 1570 was the fact that it had not been delivered before. It strengthened Elizabeth rather than weakened her; by encouraging Protestant loyalty, by discouraging Catholicism, which now became tantamount to disloyalty.

Norfolk had been lucky in 1569 in only being put in the Tower, but he was a weak man who learned nothing. In 1571 he allowed himself for the second time to be involved in a plot by which he was to marry Mary, a rebellion in England was to be aided by a foreign invasion, Elizabeth was to be deposed and Mary made Queen. This was the Ridolfi plot of 1571, as a result of which Parliament demanded the execution of Mary, but Elizabeth refused and refused also her assent to a bill depriving Mary of all interest in the English throne. For a moment she did agree to sending Mary back to Scotland to be put to death, provided that guarantees were given that she would not be kept there alive, and on no account was Elizabeth's name to be mentioned in the negotiations. But the Scots would not agree, and Mary remained in England. But Spain was now clearly hostile and the end of the third civil war in France left that country free to attack England. Elizabeth therefore resorted to the old time-saving (or time-wasting) device of marriage negotiations. The *Politiques*, the moderate Catholics, were now in power in France and were ready for an alliance with England as a counter-weight to Spain. It was proposed that Henry, Duke of Anjou, brother of Charles IX and heir to the French throne, should marry Elizabeth. Nothing came of this, as Anjou on religious grounds refused to marry a Protestant. Then came the Massacre of

St. Bartholomew (1572), which looked as if it must put paid to any Anglo-French alliance. Elizabeth kept the French ambassador waiting for three days for an audience. When it took place, she received the ambassador in dead silence with her councillors and ladies standing round. In the end she accepted his explanation, for in truth she could not afford to break with France. Within a few months she and Catherine de Medici were negotiating a marriage between herself and Charles IX's younger brother, Francis, Duke of Alençon (later Anjou). He was more than twenty years younger than Elizabeth, a dwarf, ugly and pock-marked. From 1572 to 1584 she kept her 'frog' on tenterhooks, until he died in that year unmarried. This proposed marriage was very unpopular and was openly attacked by Sidney, and indirectly by Spenser (in *Mother Hubbard's Tale*).

Elizabeth's marriage negotiations with the Duke of Anjou were closely tied up with the revolt of the Netherlands against Spain which began in 1568. This produced inside the Spanish dominions a Protestant party corresponding with the Huguenot party inside France. From 1561 to 1563 Elizabeth had given some help to these Huguenots: she got little advantage out of it and she spent more money than she could afford. When the Netherlands revolted, there were statesmen in England, like Walsingham, who wanted Elizabeth to go all out in support of these Continental Protestants. She refused, for she knew that a religious war could only split England from top to bottom. On the other hand, she recognized the opportunities which these revolts gave her to weaken her enemies abroad. She was therefore ready to give secret and limited aid, which later through force of circumstances became open and considerably greater, but she did this, not on religious grounds, but simply on grounds of policy. In the 1570s she helped the Dutch, because she did not want a Dutch Protestant victory as a result of French help — that would have subordinated the Netherlands to France and brought France much too near the English Channel ports. So it was that, when the Dutch turned to the Duke of Anjou for help against Spain, Elizabeth at once began her prolonged marriage negotiations with Anjou. The Queen was criticized for never giving enough help to bring victory to the Huguenots or the Dutch, but she never wanted them to be victorious. She was concerned much more to stoke the fires and keep the rebels fighting in order to weaken her enemies abroad. It was not the salvation of French or Dutch Protestantism which Elizabeth had in view: it was the salvation of England.

In 1584 things came to a head. Anjou died, which ended the marriage plans; William the Silent was murdered, which left Elizabeth the unwilling leader of Protestantism in Europe. Spain had apparently strengthened herself by the conquest of Portugal, and Parma had all but finished off the Dutch revolt. Once Philip was free of the Dutch he would turn his attention to the invasion of England, with a convenient jumping-off ground in the Netherlands. Reluctantly Elizabeth realized there was nothing for it but to send immediate help to the Dutch — hence Leicester's expedition of 1585 and Drake's voyage to the Spanish Main. Leicester proved a complete failure; Drake was brilliantly successful. But at home difficulties were piling up. The Puritans were voicing their discontent; the arrival of the missionary priests showed all too clearly the potential danger from the Catholics. Persecution of the Catholics increased and the roll of Catholic martyrs mounted. Always Elizabeth tried to mitigate the severities and to separate religion from politics. But on the home front the root of the danger lay in Mary, Queen of Scots. She was the centre of every Catholic plot. The revelations made by Throckmorton in 1583 drove Cecil and Walsingham to entrap Mary beyond escape. The Babington plot of 1586 sealed her fate: she was tried, condemned and sentenced to death. The problem was to bring Elizabeth to sign the death warrant. For months she hesitated, then at last she gave way and on 1 February 1587, she signed it. Mary was executed at Fotheringay on 8 February. Elizabeth flew into a passion: she went into mourning, she railed at her ministers, she sent her Secretary Davison to the Tower, and she protested that the warrant had been sent off without her knowledge or consent. But Davison's salary was paid all the time he was in the Tower. If this was play-acting, as most of it was, it was wasted effort, for scarcely a tremor appeared on any political seismograph in Europe. Elizabeth's hesitations had arisen from a struggle between her personal feelings and her political instincts. As usual, her political instincts triumphed, but as usual she did her best to get rid of the responsibility.

The execution of Mary Stuart immensely strengthened England, for it removed the only conceivable alternative to Elizabeth in the eyes of the English Catholics. Elizabeth's main objective was now achieved: England was united and able to meet the invader. When in 1588 the Spanish Armada came, the government had no need to worry about Catholic Quislings. The ships built by Hawkins, Drake's offensive expeditions before the battle and his seamanship during the battle, the co-operation and commonsense of Howard of Effingham, the stage-management by Leicester at the camp at Tilbury, and not least the heroic leadership of the Queen herself, saw England through the sixteenth-century Battle of Britain. Elizabeth's speech to her troops at Tilbury remains one of the greatest in the English language.

> My loving people, we have been persuaded by some that are careful of our safety to take heed how we commit ourselves to armed multitudes for fear of treachery. Let tyrants fear. I have always so behaved myself that, under God, I have placed my chiefest strength and safeguard in the loyal hearts and goodwill of my subjects. And therefore I am come amongst you, as you see at this time, not for my recreation and disport, but being resolved, in the midst and heat of the battle, to live or die amongst you all; to lay down for my God and for my kingdom and for my people my honour and my blood, even in the dust. I know I have the body of a weak and feeble woman, but I have the heart and stomach of a king, and of a king of England too; and think foul scorn that Parma or Spain, or any prince of Europe, should dare invade the borders of my realm . . .

For thirty years Elizabeth had striven to unify the country against foreign invasion. That invasion had come and been defeated. The Queen was at the height of her fame and popularity. But she had fifteen years more to live and to govern the country. These were to prove years of anti-climax. She was to remain, but her old friends and advisers were slipping away. By 1596 they had all gone — Leicester, Knollys, Hatton, Walsingham, Hawkins, Drake, Frobisher, and two years later Burghley died. The Queen was virtually alone, only Burghley's son, Robert Cecil, and Whitgift were there to help her. The Elizabethan system was beginning to creak as early as 1588, when the Martin Marprelate attacks were launched against episcopacy in general and Archbishop Whitgift in particular, Elizabeth's 'little black husband'. The religious feuds were to go on for the rest of the reign and to them were added quarrels between the Crown and Parliament in which Peter Wentworth appeared at last to be attacking, if not monarchy itself, at least the monarch, for which Elizabeth sent him to the Tower. The session of 1597–8 was rowdy enough, and Elizabeth vetoed twelve bills of small importance: that of 1601 was even more violent — 'more fit for a grammar school than a court of Parliament', said Robert Cecil, while the Commons 'hawked, spat and hemmed'. The Queen also fell foul of the Commons over monopolies in 1597 and again in 1601, when she was compelled to give way, which she did with all her old skill and graciousness. War continued in the Netherlands; in France, where she had to support Henry of Navarre; in Ireland, where a long and expensive struggle showed few signs of ending. As a result the national finances became dangerously involved and Elizabeth had to call Parliament and ask for supply, a course particularly odious to her. At court new and young men, impatiently waiting for new policies, for promotion and for opportunities for fame and fortune, spent their time quarrelling and building factions. In her old age the Queen tried desperately to recreate the atmosphere and relationships of her youth and she turned to Robert Devereux, Earl of Essex, on whom she lavished honours, offices and affection, only to find out — for her judgement of men never failed her — that he was worthy of none of them. In him was centred all the discontent of the young courtiers. His rebellion in 1601 was a direct challenge to the whole Tudor system and to the Queen herself. She met it with invincible courage — she was barely restrained at the age of 68 from going out into the streets to see whether any rebel dared fire a shot at her. The rebellion failed, and Essex was executed in February 1601. Once again she was forced to decide between her personal feelings and her public duty, and once again duty won, but it must have been a terrible blow to send to the block the stepson of her once beloved Robert Dudley, Earl of Leicester.

For another year Elizabeth remained in good health and good spirits, but by 1602 she was beginning to lose vitality and interest, she was convinced that she was going to die; she began to refuse food, to decline to take any medicine and even to go to bed. Finally she lost her power of speech, but not her wits and understanding. She died early in the morning of 24 March 1603.

Elizabeth had reigned for forty-five years, the longest reign since

Edward III's and until George III's. It was one of the great creative periods in English history — in the realm of literature, of music, of architecture, in the art of limning, if not in that of painting, in exploration and the expansion of trade. Men saw Elizabeth as the inspiration of their work and the idol of their worship. She became Gloriana, the 'Faerie Queen', and we still call those forty-five years the 'Age of Elizabeth', the 'spacious days of good Queen Bess'. And yet the writers got nothing out of her for all their flattering patriotism: the sailors could only expect her support if their voyages caused no diplomatic trouble and — more important — produced a handsome profit. Nor would she risk money on 'plantations' overseas: Elizabeth was no expansionist. She was a conservative through and through, an admirable conservative builder in her early years, a dangerous and obscurantist conservative in her later years, with the result that she left to her successor, James I, a number of unsolved problems — the relations of Crown and Parliament, the desperate state of the national finances, the religious problem of the Puritans and Catholics.

How, then, did this extraordinary woman succeed in identifying herself with the age in which she lived — for it was not only the English who recognized her qualities? Pope Sixtus V said of her, 'she is certainly a great Queen and were she only a Catholic she would be our dearly beloved. Just look how well she governs! She is only a woman, only mistress of half an island, and yet she makes herself feared by Spain, by France, by the Empire, by all.' The answer seems to be by skill and by character. The cult of monarchy reached its height in England in Elizabeth's reign. (By the end of the reign this idea was already a trifle *démodé*.) A semi-religious, almost a semi-deified idol was exactly what the English people needed, looked for and enthusiastically accepted as a rallying point for their national life and their individual patriotism. Elizabeth recognized this opportunity and exploited it to the full. It suited exactly her own sense of nationalism, her innate vanity and that vein of vulgarity which was never far below the surface of her character. At the same time, it called forth the best that was in her — her unfailing sense of duty and service, her usually invincible courage, her uncanny judgement of men, and her astonishing ability to remain regal and yet never to lose the common touch. Her love of dresses and jewels delighted her subjects, her enjoyment in showing herself to her subjects was only equalled by their enthusiasm at her progresses: her wit, her repartee, her eloquence and her graciousness were only heightened by her frequent loss of temper, her violent oaths, her beer-drinking and her conforming to the conventional habit of spitting. People felt that she was the finest example of one of themselves. In an age which was on the whole savage and cruel, she could be and was ruthless and savage — as after the rebellion of the Northern Earls. She could be furious, abusive and formidable, yet (as Sir John Harington said) her smile 'was pure sunshine'. She could be disloyal to her ministers, but she never lost their loyalty: she could speak the most bitter words, yet she could write the most enchanting and heart-warming letters. She could hesitate and vacillate, change her mind and be criminally cautious, yet she could take the most dangerous risks against the wishes of her ministers and prove herself right. She had a wonderful flair for politics and a most discerning eye in foreign affairs — more discerning than those of her ministers. Nothing is more remarkable about her than the immense impression she made, even in her old age, on the foreign ambassadors who visited her. They might remark on her black teeth and her low-cut dresses, they might feel that she was 'strangely attired', they might note her loss of temper and her restlessness, but they all recognized her extraordinary grasp and understanding of the European political stage. Much of her financial tight-fistedness was due to her recognition that taxation caused more discontent than anything else: much of her shirking of responsibility is to be explained by her recognition that on her depended the unity and safety of the country: better that ministers and bishops should bear undeserved unpopularity than that the *mystique* of royalty should be undermined. The secret of her astounding success she herself revealed in her last speech: 'though God hath raised me high, yet this I count the glory of my reign, that I have reigned with your loves.'

J. E. Neale, *Queen Elizabeth I*, 1934.
C. Morris, *The Tudors*, 1955.
J. Hurstfield, *Elizabeth I and the unity of England*, 1960.
C. Haigh (ed.), *The Reign of Elizabeth I*, 1984.
P. Williams, *The Tudor Regime*, 1979.
C. Haigh, *Elizabeth I*, 1988.
J. Ridley, *Elizabeth I*, 1987.

WILLIAM CECIL, LORD BURGHLEY (1520–1598), statesman, was the son of Richard Cecil and his wife, Jane Heckington
of Lincolnshire. His grandfather, David Cecil, had thrown in his
lot on the side of Henry VII at Bosworth Field and thus laid the
foundations of the family fortunes. He became a member of Henry's
Yeomen of the Guard, and Richard held several minor appointments
at Court.

William was educated at the grammar school in Grantham and
then at the grammar school at Stamford. In 1535 he went to St.
John's College, Cambridge, where he proved himself a first-class
classical scholar and became friends with such men as Cheke and
Ascham. In 1542 he fell in love with and married Cheke's sister,
Mary, but his father looked askance at the marriage, for Mary's
mother was only an innkeeper in Cambridge. There was one son of
the marriage, Thomas, who never got on well with his father, and it
cannot be said that William ever showed him much affection or
consideration. Later, he became the first Earl of Exeter. It may have
been because of this indiscreet marriage that William left Cambridge
without a degree.

Mary died in 1544. The next year William married a very
remarkable woman, Mildred Cooke, a noted Greek scholar and
Protestant, who was to influence William's life considerably in the
future. Mildred's sister, Anne, married Nicholas Bacon, later
Elizabeth's Lord Keeper and father of Sir Francis Bacon.

Richard Cecil's position at Court ensured William's being noticed
by Henry VIII, but the truth is that only a little is known about
William's life before he became Secretary of State to Elizabeth I,
when she came to the throne. Probably thanks to Cheke and
Ascham, who were tutors to the King, Edward VI, and to the
Princess Elizabeth respectively, William entered the secretariat of
Protector Somerset in 1547. He went with Somerset to Pinkie
Cleugh: he was made Master of Requests during the winter of 1547,
and in the next year he became Somerset's private secretary. About
this time he entered Parliament for Stamford. He sat on a commission to enquire into Anabaptism and on another to review the books
printed in England dealing with religious matters. On the fall of
Somerset (1549) Cecil spent two months in the Tower (1550), but
on his release he was appointed Principal Secretary of State by
Northumberland. Cecil was now beginning to appear as one of those

William Cecil, Lord Burghley
(Artist: Unknown)

professional politicians who find their way into every successive government. It was in this year that Princess Elizabeth appointed him her Surveyor (or estate agent), but the duties were carried out by a deputy and Cecil seems to have had little direct contact with Elizabeth. In 1551 he was knighted, in 1552 he was made chancellor of the Order of the Garter, a post which he had to surrender when Mary I came to the throne. When Northumberland hatched his plot for putting Lady Jane Grey on the throne, Cecil played a most ambiguous part. When he was compelled to sign the 'device', he protested that he signed only 'as a witness': during the nine days when Lady Jane was Queen, Cecil seems to have done as much as he could secretly to thwart Northumberland's plans. So adroit was his conduct that Mary I gave him a general pardon and renewed his commission as Justice of the Peace for Lincolnshire. In the course of her short reign Cecil was twice employed on diplomatic embassies, once to fetch Cardinal Pole to England and once to share in the attempts to make peace between the Emperor and the King of France. He seems also to have played a fairly important part in the 1555 Parliament, especially as a drafter of bills and over a bill to check enclosures.

For at least a fortnight before Mary died Elizabeth was making arrangements for her succession. She had already chosen her Principal Secretary of State, so that at the first meeting of her Privy Council she appointed William Cecil to that position with the well-known tribute, 'I give you this charge that you shall be of my Privy Council and content to take pains for me and my realm. This judgment I have of you, that you will not be corrupted by any manner of gift and that you will be faithful to the state; and that without respect of my private gain will you give me that counsel which you think best, and if you shall know anything necessary to be declared to me of secrecy, you shall show it to myself only. And assure yourself I will not fail to keep taciturnity therein and therefore herewith I charge you.' Thus began forty years of partnership between Queen and minister, the longest in English history. Often Cecil criticized his mistress, often Elizabeth railed against her minister; after Mary, Queen of Scots, was executed, her fury was so great that Cecil dared not go to Court. But through all the stresses and strains the trust was never betrayed and the support was never withdrawn, and when at last, worn out and dying, Cecil was visited by the Queen as he lay in bed, she fed him 'with her own princely hand'. A short while before she had written to him that he was 'to her in all things and shall be Alpha and Omega.'

During these forty years, from 1558 to 1598, Cecil held three chief offices of state. From 1558 to 1572 he was Principal Secretary of State. He had to handle all the routine business of the Council and its relations with the Queen: he was responsible for the administration of foreign policy; he had to be well informed about all matters of defence, of public finance, of public relations between the Crown and the country, of the Church of England and its enemies. This involved him with jealous colleagues, jealous courtiers and a very temperamental mistress (Conyers Read, i, p. 121). From 1561 until 1598 he was Master of the Court of Wards, a post of immense importance, since wardship was, or should have been, one of the chief sources of revenue to the Crown, and also the most lucrative post for its holder. It was through the profits which he derived as Master that Cecil built up the huge income which enabled him to live in style and to build his great houses of Theobalds and Burghley. (For a full discussion of Cecil's emoluments from this office, see Hurstfield, *The Queen's Wards*.) From 1572 to 1598 Cecil was Lord Treasurer, the most important of all the offices. As Lord Treasurer he administered the royal finances and he also presided over the Court of Exchequer. In this capacity, as well as in that of Master of the Court of Wards, Cecil filled an important place in the English judiciary.

A biography of Cecil, therefore, is really a history of England from 1558 to 1598, a period to which Froude devoted three solid volumes. Not much more can be attempted here than to indicate Cecil's political and religious views and policies and to try to show what sort of a man he was. And here one is met at once with a further difficulty. If there is an appalling mass of letters and memoranda available to the political biographer — over one hundred folio volumes at the British Museum, over two hundred folio volumes at Hatfield House, and an incalculable number of state papers at the Public Record Office — only a very small number of Cecil's outgoing letters survive, and of his purely personal and family correspondence only one doubtful letter to his wife.

In 1571 William Cecil became Lord Burghley, the only one of Elizabeth's ministers to receive a peerage. The next year he was made a Knight of the Garter. In 1589 he suffered a grievous loss in the death of his wife. He had nine more years of life ahead of him, during which he suffered much ill health, especially from gout, and was forced to ride round his estates on a mule: the last five years he grew increasingly feeble and had to be carried wherever he went; he was also extremely deaf. But his mental powers never decayed and in his seventy-eighth year he still sat with the Privy Council. His son, Robert, was made Principal Secretary in 1596 and for the last two years of Burghley's life Robert took over virtually all the routine business of government. Burghley died on 4 August 1598.

'Perhaps the greatest of his achievements was that he managed by great tact, great wisdom and great integrity of purpose, along with a nice sense of what was practicable and possible, to advance from strength to strength' (C. Read, i, 122), so that he became indisputably the Queen's first minister. Regarded as a 'new man', he was hated by the older families, but not even Leicester's attempts to drive him from office succeeded. One reason for the Queen's unfailing support was that her views on policy were very close to Burghley's views. Burghley was essentially a conservative, by instinct as well as by reason opposed to rash schemes and extreme methods. He saw as clearly as did Elizabeth that the two threats to the safety of England were in fact one and the same threat, that the dangers from foreign invasion were inextricably bound up with the religious dangers at home.

In foreign policy both saw that for England, geographically placed as she was in relation to France and Spain, both Catholic countries, war was to be avoided as long as possible. Both realized that the nation's resources were not equal to a prolonged conflict. Both believed that unity was essential, if war came, and that to go to war on religious grounds would not produce national unity. Both understood that the survival of England was bound up with the survival of the Netherlands, and therefore both reluctantly accepted war with Spain in the Netherlands, when it became clear that diplomacy would no longer serve.

In religion Burghley was never publicly a Puritan — he quarrelled more often with the Puritans than he agreed with them, but nothing shows more clearly his common sense than his warning to Whitgift in 1584 not to attack the Puritans in a manner 'as I think the Inquisitors of Spain use not . . . to trap their prey'. He also made the

Puritan Travers tutor to his children and protected his relation, Robert Browne, the separatist.

As a financier Burghley was always a conservative. Indeed, it has been charged against him that, inheriting an old-fashioned and inefficient system of national finances, he did nothing to reform and modernize it, being content merely to improve where he could. Certainly as Master of the Court of Wards he accepted the conventions of his times by which salaries of state officials were supplemented by gifts and profits incidental to the sale of wardships, and by his efficiency he greatly furthered his own interests, even at the expense of the Queen.

But at the same time he was developing and putting into practice an economic policy of first rate importance. By 1561, with the help of Gresham, he had restored a sound currency with a new silver coinage, minted at a profit to the Crown. He set about reducing ordinary expenditure and also making the defences of the country independent of foreign sources for gunpowder and naval stores. He developed mining for copper and tin and the growing of hemp: he paid bounties on shipbuilding, repaired harbours and made the people eat fish, not only in Lent, but on two days a week all the year round, in order to expand the fisheries which in turn expanded the number of mariners. He looked on piracy as 'detestable', pinning his faith rather on the finding of new markets and on encouraging foreigners to migrate into England. His whole policy was codified in 1563 in the Statute of Labourers. Mediaeval usury laws were abolished and interest was legalized up to ten per cent. Indeed, Cecil was proving himself to be one of the earliest of the long line of conservative reformers. (K. Feiling, *A History of England*, pp. 391, *ff.*)

In one department of government Burghley was invaluable to the Queen — as her public relations officer. He was an indefatigable writer of pamphlets and he would use foreign channels for promoting English policy. His literary style was unattractive, but his great merit was that 'he never sought to display his own cleverness... or to advance his own interests. He sought only to promote the cause and serve his mistress' (C. Read in *Elizabethan Government and Society*, 1961).

William Cecil, Lord Burghley, must be accounted one of the greatest of English statesmen. For forty years (together with

Elizabeth, who always had the final say) he guided the country through a maze of dangers at home and abroad. But there was nothing of the saint or of the hero in him, little of the genius. Camden wrote of him that 'of all men of genius, he was the most of a drudge; of all men of business the most of a genius'. In religion he was an upright, God-fearing man, who held faithfully to the Christian faith, but who cared little about its particular form. He could never have survived the religious difficulties of his earlier years, if he had not been unheroically pliant in the days of Northumberland and Mary I — and it was as well for England that he did survive. He could never have maintained himself in office under Elizabeth I, if he had not been as wary and cunning as a fox. He could never have saved England from sedition, privy conspiracy and rebellion, if he had not been ready to use all the weapons available in his time, which included the use of torture — but he never condoned political assassination — and to be resolute to the verge of ruthlessness, as he was over Mary, Queen of Scots. By superhuman industry, by devotion to his Queen and country and by subordinating himself to the service of both, he, as much as the younger Pitt, became the pilot that weathered the storm.

In his private life Burghley was a devoted son, a faithful husband and a loving father, except to the unsatisfactory Thomas. Although he lived in sumptuous style, he himself ate very little and seldom drank wine. His chief recreations were gardening and reading in Latin, French and Italian books (seldom in English), or riding upon his little mule. He was blessed with an unfailing memory, which enabled him to dispatch business quickly. To his friends he was by nature kind, courteous and affable, and very loyal, as Robert Browne, the Separatist, discovered. His whole life bears witness to the advice he gave his son, Robert: 'serve God by serving of the Queen, for all other service indeed is bondage to the devil'.

C. Read, *Mr. Secretary Cecil and Queen Elizabeth*, 1955. *Lord Burghley and Queen Elizabeth*, 1960.

J. Hurstfield, *The Queen's Wards*, 1958.

J. Hurstfield, *History Today*, December, 1956.

C. Read, 'William Cecil and Elizabethan Public Relations', in S. T. Bindoff *et al.* (eds.), *Elizabethan Government and Society*, 1961.

B. W. Beckingsale, *Burghley: Tudor Statesman*, 1967.

SIR FRANCIS WALSINGHAM (1532–1590), Secretary of State, was the only son among the six children of William Walsingham of Footscray in Kent and of his wife Joyce, daughter of Sir Edmund Denny of Cheshunt in Hertfordshire. His father died in 1533, and Joyce married Sir John Carey, uncle of the first Lord Hunsdon. Francis went up to King's, Cambridge, in 1548 and came down probably in 1550 without having taken a degree. The Denny family had strong Protestant leanings and King's was one of the most Protestant colleges in Cambridge, under its Provost Cheke: Francis must have been influenced by his surroundings, the more so since his tutor, Gardiner, was also a strong Protestant, and in 1549 Martin Bucer arrived in Cambridge and became Professor of Hebrew, being himself one of the greatest of the Protestant scholars. Francis was to be all his life an ardent and uncompromising Protestant.

Between 1550 and 1552 Walsingham was abroad learning the French and Italian languages. He was by nature a facile linguist, and this gift was to be the foundation of his political success when he entered the Queen's service in 1568. He was entered as a member of Gray's Inn in 1552, but the next year the Catholic Mary Tudor succeeded to the throne and Walsingham left the country, ostensibly on the grounds of religion. Conyers Read suggests that possibly there were other reasons: that he might have been involved in the Protestant plots of Northumberland and Wyatt (*Sir Francis Walsingham*, i, 22). During this exile he was at Padua University where he was appointed Consularius of the English Nation in the Faculty of Civil Law, a post he held from 1555 to the spring of 1556. During his sojourn in Italy he not only perfected his Italian, but he also learned much law and studied the political systems of Continental countries. It is possible that before he returned home he visited Switzerland and had contacts with English Protestant exiles in Basle, Strasbourg and Frankfurt. He was certainly back in England in 1560, by which time Elizabeth I was on the throne.

In 1562 he was returned for the first time as M.P. for both Banbury and Lyme Regis: he chose to represent Lyme Regis. In that year he married a widow, Anne Carleill, who died in 1564 and gave him no children. Two years later he married the widow of Sir

Sir Francis Walsingham
(Artist: Attributed to J. de Critz the Elder)

Richard Worsley of the Isle of Wight, by whom he had one daughter, who married Sir Philip Sidney, and one who died early. In 1568 he entered the service of the Queen, and he remained her most loyal servant for the next twenty-two years, up to the day of his death.

No doubt it was Walsingham's knowledge of foreign languages and the contacts which he maintained with friends abroad which first commended him to Burghley. In 1568 Walsingham supplied Cecil with a list of all persons arriving in Italy who might be dangerous to the Queen and her government. In 1569 he was employed by the government's secret service in London and he played a part in unravelling the Ridolfi plot, although at one point he was completely hood-winked by Ridolfi.

From 1570 Walsingham was employed almost entirely on foreign affairs. In that year he was in France trying to secure toleration for the Huguenots. He was engaged in the matter of Elizabeth's projected marriage with Anjou. And in December of that year he supplanted Norris as ambassador in Paris. In conjunction with Sir Thomas Smith he negotiated the Treaty of Blois (1572), but friendship with France was disturbed by the Massacre of St. Bartholomew (24 August 1572), which event left a lasting impression on Walsingham and much increased his Protestant fanaticism. In 1573 he left Paris and was made Secretary of State, a position he held until his death in 1590.

His administration of what we should now call the Foreign Office was shared to a large extent with Burghley, but it must be remembered that in foreign affairs the final decisions were Elizabeth's decisions. Broadly speaking, Burghley and the Queen saw eye to eye in foreign affairs, and broadly speaking their policy was to play for time and to avoid committing themselves to one side or the other. This was diametrically opposed to Walsingham's views. He was not, like Burghley, a politician who was ready to trim his sails to suit the weather. Walsingham was an ardent Puritan and a man of inflexible principle. He had made up his mind that the one thing necessary for the safety of the country was the utter defeat of Spain and the removal of Mary, Queen of Scots. He was, therefore, uncompromisingly in favour of an alliance with Huguenot France and active intervention in the revolt of the Netherlands against Spain. James VI and Scotland must be made into friends. He was fully convinced that the struggle in Europe was not one between nation and nation, but between Catholicism and Protestantism. Walsingham was wrong in this belief. Elizabeth and Burghley had a juster understanding of the true state of affairs: that nationalism was a stronger force in Europe than religion. Walsingham was fearlessly outspoken to the Queen in advocating his policy and trying to persuade her that hers was wrong, and Elizabeth was often driven to outbursts of fury against him. But she continued to use him in all her diplomatic business. At first sight this is inexplicable, but probably the reasons are these: first and foremost, she knew that she could trust Walsingham to do his best to achieve her policy, however much he himself was personally opposed to it. She never doubted his abilities or his loyalty. In 1578 he was sent to the Low Countries to pursue a policy which Elizabeth knew well enough was exactly the opposite to what Walsingham approved. Walsingham bitterly resented the vacillations and procrastinations of the Queen, yet he accepted, 'with never so ill a will', a mission to Scotland which might involve him in humiliation (1583). He must have had one moment of pleasure when in 1585 he was able to negotiate with the Dutch commissioner in London the terms on which the Queen was ready to support the Netherlands against Spain. But even then by her vacillation and parsimony Walsingham was 'utterly discouraged'. From first to last Walsingham never had any success with the Queen in advocating his policy and methods.

A second reason for using Walsingham was that he was always able to supply the fullest and most reliable information. His secret service was extraordinarily efficient. On it he spent the whole of his private fortune, so that he died in the utmost poverty. He had at times in his pay fifty-three agents in foreign courts and eighteen other spies. He would get the fullest information from thirteen towns in France, seven in the Low Countries, five in Spain, five in Italy, nine in Germany, three in the United Provinces, three in Turkey. He was both patient and ingenious in ferreting out the plots raised against Elizabeth, as, for example, the Parry and the Babington plots. Many of his agents were disreputable characters — he employed Christopher Marlowe — and Walsingham himself employed Machiavellian methods, but there is no conclusive evidence that he ever strained the law or justice against his victims. There was no cruelty in Walsingham: he regarded the Catholics as political dangers and as such they must be got out of the way, but he was strongly opposed to making them into martyrs: he preferred to have them detained or deported, and he once had an idea of founding an American colony for them. Only against Mary, Queen of Scots, 'that devilish woman', as he called her, was he determined to go to extremes, for he believed that she was the cause of all the trouble and that as long as she lived Elizabeth and the country were in the direst danger. After her execution he set about organizing the defences of the country against the Spanish invasion, which he clearly foresaw. Burghley told him 'you have fought more with your pen than many here in our English navy with their enemies'.

Ardent Protestant as Walsingham was, he was no fanatic. Camden called him 'a most sharp maintainer of the purer religion', but Walsingham himself understood that unity was essential, if English Protestantism was to survive. 'I would have all reformation done by public authority: it were very dangerous that every private man's zeal should carry sufficient authority of reforming things amiss.' He also held that men's consciences were 'not to be forced, but to be won and seduced by the force of truth, with the aid of time and the use of all good means of instruction and persuasion'. On the other hand, breaches of the law and peace and order he would have visited with the sternest measures.

Walsingham was a man who kept up with his times. He was a great supporter of all overseas adventures and he subscribed to Fenton's voyage in 1582–3: he took Richard Hakluyt into his pay, and Hakluyt dedicated the first edition of his *Voyages* to him; he corresponded with Lane, the explorer of Virginia, with Grenville and with Gilbert. He was greatly interested in the literature of his time and he was known to all the leading men of letters. All forms of learning earned his admiration and often his patronage — he founded a Divinity lecture at Oxford and he gave a polyglot Bible to King's College, Cambridge. Worldly honours did not much interest him, and Elizabeth was chary of rewarding her public servants — only Cecil was given a peerage. Walsingham's reward was a knighthood (1577). He was also made Chancellor of the Duchy of Lancaster (1587) and Chancellor of the Order of the Garter (1578).

Walsingham died on 6 April 1590. The news reached Philip II of Spain in a letter from a Spanish agent in England, who wrote 'Secretary Walsingham has just expired, at the which there is much sorrow'. Philip scribbled in the margin 'There, yes! But it is good news here'. That would have satisfied Walsingham as his epitaph.

Conyers Read, *Sir Francis Walsingham*, 1925.

ROBERT DUDLEY, EARL OF LEICESTER (1533–1588), was born on 24 June 1533 (Elizabeth I was born on 7 September 1533), and died on 4 September 1588. He was the fifth son of John Dudley, Earl of Warwick, Duke of Northumberland (executed 1553), and a grandson of Edmund Dudley, Henry VII's finance minister, who was also executed. At an early age he was brought into the society of Edward VI and of the Princess Elizabeth, and shared some of his education with them; thus Roger Ascham taught him Latin, as he did Elizabeth. Robert was well educated and showed a preference for mathematics.

On 4 June 1550, he married Amy Robsart of Norfolk, a marriage which William Cecil described as 'begun in passion, ended in mourning'. Robert was then seventeen; in 1552 he became M.P. for Norfolk and he supported his father's attempt to exclude Mary Tudor and Elizabeth from the throne in order to make his sister-in-law, Lady Jane Grey, Queen. On the failure of this conspiracy Robert was arrested and put in the Tower, where his wife was allowed to visit him — a sign that she and Robert were then on good terms. In January 1554 Robert was sentenced to death, but after a year he was released and pardoned, probably because Philip II wished to win over the English nobility. Dudley was just the sort of young man whose jousting expertise would make him an ornament at the royal court. In 1557, when war between France and England broke out, Robert and his family were restored in blood. In return, Robert raised troops to serve abroad, and he fought at the battle of St Quentin, where the English served most bravely under Spanish command.

On the accession of Elizabeth I Dudley lost no time in appearing at Court. He was made Master of the Queen's Horse — a post for which he was peculiarly suited by his knowledge of horses, his superb skill as a horseman and his great administrative powers. On 23 April 1559 he was created a Knight of the Garter. This rapid advance in the royal favour made Dudley exceedingly unpopular with the older families, such as the Duke of Norfolk and his friends, and their hatred was only increased by the palpable fact that the Queen was infatuated with this son of a man who had been executed for treason. Already the Spanish ambassador was writing to Philip II of Robert Dudley as 'the king that is to be'.

Most of Elizabeth's favourites were given nicknames by the Queen. Robert Dudley she named her 'eyes', which explains the symbol OO which he frequently used in his letters to Elizabeth in

Robert Dudley, Earl of Leicester
(Artist: Nicholas Hilliard)

place of his own name. Leicester's enemies called him 'the gypsy'.

There is plenty of evidence to prove that Dudley, throughout the years 1558 and 1559 was on excellent terms with his wife, but there were plenty of malicious tongues to suggest that Amy was an obstacle in the way of Dudley's highest ambition and that he was planning to be rid of her. On Sunday, 8 September 1560, Amy was found dead at the foot of the stairs in the house of a family friend at Cumnor, near Oxford. Every kind of rumour spread like wildfire: the Spanish ambassador has been represented as writing to Philip II that the Queen had told him of the death the day before it happened. There is not a shred of evidence for this. Inevitably, Amy was said to have been murdered at the instigation of her husband. Again, there is no evidence to prove this. The most convincing discussion on the cause of her death is to be found written by Professor Ian Aird in the *English Historical Review*, 1956, where he uses modern medical science to show that the most likely cause of death was a fall brought about by cancer of the breast, from which it is known that Amy Robsart was suffering. Robert Dudley took all possible steps to ensure that the inquest was held before a wholly impartial jury, which returned a verdict of accidental death. This was not enough to clear Dudley in the eyes of the world, nor was he helped by the fact that his relations with the Queen became closer and closer after Amy's death.

In 1562 Dudley was sworn of the Privy Council and chosen as High Steward of Cambridge University: two years later he was created Baron Denbigh and Earl of Leicester and became Chancellor of Oxford University. In the previous year (1563), when Mary, Queen of Scots, was in search of a husband, Elizabeth made the staggering suggestion that she should marry Robert Dudley, and it has been thought that the grant of an Earldom was a move in this diplomatic game, for it was urgent that neither a Spaniard nor a Frenchman should marry the Scottish sovereign. What were Elizabeth's motives, or how genuine was her offer, will never be known: what is certain is that Dudley had no intention of sacrificing his chances of marrying Elizabeth by accepting Mary Stuart, and he himself called the whole proposal a 'fetch'. The episode was closed when Mary married Darnley.

In 1566 the Archbishop of Canterbury, Matthew Parker, issued an ordinance to impose uniformity in church ritual and vestments. The Puritans turned to Leicester for help and it became apparent that he was prepared to offer them some support. His reasons for doing so are obscure: Strype believed that Leicester had joined that party 'on some displeasure with the Archbishop and for other ends'. (P. Collinson, *Letters of Thomas Wood 1566–77*, Introduction). From this time forward Leicester became a bitter opponent of the Catholics. Years later this was to cause him much grief. In 1566, when the Queen was being entertained by Oxford University, a young man of the name of Edmund Campion made a speech in front of her of such brilliance and charm that she specially commended him to Leicester. Leicester proved a faithful and generous patron, and Campion freely acknowledged the debt when he dedicated his *History of Ireland* to Leicester in 1571. In 1581 Campion was arrested as a Jesuit missionary. The Queen and Leicester both personally interviewed Campion and Elizabeth did her best to save the young man's life, but he refused all her generous offers. When he came to be hanged and quartered, the executioner had orders that Campion was not to be cut down from the gallows until he was dead. It seems likely that those orders came from Leicester.

The arrival in England of the Queen of Scots in 1568 and her imprisonment raised all kinds of difficulties for the government. In 1569 a plot was hatched to rescue Mary from her prison at Tutbury and to marry her to the Duke of Norfolk. For some reason Leicester supported the idea of her marrying Norfolk, but he was not privy to the Rising of the Northern Earls and he lost none of the Queen's favour through it.

About this time — perhaps as early as 1568, certainly by 1573 — Leicester became embroiled in what was probably his worst indiscretion: he had a liaison with Douglass, widow of Lord Sheffield and sister of Lord Howard of Effingham. Whether Leicester married Lady Sheffield or not is unclear; if he did so, it was in the strictest secrecy and was never acknowledged in his lifetime. There was a son by this misalliance, who was named Robert and was recognized by Leicester as his son. He was given the best possible education and grew up to be very like his father. He eventually married Alice Leigh, of Stoneleigh, in Warwickshire, by whom he had several daughters. He left wife and children and went to Italy in company with his lovely cousin, Elizabeth Southwell, dressed as a boy, and made a name for himself as a navigator, explorer and naval architect.

On 7 May 1574, the first royal patent granted to actors in this country was given to Leicester for 'Lord Leicester's Men', the chief of whom was James Burbage. He had already in 1571 founded by Act of Parliament a hospital for twelve poor men at Warwick, which still exists.

1575 saw the marvellous entertainment which Leicester provided for the Queen at Kenilworth, and which Shakespeare is supposed to have witnessed as a boy of 11 and to have commemorated later in his *Midsummer Night's Dream* in Oberon's vision (II, ii, 98 *seqq.*), with its hidden reference to the Queen and Lady Sheffield:

> Cupid alarmed, a certain aim he took
> At a fair vestal throned by the west
> And loosed his love shaft smartly from the bow
> As if to pierce a hundred thousand hearts ...
> Yet marked I where the bolt of Cupid fell,
> It fell upon a little western flower,
> Before milk-white, now purple with love's wound
> And maidens call it Love-in-Idleness.

But Lady Sheffield was not Leicester's one and only mistake. There had been staying at Kenilworth for the festivities Lettice, the Countess of Essex, daughter of Sir Francis Knollys and mother of Robert Devereux, second Earl of Essex, who was to become the favourite of Elizabeth in her old age. Already Leicester was making love to her (1575) and in 1578, when he knew that Lettice was pregnant, he married her secretly without the knowledge or the permission of the Queen. Of course he was accused, falsely, of having poisoned the Earl of Essex, her husband, who had died in 1576. When the Queen heard the news, she was furiously angry, but she soon recovered her temper and Leicester was forgiven. Not so Lettice, for whom Elizabeth preserved an undying hatred and whom she would refer to as 'that she-wolf'. There was one son by this marriage, Robert, who died at the age of three and lies buried in the Beauchamp Chapel in St. Mary's, Warwick, 'the noble impe ...a child of great promise'.

Leicester's marriage to Lettice proves that he had by 1578 abandoned all hopes of marrying Elizabeth. But his ambitions were still enormous. He probably had hopes of becoming the ruler of the Dutch Protestant provinces: he proposed in 1582 that his small son Robert should marry Arabella Stuart, the niece of Mary, Queen of Scots, and first cousin to James VI of Scotland, whereby the crown of England might come into his own family. In 1583 he made the rash suggestion that one of the daughters of Lettice by her first marriage should marry James VI — a suggestion which roused the fury of Elizabeth in her hatred of the 'she-wolf'.

All this time the dangers from Catholic plots and Mary, Queen of Scots, were causing alarm. It is probable that Leicester was the originator of the idea to form an association for the protection of the Queen's life (1584). In the same year there appeared a virulent and malicious pamphlet, *The Copy of a Letter written by a Master of Art at Cambridge*, better known as *Leicester's Commonwealth*. It was written by the Jesuit, Robert Parsons, in part on the basis of information supplied by former courtiers like Charles Arundell. The pamphlet was published abroad and was a shrewdly written and entertaining piece of propaganda, directed against Leicester, repeating all the old stories, rumours and gossip. As historical evidence the pamphlet needs corroboration; as a proof of Leicester's unpopularity it cannot be ignored. Sir Philip Sidney wrote a passionate defence of his uncle in reply.

In 1585 the United Provinces in the Netherlands offered Elizabeth the sovereignty of these states. She absolutely declined in any circumstances to accept. She saw clearly that England could only survive so long as both her enemies, France and Spain, survived, the one to balance the other. She saw as clearly that an independent Netherlands would be unable to withstand a powerful France, and she was proved right in the eighteenth century. Her policy was to try to restore all the Netherland provinces to their ancient liberties 'wherein they lived before the persecutions and oppressions begun by the Duke of Alva', but they must remain Spanish (*Elizabethan Government and Society*, Wernham, pp. 345–6). Reluctantly she agreed to go to war in defence of the Dutch Protestants and she sent an expeditionary force under the command of Leicester. He landed at Flushing on 10 December 1585. He received a tumultuous welcome which entirely turned his head, as his letters home show. He wrote to Burghley that the Dutch would serve under himself with a better will than they had under William the Silent. And he publicly announced that the total expulsion of the Spanish from the Netherlands would be accomplished in one summer's campaign.

On 1 January 1586, the States General offered him the office of Governor of the United Provinces. Before he left England, the Queen had made perfectly plain to him that he was not to take any oath of allegiance or accept any powers which would involve her in responsibilities beyond the limited ones to which she was committed. Leicester accepted the offer of the States General. Elizabeth was furiously angry; she wrote to Leicester, 'How contemptuously we conceive ourselves to have been used by you ... We could never have imagined, had we not seen it fall out in experience, that a man raised up by ourself and extraordinarily favoured by us above any other subject of this land, would have in so contemptible a sort broken our commandment . . .' She was at least as angry that she had now been committed to detaching the Netherlands from Spain (Wernham, *ibid.*).

It soon became evident that Leicester was utterly unsuitable for the command of any army. He lacked experience, he was so arrogant that soon the States General repented of their action, and he proved himself totally unable to work with any of his military commanders. He made no attempt to control the finances of the campaign, which further inflamed the Queen. In 1586 he returned to England and was able to make up his quarrel with the Queen, but militarily his campaign had proved a failure, its only successes being the capture of the forts of Zutphen and Deventer, at the price of the death of Sir Philip Sidney.

Leicester's return was said to be necessary so that he could sit in the 1587 Parliament, which was to settle the fate of Mary, Queen of Scots. Leicester was violently in favour of her being executed at once and when it seemed that the Queen would refuse to agree, Leicester is said to have advised 'the sure but silent operation of poison and sent a divine privately to Walsingham to convince him it was lawful'. (Camden.)

Things in the Netherlands were going from bad to worse, and when Sir William Stanley betrayed Deventer to the enemy and Yorke did the same at Zutphen, the States General urged that Leicester should be sent back. He went back, but he did nothing effective and was finally recalled home in November 1587. He was at once on the best of terms with the Queen, and when preparations were being made to resist the Spanish Armada, Leicester was put in charge of the camp at Tilbury with the title of 'lieutenant and captain-general of the Queen's armies and companies'. But once again he proved himself unable to work harmoniously with other men. All the same, it was he who saw the possibilities in the Queen's suggestion that she might visit the troops at Tilbury, it was he who stage-managed her arrival and her triumphant review of her army, culminating in what has become one of the most famous speeches in the English language.

At the end of August 1588 Leicester decided to go to Buxton to take the waters. On his way he stopped at his house at Cornbury in Oxfordshire, and there on 4 September in the morning he died 'of a continual burning fever' (Camden), probably of malaria, at the age of fifty-five. He lies buried in the magnificent tomb set up by his wife, Lettice, in the Beauchamp Chapel of St. Mary's, Warwick.

Robert Dudley, young, handsome, athletic, charming, ambitious, self-confident, might have cast his spell on any young lady. Deliberately he aimed his shaft at the first lady in the land and the shaft went home. There can be no doubt that Elizabeth was deeply in love with him and he was as devoted to her. There can be equally little doubt that she was never his mistress. Hers was the more disinterested love; his may well have been tainted with ambition. Both longed for their love to be consummated, but what Elizabeth the woman would gladly have given and received, that Elizabeth the Queen saw clearly could not be. The unity of England depended on her remaining unmarried in every sense of the word. Dudley could and did find physical satisfaction with other women, but without love. The Queen could have love, but no physical satisfaction. Both were sacrificed to inexorable circumstances. Leicester, middle-aged, corpulent, red-faced and white-haired, arrogant, intolerant, touchy, still showed his devotion to Elizabeth and to the Queen: she returned it to the day of his death. What the strains and stresses of that rare courtship must have been we may partly guess from the wild tantrums of Elizabeth and the furious insolence or the black despair of Robert. When he died, she had still fifteen years of life ahead of her. Is it mere coincidence that in her old age she turned for comfort to Robert Devereux, Earl of Essex, step-son of Robert Dudley, Earl of Leicester?

R. B. Wernham, 'Elizabethan War Aims and Strategy' in S. T. Bindoff et al. (eds.), Elizabethan Government and Society, 1961.

P. Collinson (ed.), Letters of Thomas Wood, Puritan, 1566–77, 1960.

D. Wilson, Sweet Robin, 1981.

D. C. Peck, Leicester's Commonwealth, 1985.

P. J. Holmes, Journal Ecclesiastical History, 1981.

A. Haynes, The White Bear, 1987.

ROBERT DEVEREUX, 2nd EARL OF ESSEX (1567–1601), favourite of Elizabeth I, was born on 10 November 1567, and died on 25 February 1601. He was the son of Walter Devereux, Earl of

Essex, and his wife, Lady Lettice Knollys, who was herself daughter of Sir Francis Knollys and grand-daughter of Mary, sister of Anne Boleyn. He was, therefore, a cousin of the Queen on her mother's side, a relationship which may in part account for the extreme favour and leniency which the Queen showed to him. He was also step-son to Robert Dudley, Earl of Leicester, which is more likely still to account for Elizabeth's affection for him. His father died in 1576 and thus Robert became Earl of Essex at the age of 9. His early years were spent in the household of Lord Burghley and he proved himself to be a genuinely able and precocious child. He went to Trinity, Cambridge, under Whitgift (1577), took his M.A. in 1581, and first appeared at Court in 1584. Two years later (1586) he was created a knight-banneret for his courage at the battle of Zutphen, where Sir Philip Sidney was killed. On his return home he at once attracted the notice and favour of the Queen and in 1587 was made her Master of Horse, a fact the more remarkable, because his mother had married Robert Dudley, Earl of Leicester, to the Queen's fury. In 1588 he was made a Knight of the Garter. But even so early on as this, there were quarrels and scenes between the Queen and Essex. In 1588, Essex raised a force which assembled with the army at Tilbury to meet the Spaniards, should their Armada effect a landing.

In 1589 Essex joined himself to the party of Don Antonio, the Pretender to the throne of Portugal. He was unhappy at Court, quarrelling with Ralegh and the Queen, so much so that Elizabeth was saying 'by God's death it were fitting some one should take him down and teach him manners!' Therefore, when the Drake-Norreys expedition was sent against Spain in 1589, Essex determined to join it. He knew the Queen would veto his going. He slipped away privately and succeeded in joining the official expedition. He proved an encumbrance, achieved some distinction — his courage was never in doubt — but furious letters from Elizabeth entailed his immediate return to England. When he met the Queen, all was forgiven him.

In 1590 Essex secretly married Frances, the daughter of Walsingham and the widow of Sir Philip Sidney. This aroused another angry scene with Elizabeth, but in a few months Essex was again restored to favour. The next year (1591) he was given command of a force which was sent to help Henry of Navarre. He behaved with much courage and he succeeded in capturing Gournay. But he earned a

Robert Devereux, 2nd Earl of Essex
(Artist: M. Gheeraerts the Younger)

reproof from the Queen for creating twenty-three knights, too large a number to please Elizabeth, who hated to see knighthood cheapened. Twice he was recalled temporarily to satisfy Elizabeth that he was not risking his life rashly, and then in 1592 he was finally summoned home.

Between 1592 and 1596 Essex set about building up his political reputation at Court. He became the rallying point for all those who resented the monopoly of power by the Cecils: chief among these was Francis Bacon. Essex had genuine affection for Bacon, but his persistent and often ill-judged attempts to obtain political promotion for Bacon led to further quarrels with Elizabeth. Essex concentrated on foreign affairs and made Anthony Bacon, brother of Francis, his chief adviser. He built up a well-organized system of intelligence and he drew information from all parts of the Continent, corresponding with Henry of Navarre and James VI of Scotland. In 1593 he was made a Privy Councillor. The year before Don Antonio had arrived in England and attached himself to the Essex party. It was largely through him that Essex brought to the gallows Dr. Rodrigo Lopez, the Queen's physician, on a charge of plotting to murder the Queen (1594), but not before Elizabeth had called Essex 'a rash and temerarious youth'.

In 1596 Essex was appointed General-in-Chief of the land forces and also put in command of one of the five squadrons which formed the Cadiz expedition under Lord Howard of Effingham. The expedition was a resounding success: the Spanish fleet was totally defeated and Essex landed his army and captured Cadiz (22 June 1596). The fleet then sailed to Cape St. Mary, where Essex landed a force and entered the town of Faro. He got little out of it, but he came away with the library of Jerome Osorio, Bishop of Algarve. The books eventually passed to the Bodleian. Essex then tried to persuade Howard to attack Lisbon and intercept the Spanish treasure fleet, but Howard refused, and on 10 August Essex reached Plymouth, the generally recognized hero of the expedition.

Essex was now at the height of his fortunes. His very success made him enemies at Court, and the Queen was angry that her share of the profits of the Cadiz expedition was so small. When the treasure fleet entered the Tagus two days after the English had left, Essex's judgement was vindicated. At once he was restored to favour with the Queen. He was popular in the country, his knowledge of foreign affairs was at least as well-informed as that of the government, and Essex House now became a miniature Court. Francis Bacon alone saw the dangers and he wrote a letter to Essex warning him not to underrate the Queen and not to overrate a military reputation. The advice was not heeded. From this moment Essex's star began to set.

In 1597 he was given command of the Islands' Voyage, an expedition sent out to capture the Spanish treasure fleet and the Azores. It was a failure, principally owing to Essex's incapacity as a commander. Again he was out of favour with the Queen. A peace was patched up, and Essex was made Earl Marshal (1597). The peace was short-lived. In 1598 Essex aided the Earl of Southampton in his secret marriage with one of the Queen's maids of honour. The Queen was furious and scenes between her and Essex were frequent. When the question arose who should command the expedition to Ireland to deal with O'Neill, Earl of Tyrone, Essex behaved outrageously, turned his back on the Queen and (according to Ralegh) told her that 'her conditions were as crooked as her carcase'. Elizabeth boxed his ears, Essex drew his sword and flung out of the Court in high passion.

Once again the two were reconciled and Essex was given command of the Irish expedition (1599). He arrived at Dublin on 15 April 1599. His whole reputation was now at stake. He had an army of 15,000 men and wider powers than had been given to any previous Lieutenant and Governor-General. He began with a minor campaign in Munster which merely wasted time, money and men. Elizabeth wrote him a scathing rebuke and forbade him to return to England. Essex then made a half-hearted advance into Ulster, but instead of fighting Tyrone he met him at a ford in the river Lagan and contrived an ignominious peace. The Queen was rightly furious. It is not impossible that Essex, who was already corresponding with James VI and knew the Queen could not live long, was gambling on his accession to the English throne and was well contented to have a friendly Tyrone in Ireland backed by a military force. Suddenly, in September, Essex deserted his army, embarked for England and arrived in the early morning in the Queen's bedroom at Nonsuch. At first she received him kindly, but then she confined him to his own house. Essex was now politically ruined. He fell seriously ill, recovered and set about building up a political party out of all those irresponsible young men who found themselves excluded from office and who clamoured for war with Spain — men like Rutland, Sir Christopher Blount and the young Earl of Southampton.

By the New Year the government was aware of what was going on. On 5 February 1601, Essex's friends arranged for Shakespeare's play of *Richard II* to be played at the Globe on the following Saturday, 7 February and the deposition scene was to be included. On the 7th the Council shut up Essex and his friends in Essex House in the Strand. On the 8th Essex with 200 men broke out and rode through the city of London, but he failed to arouse any enthusiasm or support. He was compelled to surrender. On the 19th he was tried in Westminster Hall with Southampton; Edward Coke conducted the prosecution with great acrimony and Francis Bacon basely gave evidence against Essex, who was inevitably condemned to death. He was executed on the 25th, dying with great dignity and courage. The story that Elizabeth gave Essex a ring with a promise to pardon any offence, if he sent it to her when in danger, and that Essex sent the ring from the Tower by the Countess of Nottingham, who never delivered it, is wholly apocryphal.

Essex is one of the tragic failures in English history. Handsome, brave, impulsive, loyal to his friends, generous, he won the hearts of the English people. Shakespeare twice wrote of him, once while he was in Ireland when the play *Henry V* was produced for the first time:

> Were now the general of our gracious empress,
> As in good time he may, from Ireland coming,
> Bringing rebellion broached on his sword,
> How many would the peaceful city quit
> To welcome him:

and there is a reference to him in the words applied by Ophelia to Hamlet:

> The courtier's, soldier's, scholar's eye, tongue, sword,
> The expectancy and rose of the fair state,
> The glass of fashion and the mould of form,
> The observed of all observers ...

But he was passionate, undisciplined and politically destitute of all the qualities necessary for statesmanship. He came of an old, feudal family, and his faction represents the last kick of a feudal aristocracy against the new rich, the Cecils and the Walsinghams. His great mistake was that he never understood that all his fortune depended on the favour of the Queen, and he tried to control and in the end to undermine the source from which alone his success could spring.

G. B. Harrison: *Robert Devereux, Earl of Essex*.
A. L. Rowse, 'Robert Devereux, Earl of Essex' in *The Great Tudors*, 1933.
L. W. Henry, 'The Earl of Essex and Ireland' in *Bulletin Institute of Historical Research*, 1959.
J. O'Neill, *Chosen by the Queen*, 1917. (H.N.)
R. Lacey, *Robert, Earl of Essex*, 1971.

SIR WALTER RALEGH [this spelling pronounced *Rawley*, was the one he mostly used after his father's death in 1581; although the whole family used more than 70 variations, he himself is not known ever to have used the usual modern form of RALEIGH] (1554?–1616), poet, historian, explorer, sailor, soldier, courtier, was the second child of Walter Ralegh by his third wife, and he was thus half-brother to Sir Humphrey Gilbert, his mother's son by her first husband. He fought as a volunteer in the Huguenot armies at the battles of Jarnac and Monconteur in 1569, and went to Oriel College, Oxford in 1572. In 1578 he joined with Humphrey Gilbert on an unsuccessful expedition bound for the Azores and West Indies against Spain. In 1580–1 he saw military service in Ireland, after which he returned to England to the Court at Greenwich. The story that he spread his cloak 'in a plashy place', 'whereon the Queen trod gently over, rewarding him after with many suits for his so free and seasonable tender of so fair a foot cloth' does not occur before the mid-seventeenth century. He remained at Court for many years as a favourite frequently and richly rewarded. In 1584 he was knighted.

In 1583–9 he sent out at his own expense of £40,000 six expeditions to plant a colony overseas in America, and later he sent out others, the last in 1603, but all were failures, the only tangible result being that the potato and tobacco were introduced into England and Ireland.

In 1588 he took no active part in the fighting against the Armada. In 1591 he published anonymously an account of Grenville's last fight in the *Revenge*, which later became the basis for Tennyson's

Sir Walter Ralegh
(Artist: Nicholas Hilliard)

poem. In 1592 he was imprisoned for misbehaviour with one of the Queen's maids of honour, Elizabeth Throgmorton, but he was soon released. They were married and lived at Sherborne. 1594 he sent an expedition to reconnoitre the river Orinoco, and in 1595 himself went in search of the fabulously wealthy city of Manoa in South America, known as El Dorado. The expedition was a failure. On his return he played a leading part in Essex's expedition against Cadiz. 1597 saw him back at Court and reconciled with the Queen. He then took part in Essex's abortive expedition against Spain, but his conduct led to a violent quarrel which was never healed.

When James I came to the English throne his mind had already been poisoned against Ralegh, who soon found himself in the Tower on a charge of being implicated in Watson's plot 'to surprise the King's person'. Ralegh was tried for high treason, convicted, condemned to be executed, reprieved and shut up in the Tower from 1603 to 1616. During his imprisonment he wrote his *History of the World*, beginning at the Creation, but he only got as far as 130 BC. In 1616 he was released in order to go on an expedition to find El Dorado, on the condition that, if he failed, he would return. He set sail from Plymouth on 12 June 1617. The expedition was a disastrous failure, and a fight took place with the Spanish just at the time when James I was trying to negotiate a Spanish marriage for his son, Charles, Prince of Wales. True to his promise, Ralegh returned to England, and James had him executed, largely at the demand of the Spanish ambassador (29 October 1618).

Ralegh was an intellectual genius, witty, brilliant, graceful, a poet and a great writer. He had a fearlessly independent mind, a bitter tongue and a scornful use of repartee. He was rapacious, restlessly energetic, ambitious for power and fame, an unscrupulous schemer in pursuit of success. Yet he was also extravagantly generous, adored by his wife, beloved by his servants. He never attained to political power, because the Queen never trusted his judgement, however much she enjoyed his company. He was accused of being an atheist, whereas in fact he only refused to accept without criticism orthodox opinions, and his *History of the World* proves him to have been deeply religious. His ideas were ahead of his times — he held that colonies (he would have called them plantations) would absorb surplus population, reduce unemployment at home and stimulate trade. When he laid his head on the block on the scaffold, somebody asked him if he would not rather lie with his head to the East of Our Lord's arising. Ralegh's answer was, 'So the heart be right, it is no matter which way the head lieth'.

E. Thompson, *Sir Walter Raleigh*, 1935.
V. Harlow, Introduction to *The Discovery of Guiana*, 1928.
D. B. Quinn, *Raleigh and the British Empire*, 1947.
A. L. Rowse, *Ralegh and the Throckmortons*, 1962.

A. M. C. Latham, *Sir Walter Raleigh*, 1964.

SIR CHRISTOPHER HATTON (1540–1592), Lord Chancellor, was the second son of William Hatton of Holdenby, Northamptonshire, and his wife Alice, daughter of Lawrence Saunders of Harrington in the same county. Holdenby was a parish in the Hundred of Newbottle: local pronunciation shortened the name to Holmby, and it is as Holmby House that Holdenby is now remembered, the house where King Charles I was imprisoned in 1646. Christopher's sister, Dorothy, married as her second husband William Underhill of Idlicote in Warwickshire, and it was their son, William, who sold New Place to Shakespeare at Stratford-on-Avon.

In about 1555 Hatton went to St. Mary Hall, Oxford, the Head of which was Allen, later the English Cardinal in Rome. It seems certain that the Hattons were brought up as Catholics and probable that up to the time of the Armada Christopher's religious views were that he sympathized with the English Catholics and hated the Puritans. After the execution of Mary, Queen of Scots, he became virulent against the Pope and the Jesuits. In 1560 he was entered at the Inner Temple, and here he took part in the literary and dramatic activities of the young men, rather than applying himself to the study of law. It was probably at the masque which was acted in 1561 at the Inner Temple in front of the Queen that Hatton 'danced his way into the heart of Elizabeth' (Sir Edmund Chambers). He now became a favourite of the Queen, a position which he held to the last day of his life.

For the next sixteen years Hatton was a courtier who received many favours from Elizabeth. In 1564 he was made one of her Gentlemen Pensioners and he was granted many estates and offices and an annuity of £400. In 1566 he was one of the embassy which went to Scotland to attend the baptism of James VI. The proceedings were marred by the testy behaviour of some of the Englishmen (including Hatton) who took amiss a joke perpetrated by some of the Scots at an entertainment, when some satyrs 'put their hands behind them to their tails which they wagged with their hands in such sort as the Englishmen supposed it had been devised and done in derision of them', for everybody knew that Englishmen had had tails bestowed upon them as a divine punishment for the martyrdom of Thomas Becket.

Sir Christopher Hatton
(Artist: Unknown)

In 1571 Hatton was returned as M.P. for Higham Ferrers and in 1572 and 1584 for Northamptonshire. He was at first a silent member and made no mark in the House. But further advancement came to him in 1572, when the Queen appointed him Captain of her Guard. The next year a violent Puritan, Peter Burchet, attempted to murder Hatton on religious grounds, but he mistook John Hawkins for Hatton and only succeeded in wounding Hawkins. It may be a sign of Hatton's increasing confidence and prestige that in 1573, with the help of the Queen and by very high-handed action, he compelled the Bishop of Ely to surrender to him Ely Place in Holborn (now Hatton Gardens), an episode which is inaccurately commemorated in one of *The Ingoldsby Legends*, 'The House Warming'. The year 1577 saw Hatton made Vice-Chamberlain and knighted, and his period as little more than a courtier came to an end. From then on he was the mouthpiece of the Queen in the House of Commons: it was his business to pilot government bills through the House, to prevent waste of time and debates embarrassing to the government.

Hatton found himself involved in the difficult problem of Elizabeth's projected marriage with the Duke of Anjou: at first he was in favour of it, but once he had seen Anjou in person he was so strongly opposed to it that he besought the Queen with tears in his eyes to go no further in the matter. He took some part in examining the accused in the Parry, Throckmorton and Babington plots against the Queen's life. Most important, he was on the Commission for the examination of the Queen of Scots, and it was Hatton's wise, tactful and moderate arguments which persuaded Mary to accept the competence of the Court to try her (1586). There is little doubt that it was Hatton who succeeded in persuading the unhappy Davison (Elizabeth's Secretary) to send off the warrant for the execution of Mary (1587).

These were testing times. Hatton seems to have acquitted himself so well that in 1587 he was made Lord Chancellor. This appointment has aroused passionate arguments among historians, the earlier of whom have seen in it nothing but the mere caprice of an infatuated woman, prepared to promote her favourite to the chief place in the realm, although he was wholly unsuited to the post. Later historians have taken the view that the appointment was a purely political and not a legal one. The legal side was provided for by the appointment of trained legal advisers to help Hatton on that side of his work. The view that this was a piece of sheer favouritism by the Queen is disposed of by the fact that Elizabeth was both before and immediately after the appointment doubtful whether she had done right. What she needed was somebody of sufficient strength of character and loyalty to co-operate with the new Archbishop of Canterbury, Whitgift, in suppressing the Puritans and enforcing uniformity in the Church of England. The appointment was justified by the co-operation which Hatton maintained with Whitgift. He had had to wait for more than twenty years before the Queen advanced him to an important political office.

The next year, 1588, Hatton was given the Garter and also became Chancellor of Oxford University. He died in 1591 and was buried in St. Paul's.

Christopher Hatton's place in English history has not yet been fully treated. For centuries he remained a figure of fun, a dancer and a butt for the dramatists — as in Sheridan's *The Critic*. It is true that his relations with the Queen, as judged by his letters, give some grounds to modern times for regarding him as a sycophant and nothing more. But modern times are only judging by modern standards. The tone of Hatton's letters represents only an exaggerated form of what in Elizabeth's day was looked on as the right way of approaching the monarch. There is no shred of evidence that Hatton was Elizabeth's lover, but the Queen was genuinely devoted to Hatton and in his last illness she constantly visited him, taking him broths and feeding him with her own hand. She gave him the nickname of 'lids' (*i.e.* eye-lids), which he used in his letters under the symbol of four triangles. She also called him her bell-wether and her Mutton. Hatton himself was a man with an extremely kind heart, and many letters exist from men and women in trouble thanking Hatton for the help he had given them — such people as the Catholic Pound, who published Campion's *Challenge*, and poor old Lady Egerton of Ridley, who wrote to him, 'You are the sole person in court that hath taken compassion on me, and hath given comfort unto my careful heart and, under God, kept life within my breast ... a poor, wretched, abandoned lady, no way able to yield you thankfulness worthy thereof. You are the rock I build on.' It is arguable that most of these men and women were Catholics and that Hatton was only indulging his own religious feelings, but there is plenty of evidence to show that in his examinations of accused persons, whatever their religion, Hatton used gentler and more considerate methods than most of his contemporaries.

Financially Hatton's life was a disaster. When he died he was in debt to Elizabeth to the sum of about £40,000. He spent his money largely on the most extravagant building, as at Holdenby, where his new house was looked upon as the greatest piece of building in his time. He had shares in Drake's voyage of circumnavigation, in Frobisher's voyages in search of the North-west Passage, in Fenton's voyage of 1584, and in the Cadiz expedition of 1589.

There is great need of a full-scale biography of Hatton to settle his true place among English statesmen. Scattered through the works of Conyers Read and Sir John Neale are to be found references to Hatton which go far to recognize him as a Parliamentarian of great ability and an orator much above the average. Neale calls him 'the invaluable Hatton', 'the respected, the supreme parliamentary manager' (*Elizabeth and Her Parliaments*, ii, 159), and in describing Hatton's speech in the House of Lords after the defeat of the Armada, Neale writes, 'for its eloquence, its emotion, and its stirring, confident, patriotism, as well as a withering contempt for the enemy, Hatton's speech is not unworthy of place in the treasury of England's best' (*ibid.*, 195).

Sir Harris Nicholas, *Memories of the Life and Times of Sir Christopher Hatton*, 1847.

E. St. John Brooks, *Sir Christopher Hatton*, 1946.

A. G. Vines, *Neither fire nor steel*, 1978.

SIR PHILIP SIDNEY (1554–1586), poet, statesman and soldier, was the eldest son of Sir Henry Sidney and his wife, Mary, daughter of John Dudley, Duke of Northumberland. To his contemporaries he clearly resembled one of those heroes of Greek antiquity in whom all gifts and graces were congruously blended. Educated at Shrewsbury and Christ Church, and then travelling abroad for two years (when he was in Paris on the day of the St. Bartholomew massacre), he was soon employed about the Court and sent on missions to more than one foreign potentate. To us his public career must seem one of promise rather than achievement, but there is no gainsaying the extraordinary love and admiration which he won from all who knew him. His biographer, Fulke Greville, had 'friend to Philip Sidney' inscribed on his own tombstone, and Thomas Thornton wanted it similarly recorded that he was Sidney's tutor.

Sidney's heroic death was brought about by his refusal to wear

Sir Philip Sidney
(Artist: Unknown)

armour on his thighs, out of bravado at the siege of Zutphen, fighting against Catholic Spain. Dying himself, he gave his bottle of water to a dying soldier. His death was followed by an astonishing outburst of grief from all, including the Queen. Over two hundred poetic elegies (one of which came from his devoted friend Spenser) mourned the irreparable loss of one who combined in his own life and character the qualities of the ideal Englishman.

Sidney was not only a man of diplomacy and action. His enormous pastoral romance *Arcadia* was written for the benefit of his sister in 1580–1, when his courageous protest against the Queen's projected marriage with the Duke of Anjou temporarily estranged him from her Court. He did not mean the work to be published (nothing of his was published till the 1590s), and on his deathbed he desired that it should be burnt.

The *Arcadia* is not now easy reading, being, as Horace Walpole harshly but not untruly called it, a jungle of pastoral, sentimental and heroical adventures, full of digressions and improbabilities, with much prose-poetry and tortuous convolutions. There are a few passages of rich beauty, but the main cause of the book's enormous popularity for a century and more was the newness of such a feast of romance and sentiment. Scattered among these letters — together with some disastrous experiments in classical metres — are some of Sidney's best poems, but his main contribution to English poetry was undoubtedly the sonnets which he wrote to Penelope Devereux, daughter of the Earl of Essex, entitled 'Astrophel and Stella'. Not all judges are agreed on the merits of these sonnets. Hazlitt, to the asonishment of Lamb, thought them 'jejune and frigid'; Saintsbury called the one beginning

With how sad steps O moon, thou climb'st the skies

the first perfectly charming sonnet in the English language.

The third work for which Sidney is known is his *Apologie for Poetrie* in reply to an abusive attack on the theatre by Stephen Gosson, an ex-playwright turned Puritan, who hoped to find Sidney on his side. Sidney replied with an eloquent exposition of his conviction of poetry's supremacy over all other studies, both for edification and delight. It is a work of much charm and considerable humour. The limitations of his judgement are shown by what he says of the theatre, where he insists on the rigid dramatic formalities which were shortly to be blown sky-high by Shakespeare and his fellows. But much may be forgiven the author of the famous and disarming declaration, 'I never heard the old song of Percy and Douglas that I found not my heart moved more than with a trumpet'. A critic who writes like that about poetry has the root of the matter in him.

Mona Wilson, *Sir Philip Sidney*, 1931.
E. J. M. Buxton, *Sir Philip Sidney and the Renaissance*.
H. Morris, *Elizabethan Literature*, pp. 58–66.
M. W. Wallace, *The life of Sir Philip Sidney*, 1915.
F. S. Boas, *Sir Philip Sidney*, 1955.

SIR THOMAS GRESHAM (1518?–1579), financier, founder of the Royal Exchange, was born probably in 1518, the son of Sir Richard Gresham, a well-known merchant and financier and once Lord Mayor of London, who was much employed in the business of the Crown and frequently lent money to Henry VIII. The name Gresham means 'grass-farm', and the family took their name from the village of Gresham in Norfolk. Thomas was educated at Gonville and Caius College, Cambridge, where he had taken his B.A. by the time he was 16 years of age. He seems then to have gone into business under the instruction of his uncle. In 1543 he was elected a Freeman of the Mercers' Company and he was already being employed by the Crown to buy gunpowder. It is possible that he was lending the Crown money, or else providing money for the Crown by other means, for in 1544–5 some foreign mercenaries were paid with funds which had been received from Thomas Gresham. In 1544 he married the aunt by marriage of Francis Bacon. In 1549 Sir Richard died, and Thomas and his wife moved from his father's house into a house in Lombard Street, 'at the sign of the Grass-hopper', which was the emblem of the Gresham family.

In 1551–2 Sir William Daunsell, the royal agent or King's merchant, was relieved of his post for having 'done his highness marvellous ill service'. Thomas Gresham replaced him and went to live in Antwerp, the centre of the international money market. (For the importance of Antwerp, see S. T. Bindoff, *New Cambridge Modern History*, vol. 2.)

From 1551 down to the death of Edward VI in 1553 Gresham was for the most part taken up with finding ways and means to alleviate the Crown's financial difficulties, although he also still looked after his own personal interests and business. He lived in the house of Gaspar Schetz (whose father had named his three sons after the

Magi), the chief financial agent of Charles V. He had two London agents, John Elliot and Richard Candeler, and he also had many agents all over Europe. He was usually in Antwerp for three or four months at a time, but in Elizabeth's reign he once spent as long as a year there without returning to England. In his first two years in Antwerp he crossed the Channel forty-two times. His factor at Antwerp was Richard Clough, a very astute man in negotiating loans, smuggling arms, money and foreign goods from the Netherlands into England. Clough was in the habit of writing immensely long letters, filled with detailed accounts of current events in the Netherlands, funerals, pageants, etc., but also containing very valuable political information, which Gresham used to pass on to Cecil. Gresham appreciated the value of Clough and would praise him generously, but he warned Cecil that Clough was 'very long and tedious in his writing'.

The Crown's financial difficulties were very great, brought about by wars at the end of Henry VIII's reign, by Somerset's extravagance, and to a very great extent by the inflation (rise in prices and therefore the fall in the purchasing power of money) which marked the sixteenth century. It has to be remembered that in England by the middle of the century and for some time beyond there was no class of specialized financiers or any bankers: it was the rich merchants who gave credit and discounted bills, but their capacity was limited. It was therefore frequently necessary for the Crown to seek for loans in foreign countries, which on the whole meant in Antwerp. By 1552 the interest on the Crown's debts was £40,000 and the foreign capitalists had succeeded in bringing down the rate of exchange to 16 Flemish shillings to the £1 sterling.

Gresham set about his work with a will, but in fact he had not any revolutionary ideas on how to help the Crown. He advised the Council to set aside £1,300 per week and to send this sum secretly to him in Antwerp for the redemption of debt. He would use this money to buy up small sums of sterling every day in such a way that 'it shall not be perceived nor it shall be no occasion to make the Exchange fall' — in fact, the steady demand would make it rise. He also suggested that the fleet of the Merchant Adventurers should be allowed to set sail only if the owners lent money to the King at one rate of exchange in Antwerp which could be repaid in London at another rate. The difference in the rates of exchange would operate to the King's advantage. This was a typical example of his harsh and high-handed measures — no doubt because he himself got a 'rake off' from the profits made by the Crown. Further, he advised that the Crown by the use of its prerogative should create a monopoly for itself in lead, by forbidding anyone except the Crown to export lead. The greatly enhanced price would benefit the Crown considerably.

Not much came of this so-called 'design', mainly because the Council gave up remitting £1,300 per week — much the most sensible part of the 'design' — after eight weeks, and also rejected the proposal to create a monopoly in lead, because it would make the government very unpopular. Nevertheless, within two years Gresham claimed that he had succeeded in raising the rate of exchange at Antwerp from 16 shillings to 22 shillings and was discharging the Crown's debts at this figure. He achieved this partly by giving huge banquets to the creditors, but chiefly by insisting to the Crown that it must be punctual in repaying its debts. He wrote to Northumberland, 'It shall be no small grief unto me that in my time, being His Majesty's agent, any merchant strangers should be forced to forbear their money against their wills ... To be plain with Your Grace in this matter, according to my bounden duty, verily if there be not some other ways taken for the payment of His Majesty's debts, but to force men from time to time to prolong it; I say to you, the end thereof shall neither be honourable nor profitable to His Highness'.

Gresham and Edward VI were always on good terms. The King once gave him property worth £100 p.a., saying, 'You shall know that you have served a king', and he also gave him lands from time to time, such as Walsingham Manor. Gresham once gave Edward VI a pair of long Spanish silk stockings, 'a great present', said Stow, '... for Henry VIII did wear only cloth hose or hose cut out of ell-broad taffeta'. In 1556, he gave Mary 'a bottle of fine Holland (gin) in a case of black leather'.

Besides being used as a financial agent, Gresham also acted as a source of diplomatic and political information, which he gathered from his agents scattered all over Europe.

On the accession of Mary and the execution of his friend Northumberland, Gresham was relieved of his office. Dauntsey and Dansell were reinstated, but Sir John Leigh spoke up for Gresham, and as the Queen's business in Antwerp was being badly handled —

all Gresham's work in reducing the rate of interest was undone —
Gresham was restored and went back to Antwerp. His chief problem
now was how to get the money out of the Netherlands and into
England, for a ban had been put on the export of bullion by

Sir Thomas Gresham
(Artist: Unknown Flemish)

Charles V. To begin with Gresham tried to smuggle it out in bales of pepper, but there was a limit to the amount of pepper which any one country could require and this method gave rise to suspicions. Gresham then used armour, packing the bullion in 1,000 demi-lancers' harness. How valuable this trade with England was becoming is shown by the panic into which the Flemish merchants fell at the news of Wyatt's rebellion (1554). In that year Gresham succeeded in securing from the Emperor a licence and passport for exporting 500,000 crowns in bullion from Spain, with the proviso that 'I should convey this money with as much secrecy and as small bruit as I could achieve'.

For some reason or other, from 1556 to 1558, Gresham retired into private life, but he was reinstated in Antwerp just before Mary died. Gresham hurried off to offer his services to Elizabeth — in itself a proof of how lucrative a business all this was for Gresham himself. Elizabeth received him cordially and promised as much land as any other monarch had given him and even more. Perhaps Gresham was a financier after Elizabeth's own heart — cautious, secret and above all successful. The position was very bad: debt was £226,910, whereas revenue was only £200,000: the needs of defence were heavy and expensive: what Gresham had to do was to raise loans abroad as cheaply as he could. But he himself insisted that the right policy was to borrow as little abroad as possible, to restore the purity of the coinage and to enforce the strictest economy. It is difficult to quarrel with this judgement. It is less easy to approve of his reiterated suggestion to restrict the sailing of the Merchant Adventurers' fleet, unless they agreed to what in fact was a forced loan.

During this period (1559–60) he worked hand in glove with Cecil — his letters were full of important political information. But Gresham's difficulties were very great. They were eased when Philip II recalled his troops from the Netherlands to Spain and when Elizabeth made the Treaty of Edinburgh with the Scots and French. At once the rate of interest fell at Antwerp to 10%. In 1562 Elizabeth for political reasons backed the Huguenots: Gresham wrote, 'this pen can not write you' the bad effect on credit.

Gresham had for some time urged that the coinage should be reformed. That the reform was undertaken was mainly his work. It was carried out under the supervision of Daniel Wolstrat of

Antwerp. Elizabeth made a small profit out of the transaction.

In 1559 Gresham became temporary ambassador to the Regent of the Netherlands. To adorn this office with proper dignity he was knighted. His letters to Cecil are full of political information of the highest value: he clearly foresaw the revolt of the Netherlands against Philip II, and he was very successful in bribing the Spanish officials to provide him with the fullest information. The danger to England was very great. Military stores were sorely needed. Gresham found much difficulty in supplying them from the Netherlands. He urged the manufacture of gunpowder in England, but he also spread a rumour abroad in the Netherlands that England had 200 ships ready and well-armed. In the event, he secured large quantities of ammuniton and exported them as 'velvets'. He also extracted 2,000 corselets out of the King of Spain's armoury at Malines. He was on the whole very successful in his efforts, but his financial transactions (out of which he made a pile for himself) and the secrecy of his correspondence with Cecil raised up many enemies against him who delated him to the Queen, but she knew when she was 'on to a good thing', and paid no attention to the accusations.

In 1560 Gresham had a fall from his horse and broke his leg. This seriously affected his health and he was lame for the rest of his life. He was called home the next year in order to help his recovery, but he was soon going back and forth between England and Antwerp, mainly in order to raise loans, and also sometimes on diplomatic missions.

When the government in 1568 seized the Spanish treasure, Gresham advised the Queen to have the treasure coined and put at the disposal of the merchants, from whom the government could borrow at low rates of interest. The advice was taken, and Gresham arranged the whole business.

The importance of Antwerp had for some time been declining, and Hamburg was taking its place as a mercantile centre. Gresham secretly supplied the Merchant Adventurers with money to keep two cloth fleets at Hamburg to strengthen Elizabeth's credit there. Between 1570 and 1574 Gresham was often writing to the government complaining of its dilatoriness in repaying the debts owed to English merchants. In 1574 he ceased to be the Queen's agent, as his health was bad and his leg was giving him much trouble.

Gresham does not seem to have incurred much personal risk in his loans: on the contrary, he made enormous profits for himself out of his work for the Crown, and it is clear that he was often very unscrupulous in his methods. The audit of 1574 (the last audit had been made eleven years before) showed that he had received in the interval £677,248.4s.3d. and had expended £659,099.2s.1½d. After certain deductions and allowances had been adjusted, Gresham was found to owe the Crown £100,000, but he worked out the sum so as to put the government in his debt to the tune of £11,506.18s.0¼d. The commissioners disputed his claim. Gresham got hold of a duplicate copy of his accounts, added a footnote acknowledging his claim, went off to Kenilworth where the Queen was staying and got her sanction to his claim. Armed with this, he compelled the commissioners to sign the acknowledgement.

Ten years earlier (1564) Gresham's only son had died. He therefore decided to use his immense wealth for the benefit of the public by building a bourse or Exchange. His father had originally suggested the scheme, and Clough had urged Gresham to build it in 1562. In 1564 Gresham offered to build it, if a site were provided. The Merchant Adventurers and Staplers put up the money for the site and in 1566 the foundation-stone was laid. Gresham employed a Flemish architect, one Henryke, who had a hand in some of the stone work at Burghley, which has since disappeared. The wood came from Battisford, near his own home at Ringshall in Suffolk. Clough saw to the exporting from Antwerp of most of the other materials. The building was ready for use in 1568. Two years later Queen Elizabeth visited the building and gave orders for it to be called the Royal Exchange. Gresham's building was destroyed by fire in 1666. (For an illustration, see Summerson, *Architecture in Britain 1530–1830,* plate 66A.)

Gresham also founded Gresham College in London, where free lectures were to be given (1575). This caused a quarrel with Cambridge University. He bequeathed Gresham House to the college on the death of his wife, but the plan was never very successful, although lectures are still given there (in a different building).

In 1569 Gresham was put in charge of Lady Mary Keys, sister of Lady Jane Grey, who had made an imprudent marriage. He hated the post and was continually asking to be relieved and he was replaced probably in 1573. He died very suddenly on 21 November 1579 and was buried in St. Helen's, Bishopsgate.

Sir Thomas Gresham was a shrewd, level-headed, self-confident man, blessed with foresight, a great capacity for hard work, 'a jewel for trust, wit and diligent endeavour.' He does not seem to have been a genius, and his famous law, 'Gresham's Law', that 'bad money drives out good', did no more than epitomize what many shrewd men of commonsense fully understood. He had no original ideas; he never questioned the economic ideas of his times, but he was a wonderful bargainer in negotiating loans; he recognized the evil of a debased coinage, though he probably did not recognize the evil of having two standard metals, gold and silver. He was a staunch Protestant.

J. W. Burgon *Life and Times of Sir Thomas Gresham*, 1839.
F. R. Salter, *Sir Thomas Gresham*, 1925.

SIR HORATIO PALAVICINO (*c.* 1540–1600), financier and diplomatist, was born at Genoa about 1540, the son of Tobias Palavicino, a member of the wealthy, aristocratic banking family in Northern Italy, which was closely connected with most of the powerful Italian banking firms. The family business was based on handling the Papal monopoly in alum, a commodity greatly in demand in the Netherlands and England for the cloth trade. In 1578 Horatio sold the family stocks of alum at Antwerp to the Dutch rebels in return for an import monopoly which excluded all future farmers of the Papal alum monopoly. The Dutch did not pay cash: Queen Elizabeth of England underwrote the loan in order to keep the Dutch revolt against Spain alive. In other words, she borrowed from Palavicino £29,000. In 1579 Sir Thomas Gresham, the English government's chief financial agent, died. It was necessary to find a successor, a man who had intimate knowledge of international high finance, who was an expert in currency exchange, who could handle the transfer of large sums of money from one financial centre to another, to ambassadors and secret agents, who could find the ready cash for subsidies to allies, who was ready and able to turn ambassador (or spy) himself, and whose reputation created confidence and credit. Only Horatio Palavicino fulfilled all these requirements, and on top of this he could at need act as a secret agent.

In 1586 he was given a full diplomatic mission as Ambassador to the Protestant princes in North-Western Europe to raise an army for the invasion of Eastern France. He became a naturalized Englishman and was knighted by Elizabeth. He lost the Queen's favour when she discovered the profits Horatio had made out of the 1578 loan. He had lent her £29,000: in 1592 she repaid him £4,425 of the capital, the only repayment she ever made. But by that time Horatio had cleared £41,053 in interest alone. Between 1594 and 1600 he was engaged in increasing his own wealth and investing it in land. His methods were ruthless, unsavoury and highly successful. He speculated in corn and earned great hatred for the distress he caused in time of famine by raising the price. He bought *objets d'art* for his clients; he arranged the ransom of prisoners, notably Spanish prisoners from the Armada; he lent money on the most exorbitant conditions; he tried to make a corner, but failed, in the world supply of pepper. By the time he died in 1600 he was the richest commoner in the land, worth at least £100,000, and he had accumulated 8,000 acres in three counties. He was interested in sheep-farming and devoted some 2,600 acres to pasture. At his home at Babraham in Cambridgeshire he was something of a pioneer in agriculture, in experimenting in irrigating his meadows.

Palavicino was an unpleasant man, ruthless in pursuit of wealth, harsh as a landlord. He was impetuous and emotional, but also cold and calculating. He remained on friendly and even affectionate terms with the Cecils and the Earl of Shrewsbury, yet he was notorious for the duplicity with which he treated his debtors. His intellectual powers were considerable, his abilities enormous. He spoke six languages; his interests were wide and varied — for example, he studied naval and military affairs and served at sea against the Armada. He began life as a Catholic and changed over gradually to the new faith, influenced by the cruel treatment meted out to his brother by the Pope at the time of the alum crisis in 1578 (his brother was tortured), but doubtless as much influenced by the £29,000 owed to him by a Protestant Queen. After his death his second wife married Sir Oliver Cromwell of Hinchinbrook, his son Henry (aged 14) married Catherine, Sir Oliver's daughter by a first marriage, his son Toby married her sister Jane, and his daughter

Baptina married her brother Henry. Sir Oliver was the great-uncle of
Oliver Cromwell, the Protector.

Lawrence Stone, *Sir Horatio Palavicino*, 1956.

PETER WENTWORTH (*c.* 1524–1596), parliamentary critic
of royal prerogative, was born about 1524 (not 1530, as in the
D.N.B.), He was the elder son of Sir Nicholas Wentworth of
Lillingstone Lovell, a village at that time in a piece of Oxfordshire
surrounded by Buckinghamshire, but by the time Peter succeeded his
father the village had been absorbed into Buckinghamshire. He was
twice married; first, to Letitia Lane, whose mother was a cousin to
Catherine Parr; secondly, to Elizabeth, sister of Sir Francis Walsingham. He entered Lincoln's Inn in 1542, but it was not until 1571,
when he was just on forty-seven years of age, that he entered
Parliament as Member for Barnstaple. He came into Parliament, he
said, because of his concern over the question of who was to succeed
to the throne after Elizabeth: 'I was first stirred up to deal in it . . . by
God's good motion, then by sundry grave and wise men unknown
unto me, and also by lamentable messages sent unto me by men
likewise unknown unto me.' He was to sit in six parliaments during
the next twenty-two years, as Member for Barnstaple, then Tregony,
and lastly for Northampton. He was a man 'of a whet and vehement
spirit', which got him into frequent and serious trouble with the
Queen for the attacks he made upon her, although he had a
passionate love and reverence for her.

In his first parliament of 1571 he was a member of the committee
which was formed in the House of Commons to submit a bill
dealing with the Articles of Religion to the Archbishop, Matthew
Parker. Parker asked why the Articles for the Homilies and some
other matters had been omitted. Wentworth's answer was, 'Surely
sir, because we were so occupied in other matters that we had no
time to examine them, how they agreed with the word of God.'
'What!' said Parker, 'surely you mistook the matter. You will refer
yourselves wholly to us therein.' Wentworth retorted, 'No, by the
faith I bear to God, we will pass nothing before we understand what
it is, for that were but to make you Popes. Make you Popes who list,
for we will make you none.' In this same parliament Sir Humphrey
Gilbert made a speech defending the privileges of the Crown.

Wentworth made a violent attack on Gilbert, noting 'his disposition to flatter or fawn on the Prince, comparing him to the chameleon, which can change himself into all colours saving white'.

The discovery of the Ridolfi Plot in 1571 necessitated the calling of another parliament. Wentworth was returned for the seat of Tregony. Great pressure was put on the Queen to execute Mary, Queen of Scots, or at least to attaint her: Elizabeth preferred to delay the attainder, but she sent for the committees of both Houses and treated them with such tact that the Commons moved a resolution that the thanks of the House be given to her. Wentworth opposed the resolution to return thanks, 'the which for my part I did not think her Majesty had deserved, so that my speech was to stay thanks'.

Parliament met again after an interval of three and a half years, in February 1576. During the interval Wentworth brooded on his experience in the Commons. He thought the House was too subservient to the Queen. On the 8th Wentworth made a resolution on liberty of speech. He forthrightly attacked the Queen for the 'great faults' she had committed. 'It is a dangerous thing in a Prince unkindly to intreat and abuse his or her nobility and people, as her Majesty did the last Parliament . . .' Sir John Neale has called this 'the most remarkable speech hitherto conceived in the Parliament of England . . . He was wrong, utterly wrong in his own generation; but the future hallowed his doctrine. He, indeed, as much as any of his colleagues, shaped that future' (*Elizabeth and her Parliaments, 1559–1581*, pp. 318–25). The House stopped him, committed him to the serjeant's ward and appointed a committee to examine him 'for the extenuating of his fault'. As a result Wentworth was sent to the Tower, where he remained for rather more than a month: then the Queen ordered his release and sent a very magnanimous message to the House of Commons. Wentworth was brought to the bar of the House, where he made a humble submission on his knees and was then allowed to take his seat again.

In 1579 Wentworth was in trouble with the Council. His bishop complained that many Puritans were resorting to his house at Lillingstone Lovell, where they received the Sacrament in Puritan fashion. Sir John Harington noted that Wentworth was 'a man of great accompt with all of that profession' in his neighbourhood. Wentworth was not a member of the 1584/5 Parliament, but he was returned for Northampton to the Parliament of 1586/7, made necessary by the Babington Plot. An attempt to reform the Church along Presbyterian lines failed in the Commons, because the Queen put a stop to it. Wentworth held that she thereby infringed the rights of the House. He therefore determined to make the Commons define their own rights to freedom of speech and no longer accept a definition laid down by the executive. He proposed to the House a series of questions, the answers to which would remain as the rulings of the House. Once more Wentworth, and four others, were sent to the Tower, not apparently for any speech made by them in the House, but for 'conferences in matters of religion' held outside the House where privilege did not arise. In fact, an organized campaign against the Elizabethan church settlement was being made, and the Queen would have none of it. The Puritans had only narrowly failed to win their case in Convocation in the '60s. They were now fighting in Parliament. Puritanism was also changing its character: in the past it had been a protest of Puritan clergy against religion being subordinated to politics. By Wentworth's time in the '80s it was beginning to be a protest of Puritan squires against control of the state by the bishops.

Up to this point Wentworth had been the champion of free speech, for he saw that the way for the Puritan cause to triumph was to make it a struggle for privilege in the House of Commons. If he could win freedom of speech there, the Queen could no longer put a stop to the attacks on the Church. From 1587, however, he ceased to think in terms of parliamentary privilege and became entirely taken up with the problem of the succession to the throne.

It is not known when Wentworth was released from the Tower. In 1587 he drafted A Pithie Exhortation to her Majestie for establishing her succession to the crowne. The tract urged the Queen to nominate the heir to the throne: it drew a fearful picture of what would happen to England if she were to die without having established her successor: and it also warned her of the dreadful fate which would befall her own body and her own soul. Wentworth failed to win any sympathy for his course of action, and when the Parliament ended, nothing had been done. In 1590 he tried to interest the Earl of Essex in his plan, but news of what was in his tract leaked out and he was summoned before the Council and put in the Gatehouse (August 1591). For a second time he tried to use

Burghley to bring the Queen over to his way of thinking, and of course failed. He was treated very leniently and was released on 21 November.

Ever an optimist, Wentworth was now convinced that the Queen would call a parliament and declare the name of the heir to the throne. When she did call a parliament in 1593, he fully expected this to happen. He prepared a campaign for the House of Commons and called some friends together to discuss his speech, the bill he had drafted, a petition to the House of Lords, a thanksgiving if the Queen agreed, and an attack on her if she refused. Few were ready to support Wentworth's scheme and then news of his intentions leaked out. He was summoned before the Council and once again found himself in the Tower. He never left that prison. He was not badly treated: he had considerable liberty and his wife was allowed to be with him. In 1594 he wrote his *Discourse containing the Author's opinion of the true and lawful successor to her Majesty* (published 1598). This was an answer to Father Parsons' *Conference about the Next Succession to the Crown of England*, in which the Jesuit repudiated the doctrine of divine hereditary right and implied that Parliament could make null the hereditary right of James VI of Scotland to the English throne. Wentworth refuted Parsons' arguments and supported the right of James to succeed Elizabeth. He had previously been against the Scottish claim, perhaps because he was opposed to the succession of Mary, Queen of Scots. Her execution removed this stumbling block, but Wentworth found himself opposing Parsons for allegedly over-exalting Parliament. (Neale, *Elizabeth and her Parliaments, 1584–1601*, p. 262). Efforts were made to secure his release, but these for unknown reasons failed. Wentworth died in the Tower in 1596.

The Queen's policy on the succession problem was subtle, characteristic and successful: not to take action when no action was needed, to keep the succession uncertain, to dangle it in front of James VI, 'to be given or withheld according to his behaviour' (Neale, *Elizabeth and her Parliaments, 1584–1601*, 251–2). Wentworth wanted to wreck that policy: Elizabeth could only treat him as she did. He was wrong from first to last, but he was a man of passionate conviction, passionately devoted to the Queen and to his country, but he totally lacked self-criticism. One of his contemporaries said of him that 'Mr. Wentworth will never acknowledge himself to make a fault nor say that he is sorry for anything he doth speak'. The Queen once said of him, 'Mr. Wentworth has a good opinion of his own wit'. In his fight for freedom of speech he was far ahead of his own times: but he would not have extended freedom of speech to his opponents: it was lucky for the Stuarts that Wentworth was not in the House of Commons in days when he would have found much more support than he found in his own day: it was lucky for Wentworth that he was dealt with by a comparatively lenient sovereign, for he would have had shorter shrift from Charles I than he got from Elizabeth. Wentworth was a symbol of his own age — the fiery spirit of Essex and Ralegh burned as high in him; but he was also a pointer to the future, a forerunner of Pym and Hampden, but not a progenitor of the Earl of Strafford.

Sir John Neale, *English Historical Review*, 1924; *idem, Elizabeth and her Parliaments*, 1953.

MARY, QUEEN OF SCOTS (1542–1587), was the third child and only daughter of James V of Scotland and of his wife, Marie de Guise. The rout of the Scottish army at Solway Moss had taken place on 24 November and Mary was born on 8 December. It is said that in his despair over the military defeat James V, on hearing the news of the birth of his daughter, cried out, 'it came with a lass and it will pass with a lass', and turned his face to the wall and died on 14 December. Mary was, therefore, one week old when she became Queen of Scots. Negotiations at once began for her marriage with Edward VI of England, but these were frustrated on religious grounds by Cardinal Beaton. On 10 September 1547 Protector Somerset, determined to bring about the marriage, defeated the Scots at Pinkie Cleugh. The Scots now made a marriage alliance with the French, and on 7 August 1548, at the age of 6, Mary sailed for France to marry the Dauphin, Francis, son of Henry II and Catherine de Medici.

Mary was brought up at the French court with the children of the royal family. Her education was carefully supervised and gave her all the Renaissance accomplishments. Throughout her life she wrote French most easily, although she was, of course, fluent in Scots and even learnt some English while in captivity here. The French Court was soon impressed by her intelligence, her charm, her beauty and personality. She was brought up a strict Roman Catholic in the midst of a cultured and far from strict Court, but the freedom of the Court would seem to have affected her more than the strict discipline of the Church, if one is to judge by her later history. Yet, in truth, her position was an impossible one. She had never known Scotland, yet she was Queen of that country: she married on 24 April 1558 a weak and sickly husband, Francis, heir to the French throne. She might thus combine the two kingdoms of France and Scotland, and she was heir to the throne of England. Yet before her marriage she had signed away Scotland to France, on the terms that if she died without an heir Scotland was to go as a free gift to the King of France, with all her rights to the English throne, and any assent she might be compelled to make to any different arrangement by the Scots was to be null and void from the start. That that was a betrayal of her native country cannot be denied, but what did her native country mean to a girl of sixteen who had left it at the age of six?

In the year when Mary married Francis (1558) Mary I of England died and the Protestant Elizabeth came to the English throne. Mary at once claimed the English throne on the grounds of Elizabeth's illegitimacy. She quartered the arms of England with those of France and assumed the style and titles of the ruler of England — and she used them even after her accession to the French throne, on the death of Henry II, in 1559. The English Queen was not unreasonably incensed.

On 10 June 1560 Marie de Guise died, which removed the Regent and created a feeling in some Scottish minds that the real Queen ought to return. On 5 December Francis II died and Mary was left a widow at the age of 18, with no throne in France, excluded from Court by the jealousy of the regent, Catherine de Medici, and with the prospect of returning to Scotland, where the Roman religion was proscribed and the Reformation was in full swing under John Knox. The Protestant lords were trying to arrange a marriage between James, the second Earl of Arran, who was heir to the Scottish throne after Mary, and Elizabeth of England. Scotland was a wild, uncivilized and heretical country, turbulent and split into factions. To return from France to Scotland was an act of great courage, especially as few of the lords seemed to want Mary. Elizabeth refused the Arran marriage: at once a reaction in favour of Mary set in.

Mary, Queen of Scots
(Artist: After Nicholas Hilliard)

The period of the negotiations for her return shows Mary at her best. She offered to forget all troubles of the past, she wanted to be recalled by the Scots, and she agreed not to interfere with the new Protestant religion of Scotland. But even at that moment she was playing a double game. She had not made up her mind to go back. She was desperately anxious to marry. The Guises backed her, hoping to recover their influence in French politics. But all proposals for Mary's marriage were thwarted by Catherine de Medici. At last Mary determined to go back to Scotland. It was an inauspicious moment from the point of view of Elizabeth. Mary was heir to the English throne: she was a Catholic, and the treaty of Edinburgh between Elizabeth and the Scottish Protestant lords was as yet unsigned. Trouble was bound to ensue.

Mary sailed from Calais on 15 August 1561. She had a cheerless journey, she was delayed outside Leith by a dense fog (Knox saw in this 'the sorrow, dolour, darkness and all impiety' which her arrival betokened), and no preparations had been made for her at Holyrood. Mass was said in her private chapel on the first Sunday, which resulted in a stormy interview between Mary and Knox, who came away impressed only by 'her proud mind, crafty wit and indurate heart'. (Knox is no reliable witness.) And indeed her passions — always so much stronger than her political judgements — led her into a great error. She had told Moray that she did not want to interfere with the religion of Scotland: but in fact she had already told the Pope that she meant to restore Catholicism to Scotland. And now she burst out at Knox: 'Ye are not the kirk I will nourish. I will defend the Kirk of Rome, for I believe it is the true Kirk of God.'

Efforts have been made to see Mary as a successful ruler of Scotland in the years 1561-7. She did not convince Knox, who noted that 'in the council she kept herself very grave: but as soon as ever her French fillocks and fiddlers and others of that brand gat the house alone, then might be seen skipping not very comely for honest women'. Knox thought that rather than work at the business of being a Queen, she preferred to 'shoot at the butts' and to hawk. It is true that Mary's *politique* policy restored a degree of religious peace to Scotland, and that for a while she was able to keep order among the troublesome Scottish nobles. She established quite friendly relations with Elizabeth of England, but her negotiations failed to obtain any recognition of her claims to the English succession, and Elizabeth remained suspicious of her. Within a short time, Mary's government in Scotland was to be challenged, especially after her disastrous marriage to Darnley.

Mary's prime objective when she returned to Scotland was marriage. She wanted at first to marry Don Carlos, son of Philip II, and thus to combine in her own person the thrones of England, Scotland and Spain. To accomplish this she was ready to restore

Catholicism in Scotland. But the Guises were opposed to and prevented the marriage. Elizabeth suggested Robert Dudley, Earl of Leicester, but in 1565 there arrived in Scotland Henry Stuart, Lord Darnley, the elder son of the Earl of Lennox and Margaret, daughter of Margaret Tudor, sister of Henry VIII, and the Earl of Lennox. Thus Darnley was heir to the English throne after Mary herself. He was aged 19, extraordinarily handsome, very athletic, of the meanest intelligence, arrogant, wilful and vicious. Whether Mary did in fact fall in love with Darnley has been disputed. That she did would seem to be her only justification. If the marriage was simply a political move to strengthen her claim to the English throne, her intelligence failed to reveal to her that Darnley, a Catholic, could only further bind together the English and the Scottish Protestants, could only alarm the Scottish Protestant lords for the safety of their lands, and threaten the hopes of the Hamiltons of reaching the throne of Scotland. At any rate, she married him, perhaps secretly in March, certainly publicly in July 1565. From this ill-judged marriage sprang most of Mary's future troubles.

Darnley was hateful to the Scottish lords, largely on account of his arrogance, his imprudence and his viciousness. Hateful also was David Riccio, one of Mary's musical quartet whom she now raised to be her Foreign Secretary. Moray headed a rebellion, which Mary succeeded in putting down, but she had already found out her mistake in marrying Darnley. His discontent that she refused to give him the Crown Matrimonial (that is, official recognition by parliament of his position as her equal as King and the reversion of the throne to him, were Mary to die first), his weakness of character, and his accusations that she was Riccio's mistress, soon turned her love to hatred. The murder of Riccio in 1566 was followed by the imprisonment of the Queen by the lords, but Mary escaped with Darnley, with whom she put up as well as possible until her son was born in June 1566. It is at least probable that she was already in love with Bothwell and anxious to be rid of Darnley. He had just married Jane Gordon, sister of the Earl of Huntly, but within a matter of weeks he had made up his mind to secure the Scottish throne by marrying Mary. When Darnley fell ill at Glasgow — it was said of smallpox, almost certainly of syphilis — Mary attended him frequently, then fetched him away to an isolated house outside Edinburgh, Kirk o' Field, where he might have better air than in the city, the arrangements being left in the hands of Bothwell. She left Darnley there late in the evening of 9 February 1567 and went in the company of Bothwell to Holyrood. Early in the morning of the 10th the house at Kirk o' Field was blown up and the body of Darnley was found under a tree, uninjured by the explosion: he had been strangled before the explosion took place. There is no proof that Mary had any hand in the murder of her husband, or that she even knew it was to take place, since the only purported evidence contained in the Casket Letters must on the whole be rejected. Yet, if she was wholly innocent, her subsequent behaviour with the universally accepted murderer, Bothwell, requires much more explanation than has so far been forthcoming. She made no attempt to exonerate herself when the populace was vociferously accusing her, as she went through the streets. She showered favours on Bothwell, probably agreed to a collusive abduction, and within three months of Darnley's death she had married the by then divorced Bothwell (16 May 1567). Never had Mary behaved with less wisdom or discretion.

Once again Mary's passions had outrun her judgement — or so one is justified in saying, until further evidence in her favour is available. Fairly or unfairly, all Europe turned against her — France, Spain, the Pope and her own subjects. The Scottish lords raised an army against her, Mary and Bothwell gathered a small force (mostly adherents of Bothwell's) to meet them. At Carberry Hill, seven miles outside Edinburgh (June 1567), the two sides met, but Mary's army dwindled away without any battle being fought. She was forced to abdicate and was imprisoned in a castle on Loch Leven. Bothwell escaped to Norway. In 1568 Mary escaped from Loch Leven, raised a force to meet her half-brother, the Regent, Earl of Moray, but she was defeated at Langside, and then crossed the Border into England. Mary is sometimes described as 'fleeing' into England, but she could safely have stayed in Scotland, where her supporters were rallying, or have returned to France, to seek the help of her family. To put herself into Elizabeth's hands was to commit an act of gross political miscalculation. Elizabeth never released Mary, keeping her in one place of imprisonment or another for the next nineteen years. For the first few years, Elizabeth entered into discussions with the Scots and French to achieve Mary's restoration to the throne of Scotland, but all negotiations of this sort failed.

Mary now became the centre, witting or unwitting, of Catholic plots against the life of Elizabeth. Without doubt the extreme Catholics used her for their own ends: without doubt Mary was a party to their plots. She came to approve political assassination too many times for Elizabeth to feel safe or for anybody to believe her protestations. When her brother Moray was murdered (1570), she wrote to Cardinal Beaton that 'she was the more indebted to the assassin that he had acted without her instigation': but she told Moray's widow that the murder was done 'against our will'. She agreed to the plot by which she was to marry the Duke of Norfolk: she was a party to the Ridolfi plot (1571) which was linked with Norfolk's plot: she was pleading with Elizabeth for kindness and at the same moment she was hand in glove with Throckmorton in his plot for the invasion of England and the taking off of Elizabeth (1583): by her own actions she hopelessly entangled herself in the Babington Plot (1586), for she dictated a letter to Babington which gave her consent to a rising on her behalf which was to include the murder of Elizabeth. Her arrest, trial and condemnation followed inevitably. For a long time Elizabeth refused to sign the death warrant, but at last she gave way, and Mary was beheaded at Fotheringay Castle on 8 February 1587.

It is doubtful, however, whether the plots in which Mary engaged were very dangerous to Elizabeth, and Mary's imprisonment in England made the task of conspirators more, not less difficult. Elizabeth gained a great deal from having Mary in prison in England; above all, it tied the Scottish opponents of Mary closely to the English side, and it established a close, lasting alliance between Scotland and England for the first time in the history of what had previously been extremely hostile nations.

Mary Stuart has been fortunate in her biographers beyond her deserts. Largely through her dignity and courage at her execution, the spell which she failed to exert on most of her contemporaries she has succeeded in casting on her modern biographers. Mary, Queen of Scots, has become a legendary figure, a shamefully wronged woman, beautiful (Clouet has done his very good best for her), pathetic, romantic and pitiable. Swinburne wrote of her that 'the world never saw more splendid courage at the service of more brilliant intelligence'. That is a travesty of the truth.

It is doubtful how much intelligence she had: it failed her over

Darnley and over Bothwell. She had some courage, as in deciding to return to Scotland from France — but what other choice was open to her? That courage failed her after Carberry when, in the Provost's house in Edinburgh, she was seen at the window half-naked and screaming for help. It failed her again after Langside, when she fled to England as fast as a horse could carry her, before her cause was irretrievably lost. And it is difficult not to feel that much of her behaviour in prison in England was unheroic.

It is easy to say that no woman, placed in Mary's circumstances, could have succeeded where she failed. It is as easy to say that in any other circumstances Mary would as surely have ruined her own life. She was a woman destitute of all moral sense, incapable of self-sacrifice, concerned only with her own selfish ends. It is not even true that she remained faithful to the Catholic religion: she abandoned it in order to get the Scottish throne; she would have abandoned it, if there had been the slightest chance of her winning the English throne through the English Protestants. And she, the Queen, had not enough authority or will to marry Bothwell according to the Roman ceremony. Mary, Queen of Scots, is pitiable in that she had not enough character to control her passions: it is only by falsifying values, Protestant or Catholic, that she can be called admirable.

From her folly and suffering, however, the union of England and Scotland, in the person of her son, James VI and I, was to be born.

G. Buchanan, *The Tyrannous Reign of Mary Stewart*, ed. Gatherer, 1958.

A. Fraser, *Mary, Queen of Scots*, 1971.

G. Donaldson, *Mary, Queen of Scots*, 1974.

M. Lynch (ed.), *Mary Stewart*, 1987.

HENRY STUART, LORD DARNLEY (1546–1567) second husband of Mary, Queen of Scots, was born at Temple Newsam in Yorkshire in 1546. He was the second but eldest surviving son of Matthew Stuart, Earl of Lennox, and his wife, Lady Margaret Douglas, Countess of Lennox, daughter of Margaret Tudor, widow of James IV of Scotland, by her second husband, the Earl of Angus: Margaret Tudor was the aunt of Elizabeth I, therefore Darnley, who had been born in England and was an English subject, was next legal heir to the English throne after Mary, Queen of Scots, if Elizabeth were to die childless. In 1560 de Quadra, the Spanish Ambassador, reported to Philip II that if that were to happen the English Catholics would put Darnley on to the English throne. The Countess of Lennox — 'a very wise and discreet matron' (Sir James Melville's *Memoirs*, 1929 ed., p. 99) — was at that time correspsonding with the Scottish Catholic lords about marrying Darnley to Mary, Queen of Scots. The Countess and Darnley, therefore, found themselves shut up in the Tower for a time by Elizabeth, who thought it worth while to deny the legitimacy of the Countess on the grounds that her mother had got a Papal divorce from Angus (1527) and that the Scottish estates had declared her to be a bastard. Mother and son were soon released, and Darnley was daily at Elizabeth's court.

In 1564 Sir James Melville was sent by Mary to Elizabeth to get permission for Darnley to visit Scotland in order to 'see the country'. At that moment Elizabeth was suggesting that Mary should marry Robert Dudley, Earl of Leicester, but she very well knew the real purpose of the visit, for she said to Melville, 'ye like better of yon long lad, pointing towards my Lord Darnley ... My answer was that no woman of spirit would make choice of such a man, who resembled more a woman than a man. For he was handsome, beardless and lady-faced' (Melville, *ibid.*, p. 92). All the same, probably because she feared that Mary might in fact marry Leicester, Elizabeth sent Darnley to Scotland, 'in hope that he being a handsome, lusty youth, should rather prevail, being present, than Leicester who was absent' (*ibid.*, p. 101).

Darnley arrived at Wemyss Castle on 17 February 1565, where he stayed with Mary for two or three days. It is probable, though disputable, that Mary at once fell desperately in love with 'the properest, and best proportioned long man that ever she had seen: for he was of a high stature, long and tall, even and straight' (Melville, *ibid.*, p. 107). Darnley was indeed handsome and notably athletic, by repute a good musician on the lute; but his intelligence was of the meanest and he was vain, arrogant, irritable and vicious by the time he was twenty years of age.

The marriage between Darnley and Mary was greatly encouraged by Riccio, who was by this time rapidly advancing in the Queen's favour and confidence. In April Darnley fell ill of the measles, and Mary was assiduous in her attentions to him. She knighted him and created him Earl of Ross and later Duke of Albany. On 29 July their public marriage took place in the chapel of Holyrood (1565).

From the moment that he arrived in Scotland Darnley was hated by the Protestant lords, because he was a Catholic. In next to no time he was universally hated for his extreme unwisdom. He chose as his friends the most disreputable of the Scottish nobles, his pride was 'intolerable' and 'his words not to be borne'. Politically he was a menace, for he could not keep his tongue quiet — 'few durst advertise him, ... because he told all again to some of his own servants, who were not all honest' (Melville, *ibid.*, p. 145). Then he took to drink and treated the Queen so shamefully in public that she 'left the house in tears'. Mary knew now what a fatal marriage she had made. She refused Darnley the Crown Matrimonial and she began to advance Riccio to the political importance which should have been Darnley's. Darnley's position was becoming increasingly difficult and there were some of his relations who were offended by his humiliation.

Hated as Darnley was, Riccio was soon even more hated, as a Catholic, as a foreigner, and for his arrogant behaviour. He was virtually the Queen's Prime Minister and all business was conducted by him. Darnley's Catholic friends and Protestant enemies now combined for a moment to murder Riccio. Darnley was not only privy to the plot, but he insisted on being present at the murder, because so great had his hatred for his wife become that he accused her of being Riccio's mistress. Riccio had done him 'the most dishonour that could be to any man'. On Saturday evening, 9 March 1565, Darnley admitted the conspirators — Moray, Morton, Ruthven and others — into Holyrood and led them up by the private staircase into the room where Mary was dining with Riccio. After the murder was committed, it was Darnley's dagger which was left in Riccio's side — borrowed for the purpose by the nobles, who were determined to make him appear as the instigator of and sharer in the deed.

For political reasons Mary could not at once break with Darnley. She promised him his proper position as her husband. Darnley told her 'all that he knew of any man' in the conspiracy. There was a brief reconciliation, but almost at once Mary discovered Darnley's share in the plot. She never forgave him, but she was pregnant and she would do nothing to jeopardize the legitimacy of her child. She began to favour Moray, Maitland and others who hated Darnley. His position was impossible and he determined to leave the country. The nobles met at Craigmillar and determined to be rid of Darnley. Darnley refused to attend the christening of his son at Stirling, left for Glasgow to find a ship to take him abroad, but he fell ill, almost certainly of syphilis, and could not go. Mary was now in love with Bothwell, but she brought about a reconciliation with Darnley and persuaded him, when he was convalescent, to go with her to Edinburgh. She took him to an isolated house at Kirk o' Field, outside Edinburgh, left him there on the evening of 9 February 1566 and went to Edinburgh with Bothwell. Early in the morning of the 10th the house was blown up. Darnley's body and that of his page were found under a tree, unmarked by the explosion: they had been strangled before the house was blown up.

Darnley's body was buried in the tomb of James V in the chapel of Holyrood.

DAVID RICCIO or RIZZIO (1533?–1566), secretary to Mary, Queen of Scots, was born probably in 1533. Generally reputed in his own day and for centuries since to have been the low-born son of a teacher of music at Turin, David is now thought to have come of a noble and wealthy family in Piedmont, that of Riccio di Solbitro. If this is true, then his poverty may have been a pose and his true status well known to the Queen. He is said to have had a pleasing bass voice and to have played the lute (Sir James Melville in his *Memoirs*, 1929 ed., p. 103, calls him 'a merry fellow and a good musician'), to have spent some time at the court of the Duke of Savoy, and then at the age of twenty-eight to have arrived in Scotland in the wake of Morette, who was on a mission for the Duke (1561). Mary had three *valets de chambre* who sang in her private chapel and she was looking for a fourth to complete the quartet. Riccio applied for the post and was accepted. He held this position for some years and then in 1564 the Queen's French Secretary, Raullet, was dismissed for having been corrupted by English gold, and Riccio was appointed in his place. A hostile writer, Randolph, had it that Riccio 'croope in on suspicion gathered against Raulet'. Mary was at this point planning to take the direction of policy entirely into her own hands and she feared that her French Secretary might betray her to her uncle of Lorraine. The new appointment cannot have been a great success, for Melville records that 'advices given by the Queen of England were misconstructed ... partly because David Riccio, lately admitted to be French secretary, was not very skilful in inditing French letters, which she [Mary] did write over again in her own hand' (*ibid.*, p. 23). One of the grounds for Riccio's unpopularity was that many looked on him as a Papal agent (Melville called him to Mary 'a known minion of the Pope', *ibid.*, p. 106), but he was never acknowledged as such by the Papacy.

At this point two things are certain — first, 'the extraordinary favour [which Mary] carried to that man' (Melville, *ibid.*, p. 105): secondly, that it was Riccio who was a chief supporter of the Darnley marriage. Melville again noted that Riccio was Darnley's 'great friend at the Queen's hand' (*ibid.*, p. 107). Darnley and Riccio were at first intimate friends, playing tennis together by day and sharing the same bed by night.

After Mary married Darnley, Riccio virtually became Secretary of State. It did not take Mary long after her marriage to find out what a disastrous mistake she had made. Her hatred for the insufferable Darnley grew, and as it grew Riccio attained the position which should have been that of Mary's husband. He became the Queen's adviser on all matters, even in the presence of the Scottish lords. The only road to royal favour was Riccio. Darnley demanded the Crown Matrimonial, but he was refused that and treated with (perhaps well deserved) contumely. The arrogance of Riccio became insupportable to the Scottish lords, as it was insupportable to Darnley. And his arrogance was encouraged by the Queen. Darnley's jealousy at last reached the point where he accused Mary of being Riccio's mistress. Darnley thereby played into the hands of those lords who hated Riccio. The murder of Riccio was the inevitable result.

As so often happens in conspiracies, enemies find themselves on the same side, bound together solely by hatred of a common enemy. Catholic relatives of Darnley resented his treatment by Riccio: Protestant lords saw in Riccio a Papal agent for restoring the Catholic religion in Scotland: many of both parties saw in Riccio the chief proposer for the bill to come before Parliament for confiscating the lands of those lords who had rebelled against Mary at the time of her marriage with Darnley. Morton, Moray, Lethington, Argyle, Ruthven combined to slaughter Riccio. All had a common aim, to be rid thereby of Mary. All were determined to make the murder appear the work of Darnley. Thus it was that Darnley's dagger was left in the side of Riccio. The murder took place in the evening of Saturday, 9 March 1566, in the palace of Holyrood. Riccio was dragged from the very presence of the Queen when they were at supper and struck down outside with fifty-six dagger strikes. His body was buried at first before the door of the abbey: later, by Mary's orders, it was laid in the royal tomb at Edinburgh, but then it was transferred to another part of the church.

W. A. Gatherer, introduction to G. Buchanan's *The Tyrannous Reign of Mary Stuart*, 1958.

JAMES HEPBURN, 4th EARL OF BOTHWELL (1535?–1578), third husband of Mary, Queen of Scots, was the son of Patrick Hepburn, third Earl of Bothwell, known as the Fair Earl, and his wife Agnes, daughter of Henry Lord Sinclair. He was brought up mostly in the home of his relative, Patrick Hepburn, Bishop of Moray, where he acquired a better education than was usual among the nobles of Scotland at that time. His father died in 1556, and James inherited his hereditary offices, which included Warden of the Scottish Marches and Lord High Admiral of Scotland. Bothwell was a Protestant, but he supported the policy of the Catholic Queen Regent, Marie de Guise, and opposed Arran and the reforming lords. In 1557 he commanded an expedition which raided the English border lands, and for the rest of his life he was unalterably hostile to England. In 1559 the English secretly arranged to supply the Protestant lords with £3,000 to help them against the French influence of Marie de Guise. When the money was sent north, Bothwell waylaid the conveyer of the cash and went off with it to his castle of Crichton, intending to hand it over to the Regent. Her confidence in Bothwell was so great that in 1560 she planned to send him to France to secure help in men and money, but she died in June of that year, whereupon Bothwell went on a visit to Denmark. Here he met a Norwegian girl, Anna Throndsson, whom he carried off to the Netherlands and there abandoned in great penury. She was years later to play a disastrous part in the fate of Bothwell, by giving away to Frederick II of Denmark, when Bothwell was his prisoner, the story of their early relations.

In 1560 Bothwell was in Paris and on the death of Francis II

Mary, Queen of Scots, sent him to Scotland as one of her commissioners. The next year he was made a member of the Privy Council. He was, however, in perpetual trouble because of his turbulent behaviour, especially in his relations with Arran, the nearest heir to the Scottish crown, so much so that in 1562 he was accused of trying to carry off the Queen and was imprisoned in Edinburgh. He managed to break out and then made up his mind to go back to France. On his way he was driven by a storm into Holy Island and he was detained by the English for a few months (1564). He went to France, but he was back in Scotland in March, returned to France and was thence recalled by Mary, who wanted his help against the Earl of Moray. Elizabeth I made every effort to prevent his return and sent Anthony Jenkinson with some ships to cruise off the coast of Scotland and to stop him from landing. But Bothwell gave him the slip and from now onwards he came to have increasing favour with and influence over the Scottish Queen.

In February 1565 Bothwell married Lady Jean Gordon, sister of George, fifth Earl of Huntly, which makes it clear that Bothwell had not yet formed any idea that he might marry Mary, Queen of Scots. The Huntly family was Catholic, but Bothwell remained a Protestant. He was in Holyrood on the night of the murder of Riccio (1566), but he had no knowledge of the plot and no hand in it. When he and Huntly heard the noise of the murder they went to the inner court, but they were ordered back to their rooms by Morton, who had taken control of the palace. They managed to escape by a back window and both of them went to Bothwell's home at Crichton. Mary was a prisoner in Holyrood, but she patched up a reconciliation with Darnley and they both rode by night to Dunbar, where they were joined by Bothwell. His resolute behaviour had won her admiration and her gratitude, so that from now on Bothwell's position grew more and more important. Knox wrote that Bothwell 'had now of all men greatest success and familiarity with the queen', and Sir James Melville's opinion was that Bothwell had 'a mark of his own that he shot at', to be King in the place of Darnley. In October 1566 Bothwell was severely wounded by an outlaw: as he lay ill at his castle, the Hermitage, the Queen rode over to see him and returned the same day — a distance of between fifty and sixty miles. Her love for Darnley was dead: with good reason she hated him. Had she transferred that love now to Bothwell? Was he captivated? Was he merely an adventurer in search of a crown? On an answer to these questions depends a fair historical judgement on the events which follow. We are unlikely now ever to know the real truth, since the evidence of the Casket Letters is worthless, and there is no genuine evidence on the other side. The generally accepted version of the events is as follows.

By the end of 1566 everybody was agreed that Darnley could no longer be tolerated as the Queen's husband. In December a conference was held at Craigmillar at which Bothwell favoured divorce, but the Catholic lords were not likely to agree to this. Later, a bond was said to have been signed by Bothwell, Huntly, Maitland, Argyll and James Balfour undertaking to get rid of Darnley 'by one way or other'. In January 1567 Mary went to Glasgow to see Darnley, who was ill of so-called smallpox — almost certainly it was syphilis (Gore-Browne, *Lord Bothwell*, p. 290) — and she was to take him to Edinburgh. In order that Darnley should have better air than he would get in the city, the plan was changed and an isolated house at Kirk o' Field was chosen by Bothwell, who made all the arrangements for housing Darnley. He had gunpowder brought from Dunbar and placed in the Queen's room below that of Darnley, with the intention of blowing up the house with Darnley in it. The Queen left the house late in the evening of 9 February in order to attend a ball at Holyrood and went in the company of Bothwell. Bothwell attended the ball, left about midnight and returned to Kirk o' Field, where he himself fired the train to the gunpowder. With his companions he then returned to Holyrood as soon as the explosion took place. The body of the King was found some distance from the house, without any mark from the explosion, and it was generally held that he had been strangled before the explosion took place. Bothwell himself said that the accident was 'the strangest that ever chancit, to wit, the fouder (lightning) came out of the luft (sky) and had burnt the king's house'. He then gave large presents to all his accomplices, telling them to 'hold their tongues for they should never want so long as he had anything'. There are some difficulties in accepting this version, and an ingenious attempt has been made to prove that it was Darnley who had the powder put in the house with the intention of blowing up the Queen, that rumour of this reached Holyrood during the ball, that Bothwell went to Kirk o' Field to investigate, found the powder in the downstairs room and fired the train to blow up Darnley: but Darnley woke and smelt the burning, rushed out of the house in his nightshirt into the arms of Archibald Douglas and his friends, who murdered him before the explosion took place (Gore-Browne, *ibid.*, ch. 28).

Public opinion was from the first convinced that Bothwell was the murderer, but his position at court was not in the least degree weakened. He obtained a formal acquittal in the lawcourts and he received large grants of land from the Queen. There can be no doubt that by this time Bothwell was determined to marry Mary. On 24 April 1567 the Queen was returning from Stirling to Edinburgh, when she was met by Bothwell with an armed force and was carried off to Dunbar. It is almost impossible not to believe that this so-called abduction was carried out with the knowledge and consent of the Queen. Meantime Bothwell had started a collusive action for a divorce between him and his wife, Lady Jean Gordon, on the grounds that there had been no dispensation granted when he married her within the forbidden degrees. There had been such a dispensation, and it has been discovered at Dunrobin in Sutherland-shire. On 7 May the divorce was granted and on the 15th Bothwell and the Queen were married at Holyrood (1567), according to Protestant rites. A few days before, Bothwell had been created Duke of Orkney and Lord of Shetland.

Arrogant, ruthless, self-confident, Bothwell had never been a popular man. What he had now done was in effect to have usurped the government: there was not the least chance that the Scottish lords would take that lying down. They determined to capture the Queen and Bothwell at Holyrood. Forewarned, Bothwell and the Queen fled to Borthwick Castle: when it was surrounded by Morton and Home, Bothwell escaped to Dunbar, where he was joined by the Queen in a few days. Raising a force which was composed mostly of Bothwell's men and was not a proof of public support for Mary, they met the lords at Carberry Hill. There was little enthusiasm even among Bothwell's followers: no reinforcements arrived to back the Queen: both sides began to negotiate; at once the Queen's army began to melt away. Bothwell himself created a very strong impression on the French ambassador, du Croc, who thought that if the troops had remained loyal the Queen's cause would have won under Bothwell's leadership. Bothwell tried to hazard all on a challenge to single combat: the Queen would not accept that and persuaded him to escape. He rode off unpursued to Dunbar. Bothwell and Mary never met again.

After a sojourn at Spynie with his old guardian, the Bishop of Moray, Bothwell escaped by sea, making first for Orkney, then for Shetland. He collected a number of ships and became for a time captain of a pirate fleet. Pursued by Kirkcaldy of Grange, he was arrested by a Danish ship off the coast of Norway, whence he was sent to Denmark. There he was imprisoned by Frederick II, first at Malmoe and later at Dragsholm (1573–8), where he died in abject misery, having almost certainly gone out of his mind.

F. Schiern, *James Hepburn, Earl of Bothwell*, trans. from the Danish by the Rev. David Berry, 1880.
J. Stuart: *A Lost Chapter in the History of Mary, Queen of Scots, Recovered*, 1874.
R. Gore-Browne, *Lord Bothwell*, 1937.

SIR JOHN HARINGTON (1561–1612), poet, courtier, inventor of the water-closet, was born in 1561 at Kelston, near Bath. He was the son of John Harington and Isabella Markham, who were imprisoned in the Tower at the same time as the Princess Elizabeth. John the elder was fined £1,000 for conveying a letter to Elizabeth from one of her friends while they were in prison. When Elizabeth became Queen she never forgot the loyalty of Harington and in recognition of it she became godmother to the young John.

The boy went to Eton, where he seems not to have differed much from modern Etonians. He recalled his teacher's addressing him as 'thou varay lazy fellow' — one can hear the imitation of accent. He was as disrespectful even of the Provost, who 'brake his leg with a fall from a horse that started under him. Whereupon some waggish scholars, of which I think myself was in the quorum, would say it was a just punishment, because the horse was given him by a gentleman to place his son at Eton'.

From Eton to King's, Cambridge, where he described himself as a truantly scholar who had taken little for his money. Yet he also paid a no doubt well-merited tribute to his tutor 'to whom I never came, but I grew more religious; from whom I never went, but I parted better instructed'. There is a pleasant sidelight on the Queen, who sent him a copy of her speech to Parliament (15 March 1576),

Sir John Harington
(Artist: Attributed to H. Custodis)

'and I do this, because thy father was ready to serve and love us in trouble and thrall'.

After Cambridge John turned to the study of law at Lincoln's Inn. On the death of his father (1582) he abandoned the law and went to Kelson to look to the building of the house there. Here, perhaps for the first time, he revealed his flair for mechanical inventions, not only in a fountain (originally designed by Ariosto) worked by running water, but also in a more useful, if less decorative device which was to cause himself some trouble later with the Queen, but to earn him also much gratitude with all succeeding generations, even in a short time with the Queen herself.

He was not always at Kelston, for he was frequently at Court. And here it may be noted that, in spite of two or three quarrels and dismissals, his royal godmother always had for him a deep affection, as John Harington always had for her. He was so brilliant, so gay, so witty, so clever, that he could not but charm her: but discipline had to be maintained, and Elizabeth never allowed personal feelings to undermine discipline — unless it might be with Leicester. Harington's first escapade was concerned with a translation which he made of the improper story of Giacomo in the 28th book of Ariosto's *Orlando Furioso*. The manuscript was circulated among the maids of honour at the Court. It fell into the hands of the Queen. John was exiled from Court, but one sees a wink of the eyelid in the verdict, until he had translated the whole of Ariosto's poem into English. John accomplished this by 1592, when he presented a magnificently bound copy of the work to Elizabeth on her visit to Kelston in that year. The versification may not have been above moderately good, but the volume carried a frontispiece, a portrait of Harington engraved on copper plate and signed by William Rogers, the first man to practise this art in England, probably the first book in England to be illustrated with copper plates.

The next important moment in Harington's life was the publication in 1596 of *A New Discourse upon a Stale Subject,* with the sub-title of *The Metamorphosis of Ajax.* This was published under the author's pseudonym of Misacmos. There were in fact three sections to this dissertation, but the real point of the publication was that Harington described in detail and with diagrams, and with a good many none too savoury digressions, often aimed at particular and well-known men at Court, his invention of the water-closet, on which John Harington's chief claim to fame ought to rely. (Ajax was a pun on the words 'a jakes', jakes being the Elizabethan word for a privy.) The work was issued under the initials T.C., which stood for T. C. Traveller. He explained 'how unsavoury places may be made sweet, noisome places made wholesome, filthy places made cleanly', at a cost of thirty shillings and eightpence. The Queen was much displeased, not with the indecorous passages in the book, but with veiled allusions to the Earl of Leicester. At one moment Harington was in great danger of facing Star Chamber: it is almost certain that Elizabeth's affection for him saved him from that process. But the edict went forth that that 'saucey poet' leave the Court 'till he be grown sober' (1596). By 1598 the Queen had forgiven her godson and commanded that a Harington water-closet be installed at Richmond Palace.

The next year (1599) Essex set out on his ill-fated expedition to Ireland. The Queen never trusted Essex, least of all on this military venture. She therefore sent her godson as Master of the Horse with orders 'to take account of all that passes in your expedition and keep journal thereof, unknown to any in the company: this will be expected of you. I have reasons to give for this order'. Harington had so little warning that 'I had scant time to put on my boots'. The expedition proved a total failure, and on returning to England Essex took Harington (whom he had knighted in Ireland) with him to his interview with Elizabeth. The Queen was in a furious temper and ordered Harington home to Kelston. 'I did not stay to be bidden twice. If all the Irish rebels had been at my heels, I should not have made better speed.' But before he left London he had another interview with his godmother at which he was 'cleared and graciously dismissed ... Until I come to heaven, I shall never come before a statelier judge again, nor one that can temper majesty, wisdom, learning, choler, and favour better than her Highness did at that time'.

In 1602 Harington saw the Queen for the last time and found her in 'most pitiable state'. Within three months she was dead. How deep was Harington's affection for the Queen breaks out in a letter to his wife: 'I can not blot from my memory's table the goodness of our sovereign Lady to me, even (I will say) before born; her affection to my mother ... her bettering the state of my father's fortune (which I have, alas! so much worsted), her watchings over my youth, her liking to my free speech and admiration of my little learning and poesie, which I did so much cultivate on her command, have rooted such love, such dutiful remembrance of her princely virtues, that to turn askant from her condition with tearless eyes would stain and foul the spring and fount of gratitude'.

Already by 1602 everybody of importance was taking out an insurance policy with James VI of Scotland. Harington wrote a tract *On The Succession to the Crown* (1602) in which he supported the claim of James VI to the English throne. He sent a copy to the King and with it a New Year present of a lantern so devised as to symbolize the waning light of Elizabeth and the rising splendour of James. There was also a representation of the Crucifixion with the inscription, 'Lord, remember me when thou comest into Thy Kingdom' — a typically light-hearted piece of bad taste, if not of blasphemy. The King treated Harington graciously, made him a Knight of the Bath, gave to him the properties of Harington's Markham cousins, forfeited for Sir Griffin Markham's part in the plot to put Lady Arabella Stuart on the throne, added the advowson of the rectory to the manor of Kelston, and confirmed all the properties his father had obtained through his Tudor marriage to the family for ever.

Towards the end of his life, from 1602 onwards, Harington was involved in three major lawsuits and quarrels over properties to which he tried to lay claim and some of which he tried to secure by force. He was greatly in debt and in need of money, but his methods of repairing his fortunes shew him in the least reputable light. Indeed, he was at one moment imprisoned, having promised to stand surety for the debts of his cousin, Sir Griffin Markham. He was in prison for a year, then he escaped.

In 1609 he translated the *Regimen Sanitatis Salernitanum* and entitled his book *The Englishman's Doctor*, or *the Schoole of Salerne*, perhaps for the use of James I's son, the prince Henry, for whom he had two years earlier composed the *Brief View of the State of the Church*. If none of Harington's literary productions commands much attention to-day, (in his own day his epigrams were much admired), his letters mark him as one of the great letter writers in English literature. Harington was a shrewd observer, he had a wonderful gift for what would nowadays be newspaper reporting, he was always interesting, usually witty, sometimes Rabelaisian, often serious. Some of the most intimate, alive and even moving portraits that we have of Queen Elizabeth are to be found in his letters: to his letters we owe the most vivid and forthright pictures of James I and his court, especially his vivid account of a drunken orgy, quoted in D. H. Willson's *King James VI and I*.

Ian Grimble, *The Harington Family*, 1957.
D. MacDonald, 'Sir John Harington,' *History Today*, vi, 1956.
Rev. H. Harington, *Nugae Antiquae* (collected letters), 1769.
N. E. McClure, *Letters and Epigrams*, 1930.

ELIZABETH HARDWICK (*c.* 1527–1608), 'Bess of Hardwick', was born in about 1527 and died in 1608 at a remarkable age for Tudor times. She was the daughter of John Hardwick of Hardwick Hall in the county of Derby, and of his wife, Elizabeth Leake. Bess was married four times: (1) to Robert Barley or Barlow in about 1542, but he died in 1544; (2) to William Cavendish in 1547; he died in 1557. By this marriage there were six children, and the first purpose in Bess's life was to further their interests. William became first Earl of Devon, and from him sprang the long line of Cavendish Earls of Devon and Dukes of Devonshire. Charles had a son, William, who became the first Duke of Newcastle and commanded Charles I's northern army in the Civil War. Elizabeth married Charles Stuart, Earl of Lennox, and their daughter was Lady Arabella Stuart, who might have succeeded Elizabeth I as Queen of England. Mary married Gilbert Talbot, seventh Earl of Shrewsbury, and their three daughters married respectively William Herbert, Earl of Pembroke; Henry Grey, eighth Earl of Kent; and Thomas Howard, Earl of Arundel. (3) Bess married William St. Looe in 1559, and he died in 1564 or 1565; (4) George Talbot, sixth Earl of Shrewsbury, in 1567, and he died in 1590.

Bess was imprisoned in the Tower from August 1561 to March 1562 for her connection with the clandestine marriage of Catherine Grey to Edward Seymour. She came close to being imprisoned for a second time in 1574 for the marriage of her daughter Elizabeth to Charles Stuart, a possible claimant to the throne. For sixteen years she shared with her husband, Shrewsbury, the thankless, expensive and dangerous honour of acting as gaoler to Mary, Queen of Scots (1569–85). From 1578 to 1603 she devoted herself to trying to make sure that Arabella Stuart should secure the throne on the death of Elizabeth, and that she should succeed to the Lennox inheritance. Bess failed in both objects.

If devotion to her family, with whom she frequently quarrelled, was her first passion, Bess had another purpose almost as dear to her heart: she was one of the great builders of the English Renaissance,

Elizabeth Hardwick
(Artist: Unknown)

and if her magnificent house at Chatsworth has disappeared, Hardwick Hall remains as the durable monument to a lady of character and genius.

P. M. Handover, *Arabella Stuart*, 1957.

E. Carleton Williams, *Bess of Hardwick,* 1959.
Turberville, *History of Welbeck Abbey.*
D. N. Durant, *Bess of Hardwick,* 1977.

ROBERT CARY or CAREY, 1st EARL OF MONMOUTH
(1560?–1639), was almost certainly born in 1560, the seventh son
and tenth child of Lord Hunsdon. His grandmother was a sister of
Anne Boleyn, which made Robert a cousin of Queen Elizabeth,
perhaps the reason for his intimacy with her. He will always be
remembered as the man who rode at breakneck speed on horseback
from London to Edinburgh — and took a severe fall on the way —
to carry the news of Queen Elizabeth's death to James VI of
Scotland. He may also be remembered as the writer of a short but
vivid autobiography, in which he gives a first-hand account of the
defeat of the Spanish Armada, against which he served; a miniature
portrait of Queen Elizabeth in a tantrum, because he had married
against her wishes; a lively picture of the Anglo-Scot borderland in
which he was warden of the Marches; an eye-witness' account of the
death of Elizabeth; a self-accusing description of the place-seeking
which went on in the Court of James I; a cameo of Charles I in his
nursery days, to whom he was both Keeper of the Wardrobe and
Chamberlain; he also tells how he was sent after Charles and
Buckingham on their expedition to Spain. In all this he reveals
himself as an extravagant, well-dressed man of fashion, shrewd and
clever in the pursuit of his own and of his family's fortunes, with
some understanding of diplomacy, a colourful and attractive
personality.

Memoirs of Robert Cary, Earl of Monmouth, edited by
    G. H. Powell, 1907, and by F. H. Mares, 1972.

MATTHEW PARKER (1504–1575), Archbishop of Canterbury, was born on 6 August 1504, at Norwich. He came of a well-
to-do family, but little is known of his origins and early life. He
went to Corpus Christi College, Cambridge, in 1521, where he took
his B.A. degree in 1525, perhaps in 1524. He was ordained in 1527
and in that year was elected a Fellow of the College, having refused
an offer to migrate to Wolsey's new foundation of Cardinal College,

Oxford. For the next seven years he studied the early centuries of Church history. During this period Parker consorted with the reformers who met at the White Horse Inn, and became firm friends with people such as Bilney and Latimer, but Parker differed from some Cambridge reformers in that he was never a controversialist. The debates and disputes in which he took part served only the more to turn him back to finding out historic facts, not other people's opinions. Too many of the reformers came to look on religion as a thing to be debated and not a life to be lived: Parker never fell into that error, 'he was never drawn aside into undisciplined enthusiasm' (Kennedy, p. 34). He became a popular and influential preacher in and around Cambridge, but he was once (in about 1539) attacked before Lord Chancellor Audley for alleged heresy. Audley dismissed the charge and urged Parker to 'go on and fear no such enemies'. One other fact in Parker's early days at Cambridge was to have immense influence on his later life — he became the firm friend of William Cecil (Lord Burghley) and Nicholas Bacon.

In 1535 Parker was reluctantly persuaded to accept the office of chaplain to Anne Boleyn, who gave him the deanery of St. John the Baptist College, Stoke-by-Clare in Suffolk, where he spent what were probably the happiest years of his life pursuing his interests as a scholar, improving the college and saving it from dissolution when Henry VIII attacked the monasteries. Anne also before her execution commended her daughter Elizabeth to his care. This peaceful and busy life went on until 1544, when Parker was appointed Master of his old college at Cambridge, Corpus Christi. He became Vice-Chancellor of the University and also Dean of Lincoln. His period as Vice-Chancellor involved him in some stormy episodes: he quarrelled with Gardiner, the Chancellor of Cambridge, over the performance of a scandalous play at Christ's College, and Gardiner never had a good opinion of Parker from that time onwards. He had to withstand an attack on the revenues of the Cambridge colleges by the Crown which he warded off with great tact and skill. But perhaps in the long run the most important single event in Parker's life took place on 24 June 1547, when he married Margaret Harlestone of Mattishall in Norfolk. They had been betrothed for seven years, but as long as the law forbade the marriage of clergy Parker was doomed to celibacy: in anticipation that the law would be amended by the Lower House of Convocation, Parker married this remarkable and

admirable woman. The marriage led them both into great difficulties when Mary Tudor came to the throne, and the outspoken
objections of Elizabeth, when she became Queen, to married clergy
caused both Parker and Margaret great pain and trouble. But
Margaret proved herself equal to all occasions and roused the
admiration of Nicholas Ridley to such a pitch that he enquired of
Matthew Parker whether Margaret had a sister, for if he himself
were ever to marry he could not hope for a better wife than a lady
like Mistress Parker. Even Elizabeth I was compelled in later years to
acknowledge the worth of Mistress Parker. Parker was a modest and
far from self-confident man and much of his success was due to his
wife: it is noticeable that when she died his powers began to fail
quickly.

When Ket's rebellion broke out (1549) in Norfolk, Parker
happened to be in Norwich. As the rebels used the English Prayer
Book and allowed licensed preachers to address them, Parker went to
the camp and preached a sermon from the 'Oak of Reformation'. He
gave them excellent advice, not to destroy the crops, not to shed
human blood, and not to distrust the King. It was a rash sermon to
preach in the circumstances and Parker escaped the fury of the rebels
only 'by the judicious raising of the *Te Deum*' (Kennedy, p. 62). His
purpose probably was then, as always later when he was Archbishop,
to support law and order.

It is not possible to deal fully here with Parker's relations with
Bucer, but it is necessary to record that he became a great friend of
the German theologian — Parker preached the sermon at Bucer's
funeral — and there is little doubt that Bucer had considerable
influence on Parker's views on the Sacraments. Both were by nature
moderate men of the *via media*, gentle and sincere (see Kennedy,
pp. 65-9).

When Mary Tudor came to the throne in 1553, Parker as a
married priest was deprived of his preferments and he had to
disappear into obscurity. He lived with a friend and thoroughly
enjoyed his retirement from public life and administrative duties,
but he suffered an accident when one day he fell from his horse, and
for the rest of his life suffered from a strangulated hernia which
brought him incessant ill-health and eventually killed him.

In 1558 the accession of Elizabeth opened a new chapter in
Parker's life. He himself would have liked to return to Cambridge

and restore the University, which had fallen into decay. But the problem of the Anglican Church prevented this. Elizabeth and Cecil were faced with the difficulty of holding the balance between the old Roman Catholics who still accepted the Pope as head of the Church, the Henrician Catholics who accepted the Catholic religion but repudiated the Papal supremacy, and the extreme Protestants who were now returning from exile on the Continent. It was essential to find the right man as Archbishop of Canterbury. Only a man of balanced judgement, of deep learning, gentle yet firm, conciliatory yet courageous, could successfully fill the office: only Matthew Parker had all the qualifications. He tried desperately to avoid the responsibility, but the Queen and Cecil knew that he was the right man and they compelled him to accept. Years later Parker declared that 'if he had not been so much bound to the mother (Anne Boleyn), he would not so soon have granted to serve the daughter'. He was consecrated in Lambeth Palace Chapel on 17 December 1559. This consecration by four bishops surviving in England, though without sees, is the connecting link between the old and the new succession of Orders in the Church of England.

Parker's first important piece of work was the Metropolitan Visitation of the southern province in 1560–61 to investigate how far the Act of Uniformity and the Injunctions of 1559 (a code of orders to protect the new Church from Catholic 'superstition' — e.g. the cult of saints, reverence for relics: to ensure that only sound Protestant doctrine should be taught: 'to plant true religion') were being carried out and to correct moral offences among clergy and laity. At that moment things seemed to be quiet and the nation to be accepting the new order.

By 1563 signs of the coming storm were evident. Both Parliament and Convocation were worried by fears of Papal intrigues, of the hostility of France in the south and of dangers from Mary, Queen of Scots, in the north. Measures against the Romanists were stepped up and Parker was much troubled by the prospect of religious persecution. He took pains to ensure that the measures were leniently enforced, so that for the first ten years of Elizabeth's reign life was not made too difficult for the Romanists.

With the revival of the Council of Trent, with the increase in Papal propaganda by introducing into England controversial books, and with the Puritan propaganda which was being broadcast by the

Protestant refugees and with which even some of the Anglican bishops were sympathetic, Parker set out to provide uniformity in doctrine for the Elizabethan Church. He accordingly reduced Cranmer's Articles of Religion (1563) from forty-two to thirty-eight in number (in 1571 they became the Thirty-Nine Articles) and various Homilies and Catechisms were also issued. All were intended to lay down the fundamental points of belief.

Another problem with which Parker had soon to deal was the dispute over ceremonial and ritual. There was a large party in Convocation which would have liked to destroy the whole settlement about ritual made in the Prayer Book and the Injunctions. Many clergy were taking the law into their own hands and were pulling down rood-lofts, destroying chancels and some were even turning the organs out of their churches. Similarly there was no uniformity in the vestments which the clergy wore or refused to wear. In other words, Parker was now faced with the problem of Puritanism. For the rest of his life he was continuously harassed by the disobedience of many of the clergy, by the irresolution of the Queen, and by the hostility of such courtiers as the Earl of Leicester. Parker dealt with these conflicting opponents mercifully and reluctantly. His 'Advertisements' (1566) were a compromise on the question of vestments, laying down that the surplice should be worn in the parish church and the cope in the cathedrals. He then set about seeing that these instructions were carried out. 'Execution, execution, execution of laws and orders must be the first and the last part of good governance, although I yet admit moderations, for times, places, multitudes.'

Each year the situation became more difficult, the Puritans increased in numbers and in fanaticism, and the Papacy grew more aggressive. The Rebellion of the Northern Earls in 1569, the Bull of Excommunication (1570), the massacre of St. Bartholomew (1572), persuaded the gentle Parker that strong measures were necessary and that Mary, Queen of Scots, (by now a prisoner in England) would have to be eliminated: 'If that only desperate person were away as by justice soon it might be, the Queen's Majesty's good subjects would be in better hope and the papists' daily expectation vanquished.' By dint of patience, tact, firmness and adaptability Parker had saved the Prayer Book from the attacks of the Genevans; he had built a new Church delicately poised on the foundations of the old; a sterner policy was now needed to defend that Church, a Whitgift rather than a Parker to direct the battle.

One other achievement belongs to Parker, perhaps his greatest. He had always made it his business to see that this 'new' Church was not in fact a new Church, that it should be the old, original Church revived. His study at Cambridge of the early centuries of the Church's history, his refusal to be moved by anything other than historical facts, his study of the Anglo-Saxon language, his collecting of ancient documents, were all directed towards one end, to prove that the 'new' Church of England was in truth the Old Catholic Church purged from the abuses and innovations of the Middle Ages. In 1566 he paid out of his own pocket John Day to cut in brass the first Saxon type for the publications of *A Testimonie of Antiquitie*, showing, 'the ancient faith of the Church of England touching the Sacrament of the Body and Blood of the Lord ... above 600 years ago'. The book proved that it was a mediaeval innovation which forbade the clergy to marry and which restricted the receiving at the Communion to one kind.

Between 1563 and 1568 Parker was a moving spirit in preparing the Bishops' Bible, although he had not much time to give to the actual translation. He was, as Strype said, 'a mighty collector of books', not as a mere bibliophile but for a practical purpose, to help the Church of England in its struggle against Rome and the Puritans. The historian Freeman once said of Matthew Parker that it was owing to him, more than any other man, 'that there is anything to edit and anything to read about the early history of England'.

Although Parker was a modest and retiring man, hating publicity and ostentation, he had a proper regard for the office of Archbishop and for his duty as a hospitable host. He himself was very sparing in his diet, but he entertained liberally and his home life was organized on a spacious scale: he was given special leave by the Queen to maintain a body of forty retainers in addition to his regular servants. Among the many visitors who came to Bekesbourne Parker was once compelled to entertain the French Ambassador. Parker was highly suspicious of his guests, whom he looked on as religious and political spies. Parker was in many ways *naïve,* but he was also shrewd and he kept a close watch on the Frenchmen. After the party had left, Parker sat down and counted his spoons and was surprised to find that none had disappeared.

Parker died on 17 May 1575, worn out by pain and toil. He had endured much, for the Queen left him to take all the blame when he carried out her orders and they proved unpopular. He was buried in Lambeth Church and his tomb was desecrated by the Puritans in 1648. When Sancroft became Archbishop, Parker's bones were recovered and reburied, with the epitaph, *Corpus Matthaei Archiepiscopi hic tandem quiescit*. He is not the best known of the Archbishops, yet among the long line of St. Augustine's successors none has served the Church of England more faithfully and more profitably than this gentle, modest, wise and saintly man.

W. M. Kennedy, *Archbishop Parker*, 1908.
F. O. White, *Lives of Elizabethan Bishops*, 1898.
W. E. Collins, *Typical English Churchmen*, 1902.
E. W. Perry, *Under Four Tudors*, 1940.
Canon C. Smyth, *The Listener*, 30 October 1947.
V. J. K. Brook, *Archbishop Parker*, 1962.

EDMUND GRINDAL (1519/20–1583), Archbishop of Canterbury, was born in 1519 or 1520 in the parish of St. Bees, Cumberland, the son of a poor farmer. When he was fifteen he went to Cambridge, first to Magdalene College, then to Christ's and finally to Pembroke, of which he became a Fellow in 1538. Ridley was his tutor, and no doubt Ridley's influence turned him towards Protestantism. He was ordained, and in 1547 he read Bullinger's *Origin of Error*, which led him to reject the idea of the Real Presence. When in 1549 the commissioners visited Cambridge for an inspection of the University, Grindal argued with great ability and success against this doctrine in the debate staged in front of the commissioners. In that year he became Lady Margaret preacher and Vice-Master of Pembroke College. Two years later Ridley made him his chaplain, and Grindal soon became chaplain to Edward VI. By this time his reputation was so high that he was likely to be made a Bishop, but Edward VI died and the accession of Mary put an end for the time being to his success.

Taking the least heroic but the wisest line, Grindal fled abroad and stayed largely at Strasbourg while in exile, where he was much employed in trying to compose the differences among the Protestant exiles at Frankfurt. On the death of Mary, Grindal came back to

England and arrived on the day of Elizabeth's coronation, 15 January 1559. He became Master of Pembroke and then was made Bishop of London by Matthew Parker, the Archbishop of Canterbury. Grindal was an active and largely effective Bishop of London. His principal difficulty was associated with the control he exercised over his parish clergy of 'moderate puritan' views. Grindal sympathised with such men indeed he appointed several to posts within the diocese, but then found himself in the embarrassing position of needing to enforce the rules of the Church on them, especially with regard to the vestments they were required to wear as ministers. In the end, he was forced by Parker to dismiss thirty-seven Puritan clergymen who opposed the Anglican clothing as too ornate and Popish (1566). Had Grindal taken a tougher line earlier, he might have avoided this damaging confrontation. He dealt harshly, however, with Roman Catholics: he recommended that torture should be applied to a priest named Haverd who refused to answer the questions at his examination. Parker found Grindal 'not resolute and severe enough for the government of London'. He solved the problem by recommending that Grindal should be Archbishop of York, a diocese where he would have to root out Catholic recusancy rather than Puritanism (1570). On a more positive note, Grindal's appointment may have been intended to bring the North into some sort of conformity in the wake of the Rising of 1569.

For five years Grindal set about his work with resolution and perhaps with relish. But in 1575 Parker died, and Cecil persuaded the Queen to translate Grindal from York to Canterbury. It was a mistake. Grindal and the Queen never saw eye to eye, for their views on politics and religious policy were diametrically opposed. They fell out eventually over the question of 'prophesyings', clerical meetings for the exposition and discussion of scripture. They were not 'revivalist' meetings, but rather 'refresher courses' (C. Morris, *Political Thought*). The Queen wanted them forbidden: Grindal felt that the meetings might have been abused, but that it was enough to cure the abuse and to maintain a form of study which he believed did much to raise the standard of the clergy. In 1576 the Queen straightly commanded him to suppress all prophesyings. Grindal refused and wrote her a polite, sensible and admirable letter explaining his reasons and reminding her that it was her duty to consult her clergy in matters of religion. The Queen's answer was an order to suppress the meetings. Grindal refused, and the Queen suspended him from his office.

Grindal's suspension after only a hundred days in office may have owed something also to courtly factions, since he had offended an Italian physician, influential with Sir Christopher Hatton. It may also be connected with the broader struggle in Court and Council between the godly, who were supporters of an aggressive foreign policy and the persecution of Catholics at home, and on the other hand a more moderate group who opposed such proposals.

For seven years, Grindal remained Archbishop, but was prevented from exercising his office. His complete deprivation and his resignation were discussed, but no decision was reached before he died on 6 July 1583. He was a man able, learned and of much charm; he had many friends, among whom he counted Spenser and Whitgift; he liked music and was fond of gardening, and sent grapes to the Queen. But he was unsuited to high ecclesiastical office in the times in which he lived, because he refused to toe the official line. He always wanted to improve the standard of the clergy and he spent money on educational benefactions. But he failed to give Elizabeth the obedience she required from an Archbishop of Canterbury and paid the penalty.

C. Morris, *Political Thought in England, Tyndale to Hooker*, 1953.
P. Collinson, *Archbishop Grindal*, 1979.

JOHN WHITGIFT (1530–1604), Archbishop of Canterbury, was born at Grimsby in 1530. His father was a wealthy Grimsby merchant; his uncle Robert was Abbot of Wellow, near Grimsby, and it was his uncle who took him under his care and sent him to St. Anthony's school in London, where had also been Sir Thomas More and Archbishop Heath. He lived with his aunt, but she threw him out because he refused to attend 'morrow mass', the first mass of the day, and would not be persuaded by some of the canons of St. Paul's.

On the advice of his uncle, his father sent John to Queens' College, Cambridge, but the boy soon migrated to Pembroke (1550), where Nicholas Ridley was the non-resident Master and Grindal was President, and also Bradford, later the Marian martyr, was a Fellow, and became Whitgift's tutor. So promising a pupil did

John Whitgift
(Artist: Unknown)

Whitgift prove that when his father's finances were affected by losses at sea, Ridley made the son a Bible Clerk, which enabled him to remain at Cambridge.

Whitgift justified the privilege. His success was swift and steady:

1553–4, B.A.; 1555, Fellow of Peterhouse; 1557, M.A.; 1560, ordained chaplain to Cox, the strongly anti-Roman Bishop of Ely and Rector of Teversham; 1563, B.D. and Lady Margaret Lecturer in Divinity; 1567, D.D., Master of Pembroke, and immediately Master of Trinity. This last appointment was made in order to strengthen the Heads of Houses to deal with the growing trend in Cambridge towards Presbyterianism. In 1567 he became Vice-Chancellor and Regius Professor; in 1568, prebend of Ely. Being now far better off than ever before, he resigned the Regius Professorship and was succeeded by the holder of the Lady Margaret Chair: the latter was succeeded by Cartwright, and thus Whitgift had unwittingly provided Cartwright, later one of the leaders of Presbyterianism in England, with the chance which he wanted. In 1571 Whitgift became Dean of Lincoln and Parker gave him a dispensation to hold at one and the same time the Deanery of Lincoln, the prebend of Ely, the Mastership of Trinity and the Rectory of Teversham. In 1572 he became Prolocutor of the Lower House of Convocation (*i.e.* President). In this year there was published the very popular and successful *Admonition to the Parliament*, which advocated that the Church of England should be reformed on the Presbyterian model. Whitgift's *Answer* was the most learned and powerful defence of the Anglican settlement until Hooker's *Ecclesiastical Polity*.

In 1577 Whitgift was made Bishop of Worcester and soon after Vice-President of the Marches of Wales, while Sir Henry Sidney was away in Ireland. He proved himself a diligent, courageous and successful Bishop, and a most able administrator in the difficult circumstances of the Welsh Marches.

In 1583 Grindal, Archbishop of Canterbury, died. He had been an unsuccessful Archbishop, and when Whitgift was appointed to succeed him, he found a difficult and dangerous situation, in which ecclesiastical law was ignored, uniformity did not exist and the foundations of the Elizabethan settlement were being undermined. Between his appointment and his death he had restored peace and quiet to the Church, at least for the time being. He had enforced the law, more often by tact than by violence, but he was never afraid to deal boldly with dangerous opponents, and he had made many improvements in the administration of the Church. Both the Queen and Burghley had complete confidence in him, as is shown by his being made a member of the Council, the first ecclesiastical member since the beginning of the reign.

He saw that the first thing to be done was to enforce the law, especially on the Puritans. He set about doing this by his Articles of 1583. The intention was to remove clergymen who would not agree with the doctrine, liturgy and constitution of the Church of England as by law established. Whitgift attempted to enforce conformity on Puritans through the Court of High Commission, using the *ex officio* oath to do so (an oath which bound them to give evidence of their opinions even if it might incriminate themselves). He was only partially successful, owing to the powerful support which the Puritans were able to mobilize against his inquisitorial methods. He saw also that there were genuine grievances against serious short-comings in the Church: he set about remedying these by his Articles of 1586 which had to do with clerical education and preaching. He was determined to repress nonconformity, but he was also deter-mined not to create Puritan martyrs as Mary Tudor had created Protestant martyrs. As time went on, he gradually reduced the severity of his rule and treated the Puritans with sympathy and kindness — he even welcomed Cartwright, when that extremist went to Warwick to Leicester's Hospital, now known as Lord Leycester's. But the Puritans never ceased to revile and calumniate him.

The variety of his work was enormous. He saw to it that the five vacant bishoprics were filled: he defended pluralism in order to improve the low standard of living and the penury of the clergy: he set about reforming the ecclesiastical courts, which were very unpopular owing to their dilatory ways, their expense and their extortions: he enforced orderliness at the two hospitals at Canter-bury and also at All Souls College, of which he was Visitor. He realized that it was part of the Church's duty to back up the social and economic policy of the government, so that in 1597-8 he instructed all the bishops to see that the laws against vagabonds and sturdy beggars were properly enforced. Being a bachelor and a wealthy pluralist, he had a good deal of money at his disposal, and this he spent lavishly, not only in entertaining on a scale worthy of his office, but on the relief of the poor, as when he founded the Hospital of the Holy Trinity at Croydon, and also on education, when he founded a free school at Croydon, still known as Whitgift

School. He gave much attention to the training of young men both at Trinity, Cambridge, and at Lambeth: he founded a Bible Clerkship at Peterhouse.

Whitgift was essentially an administrator rather than a spiritual theologian. His work was to lay the foundations of a secure Church on which others could build. The last ten years of his life saw the beginnings of this building which was later to develop according to the more theological, spiritual and Catholic conceptions of men like Lancelot Andrewes. It is to Whitgift's great credit that he recognized both the need and the opportunities for this beginning and encouraged the younger men to use them. The most notable example is the backing he gave to Hooker in writing the *Ecclesiastical Polity*.

One remarkable characteristic of Whitgift was his ability to subordinate his own instincts and inclinations to the general needs of the times. He was himself, if he could have had his own way theologically, a Calvinist, but he saw clearly that it was not right to try to inject Calvinism into the Anglican Church as established in 1559. When the great attempt was made in 1595 by the Cambridge divines to get the Archbishop to pronounce clearly in favour of Calvinistic doctrines, Whitgift summoned a conference to Lambeth and as a result he issued the Lambeth Articles which, while they conceded a good deal to the Calvinists, made some significant alterations in the original proposals and prevented the attempt to read a full Calvinistic doctrine into the old Thirty-nine Articles.

When Elizabeth realized that she was dying, she sent for her 'little black husband' and Whitgift was with her to the end. He himself was now over seventy and worn out. He took some part in the Hampton Court Conference, but the immediate future lay with Bancroft, and Whitgift died on 29 February 1604. He was buried in the parish church at Croydon.

'He was of a middle stature, of a grave countenance and brown complexion, black hair and eyes; he wore his beard neither long nor thick.' He lived in splendour with a large army of retainers and he was on great occasions served 'upon the knee,' 'for the upholding of the state that belonged unto his place'. Strype called him a 'man born for the benefit of his country and the good of his church'. His biographer, Sir George Paule, wrote, 'happy surely was it for that crazy state of the Church (for so it was at this Archbishop's first coming and long after) not to meet with too rough and boisterous a physician'. Queen Elizabeth, that shrewd and difficult lady, said 'She pities him because she trusted him, and had thereby eased herself by laying the burthen of all her clergy-cares upon his shoulders; which he managed with prudence and piety.' Izaak Walton has drawn a characteristically friendly sketch of him — 'he was noted to be prudent and affable, and gentle by nature.' Characteristically, Macaulay has dismissed him in a few lines which reveal his misunderstanding of Whitgift, 'a narrow-minded, mean and tyrannical priest, who gained power by servility and adulation, and employed it in persecuting both those who agreed with Calvin about Church government, and those who differed from Calvin touching the doctrine of Reprobation' (*Essay on Lord Bacon*). Perhaps those who knew him best may pass the final judgement. When about 1571 Whitgift had it in mind to leave Cambridge, the Heads of Houses wrote to Cecil, the Chancellor, that should the Vice-Chancellor leave, 'the whole body of the University would lament', for he was 'wise, learned and wholly bent to the execution of good laws and statutes.' 'They could not want (*i.e.* do without) him'.

H. C. Porter, *Reformation and Reaction in Tudor Cambridge*, 1958.
Izaak Walton, *Lives*.
V. J. K. Brook, *Whitgift and the English Church*, 1957.
P. M. Dawley, *John Whitgift and the Reformation*, 1955.

JOHN JEWEL (1522–1571), Bishop of Salisbury, was one of a family of ten, the children of John Jewel of Berrynarbor in North Devon. His education began at Barnstaple School, whence he went in 1535 to Merton College, Oxford. His tutor was Parkhurst, later Bishop of Norwich, who recommended him after four years to migrate to Corpus Christi College. He took his B.A. degree in 1540 and soon became a Fellow of his new college. In 1547 Peter Martyr, a Florentine reformer who became Regius Professor of Divinity at Oxford, arrived in Oxford and Jewel came much under his Protestant influence. In 1552 Jewel took the degree of B.D. and became Public Orator just in time to have to make the oration congratulating Queen Mary on her accession. Weakly he subscribed to religious doctrines which he did not believe, gave up his Protestantism, and then fled abroad to Frankfurt (1555), where he acknowledged his

John Jewel
(Artist: Unknown)

weakness and recanted his recantation. He moved about among the
Protestant exiles in Frankfurt, Strasbourg and Zurich, then toured
Italy and spent a short time at Padua.

On the death of Mary, Jewel returned to England (1559) and was
consecrated Bishop of Salisbury. By nature and instinct, by upbringing and education, Jewel was sympathetic towards the Puritans. He
had a supreme contempt for what he called 'the scenic apparatus of
divine worship'. Vestments he labelled 'theatrical habits' and

'ridiculous trifles': the cope was a 'comical dress', the linen surplice 'a vestige of error'. This 'rubbish' and these 'fooleries' he wished to see done away with, because they could only disturb 'weak minds'. But what makes Jewel a notable figure in the history of his own times is that he was capable of seeing these 'trifles', not merely as trifles and therefore to be abolished, but also as trifles which mattered nothing in comparison with the vital necessity of preaching the gospel and the Word of Life. Therefore he put up with these 'fooleries', because he recognized that 'the doctrine (of the Anglican Church) is everywhere most pure' and must be maintained against the Romish errors. To this work the rest of his life was dedicated. Even so, he felt so strongly that everything must be done in a decent and orderly way that he was prepared to enforce things which in his heart he disliked against the Puritans, with whom he had much in common.

To the defence of the established Church Jewel brought the help of his profound learning, his deep piety and his unselfish sense of service. He set great store by education and he tried by incessant preaching throughout his diocese to raise the standard of his clergy. His most important piece of writing was his *Apologia Ecclesiae Anglicanae* (written in Latin in 1562 and translated into English in 1564 by Ann Bacon, mother of Francis Bacon), in which he justified the position of the Anglican Church and transferred the accusation of innovations to the Church of Rome. The *Apology* did not define Anglican beliefs: that explanation had to wait for Hooker. Jewel was a gentle, kindly, hospitable man, generous and courteous, yet he was ungenerously discourteous to the Roman Church, whose clergy he assailed in vulgar terms and whose Pope he denounced as the 'hangman of the Church'.

Jewel was a great patron of friendless and needy scholars, and he kept a kind of school in his palace at Salisbury where he trained poor boys of intellectual promise: it was here that Richard Hooker found the encouragement and often the financial aid which enabled him to stay at Oxford. In appearance Jewel was worn and emaciated, and in his later years he seemed a living skeleton. He wore himself out by going round his diocese preaching, maintaining that a Bishop 'should die in his pulpit'. Being booked to preach at Laycock, although too ill to keep his appointment, he insisted on doing so. When the service was ended he rode to Monckton Farleigh, where he went to bed and died, 23 September 1571.

F. O. White, *Lives of the Elizabethan Bishops*.
J. E. Booty, *John Jewel as apologist of the Church of England*, 1963.

WILLIAM WHITTINGHAM (1524? –1579), Dean of Durham, was born at Chester probably in 1524. He was educated at Brasenose College, Oxford. He became a B.A. and in 1545 a Fellow of All Souls, in 1548 Senior Student of Christ Church. At the age of twenty-six he was given leave by his college to travel in France, Germany and the Low Countries for three years. Most of that time was spent at Louvain University, where he married a strongly Protestant lady, and he became so proficient in the French language that he was often employed as an interpreter at the English embassy in Paris. There is no reason for accepting the idea that his wife was a sister of Calvin.

He returned to England just in time for the Nine Days' Reign of Lady Jane Grey. He was an extreme Protestant, and the accession of Mary to the throne made it dangerous for him to remain in England. With some difficulty he escaped overseas via Dover to France. On being questioned by the innkeeper at Dover, Whittingham replied that he was going abroad 'because the Whore of Rome was again erected amongst them'. The innkeeper was on the point of sending the party to a magistrate, but he was in some way cajoled into describing his female dog as 'one of the Queen's kind', after which Whittingham was free to go on his travels.

He went to Frankfurt (June 1554), where he soon became involved in a violent dispute with other Protestants over the use of the Prayer Book. Most of the English exiles wanted to use Cranmer's Second Prayer Book, but Whittingham and John Knox wanted to start a new Church with a Prayer Book of its own, much more extreme than their opponents cared for. So violent was Knox that he was expelled from the city. Whittingham soon followed him to Geneva (April 1555) with his party of twenty-seven supporters. Here was 'erected' the sort of Church which Knox and Whittingham wanted. Whittingham was twice elected a 'Senior' or Elder of this Church (1555 and 1556); he was then appointed Deacon (1558) and in 1559 he succeeded Knox as Minister.

During this time Whittingham was largely taken up with producing a new translation of the New Testament (1557), notable for its being the first English Bible to be divided into chapters and verses. His chief literary work was the 'Geneva Bible', known more vulgarly as the 'Breeches Bible', and closely connected with the name of Coverdale, but there is no doubt that Whittingham was responsible for most of the translation of the New Testament (1560). This book was the first to omit the Apocrypha and it became a popular Bible in English households, even after the Authorized Version of 1611.

The Prayer Book, known as the Genevan-English Order, published in 1556, was remarkable for the metrical versions of the Psalms which were included for congregational singing. This practice became very popular, and gradually there were introduced into the Book of Common Prayer metrical versions of passages from the Scriptures, such as those by Sternhold and Hopkins. Whittingham was the man who saved this practice from disappearing and who made it popular by his skill in selecting suitable tunes.

The accession of Elizabeth opened the way to a return to England. Whittingham was delayed by remaining in Geneva to complete the publishing of the Geneva Bible, but he was home in 1560 and attached himself to Ambrose Dudley, Earl of Warwick, and his brother Lord Robert Dudley, the future Earl of Leicester. In 1562 war broke out between England and France, and Warwick was sent to defend Havre: Whittingham went as his chaplain. It is said that his diligence in preaching was only equalled by his 'vigilance in discovering stratagems'. He preached always in armour and 'as the old captains and soldiers of Berwick would say, many years after, that — when any alarum came whilst he was preaching, he would be on the town walls as soon almost as any man'.

The reward for this service by the Church Militant was the Deanery of Durham (1563). He proved in many ways to be an excellent choice: he paid strict attention to his religious activities, holding two services a day and giving three or four hours a day to teaching the children: he was socially a great success, living 'in the great love and liking of his neighbours, for his affability and bountiful hospitality': and when he saw the Rebellion of the Northern Earls about to break out, he made every effort to persuade the Bishop to take military measures in time, but he failed to move the timid Pilkington. He had better results at Newcastle, where by means of his efforts 'the rebels never dared attempt of the siege of that town'.

On the other hand, he ignored the Act of Uniformity and introduced into Durham Cathedral Genevan principles which he was compelled to abandon, when in 1566 Archbishop Parker published his 'Advertisements' to regulate such things as the out of doors dress of the clergy and the use of the surplice, as well as enforcing kneeling at the Communion. He also embarked on a policy of iconoclasm: he broke up the image of St. Cuthbert in the cloisters, he removed grave-covers to use as paving-stones, stone coffins as cattle troughs and stoups for steeping 'their beef and salt fish in, having a conveyance in the bottoms for letting forth the water, as they had when they were in the Church'. He lowered the frater roof and sold the lead for £20, while his wife burned the banner of St. Cuthbert. These actions could be defended on the grounds that the Queen had re-enacted the Injunction of 1547 for the removal of superstitious ornaments.

Whittingham was a difficult man and one not easily handled. He flatly refused to succeed to the office of Secretary of State in 1572. He boldly and successfully withstood his own Bishop when Sandys, the new Archbishop, ordered Barnes, Pilkington's successor, to visit the cathedral. Whittingham told the janitor to lock the door, the Bishop tried to prevent him, the Dean 'did a little interrupt him, taking hold of his gown', and kept the Bishop out. Whittingham was then involved in other disputes: he was accused of adultery and of drunkenness, neither charge being well established: it was brought against him that he had never been properly ordained — nor in fact had he been ordained in the strict sense of the word, only 'ordered' as a minister at Geneva. Before any decision was arrived at on this point, Whittingham died at Durham in 1579.

He remains historically as an excellent example of that type of extreme Protestant who had little patience with the *via media* which Elizabeth wished to follow in matters ecclesiastical.

James Wall, *The Church Quarterly*, 1936.
S. L. Greenslade, *Durham University Journal*, 1945–8.
W. Whittingham, *The Troubles at Frankfurt*, (ed. E. Arber, 1908).

JOHN DE FECKENHAM (1518?–1585), last Abbot of Westminster, deserves a longer biography than the space available in this book will allow. The main facts of his life can be shortly stated. He was the son of poor peasants named Howman who lived in Feckenham Forest, Worcestershire. The parish priest spotted the boy's abilities and a place was found for him in the monastery at Evesham. After becoming a monk, he was known as John of Feckenham. He went to Oxford to what is now Worcester College: he took the degree of B.D. in 1539 and went back to the monastery at Evesham. This foundation was dissolved in 1540. Feckenham was then appointed to the benefice of Solihull and became chaplain to Bishop Bonner. Under Edward VI, when Bonner was deprived, Feckenham was sent to the Tower. When Mary came to the throne, he was released and made Dean of St. Paul's. In 1556 he was entrusted with restoring the convent at Westminster. When Elizabeth came to the throne, Feckenham was a steadfast opponent of her ecclesiastical settlement; he refused the Oath of Supremacy, and he and his monks were ejected (1559). Between 1559 and his death in 1585 Feckenham was almost the whole time in some sort of restraint. In 1560 he was sent to the Tower: in 1563, he was released and put under the eye of Horne, Bishop of Winchester, who thought he could convert Feckenham, but failed to shift him a single inch. Therefore Feckenham was sent back to the Tower (1564) and later to the Marshalsea. In 1574 he was released on bail, but the Bishop of London objected to his being free to corrupt Londoners and he was in 1577 sent to live with Cox, Bishop of Ely. In 1580 Cox petitioned that he might be relieved of this incubus, and Feckenham was sent to Wisbeach Castle, a damp, wretched and half-ruined place, where he spent the last years of his life in much more severe conditions. He died there in 1584. What makes Feckenham such an admirable and interesting man is that he never compromised with his conscience for a moment: he never wanted Protestants to be maltreated: he is alleged to have saved twenty-eight people from burning under Mary: he was a most accomplished preacher and acute debater: he never showed violence or venom or vulgarity in his sermons and disputations: and he took all that befell him with a wonderful serenity. He ministered to Lady Jane Grey before and at her execution.

But more than that: he seemed always to have command of very large sums of money. These he spent wholly either indirectly relieving the poor or else in building for the benefit of everybody.

Feckenham must be looked upon, not as an important character in

Tudor history, but as one of the most attractive and genuinely Christian churchmen of his times.

RICHARD DAVIES (1501–1581), Bishop of St. David's, was the son of a Welsh vicar, was educated at Oxford and took his degree in 1530. Under Edward VI he was given two livings in the diocese of Lincoln, of which he was deprived by Queen Mary. He and his wife then went into exile at Geneva, where they suffered greatly from poverty. When Elizabeth came to the throne, they returned to England and he became Bishop of St. Asaph in 1560. The next year he was translated to St. David's. He became the trusted adviser to Matthew Parker and to Burghley on Welsh ecclesiastical matters.

Davies was a good scholar and linguist and he is to be remembered as the man who gave to Wales the Prayer Book and the New Testament in Welsh (1567), but the translation of the New Testament was almost entirely the work of Salesbury. Davies and Salesbury shared the expenses of producing these books. They intended to bring out a Welsh version of the Old Testament, but they quarrelled over 'the general sense and etymology of some one word' and the plan was never realized. Davies also had a hand in the Bishops' Bible of 1568. He died on 7 November 1581.

F. O. White, *Lives of Elizabethan Bishops.*

WILLIAM SALESBURY (*c.*1517–*c.*1600), translator of the Scriptures into Welsh, came of an old and distinguished Norman-Welsh family and was educated at Oxford, where he became a strenuous supporter of the reforming movement in religion. He published many books to further the Reformation. In 1547 he published his English-Welsh dictionary, and in 1567 he collaborated with Bishop Davies in translating the New Testament and the Prayer Book into Welsh, he himself translating all the New Testament except the pastoral epistles and the Revelation. His printed Welsh had a very odd appearance owing to his theory that the Welsh words should be spelt as nearly like their supposed Latin originals as he could make them. He is said to have pursued his studies in a secret room which could be entered only by climbing up the chimney.

WILLIAM MORGAN (*c*.1541–1604), Bishop of St. Asaph, was educated at St. John's College, Cambridge, and between 1575 and 1588 he held four livings in Wales. He made a translation of the Bible into Welsh, but he met with much local opposition and he was delated to the Bishop, who refused to take any action. Morgan was then reported to Archbishop Whitgift and was summoned to Lambeth. He succeeded not only in convincing Whitgift that he was perfectly capable of making a sound translation, for he knew both Greek and Hebrew, but he also won the support of the Archbishop, who promised to defray all the expenses of producing the book. The Bible was published in 1588, an independent translation made directly from the original. Many of the changes made in the English Revised Version were taken from Morgan's translation.

In 1595 Morgan was made Bishop of Llandaff and he was translated to St. Asaph in 1601. He proved himself an admirable Bishop, a sound administrator and a firm and incorruptible man, but he seems to have had a good many quarrels with people who were less scrupulous than himself. He died on 10 September 1604. There is a biography of him by C. Ashton published in 1888 to commemorate the tercentenary of the Welsh Bible.

F. O. White, *Lives of Elizabethan Bishops.*

ALEXANDER NOWELL or NOEL (1507?–1602), Dean of St. Paul's, author of much of the Prayer Book Catechism, was born perhaps in 1507 or 1508 (1506, 1510, 1511 have also been given) at Whalley, in Lancashire. He was educated at Brasenose College, Oxford, became a Fellow of the college, Public Reader of Logic in the University, and after he was ordained he became Master of Westminster School and Prebendary of the Abbey (1551). Being given a licence to preach, Nowell soon acquired a great reputation as a preacher, and during the reign of Edward VI he 'preached in some of the notablest places and auditories in the realm'. When Mary came to the throne, Nowell was returned to Parliament as Member for Looe in Cornwall, but he was not allowed to take his seat on the ground that 'having a voice in Convocation' he was not eligible to sit in the House of Commons. He then went abroad and joined the Marian exiles. On Mary's death Nowell returned to England and was made Archdeacon of Middlesex, a Canon of Canterbury and a Canon of Westminster.

In November 1560 he was recommended by Elizabeth 'for his goodly zeal and special good learning, and other singular gifts and virtues' for election as Dean of St. Paul's. Nowell soon afterwards married, and Archbishop Parker wrote that, if the Queen would have a 'married minister' for Provost of Eton, there was none comparable with Nowell. The Queen would not have a married minister. Some of Nowell's sermons were bold rather than tactful and he was in trouble more than once. On 1 January 1562 he placed a richly bound prayer-book with pictures of the saints and martyrs on the Queen's cushion in St. Paul's as a New Year's gift: Elizabeth sent the verger to fetch her old book, and after the service was over she went to the vestry and soundly rated the Dean for infringing her proclamation against 'images, pictures and Romish relics'. In 1564 he was preaching a Lenten sermon before the Queen and spoke slightingly of the crucifix. The Queen called out, 'To your text, Mr. Dean — leave that, we have heard enough of that', and so confounded was Nowell that he could not finish his sermon. His boldest sermon was that in which he took the Queen to task for not marrying and providing an heir to the throne, with the Queen sitting listening. 'All the Queen's most noble ancestors have commonly had some issue to succeed them, but Her Majesty yet none.' ... 'If your parents had been of your mind, where had you been then?'

In 1562 he became Rector of Much Hadham, Canon of Windsor in 1594 and Principal of Brasenose in 1595. He died in 1602. He was twice married, but he had no children. He was a fine scholar, a skilful debater, a learned theologian: he was held to be an authority on educational matters and he endowed a free school at Middleton. He was also a devoted and accomplished fisherman and is said accidentally to have invented bottled ale, for when one day he was fishing in the Ash at Much Hadham he left a bottle of ale in the grass beside the river and a few days later found the contents effervescent.

Nowell is to be remembered as the author of three catechisms: (1) the 'Large Catechism' approved by Convocation in 1563 and printed in 1572; (2) the 'Middle Catechism', an abridged version of the Large; (3) the 'Small Catechism' of 1572, which was almost identical with that in the 1549 Prayer Book and of which Nowell was probably the author: he was also the author of the first part of our present catechism, the second part being added in 1604 as a shortened and altered version of Nowell's.

R. Churton, *Life of Nowell.*

CUTHBERT TUNSTAL (1474–1559), Bishop of Durham, was born at Hackforth in Richmondshire (*i.e.* Yorkshire) in 1474. He was the son of Thomas Tunstal by his second wife, the daughter of Sir John Conyers, whom he did not marry until some years after the birth of the son. In 1491, at the age of 17, Cuthbert went to Oxford to Balliol College, but owing to an outbreak of the plague he left Oxford and migrated to Trinity College, Cambridge, where he stayed until 1499, when he travelled abroad to Padua. At Oxford he knew More, Grocyn, Linacre and Colet, and his chief academic interest was in mathematics. He became a Fellow of Trinity, and when he was at Padua he met some of the Renaissance leaders, such as the printer and publisher, Aldus Manutius. He was at Padua for six years and returned to England in 1505, after a visit to Rome.

By this time Tunstal certainly knew Greek and Hebrew; 'he was a very eloquent Rhetorician, a passing skilful mathematician (famous especially for Arithmetic, whereof he writ a work much esteemed), a great lawyer ... and a profound divine ...' (Bishop Godwin). He was not ordained until 1509, but (as was quite usual) even before this preferments had been showered on him, so that he was both Prebendary of Lincoln and Archdeacon of Chester. In 1515 Warham made him his Chancellor, and Tunstal's public life had begun. For the next seven years he was for the most part employed on diplomatic work. In 1521 he went on an embassy to the Emperor Charles V; the Lutheran movement was beginning, and Tunstal came away with a very bad impression of what he had seen of the Reformation in Germany. In 1522 Warham appointed him Bishop of London because 'he was a man of so good learning, virtue, and sadness, which shall be right meet and convenient to entertain ambassadors and other noble strangers at that notable and honorable city in the absence of the King's most noble grace'.

In 1522 he published his work on arithmetic, *De Arte Supputendi*, which he dedicated to his best friend, Sir Thomas More. This was the first work wholly on arithmetic to be printed in England, but it was never translated into English, and of its eight editions only the first was printed at home.

In 1523 Tunstal was made Keeper of the Privy Seal and he was now one of the most important civil and ecclesiastical servants of the Crown. But he did not neglect his diocese, where he set about dealing with a revival of Lollardy under the influence of the Lutherans. He had already in 1523 refused Tyndale's application to become one of his chaplains. Now in 1526 he prohibited various heretical books, including copies of Tyndale's New Testament. Three years later (1529), so determined was he to root out heresy, he bought up all the copies he could find of Tyndale's book in order to burn them. In fact, he only thereby increased the financial profits for Tyndale and enabled him to go ahead with more printings. Tunstal could never be called wordly-wise.

Tunstal remained Bishop of London until 1530: in that year he was translated to Durham by Papal Bull to succeed the fallen Wolsey. He was to hold this see from 1530 to 1552 and again from 1553 to 1559, being deprived in 1552 by Northumberland, reinstated by Mary, and deprived again by Elizabeth in 1559. He was essentially a conservative, in the true meaning of that word. Like nearly all the bishops of his time he accepted quite easily the abolition of the Papal jurisdiction in England: he could not at first accept the Royal Supremacy: but he was a loyal Englishman, and it needed only a tactful letter to bring him round to Henry VIII's point of view. Henry wrote to him that he had no intention of usurping spiritual jurisdiction, and Tunstal was satisfied (1536). In 1530 he had been made the President of the Council of the North. When the Pilgrimage of Grace broke out in 1536 — he described it as 'worse than the Turks' — he fled from Auckland. Tunstal was not a strong man and should never have been made President of the Council of the North, and indeed he lost the job in 1537.

When Edward VI came to the throne, Tunstal conformed to most of the ecclesiastical changes up to the time of Northumberland. But like many conscientious and generous-minded men, anxious to be reasonable, there was a point beyond which Tunstal could not be moved. He voted against the First Act of Uniformity and in 1552 he was deprived of his bishopric and imprisoned. It was also in part Northumberland's determination to secure the revenues of the see of

Durham for himself and his friends which brought about the final breach between them.

On the accession of Mary I Tunstal was released and reappointed to the see of Durham. He went to Gravesend to welcome Reginald Pole to England, and he was at Mary's right hand at her coronation. When Elizabeth came to the throne (1558), Tunstal took no part in her coronation. In 1559 he refused the Oath of Supremacy and was deprived of his bishopric. He had also refused to take part in the consecration of Matthew Parker as Archbishop of Canterbury. He was inevitably deprived of his see and he was sent to live with Parker, who treated him with the greatest kindness. He died on 18 November 1559. Too often he was a man whose strength of character never quite matched his first-class abilities: but in general he preserved holiness in very unholy times.

C. Sturge, *Cuthbert Tunstal*, 1934.
G. H. Ross-Lewin in *Typical English Churchmen*, series iii.
L. Baldwin Smith, *Tudor Prelates and Politics*, 1953.

RICHARD HOOKER (1554–1600), author of the *Laws of Ecclesiastical Polity*, was born at Heavitree in Exeter in 1554 and died at Bishopsbourne near Canterbury in 1600. He came of a good but not wealthy family. His uncle had been Chamberlain of Exeter and once M.P. for that city. It was thanks to his uncle's generosity that Richard was kept at school, and the boy proved so promising a scholar that his uncle introduced him to Jewel, Bishop of Salisbury. On him the boy made so good an impression that Jewel provided his parents with a pension and sent Richard to Corpus Christi College, Oxford (1568). This college was rather Puritan, but Hooker formed his own views.

At Oxford Hooker made excellent progress so that he soon acquired a reputation as a scholar and a tutor, and he was so diligent that he was absent from College chapel only twice in four years. In 1571 Jewel died, but the Master of the college saw to it that Hooker was able to remain at Oxford. In 1573 he was elected to a scholarship, in 1577 he took his M.A. and in 1579 was elected a Fellow of Corpus. In 1579 he became Reader in Hebrew to Oxford University. In that year for some unknown reason Hooker and several other Fellows were expelled from the college, but they were reinstated on appeal to the Visitor. In 1581 Hooker was ordained and in the same year he preached at St. Paul's Cross.

From this point the story of Hooker's life has always been based upon the account given by Izaak Walton in his *Life of Mr. Richard Hooker*, but Professor C. J. Sisson in his *The Judicious Marriage of Mr. Hooker* (1940) has conclusively shown that account to be radically wrong. Hooker was not married in 1582, but on 13 February 1588, to Joan Churchman, in the parish church of St. Augustine's, Watling Street, as is proved by the entry in the parish register. He is known to have been at Corpus Christi College in 1582: he was presented with the living of Drayton Beauchamp in 1584, but there is no evidence that he ever resided there. By 1584 the challenge launched by the Puritans against the established Church demanded an authoritative answer from a first-class scholar and writer. The leaders of the Anglican Church saw the right man in Hooker. His appointment as Master of the Temple in 1585 was the first step in this counter-attack. In 1584 Hooker left Oxford and went to live in London with John Churchman, the father of his future wife, Joan. There is dispute over Walton's amusing account of the Churchman family and of the disastrous results of Hooker's marriage. The Churchman family were well-to-do and reputable people, (John rose to be Master of the Merchant Taylors), and their house in Watling Street came to be the headquarters from which the counter-attack on Puritanism was organized and launched by Hooker's supporters in the form of *The Laws of Ecclesiastical Polity*. Hooker first went to live there in 1584; he lived there all the time he was Master of the Temple, and he continued to live there with his family after his marriage.

When Hooker became Master of the Temple, he was confronted with Walter Travers, a violent Calvinist, who was the afternoon lecturer. Hooker was strongly opposed to the Calvinist system, so that 'the pulpit spake pure Canterbury in the morning and Geneva in the afternoon' (Fuller). Relations between the two grew tense, and Travers at last accused Hooker of heresy for saying that 'he doubted not but that God was merciful to many of our forefathers living in popish superstition, inasmuch as they sinned ignorantly'. In 1591 Hooker was given the living of Boscombe, near Salisbury. The Librarian of Salisbury Cathedral has lately revealed that Hooker did reside at Boscombe. So the books he needed for his work were in that library and are still there, heavily annotated on the shelves given by Bishop Jewel. Izaak Walton is thus vindicated at the expense of Professor Sisson.

Hooker completed the first four books of the *Laws of Ecclesiastical Polity* in 1593, and they were published in that year, not (as is usually stated) in 1594. Every political argument demanded haste in publishing his work, so that it should coincide with the passing of the Conventicle Act of 1593, which was aimed against 'seditious sectaries and disloyal persons' who assailed the ecclesiastical supremacy. The bill was thus aimed against the Puritans and not the Romanists. The printing of the *Ecclesiastical Polity* was completed on the very day on which Sandys made a speech in the Commons urging that stronger measures should be added to the bill (13 March 1593).

Hooker's chief purpose was to defeat the Puritan demand that the Anglican Church should be organized on the Genevan system. Dr. A. L. Rowse in his *The England of Elizabeth*, (p. 476), writes, 'In the fifteen-nineties the fact that the Church had won its battle is witnessed by the flood of apologetic literature on its side, culminating in a great work, Hooker's *Laws of Ecclesiastical Polity*'. Yet the fact remains that Hooker was unable to find a publisher in 1593. The publishers held that religious works, especially on the episcopal side, would not sell. The generous Sandys came to the rescue and undertook to bear all expenses and to guarantee the publishers against any losses they incurred. And the publishers were right, for it took eleven years to sell 1,200 copies, whereas the Genevan Bible was selling at the rate of thirty-four editions between 1593 and 1603 (Sisson, pp. 50-70).

Hooker's reward from the Queen was the living of Bishopsbourne, near Canterbury. Here he died on All Souls' Day, 1600, 'meditating the number and nature of the Angels'. The fifth volume of his book had been published in 1597 and at his death he left three more volumes very nearly ready for the printers. (For the story of the suppression of these manuscripts, see Sisson, and also R. A. Houk's edition of Book 8, 1931).

Izaak Walton is not to be blamed for the errors in his biography, for he was given false information, but one may accept his description of Hooker as 'an obscure, harmless man, a man in poor clothes, his loins usually girt in a coarse gown or canonical coat; of a mean stature and stooping, and yet more lowly in the thoughts of his soul'. Fuller noted his 'dove-like simplicity' and went on to describe his preaching. 'Mr. Hooker's voice was low, stature little, gesture none at all, standing stone-still in the pulpit, as if the posture of his body were the emblem of his mind, unmovable in his opinions. Where his eye was left fixed at the beginning, it was found fixed at the end of his sermon: in a word, the doctrine he delivered had nothing but itself to garnish it ... His style was long and pithy, driving on a whole flock of several clauses before he came to the close of a sentence; so that, when the copiousness of his style met not with proportionable capacity in his auditors, it was unjustly censured for perplexed, tedious and obscure.'

Hooker's memorial is, of course, his *Laws of Ecclesiastical Polity*. What he did was not only to explain why the Anglican Church could not accept the Roman doctrine, but also to explain fully and clearly what was the doctrine of the Anglican Church. Further, he demonstrated that Puritanism was a danger as much to the political as to the ecclesiastical stability of the State. What marks out Hooker's book from all other controversial literature of his time is its 'utter calm, the great charity of the language, the peace in which it is all thought out' (P. Hughes, *The Reformation in England*, vol. 3, p. 218). Eschewing the normal methods of violent language and vilification, Hooker brought reason to bear on theological matters. Relegating to the background ephemeral problems, he built his argument on the real fundamental points at issue. These he argued with courtesy and moderation. Nor was he afraid to concede points to the other side. While he could write, 'Think ye are men, deem it not impossible for you to err', he could also grant that 'the word Presbyter doth seem more fit, and in propriety of speech more agreeable than Priest with the drift of the whole Gospel of Jesus Christ'. But there is a firmness in his moderation and he is not afraid to use strong language: he denied that customs were necessarily dangerous simply because the Roman Church used them. But he also wrote, 'with Rome we dare not communicate concerning sundry her gross and grievous abominations, yet touching those main parts of Christian truth wherein they constantly still persist, we gladly acknowledge them to be of the family of Jesus Christ'.

The Anglican Church has been marvellously blessed in Cranmer's

Prayer Book, in the Authorized Version of the Bible and in Hooker's *Laws of Ecclesiastical Polity.*

Best ed. of Hooker's works is that of J. Keble, 1836, revised by Church and Paget, 1888.
I. Walton, *Life of Mr. Richard Hooker.*
C. J. Sisson, *The Judicious Marriage of Mr. Hooker,* 1940.
C. Morris, *Political Thought in England, Tyndale to Hooker,* 1953.
S. Archer, *Richard Hooker,* 1983.

JOHN FOXE or FOX (1517–1587), martyrologist, author of *The Book of Martyrs,* was born in 1517 at Boston, in Lincolnshire. He came of good burgess stock; 'his father and mother were of the commonalty of that town' (Boston), but while John was still young his father died and his mother married Richard Melton, who came from the neighbouring village of Coningsby, whose rector was one John Hawarden: this Hawarden was also a Fellow of Brasenose College, Oxford; later he was to become the Principal. When Hawarden met John Foxe in 1533, he was so struck by the promise of the young man that he persuaded his stepfather to send him to Brasenose, Oxford, where Foxe arrived in 1534. It is likely that he learned Latin at Magdalen College School: he became a B.A. in 1537 and a Fellow of Magdalen College in 1539, an appointment which he held for about seven years. He became lecturer in logic in 1539 and took his M.A. degree in 1543.

During these years Foxe studied theology, and by the time he was twenty-five he had read the Greek and Latin Fathers and had acquired some knowledge of Hebrew. It might be expected that the next step would be ordination, but it was not so. Foxe gradually adopted the reforming views of the Reformation and therefore he came to reject the doctrine of the celibacy of the clergy: therefore he refused to be ordained and therefore he lost his Fellowship.

Out of employment, Foxe turned his mind to school-mastering, but he could find no opening; therefore he accepted an offer to become tutor in the household of William Lucy at Charlecote Park in Warwickshire. He spent but a year here, during which time he married Agnes Randall of Coventry (1547). Thence he moved to London, destitute of money, but suddenly an offer was made to him to become tutor in the house of the Duchess of Richmond, widow of

Henry FitzRoy, Henry VIII's illegitimate son, to the children of her brother, the Earl of Surrey, who had in that year been executed by Henry VIII. Thus began the long friendship between John Foxe and Thomas Howard, aged eleven, who was later to become the Duke of Norfolk and himself to be executed under Elizabeth. Another boy came under his care at the same time, Charles Howard, later to command the English fleet against the Armada as Lord Howard of Effingham.

In 1550 Foxe was ordained deacon by Nicholas Ridley — by that time marriage of the clergy had been legalized — but he was not ordained priest until 1560.

On the accession of Mary Tudor the Duke of Norfolk was released from the Tower and recovered the guardianship of his grandchildren, with the result that Foxe was once again out of employment. Besides which, he was too well known as a Protestant to be safe under the new government of the Papist Queen. Therefore with the help of his patron Thomas Howard, now the new Duke of Norfolk, he escaped overseas to Strasbourg, taking with him the manuscript in Latin of his history of the Church from the time of Wyclif, which was in fact the nucleus of his later book, *Actes and Monumentes* or *The Book of Martyrs*. This history was published in Strasbourg in 1554. From Strasbourg Foxe moved to Frankfurt and then to Basle, and it was here that he began an enlarged edition of the history. He was involved to some extent in the quarrels among the English Protestant exiles in Germany, rather as a peacemaker than as a disputant, but his principal work was the making of his new book on the Marian martyrs.

When Mary died in 1558, Foxe did not at once return to England: he waited to see his book through the press. But in 1559 he was back in England, entirely penniless. His faithful friend and patron, the Duke of Norfolk, gave him lodgings in his London house in Aldgate, where Foxe mainly resided for the next ten years. In 1560 he was ordained priest by Grindal, Bishop of London. Three years later John Day published the magnificent English edition of the *Actes and Monumentes*. The book was immensely popular, and the Queen commanded a copy to be set up in every parish church. The book was dedicated to the Queen, who in return presented Foxe with the prebend of Shipton in Salisbury Cathedral. But there were bitter opponents of the book who attacked it violently and abusively —

'that huge dunghill of your stinking martyrs, full of a thousand lies' (Thomas Harding). A second edition was published in two folio volumes in 1570, a third edition in 1576 and a fourth edition in 1583.

Modern historians have also criticized the accuracy of Foxe's stories, notably S.R. Maitland, J.S. Brewer, J. Gairdner and Sir Sidney Lee. Their attacks are mostly concerned with the pre-Marian section of the book, and it is true that Foxe in this part of the work was inaccurate and interpreted the episcopal registers wrongly, but in the way which he thought to be the truth. The Marian section is on the whole open to very little criticism. Professor Rupp maintains that 'Foxe's *Book of Martyrs* is not accidental to English Protestantism; it holds a unique place in the making of the English Protestant tradition, one by which the memorial of events became itself an event. Foxe's *Book* counted in English history as much as Drake's Drum' (E.G. Rupp, *The English Protestant Tradition*, p. 208). It was probably the only book besides the Bible which poor men read for a hundred years. Foxe's book helped create in the English a sense of patriotism, a feeling that they, like the children of Israel, were God's Elect or chosen people.

John Foxe was a most unworldly man, caring nothing at all for money, success, the pleasures of this life; eating little, sleeping little, studying much, praying much. He hated cruelty in every form and lost no opportunity of trying to stop it. 'I can scarce pass the shambles where beast are slaughtered, but that my mind secretly recoils with a feeling of pain.' In 1551 he wrote a tract against the death penalty for adultery — 'I think it neither useful nor necessary ... What sort of a remedy is it which takes away the life of a sick man?' He alone pleaded for the life of Joan Bocher, as he also pleaded for the lives of the Anabaptists in a personal letter he wrote to the Queen, a wonderful piece of pleading (1575). He tried to save the life of George van Parris, another martyr, in 1551, and he expressed the most severe disapproval of the burning of Servetus in 1553.

But Foxe was no crank and no weakling. He viewed with horror the misgovernment of Northumberland and wrote a tract arguing in favour of a revival of excommunication as a discipline for the times. It was high courage to write personally to the Queen on the burning of the Anabaptists. It was not less courageous in 1569 to write to his friend and patron, the Duke of Norfolk, warning him against the proposed marriage with Mary, Queen of Scots, a letter in which plain speaking was in no way weakened by the courteous tone of the letter. Foxe visited Norfolk in the Tower and he attended him at his execution. Norfolk left him a pension of £20 a year.

Foxe died on 18 April 1587, and was buried in St. Giles's, Cripplegate.

T. F. Mozley, *John Fox and His Book*, 1940.
Simeon Fox, a memoir printed in the 1641 edition of the *Actes and Monumentes*.
S. R. Maitland, various articles in the *British Magazine* between 1837 and 1847, some of which have been reprinted in *Essays on Subjects Connected with the Reformation*.
H. Morris, *Elizabethan Literature*, 1958.
W. Haller, *Foxe's Book of Martyrs and the Elect Nation*, 1963.

ROBERTO DI RIDOLFI (1531–1612), conspirator, was born at Florence in 1531 and died at Florence in 1612. He came of a good family, many of whom were senators and supporters of the Medici. Roberto was brought up as a banker and as such he built up a business with London merchants. After Mary Tudor came to the throne and had married Philip II of Spain, Ridolfi visited England and soon settled down there. He was a strong Catholic and became intimate with many of the leading Catholic families in England. In much the same way as Horatio Palavicino, he established his reputation and integrity as a banker, not only with his business connections, but also with Cecil and the government, who often employed him in financial affairs. It is odd that the accession of Elizabeth in no way lessened Ridolfi's importance and influence. He was able to keep up a large correspondence with friends and agents in Italy, even with the Papacy, and he was in close touch with both the Spanish and French ambassadors in London. Secretly, he held the position of Papal agent in England from 1567 onwards. His banking facilities brought him into contact with the Duke of Norfolk and other leaders in the plot which developed first in 1568 to marry Norfolk to Mary, Queen of Scots, to secure her recognition as the heir to the throne and possibly to restore Catholicism in England.

This plan fitted in with Ridolfi's genuine sympathy with the discontent of the English Catholics, the more so because he had been charged by the Pope to act as his secret agent in England. Ridolfi set himself to form a league of English Catholic nobles. He was in the pay of both France and Spain, and thus he was in an excellent position to be the go-between among the Pope, the conspiring English peers, the French and Spanish ambassadors and Mary Stuart's agent, the Bishop of Ross.

In 1568 Ridolfi consulted with de Spes, the new Spanish Ambassador, how the lot of the English Catholics could be improved. In December he gave a letter of credit for twelve thousand ducats to Sir Thomas Gresham for the use of an Englishman who was going abroad. In the autumn of 1569 he sent to the leaders of the Northern Earls' Rebellion twelve thousand crowns from the Pope with a promise of a further ten thousand to come. Up to this point the English government was wholly ignorant of what was going on, but in October Cecil became aware that Ridolfi was receiving large sums of money from abroad and was distributing it among the Bishop of Ross and some of Norfolk's servants. On 7 October Ridolfi was arrested and sent to Walsingham for examination.

To Walsingham Ridolfi admitted that he had paid over money to the Bishop of Ross and to the Duke of Norfolk, and he further admitted that he had been 'made privy to the matter of marriage betwixt the Queen of Scots and the Duke'. On a second examination Walsingham failed to extract any further evidence against Ridolfi, whose house was now searched and his papers seized. Nothing more was discovered against him. He remained with Walsingham until 11 November, when he was released on condition that he kept to his own house at the Queen's pleasure and gave an undertaking not to meddle in affairs of state, and he had to provide bail of £1,000. In January 1570 he was returned his bail and completely freed. It is extraordinary that he got off so lightly. With great skill he had explained his disbursements of money as part of his normal business of banking. He could account for his connection with the Spanish embassy, because Cecil had employed him to negotiate over the seizure by England of the Spanish treasure ships in 1568. His connection with the French embassy does not seem to have been known. It is possible that Cecil and the Queen hoped to use so able and well-informed a man for their own purposes, a view which is supported by the fact that Cecil had Ridolfi to dine on 22 June 1569 to discuss the Spanish negotiations.

It has been suggested that Ridolfi became a government spy or *agent provocateur*, and hence that the Ridolfi Plot was fabricated by Cecil to entrap Norfolk and Mary. There is, however, very little evidence which directly supports such a view.

After his release in 1570, Ridolfi was in a position to go ahead with his plans. He was trusted by everybody, except by Alva in the Netherlands, who never had any confidence in him. Ridolfi began to co-ordinate the plot for Norfolk's marriage with the Spanish plot for the invasion of England. He made a list of forty peers who, he was convinced, would rise against Elizabeth. Mary Stuart approved his plans; the two plots were fused; the English Catholics were to rise; an invading army was to overthrow Elizabeth and her govern-ment; Mary would marry Norfolk and replace Elizabeth on the English throne: this was what is known as the Ridolfi Plot. Ridolfi went abroad in order to explain the new scheme to Alva, Philip II and the Pope, 24 March 1571. Even now Cecil believed that Ridolfi was working on the English side.

Ridolfi went first to Alva, who refused to move a single man until the English Catholics had actually risen in revolt. He then left for Rome, but he sent three letters to the Bishop of Ross, the Duke of Norfolk and Lord Lumley by Charles Baillie. Baillie was arrested at Dover: the letters were in cipher, but Baillie's confession at last opened the eyes of the government to the truth about Ridolfi.

In Rome Ridolfi found the Pope encouraging and he went on to Spain bearing a written approval of his scheme from the Pope. In Madrid he was asked whether it would be possible to assassinate Elizabeth, and Ridolfi assured Philip that it could be done. Philip finally agreed that as soon as Elizabeth was dead Alva should invade England. Ridolfi wrote triumphantly to Mary, Norfolk and the Bishop of Ross, but they never received the letters from de Spes, for in September the government had got all the information it needed. Norfolk and many others were arrested; Alva refused to stir in the Netherlands; it was impossible for Ridolfi to return to England. The Ridolfi Plot had failed.

Ridolfi returned to live in Florence, where he became a senator. He died on 18 February 1612.

F. Edwards, *The Dangerous Queen*, 1964.
F. Edwards, *The Marvellous Chance*, 1968.

FRANCIS THROCKMORTON (1554–1584), conspirator, was a member of the large and well-known West Midland Catholic family, whose name sometimes appears as Throgmorton. The family seat was and is still at Coughton Court in Warwickshire. The Throckmortons intermarried with many of the leading, and especially Catholic, families, such as the Digbys and Catesbys, and their history is closely connected with that of the staunch Roman Catholic families of the sixteenth and early seventeenth centuries. Although they were not directly involved in the Gunpowder Plot — Mr. Thomas Throckmorton had prudently gone abroad — before going he had loaned Coughton Court to Digby, and it was there that the wives of the 1605 conspirators had waited for the news of the Gunpowder Plot. Long before that date, the family was directly and disastrously involved in what is known as the Throckmorton Plot, in the person of Francis Throckmorton, although he was no more than the agent carrying out other men's instructions.

Francis was the son of Sir John Throckmorton of Feckenham in Worcestershire, and Sir John was the seventh of eight sons of Sir George Throckmorton of Coughton Court, Warwickshire, and the brother of Sir Nicholas Throckmorton, the Elizabethan diplomatist. Francis, after matriculating at Oxford in 1572, in 1576 was entered as a student of the Inner Temple. In 1580 he went abroad with his brother Thomas: as an ardent Catholic he visited the English Catholic exiles on the Continent and he heard plans for restoring the Catholic religion in England by means of a foreign invasion. He heard the story in France, he heard it in Madrid: in Paris he met Charles Paget and Thomas Morgan, the agents of Mary Stuart, and imbibed the same story. Put shortly, the plan was one devised by the Duke of Guise: his armies would invade Scotland and England at one and the same moment. He had originally intended to murder Elizabeth, but he gave up that idea. The English Catholics were to be roused against the government and Mary Stuart was to be put on the throne. The whole cost of the adventure was to be financed by the Pope and the King of Spain. Guise himself was to lead the invasion on the south coast of England.

Walsingham was well aware that some such scheme was being

planned, but he had no detailed information. He therefore set a spy to work in the French embassy, a Frenchman who signed himself Fagot. It was Fagot who gave Walsingham the clue that he needed, when he wrote to him, 'the chief agents of the Queen of Scots are Mr. Throckmorton and Lord Henry Howard. They never come to the ambassador's house except at night' ... 'On the 29th April le Sieur Frocquemorton visited the ambassador's house'. At once Walsingham set spies to work on Throckmorton and early in November Throckmorton was arrested and his papers seized: these contained a list of Catholic noblemen, a plan of harbours suitable for landing military forces and a number of 'infamous pamphlets against her Majesty printed beyond the seas'. There is no doubt that Throckmorton had also organized communication between Morgan and Mary, Queen of Scots, and also the Spanish ambassador, Mendoza.

At his first examination Francis denied all knowledge of the papers: they had been 'foisted' upon him by the searchers of his house. Being urged to confess and being promised pardon if he would do so, he still refused to admit anything. He was then sent to the rack in the Tower, but he still refused to admit anything. Sent to the rack a second time, he collapsed and agreed to make a full confession. His confession did not in fact cover the whole conspiracy, but it probably covered all that Francis knew. The damning evidence against him was the confession that 'he had set down in his own hand certain special havens for the landing of forces' and had also 'noted the number of persons of power as he thought fit to be drawn to that action with the aptness of their dwellings to each port'. He also admitted that on this calculation the Duke of Guise had decided on Arundel in Sussex as his port of landing for the invasion of southern England.

In view of this confession and of the written evidence to support it, there could be no result but the execution of Throckmorton at Tyburn. One other result of this so-called Throckmorton Plot was the expulsion of the Spanish Ambassador, Mendoza, from the kingdom, since he had known all the details and was deep in the whole design.

A. L. Rowse, *Ralegh and the Throckmortons*, 1962.

WILLIAM PARRY (*d.* 1585), conspirator, was the son of Harry ap David of Flintshire, a man of good family, and his second wife, Margaret, daughter of the Archdeacon of St. Asaphs. His original name was William ap Harry. According to his testimony, his father died about 1566, aged 108, leaving fourteen children by his first marriage and sixteen by his second. No date is known for William's birth. He was executed on 2 March 1585.

William was educated at a grammar school in Chester, from which, after several attempts, he escaped and went to London. Here he married a widow, Mrs. Powell, who brought him some wealth. He entered the household of William Herbert, the first Earl of Pembroke, with whom he remained until the Earl died in 1570, when Parry entered the Queen's service. A second marriage with a widow, Catherine Heywood, brought him several manors in Lincolnshire and Kent, which involved him in some litigation in 1571. He was a profligate and extravagant young man and he very soon squandered all his resources and was being pursued by creditors. He therefore applied to Burghley to be employed as a spy abroad, doubtless in order to elude the creditors. He tried to ingratiate himself with the English Catholics abroad, to worm out of them their secrets which he could send on to Burghley. He returned home in 1577 and was constantly applying to Burghley for financial help. In 1579 he suddenly disappeared overseas without a licence to leave the country: he was home again in 1580. Pestered again by creditors, Parry violently assaulted one of them, Hugh Hare, for which he was convicted and sentenced to death, although he complained that the Recorder 'spake with the jury and the foreman did drink'.

Pardoned by the Queen, Parry in 1582 asked leave to travel abroad. He continued to pretend that he was searching out the secrets of exiled Catholics, but in fact he was beginning to take the Catholic side. He urged a more lenient policy towards them in England and he pleaded for a pardon for some of the best of the exiles. Then he fell in with Charles Paget and Thomas Morgan, agents in Paris of the Queen of Scots. After reading some of the writings of Cardinal Allen, Parry allegedly began to ponder on the lawfulness of murdering princes for the sake of religion, with special reference to Queen Elizabeth. But he still played a double game: on 10 May 1583 he wrote to Burghley, 'if I am not deceived, I have shaken the foundation of the English Seminary at Rheims and utterly overthrone the credit of the English pensioners at Rome'.

In January 1584 Parry was again in England. He went straight to Court and had an interview with Elizabeth. To her he confessed that he had had dealings with the Pope, Paget and Morgan to attempt 'somewhat' against her life, but he protested that he had done this only in order to 'discover the dangerous practices devised and attempted against her Majesty by her disloyal subjects and other malicious persons in foreign parts'. In March he received a letter from Cardinal Como which gave some colour to this story. This letter Parry shewed to the Queen, who pardoned his offences and provided him with a seat in Parliament (1584). He at once got into trouble for violently opposing an anti-Catholic bill and he was imprisoned for a few hours until released at the command of the Queen.

Short once more of money, Parry took up spying again. He selected a man named Edmund Neville, who may have been a cousin of Parry's, and to him he proposed a plot to assassinate the Queen. It is possible that Parry was only trying to extract from Neville some admission which could be used against him. Neville, however, revealed Parry's suggestion to one of the courtiers, who at once went with the information to Elizabeth. Parry was arrested, accused of compassing the Queen's death, partly on Neville's evidence, chiefly on the evidence provided by Parry himself in his confession to the Queen in January 1584.

It is difficult to be sure that Parry was really guilty. That he was technically guilty in discussing the murder of the Queen without any authority from a minister to do so as a trap is certain. Whether he ever intended to murder the Queen is another matter. Parry was a vain, weak and vacillating man, with an inflated idea of his own importance. It is unlikely that he would ever have had the resolution to carry out such a deed. When he was examined by Walsingham, he passionately protested that he had never mentioned such a matter to anybody since his return from France. He spent the night at Walsingham's house: next morning he asked for an interview and told Walsingham that he now remembered that he had mentioned to a kinsman of his a statement he had read in a book about the lawfulness of killing princes for the sake of religion. Confronted with Neville, he denied again that he had talked of murdering Elizabeth. Examined a third time, Parry made a full confession, wrote it out and confirmed it in a letter to the Queen. The most charitable thing is to suspect that he was not entirely sane. He was hanged at Westminster on 2 March 1585.

Conyers Read, *Sir Francis Walsingham*, 1925.

SIR ANTHONY BABINGTON (1561–1586), conspirator, whose name has been given to the plot (Babington Plot) against Queen Elizabeth (although he was not the originator of it) because he appeared to be, and in many respects was, the leader of the English Catholics in it. He was born in October 1561 at Dethick in Derbyshire: he was executed at Tyburn on 20 September 1586. He came of an ancient and wealthy family, with one branch of which in the nineteenth century the historian Thomas Babington Macaulay was connected. Anthony was the third child and eldest of three sons born to Henry Babington by his second wife, Mary Darcy, granddaughter of Thomas, Lord Darcy, who was executed for his part in the Pilgrimage of Grace. Henry died in 1571 when his son and heir, Anthony, was ten years old. Anthony became the ward of his mother, but her second husband, Henry Foljambe, and Philip Draycot of Paynsley in Staffordshire, had most of the care of Anthony's education. All three families were at heart Catholics, even if they conformed outwardly to the new state religion, and Anthony was brought up as a Catholic, especially when he was staying at Paynsley. He was at Dethick until 1577, but he made many visits to Paynsley, where he met and eventually married (1579) Margaret, Philip Draycot's daughter, when he was eighteen years old. Before his marriage he was for a short time in the household of the Earl of Shrewsbury at Sheffield, when Shrewsbury was gaoler of Mary, Queen of Scots, where he acted as page to Lord Shrewsbury. Whether he ever met Mary Stuart is doubtful, but certainly he conceived a great admiration for her.

In 1580 Anthony made a six months' tour of France, spending his time chiefly in Paris and Rouen. It was here that he first met Chidiock Tichborne, a recusant English exile, who was later to be executed at Tyburn on the same day as Anthony (1586). In Paris he was visited by Thomas Morgan, one of Mary Queen of Scots' agents, who introduced him to her ambassador, the Archbishop of Glasgow.

On his return to London (1580) Babington entered as a student at Lincoln's Inn. He was a handsome, charming, intelligent and wealthy young man, popular at Court, where he met other young bloods who were Catholic admirers of the Queen of Scots. Anthony lodged near Temple Bar. One day he received a letter from Queen Mary, conveyed to him by a Mrs. Bray of Sheffield (Staffs.). From this letter he learned that Morgan and the Archbishop of Glasgow had recommended him to the Scots Queen. Shortly afterwards he was visited by the Secretary to the French embassy who brought him a packet from Morgan. In it was another packet which Morgan asked Babington to convey to the Queen of Scots. This packet he succeeded in getting to the Scots Queen, the first of a series, as Babington admitted in his final Confession, although he could not recall more than five letters in all. In 1585 the Scots Queen was transferred to the much more vigilant care of Sir Amyas Paulet at Chartley, and Babington's work as a postman came to an end.

In the early 1580s he was one of the Catholic laymen who helped the Catholic missionaries in England. Babington took an active and dangerous part in aiding their movements about the country from house to house.

A plan to travel to Italy and perhaps even to settle in that country came to nothing, because Babington was unable to get a licence to leave the country (1586). In the spring he moved his lodgings from Temple Bar to Hern's Rents, Holborn, near to Lincoln's Inn Fields. Twice he received packets from Morgan to forward to Queen Mary, but he refused to help. Then, towards the end of May 1586, Ballard returned to England and called on Babington at his lodgings. They were well acquainted with each other. Ballard gave Babington an account of an interview he had had in Paris with Mendoza, the Spanish Ambassador. He explained that there was a plot arranged for the rising of the Catholics in England; this was to be supported by a foreign invasion; Queen Elizabeth was to be murdered and Mary Stuart was to be released and put on to the throne of England. At first Babington was sceptical: Ballard overcame his doubts. Babington discussed the plan with his young Catholic friends. He then decided he had better flee the country and he applied to Walsingham for a licence to travel abroad. This brought him into contact with Robert Poley, one of Walsingham's agents. Poley ingratiated himself with Babington and got from him many of the details of the plot. Babington discussed with him the lawfulness of murdering Elizabeth. All this information Poley passed on to Walsingham.

In April 1586 Morgan had written to Queen Mary advising her to send a friendly letter to Babington and enclosing a draft for such a letter. Walsingham intercepted this correspondence and kept it for future use. When Poley revealed to Walsingham that Babington was talking about the lawfulness of murdering Elizabeth, Walsingham at once sent on Morgan's letters to Mary. On 25 June 1586, Mary wrote to Babington, and he received the letter on the 29th — of course, after Walsingham had read it. Babington sent a reply, and one of Walsingham's agents took it to Chartley, where Mary received it on Saturday, 9 July in a cask of beer — the machinery which Walsingham had devised by which all Mary's correspondence passed in and out of Chartley with the secret knowledge of Sir Amyas Paulet. Thus all Mary's letters were known to the government without Mary's suspecting. On 18 July Mary sent Babington an answer, which he received on the 29th. This was the letter which brought Mary, Queen of Scots, to the block. In brief it may be said that Babington had written to Mary details of the plot, including the plan to murder Elizabeth: Mary replied, approving of everything, including the murder of Elizabeth. An enormous literature has grown up dealing with the question whether the whole of Mary's letter, as produced at the trial, was genuine or whether that part of it approving of the murder of Elizabeth was forged by Walsingham.

Walsingham had now all the information he needed. He played the Babington fish for several days, anxious to extract from him the fullest information. He probably played one day too long. When Babington heard of Ballard's arrest, he wrote a protest (according to Camden, and there is no reason to disbelieve his version) to Walsingham, who replied that Babington would be in similar danger if he did not take refuge in Walsingham's house. Babington did so, but finding himself a prisoner, he invited Walsingham's servants to supper and, pretending to pay the bill, he escaped to St. John's Wood. There with a few friends he hid himself, until he was driven by hunger to the house of a friend. There he was captured and imprisoned in the Tower.

It is possible to sympathise with this romantic and generous-minded young man, but it is impossible to regard him as a hero,

except at the moment of execution. He was a half-hearted conspirator and at the trial he played the meanest part of them all,
(Conyers Read, *ib.*), putting all the blame on Ballard, which Ballard
gallantly accepted. Sentence of hanging and quartering was passed.
Babington wrote an abject letter to Elizabeth crying for mercy. He
offered £1,000 to a friend, if he could secure his release. On
20 September 1586 he was executed at Tyburn. To his credit it must
be recorded that an eye-witness wrote that Babington, who had to
watch the appalling execution of Ballard first, shewed 'a sign of his
former pride' by standing, instead of praying on his knees, 'with his
hat on his head as if he had been but a beholder of the execution'.
When his turn came, he died in such 'diabolical tortures' that when
Queen Elizabeth heard the story she ordered that the rest of the
conspirators should be hanged until they were dead.

J.H. Pollen, *Mary Queen of Scots and the Babington Plot*, 1922.

RODRIGO LOPEZ (*d.*1594), Physician-in-Chief to Queen
Elizabeth I, came of a Portuguese Jewish family. Little is known of
his early life. He married the eldest daughter of Gonsalvo Añes, more
usually known as Dunstan Añes, by whom he had two sons and three
daughters. His brother-in-law was Alvaro Mendez, councillor to
Sultan Murad, who created him Duke of Metilli. Thus Lopez had
distinguished relations in many parts of Europe. He was driven from
Portugal by the Inquisition and settled in England in 1559. Lytton
Strachey in *Elizabeth and Essex* calls him a practising Christian, but
Lucien Wolf in his *Jews in Elizabethan England* quotes evidence to
show that Lopez was a practising crypto-Jew and that Burghley was
well aware of it.

Lopez set up in London as a doctor and was so successful that he
became the first house physician at St. Bartholomew's Hospital.
Leicester and Walsingham became his patients, and in 1586 he was
appointed Physician-in-Chief to the Queen, who treated him with
great generosity. He was now a well-known and prosperous man,
with a son at Winchester College, a house in Holborn, and an
assured position at Court. His very success, however, and his being a
foreigner and a Jew, brought him many malicious enemies.

After Spain had incorporated Portugal in the Spanish Empire, the
pretender to the Portuguese throne was Antonio Perez, known as

Don Antonio. Lopez, of course, sided with Antonio against Spain. It was partly on the advice of Lopez that Elizabeth sanctioned the Drake-Norris expedition of 1589 to restore Don Antonio to the throne. That expedition was a failure, and the Earl of Essex, who was the leader of the anti-Spanish party in England, brought Antonio back to England in 1590 to act as a cat's-paw in his political ambitions. Lopez got to know Essex at court and agreed to act as interpreter between the Earl and Antonio. Relations between Lopez and Essex soon deteriorated, and in 1593 Lopez rashly criticized the Earl to Antonio, who passed on the criticism to Essex.

Spanish spies were all the while plotting to get Antonio's servants to murder Antonio and the Queen. Lopez became involved in the first part of the plan, but he showed no sympathy with the idea of murdering Elizabeth. The plot reached the ears of the Council, Lopez was at once under suspicion, and Essex saw his chance to have his revenge on the Jew. When he examined Lopez's papers nothing incriminating was found, but that did not deter Essex. Some of Antonio's servants were arrested, and under torture they brought charges against Lopez which led to his arrest. He was put in the Tower (1594) and was tried by a special tribunal over which Essex himself presided. Inevitably Lopez was found guilty and condemned to death. For three months the Queen delayed signing the death warrant, but she gave way at last, and on 7 June Lopez was drawn on a hurdle to Tyburn, where he was hanged and quartered. Camden records that on the scaffold Lopez declared that 'he loved the queen as well as he loved Jesus Christ, which from a man of the Jewish profession moved no small laughter in the standers-by'. There can be little doubt that Lopez was sacrificed largely to satisfy the vanity of Essex, but a point of view more hostile to Lopez will be found argued by A. Dymock.

Apart from the dramatic interest of Lopez's rise and fall, he has a claim to be remembered on another score, for there are considerable grounds for thinking that Lopez is the original of Shakespeare's Shylock.

Lytton Strachey, *Elizabeth and Essex*, 1928.
S. L. Lee, 'The Original of Shylock', *Gentleman's Magazine*, 1880.
Lucien Wolf, 'Jews in Elizabethan England', *Transactions of the Jewish Historical Society*, 1924–27.

A. Dymock, *English Historical Review*, 1894.
Martin Hume, *Transactions of the Jewish Historical Society*, 1919.

SIR THOMAS STUCLEY [there are many variations in the spelling of his name] (*c.*1520–1578), adventurer, was born probably some time before 1520. He was the third of the four sons of Sir Hugh Stucley and his wife, Jane, daughter of Sir Lewis Pollard, a Judge of the Common Pleas. There is no reason for accepting the rumour that he was the illegitimate son of Henry VIII. Nothing is known of his education, but he was probably a retainer of the Duke of Suffolk until the Duke's death in 1545. He was present at the siege of Boulogne (1544–5) and on the death of Suffolk he attached himself to the Earl of Hertford, afterwards Protector Somerset. He then returned to Boulogne, where he held the post of King's Standard-bearer at a wage of 6s. 8d. per day.

Boulogne was surrendered to the French in 1550 and Stucley returned to England to the Court of Edward VI and to the service of Protector Somerset. In May of that year he conducted the French Marquis de Maine to Scotland and back on a visit of condolence to Marie de Guise, the Scottish Queen, on the death of the Duc de Guise. In April 1551 Stucley was in France at the court of Henry II, where he made an excellent impression. It was characteristic of Stucley that he always succeeded in making a good impression at the first meeting, but he never succeeded in retaining the favour which he acquired. This may be seen in his relations with Queen Elizabeth, Burghley, Pope Pius V, Pope Gregory XIII, Philip II of Spain and many other people. He came back to England as a supporter of Somerset, but the arrest of Somerset foiled his plans, and Stucley fled back to France and entered the service of Henry II, whose confidence he at once won. Henry sent him home to England with a letter to Edward VI strongly recommending him to the King. Henry's real purpose was to obtain information which would help him in his projected attack on Calais, but Stucley used the opportunity to reconcile himself with the English government by betraying the true purpose of his mission. Northumberland, however, thought to win Henry's friendship by betraying to him Stucley's disloyalty, and he threw Stucley into prison and cancelled the previous promise to pay his many debts.

Stucley seems to have been released about 1553, but his debts drove him abroad again. Unable to return to France, he now went to the Emperor, Charles V, to whom Queen Mary had written a letter of commendation. He served under the Duke of Savoy until October 1554, when he came home with the Duke, who was paying a visit to England. Stucley was given a guarantee of freedom from arrest for his debts for six months, which enabled him to be at Court until 1555, but by then his debts had not been paid. It was essential to him that his fortunes should be repaired; therefore in that year he married an heiress, Anne, daughter of Sir Thomas Curtis, a rich City alderman. On 13 May a warrant for his arrest was issued on a charge of uttering false money. Stucley escaped overseas and again took service under the Duke of Savoy in the English force led by the Earl of Pembroke. He took part in the Duke of Egmont's victory over Henry II of France at St. Quentin in 1557.

Being still in financial difficulties and in search of quick wealth, Stucley now took to buccaneering and preyed on the French ships. Complaints against him were soon lodged with the Lord High Admiral, but Stucley's luck held and on 17 July 1558, the Admiral reported that he did not 'find the matter sufficient to charge Stucley withal'.

In 1561 Stucley was given a captaincy in Berwick where, in spite of his few resources, he lived sumptuously and gained a reputation for his 'royalty to men at arms'. In the same year he entertained lavishly and made great friends with Shane O'Neill, a friendship which was to have important results later. As a result of his extravagance Stucley had soon exhausted all the wealth of his wife and it was necessary to find a fresh source of income. Stucley therefore embarked on his famous plan for founding a colony in Florida. Once again his power to create a good impression helped him: he was able to persuade Queen Elizabeth to supply one of the ships. The plan to plant a colony was a mere blind to cover Stucley's return to piracy. For two years his exploits at sea 'were a scandal to Europe' (D.N.B.), so that Elizabeth was compelled to disown Stucley and to send some ships for his arrest. Once again he was acquitted, but he had lost the Queen money and thus he also lost her good opinion. She never forgave him.

The year 1566 was the turning point in Stucley's turbulent career. Shane O'Neill in that year asked the English government to send Stucley to him to be employed against the Scots in Ulster. Stucley went, with disastrous results. The Queen knew that Stucley hated her religious policy and that he had been carrying on treasonable correspondence for at least three years with the Spanish Ambassador and that he had accepted a pension from Philip II. She strongly suspected that Stucley's motives in going to Ireland were also treasonable. In June 1569 Stucley was accused of high treason and was shut in Dublin Castle (June to October). He had certainly proposed to Spain an invasion of Ireland, but once more the evidence was not enough to convict him and he was released. From this moment Stucley became a whole-hearted traitor.

Already he was in touch with Richard Creagh, Roman Catholic Archbishop of Armagh, and with Guereau de Spes, Spanish Ambassador in London. As soon as he was released, Stucley went to London and offered his services to Fenelon, the French ambassador, but he soon discovered that he could make a better bargain with Spain. He returned to Ireland, fitted out a ship and sailed for Vimiero on 17 April 1570, arriving there on the 24th. Stucley was received with extraordinary favour by the King, who gave him 3,000 ducats, all his daily expenses, and then a further 6,000 ducats and an establishment which was reckoned to cost the King 30 ducats a day. Stucley now lived in the most sumptuous style: he was known as the Duke of Ireland and he asked Philip to create him Duke of Leinster and his son a Marquis. It is a disputable point whether Philip did in fact knight Stucley. Some months later Stucley left Spain and moved to Rome. It is pretty certain that Philip had now become aware of Stucley's real character, partly through letters from Maurice Gibbon, Archbishop of Cashel, who wrote frequently to undermine Stucley's position. Stucley had been trying to intervene in the Ridolfi Plot, but his plan misfired. On his way to Rome, by some means or other, he commanded three galleys at Don John of Austria's great victory over the Turks at Lepanto (1571) and he won great praise for his courageous behaviour in the battle. The kudos he thus gained did something to reinstate him in Philip's favour, to whose Court he returned after Lepanto in 1572.

Between 1572 and 1578 Stucley was here, there and everywhere — in Spain, the Netherlands, in Paris, in Rome — trying to persuade the Pope and Philip II to embark on an invasion of Ireland. At last, in 1578, Stucley's efforts succeeded, largely through the help of James Fitzmaurice, a Geraldine who was violently opposed to Elizabeth's government in Ireland. Stucley won the favour first of Pope Pius V, then of Pope Gregory XIII, of the Cardinal of Como, who was Secretary of State, and of the English clergy in Rome, notably Dr. Maurice Clenog, the Provost of the English Hospital in Rome, who wrote to assure the Pope that Stucley was 'a man sent from heaven' (*divinitus*) for the English enterprise. The Pope provided 600 Papal infantry which were conveyed to the port of embarkation, the Fortezza del Re Catholico at Port'ercole. Stucley was leader of the expedition and he sailed in the *San Giovanni Battista* (possibly a Spanish ship) early in January 1578.

It was not until 4 April that he reached Cadiz. His ships were so rotten that it was necessary to refit, but Philip refused to allow him to do this at Cadiz. Stucley stayed there from 4 April to the 14th; then he sailed for San Lucar and went on to Lisbon, where he arrived probably on 17 April. Here he found that King Sebastian had no ships to offer him: instead he offered Stucley a command in his Portuguese army which was about to invade Morocco. Stucley accepted and diverted the Papal troops from the invasion of Ireland to the invasion of Morocco. He declared that he knew Ireland as well as the best, and there were only to be got there hunger and lice. He fought with great courage at the battle of Alcazar, but he was killed early in the day after a cannon-ball had cut off both his legs (4 August 1578).

'Of this man', wrote Burghley, 'might be written whole volumes to paint out the life of a man in the highest degree of vain-glory, prodigality, falsehood and vile and filthy conversation of life, and altogether without faith, conscience or religion.' Yet Stucley impressed many other people more favourably, even if wrongly and only for a time. He became the hero of more than one play and of several ballads and he appears in Chapter V of Kingsley's *Westward Ho!*

H. Simpson, *The School of Shakespeare.*
Z. N. Brooke, *English Historical Review*, 1913.
J. H. Pollen, *The Month*, 1903.

WILLIAM ALLEN (1532–1594) Cardinal ('Cardinal of England'), was the second son of John Allen of Rossall (where he was born) in Lancashire and of Jane Lister of Westby in Yorkshire.

GUILIELMUS ALANUS, S.R.E.CARDINALIS, S.T.D.
Duac. Archiēpus Mechlin. designatus; obiit Romæ
A° MDXCIV.   Edun de Boulenois fecit

Cardinal Allen
(Artist: Unknown)

In his early years he was educated at home, but in 1547 he went up
to Oriel College, Oxford. He took his B.A. in 1550; he became a

Fellow of his college in the same year and M.A. in 1554. His tutor was the Rev. Morgan Philipps, much skilled as a debater and an ardent Catholic, who later was a valuable help to Allen in the founding of Douai College. In 1556 Allen was elected Principal of St. Mary's Hall, Oxford, and he was also for a time Proctor. In about 1558 he was made a Canon of York and his future seemed assured. But the accession of the Protestant Elizabeth changed everything for the uncompromisingly Catholic Allen, so much so that in 1561 he deemed it wiser to leave England and to settle at Louvain University.

While he was at Louvain, he wrote a treatise on Purgatory which he published a few years later (1565). He was tutor to a young Englishman of the name of Christopher Blount, who was later to be executed for his part in the Essex rebellion of 1600. Blount contracted some disease which also infected Allen, and so ill did Allen become that the doctors urged him to return to England and see what his native air could do for him.

It was 1562 when Allen returned to Lancashire, and his health at once improved. Up to 1565 he devoted himself to recovering relapsed Catholics from heresy, so successfully that he became, in the eyes of the government, a menace and he was forced to leave his own county of Lancashire and move to Oxford; thence to the household of the Duke of Norfolk in Norfolk. Here he wrote his *Certain Brief Reasons Concerning Catholic Faith*. His open opposition to the religious policy of the Queen forced him once again to go abroad, and he left England in 1565 for the Low Countries, never to return. In 1567 Elizabeth issued a list of those who were to be apprehended for their 'contempt and obstinacy': 'Alen' headed the list as he 'who wrote the late booke of Purgatory'. In this year Allen was ordained at Malines and remained there teaching theology.

Now took place (1567) Allen's first journey to Rome, this time with Morgan Philipps and with Dr. Vendeville, Regius Professor of Canon Law at Douai, who wanted to persuade Pope Pius V to adopt his plan for converting the infidels. He failed in his object, but on the way home Allen persuaded him to take up the cause of Catholicism in England and the Netherlands. Allen proposed to him to found a seminary college for English students abroad.

In 1568 Allen founded such a college at Douai to enable English students abroad to have the benefit of collegiate training; to form a body of learned priests capable of restoring the Catholic religion in England; to instruct English youths in the Catholic religion who might go to Douai for their education. Allen hired a large house and began to live there in collegiate fashion with a few English and Belgian students. His great difficulty was lack of funds, but he also encountered a good deal of local opposition. His plan was, however, approved by Pope Pius V, and thus Douai became the first of those seminaries which had been ordered by the Council of Trent.

In 1569 Allen became a B.D. and in the following year the Regius Professor of Philosophy at Douai University, and in 1571 D.D. It was characteristic of his selflessness that he gave the whole of his salary of 200 gold crowns to the seminary college to improve the food and to raise the number of students which the college could accommodate.

Owing to the death of most of the Catholic bishops in England or else because they were in exile, it became necessary to find some responsible person to delegate the necessary powers to those priests who might be sent on mission to England from Douai. Allen was given, first by Pope Pius V and then by Gregory XIII, extensive powers for this purpose. The latter Pope also made a grant of 100 gold crowns a month to make Douai College financially independent. Gregory also sent for Allen to go to Rome to give him advice on a seminary college for Englishmen in Rome which he was thinking of founding. An agreement was come to by which students were to be sent from Douai to Rome as soon as the new college was ready to receive them. In 1576 Allen arrived back at Douai.

Just about this time the English students at Douai became extremely unpopular with the Dutch, principally because they regarded the English Catholics as taking the side of Philip II in the dispute between themselves and the Spanish King. So unhealthy did things become that it was deemed unsafe for Allen to remain at Douai and he withdrew to Paris (November 1576). Two years later the English college was expelled from Douai and had to establish itself at Rheims. With some prescience Allen had seen this to be inevitable and he had been preparing the ground at Rheims for the move (1578).

Meantime things had not been going well at the English College in Rome, where the English students were quarrelling so violently with the few Welsh students and with the Welsh head of the College that Allen in 1579 made his third journey to Rome, partly to deal with the quarrels, partly to try to recruit more seminary priests for England. His chief object was to persuade the Society of Jesus to take over the College in Rome and to send some of the sixty-nine English Jesuits in Rome to England. The result was that in 1580 the first Jesuits came to England, when Fathers Parsons and Campion arrived in June to lead the English mission.

Allen remained head of the College in Rheims until 1585, when he fell ill and had to go for treatment at Spa. His life was despaired of and he even destroyed his ciphers, but he made a rapid recovery at Spa and in 1585 he made his fourth journey to Rome. Probably Sixtus V had summoned him thither to take up again his share in the revision of the Vulgate which he had begun in 1579. On 7 August 1587 Allen was created a Cardinal under the title of St. Martinus in Montibus, largely at the request of Philip II, who was hoping to make use of Allen in England when she had been overcome by the Armada. Allen had no money with which to support his new position, but the Pope and Philip II saw to it that he was adequately supplied with revenues.

Allen's efforts to restore the Catholic religion in England were not confined to missionary work carried out by his seminary priests from Douai and Rheims. He realized that purely scholastic and religious attempts were proving ineffective. He therefore turned to political methods and did not hesitate both to use intrigue and to advocate armed force. He was in correspondence with Mary, Queen of Scots, and with the Guises; he was well aware of Parsons' plans for getting rid of Elizabeth from the English throne; he was for a short time involved in the Guise plan for putting James VI of Scotland on the English throne; he then became a whole-hearted supporter of the plan for substituting Philip II for Elizabeth. When the conquest had succeeded, Allen was to go to England as Papal Legate and to become Archbishop of Canterbury and Lord Chancellor. It is often said that he actually went to the Netherlands to join Parma's army of invasion, but it is certain that he remained in Rome. In two particular ways Allen made himself specially obnoxious to the English government. In 1587 he published a letter defending the surrender of Deventer, a Dutch fort, to the Spaniards by the English governor, Sir William Stanley, and of a fort near Zutphen by Rowland York. He also violently attacked Elizabeth herself in this letter. Secondly, there was published just before the sailing of the Armada from the Tagus a pamphlet entitled *An Admonition to the Nobility and People of England and Ireland, concerning the Present Wars* ... This was a violent piece of writing, justifying the Papal Bull which had excommunicated Elizabeth. It was intended by Allen to stir the English people up to rebellion in order to help the invading Spaniards.

In 1589 Allen was made Apostolic Librarian and he took a large part in the revision of the Vulgate. He had also taken a share with Dr. Richard Bristow in revising Gregory Martin's English translation of the Bible, generally known as the Douai Bible. The New Testament was published in 1582 at Rheims while Allen was at the English College: the Old Testament was not issued until 1609 at Douai after Allen's death. He also intended to revise the text of the writings of St. Augustine, but he died before he could complete the work on 16 October 1594 and was buried in the Church of the Holy Trinity attached to the English College in Rome.

Allen was without doubt the most important Englishman abroad so far as religion was concerned. He has been denounced as a traitor by English Protestants and described by Catholics as being 'graced by every species of virtue'. Everybody who met him loved him: there is no known instance of his quarrelling with anybody. He had the power to win the loyalty of all kinds of persons and to persuade all kinds of opposites to live together peaceably. He had high intellectual gifts and his religious faith was unshakable and even fanatic. His weaknesses were that he relied entirely on his own personality to achieve success: he had no ability to build a system of government for his colleges, so that, as long as he was there, things went swimmingly; when his personality was withdrawn quarrels at once broke out. Again, as long as he confined himself to purely religious and spiritual methods he achieved considerable success. But he was an unsuccessful politician and all his schemes failed. This was because the Spaniards, in whom he put his trust, were unable to defeat Elizabeth. However much one may deplore some of his methods, there can be no doubt that his motives were entirely selfless and his ruling passion was the glory of God.

The article in the *D.N.B.* is a verbatim reproduction of parts of the historical introduction to the *First and Second Diaries of the*

English College, Douai (edited by T.F.Knox for the *Records of English Catholics*), with additions from other sources, 1878.
A.O.Meyer (tr. by J.R.McKee), *England and the Catholic Church under Elizabeth.*, 1916.
J.H.Pollen, *The English Catholics in the Reign of Queen Elizabeth,* 1920.
T.F.Knox, *Letters and Memorials of Cardinal Allen,* 1882.
P.J.Holmes, *Resistance and Compromise,* 1982.

ROBERT PARSONS or PERSONS (1546–1610), Jesuit, was born at Nether Stowey in Somerset in 1546, and died in Rome in 1610. He was the son of a blacksmith who had eleven children, of whom Robert was the sixth. He was educated at Stogursey, then at Taunton, went up to Oxford, first to St. Mary's Hall, then to Balliol, of which college he became a Fellow. At heart he was a Catholic, but he twice took the Oath of Supremacy. In 1575 he left Oxford after a quarrel with his colleagues who are said to have resented his popularity with his pupils. For five months he lived in London, then he went to Padua to study medicine: after two or three months there he went on to Rome, and on 4 July 1575 he was received into the Society of Jesus.

Parsons was ordained in 1578 and was put in charge of the second year novices. It was probably Parsons who originated the idea of sending Jesuits into England. Much to his surprise he was among the first to go and was appointed the Superior of the party. Parsons, Campion and seven others set out from Rome on 18 April 1580, mostly on foot, having only a few horses. They took six weeks to arrive at Rheims, and here the party split up. Parsons travelled to St. Omer with Campion. 'He was dressed up like a soldier, such a peacock, such a swaggerer', wrote Campion, and in the disguise of a captain returning from Flanders, Parsons arrived at Dover on 16 June alone (Campion was to follow). He moved to Gravesend and thence by boat to London, where he failed to find any lodgings; therefore he went to the Marshalsea, where he knew there were many Catholics. One of them found him a home, and he summoned a synod of Catholic priests in London to meet him at Southwark, where they discussed many points of importance to the Jesuit mission.

On 18 July Parsons and Campion (who had arrived safely) met

by night to say goodbye to each other. They were joined by Thomas Pound, at whose suggestion Campion wrote his *Decem Rationes* and Parsons wrote his *Confessio Fidei*. He then began his tour of Northampton, Derby, Worcester, Gloucester, preaching and administering the sacraments from house to house. In October he was back in London, but he found that the hue and cry after the Catholics was at its height, so that he never dared stop more than two days in any one place. At last he set up a home in Bridewell, which acted as a secret centre for Catholic priests. The persecution increased, for the government was faced with a Catholic rebellion in Ireland, backed by Spanish troops, Spain was now in possession of Portugal, there was a threat from Scotland and Catholicism was on the increase in England.

At this point (1580) Stephen Brinkley set up a secret printing press near Barking, and in spite of great difficulties and dangers he succeeded in printing Parsons' *A Brief Discourse containing certain Reasons Why Catholics refuse to go to Church*. The press was removed to Stonor, near Henley (1581), where Brinkley printed Campion's *Decem Rationes*, but this led to a search at Stonor and to the capture of Campion. Parsons was at the time in Windsor Forest and he thought it safer to retire to Sussex for a short while, after which he left England and arrived on 30 August at Rouen. Here he spent the winter, his chief activity being the founding of a school at Eu, near Dieppe, for English boys. This was the first of such schools: later it moved to St. Omer, and later still it became the College of Stonyhurst in England. But Parsons was immensely busy in other directions. He was writing incessantly; he was the first man to see the necessity for saving Catholicism in Scotland, if it was to survive in England, and therefore he was negotiating with Lennox to send a Jesuit to Scotland. Meantime the Papacy and Spain were negotiating for the Enterprise — the invasion of England — without much success. Parsons determined to take a hand in the work.

From June 1582 Parsons was in Spain until April 1583, but his efforts to persuade Philip II to take active measures failed. He fell dangerously ill in Madrid and all but died. In May he was in Paris and then he met Allen at Rheims. He then travelled to Rome for three or four weeks, during which visit he extracted from Pope Gregory XIII two briefs, one to re-excommunicate Elizabeth, and one to make Allen Bishop of Durham, but these were neither published nor put into operation. In October he was in Paris, then he went into Flanders to advise the Duke of Parma about the number of English Catholics in that country and there he spent the winter. Most of 1584 was taken up in Paris with organizing the coming and going of English Catholics, sending off books, vestments, chalices, in close co-operation with Allen. It is said that at one point he was in great danger of being murdered at the instigation of the Earl of Leicester. This was because Parsons had taken the major part in publishing a libellous pamphlet called *Leicester's Commonwealth*, which was full of scurrilous abuse directed against the royal favourite and his influence over the Queen. For some months of 1585 Parsons was at St. Omer, but in September he and Allen went to Rome. The Pope was now Sixtus V, and Parsons wanted to do his third year of probation before taking his final vows as a Jesuit. Allen went to discuss the financial difficulties of the seminary at Rheims; but there is no doubt that both went in order to persuade the new Pope of the importance of the Enterprise.

For the next three years Parsons was living in Rome, first at the English College and then as Latin Secretary to the General of the Society. He took his last vows in May 1587 and he became Rector of the English College in 1588. During these years he directed the Jesuit mission to England and it was he who sent Father Garnet to England. He poured out a good deal of advice to Philip II on the invasion of England, but in fact he had little influence in getting the Armada despatched. It was certainly through his activity that Allen was made a Cardinal. Less than a month after the news reached him of the destruction of the Spanish Armada Parsons left Rome and went to Spain, where he passed the next eight or nine years in founding and managing English seminaries there. He also spent much time in inciting Philip II to renew his attacks upon England, but he also warned him that no attack would be successful unless it was supported by a strong party of Catholics inside the island. He was perfectly well aware that some of the Spanish policy had only alienated English Catholics, but there are grounds for thinking that it was Parsons' intrigues abroad which greatly contributed to English Catholics' lukewarmness towards Papal and Spanish policy. In 1594 he published his *Conference about the next Succession*, a masterly work of political philosophy in which Parsons set out the case against the theory of the divine right of kings and also argued that on Elizabeth's death, the rightful heir to the throne was Philip II's daughter, the Infanta Clara Eugenia.

After Parsons returned to Rome as Rector of the English College there in 1596 he faced a number of 'domestical difficulties', divisions within the English Catholic movement. His appointment of Blackwell as Archpriest or Superior of the mission in 1598 led to a long and bitter dispute with those among the secular clergy who resented Parsons' influence. They sent two delegates to Rome to dispute the appointment: Parsons dealt with them high-handedly and shut them up in the English College. A further delegation was sent and the matter was not finally resolved until the reign of James I. Parsons died in Rome on 15 April 1610 and lies buried beside Cardinal Allen in the church of the English College.

Parsons played perhaps the most active part of anyone in the tragic history of Catholicism in England in the reign of Elizabeth. He was committed to the restoration of what he regarded as the true faith to his mother-land. He sought to achieve this by devoting his energies and talents wholeheartedly to this end. He was one of the greatest political and religious writers of his age, he was a gifted diplomat and an educator and administrator of genius. In the end, his efforts were unsuccessful, and so for four centuries most English historians have dismissed him as a traitor.

Leo Hicks, *Letters and Memorials of Father Robert Parsons, S.J.*, Catholic Record Society, 1942.

J.H. Pollen, *The Memoirs of Father Robert Parsons*, Catholic Record Society, 1907.

P.J. Holmes, *Historical Journal*, 1980.

P.J. Holmes, *Recusant History*, 1979, 1981, 1985.

P.J. Holmes, *Elizabethan Casuistry*, Catholic Record Society, 1981.

RICHARD TOPCLIFFE (1532–1604), persecutor and torturer of Roman Catholics, came of a good county family, being the eldest son of Robert Topcliffe of Sowerby, in Lincolnshire, and his wife Margaret, daughter of Thomas, Lord Burgh, of Gainsborough. He entered Parliament in 1572 as Member for Beverley: in 1586 he was returned by Old Sarum, a constituency which he represented until shortly before his death in 1604.

He was taken into the service of Burghley in about 1573, and there is extant a letter from Topcliffe, in his execrable, even for those days, handwriting and spelling, in which he describes with relish the harsh treatment meted out to the Papists of Norwich.

From about 1586 and for the next twenty-five years Topcliffe became for his own contemporaries, Protestant or Catholic, what he has remained ever since, one of the most odious and detestable government officials in British history. 'Because the often exercise of the rack in the Tower was so odious and so much spoken of by the people, Topcliffe had authority to torment priests in his own house in such sort as he shall think good.' Topcliffe himself boasted that 'he had in his own home a machine, of his own invention, compared with which the ordinary rack was mere child's play' (D.N.B.). So loud were the complaints of both Protestant and Catholic that Burghley at one moment had Topcliffe arrested on the grounds that he had exceeded his instructions: but his imprisonment was short lived.

The most notorious cases in which Topcliffe played the part of the villain were those of Robert Southwell, the Bellamy family, Henry Walpole and Thomas Fitzherbert. The last proved such a scandal that Topcliffe found himself for a while in gaol, whence he wrote 'on Good or Evil Friday 1595' two letters to the Queen — 'two more detestable compositions it would be difficult to find.' (Dr. A. Jessop, *One Generation of a Norfolk House*.)

When Topcliffe tired of work and wanted to retire in peace, he obtained from the Queen a grant of the Fitzherbert estates at Padley Manor in Derbyshire. Here he lived from 1603 until his death in 1604.

The Revd. Sir John O'Connell, 'Richard Topcliffe', *Dublin Review*, 1934.
C. Devlin, 'Richard Topcliffe', *The Month*, 1951.

CUTHBERT MAYNE (1544–1577), the first seminary priest to be executed in England, was born in the parish of Sherwell, near Barnstaple, in 1544. He was sent to Oxford by his uncle, who had conformed to the Anglican Church; he was at St. John's College, which was at that time much affected by the Catholic revival — Edmund Campion was at that college — and Mayne became a Catholic. He took his B.A. in 1566 and his M.A. in 1570, but when

the Bishop of London, on evidence contained in some letters from
Mayne's friends overseas, sent to arrest him, Mayne left Oxford and
went abroad to the English seminary college at Douai. He spent
three years there (1573 to 1576), was ordained priest in 1575, took
his B.D. in 1576 and in April of that year he returned to England
secretly on missionary work.

Arriving safely in England, Mayne went to his own west country
and became chaplain to the Catholic Francis Tregian in his house,
Golden, in Cornwall. For a year he lived there in safety, in the guise
of Tregian's steward, and during this time he travelled about from
house to house, administering the sacraments, comforting Catholic
families and reclaiming the relapsed. Inevitably news of his presence
in Cornwall leaked out. The Sheriff was Sir Richard Grenville. After
consultation with the Bishop of Truro Grenville set off with an
armed force for Golden: he knew the house well and had not any
difficulty in arresting Mayne. He found him wearing an *Agnus Dei*
(a wax imprint of a lamb). Mayne's papers were confiscated and
among them was found a Papal Bull of Indulgence dated 1575, the
Jubilee Year, 'divers other relics used in popery ... with a special
treatise against the Book of Common Prayer'.

Mayne's trial followed the usual course and he was condemned
for treason for possessing the Bull. There was a difference of opinion
among his judges, because it was claimed that the Bull expired in
1575, but the verdict went against Mayne. He was executed on
30 November 1577, with all the horrible customs of those days.

Mayne was the first of the Catholic martyrs, neither the most
distinguished nor the most important, but he was among the
simplest and the most forthright. What Burghley and Walsingham
needed to know was how Catholics would behave, if England were
to be invaded by a Catholic power. Mayne did not hesitate: at his
final examination he said, 'If any Catholic prince took in hand to
invade any Realm to reform the same to the authority of the see of
Rome, that then the Catholics in that Realm invaded by foreigners
should be ready to assist and help them.' Mayne was a brave man
who died for his religion: he also provided the justification for the
acts of a government responsible for the safety of the realm and of its
religion as established by law.

A.L.Rowse, *Tudor Cornwall*, pp. 347, 1941.

A. L. Rowse, *Sir Richard Grenville*, pp. 134, 1937.

JOHN PENRY (1563–1593), martyr and founder of Welsh Nonconformity, came of a well-to-do family and in 1580 he went up to Peterhouse, Cambridge. In 1586 he transferred to Oxford, probably to join in a Puritan movement which was beginning there. He took to preaching, and finding that his native Wales was exceptionally backward and ignorant, he decided to approach the Government. From this moment he developed into a pamphleteer with a most forthright and rash style. He attacked those whom he believed to be the cause of the evils with violence and a total disregard for the possible consequences, including even the Queen herself in his diatribes. Between 1587 and 1590 he printed in the secret press of Robert Waldegrave a series of pamphlets which, among other things, attacked especially severely the bishops. In 1588 there came from his press, and the proofs of it were certainly corrected by Penry, the first of the Mar-Prelate tracts, known as *The Epistle*. In the next twelve months several more appeared. Penry was helped by John Udall and Job Throckmorton. Nobody to this day has discovered for certain who Martin Mar-Prelate really was. Penry suffered persecution more than once, and he was ultimately arrested and condemned to death for treason, not for the Mar-Prelate tracts. He himself denied that he was Mar-Prelate, and the evidence against him was to a large extent extracted from witnesses who had been put on the rack. The article in the *D.N.B.*, written between 1895 and 1896, accepts Penry as the author: this account should be compared with *The Notebook of John Penry 1593*, published by the Camden Society in 1944, where credence is given to Professor Dover Wilson's theory that the real author was Sir Roger Williams, although this view is not now popular. Penry was an unwise, but a highly courageous, controversialist, who was ready to die for his opinions. He was tried for treason on 21 May 1593, and was condemned to death. On 29 May, while he was having his dinner, he was suddenly told that he was to die that day. At five o'clock in the afternoon he was hanged.

The Notebook of John Penry 1593, edited by A. Peel for the Camden Society, 1944.
Dover Wilson, in *The Library*, October, 1907.

ROBERT SOUTHWELL (1561–1595), Jesuit martyr and poet, was born towards the end of 1561. He was the third son of Richard Southwell of Horsham St. Faith, near Norwich. His father was the illegitimate son of that Sir Richard Southwell who took a leading part in the destruction of the monasteries and whose unscrupulous and hard-bitten character is clearly revealed in the drawing by Holbein at Windsor Castle. The Southwells were cousins of the Cecils and the Bacons.

Robert's life began excitingly with his being kidnapped when he was an infant by a gypsy woman who was captivated by the baby's beauty in his cradle. The child was soon recovered and lived an uneventful life, the youngest in a family of three boys and five girls. In 1576 at the age of sixteen he left England with his cousin John Cotton and went to live at the English College at Douai, with the object of attending the Jesuit school nearby. Robert was at once attracted by the Jesuit order and applied for admission, which was refused him. He then moved to Rome and on 17 October 1578 he was accepted as a candidate for the order of the Jesuits. His two years as a novice were spent chiefly at Tournai; he became a full-fledged Jesuit in 1580, returned to Rome, took holy orders and became Prefect of Studies at the English College in Rome. From this moment his heart was set on one thing — to be sent on the English mission to minister to the persecuted Catholics in England. This was certain to end in martyrdom, for the penal laws against Jesuits were appallingly severe. On 8 May 1586 Southwell set out for England with Henry Garnett. They landed on the east coast in July, but Walsingham was well aware that they had arrived and from that moment Southwell was closely watched. Under the assumed name of Cotton he lived for the most part in hiding in London, but he moved about secretly into Sussex and the north country, comforting the persecuted, celebrating the Mass and making new converts to the Catholic religion, besides strengthening the weak and the relapsed. He soon won the reputation of being 'the chief dealer in the affairs of England for the papists'.

In 1589 he became chaplain to the Countess of Arundel, with whom he had rooms in her house at the Strand. Much of his time was spent in writing treatises to encourage his fellow Catholics or protests against the policy of the government, which he managed to have printed and distributed, of course anonymously, but Cecil and Walsingham were highly suspicious. Robert continued this dangerous and courageous life up to 1592, but on 20 June of that year he was arrested at the house of a Catholic friend, Richard Bellamy, who lived at Uxenden Hall, near Harrow-on-the-Hill. The Bellamy family were staunch Catholics and had been put under arrest as recusants. Southwell used to celebrate Mass there and instruct the sons and daughters. One daughter, Anne, was the first to be made prisoner and she was examined by Topcliffe. She gave away the means by which the Catholic priests were hidden in the house. Topcliffe made all arrangements to catch the next priest who arrived: that proved to be Southwell and he was easily taken. Topcliffe wrote to the Queen, 'I never did take so weighty a man, if he be rightly used.' He was imprisoned first in Topcliffe's house in Westminster, where he was brutally tortured. He was then moved to the Gatehouse where he lived in such filth and misery that his father begged the Queen either to release him or let him be imprisoned in better quarters. The Queen ordered him to be sent to the Tower, where he was allowed books and clothes and some friends to visit him. But he was thirteen times examined by members of the Council and he was tortured ten times, not by the rack, but by new forms 'each one worse than death'.

In February 1595 he was put on trial for treason, condemned to death, and on the 21st he was drawn to Tyburn, where he was hanged. He was saved from the final agonies of quartering by Lord Mountjoy, who refused to allow the hangman to cut the rope before Southwell was dead.

Robert Southwell was a man of singular beauty both of face and of mind. Strong in his religious faith, free of all rancour, with his eyes set always on the heavenly crown which he felt assured would be his, gentle yet firm, a poet, yet also a man of action, endowed with almost superhuman courage, he remains for posterity probably the most beautiful of the Catholic martyrs — only Campion can rank with him. He was a great Elizabethan poet and an excellent writer of prose.

Christopher Devlin, *The Life of Robert Southwell*, 1956.
Pierre Janelle, *Robert Southwell the Writer*, 1936.
Dom Hilary Steuert, *Downside Review*, LIV, 1936.
H. Morris, *Elizabethan Literature*, pp. 78-9, 1958.

R. Southwell, *An Humble Supplication to Her Majesty*, ed. R.C.
Bold, 1953.

EDMUND CAMPION (1540–1581), Jesuit and martyr, was
born in January 1540. He was the son of a London bookseller and he
was educated first at a London grammar school with help from the
Grocers' Company, then at Christ's Hospital, and finally at the
newly founded college of St. John's at Oxford. As a boy he had a
precociously developed gift for disputation and oratory, so that he
was selected to make a speech to Queen Mary on her entry into
London in 1553.

At Oxford Campion became a junior fellow of his college in 1557
and took his M.A. in 1564. When Elizabeth I visited the University
in 1566, Campion delivered such a successful oration to her that she
commended him to Leicester, who for many years was a generous
patron to him. In 1568 Campion was ordained deacon in the
Anglican church, but he was at heart a Romanist. Uneasy in mind, at
the invitation of James Stanihurst (father of one of Campion's most
brilliant pupils) he accepted an invitation to go and live in Ireland,
where Stanihurst was planning to revive the old Romanist college in
Dublin. The English government, however, suspected Campion of
being a Catholic, and therefore he fled in disguise to England in 1571
and thence overseas to Douai. There he was reconciled to the
Catholic church, took his B.D., and in 1572 set off on foot for Rome
to join the Society of Jesus. He spent his novitiate at Brunn and then
worked at Prague. In 1580 he was ordered by Allen, head of the
English Catholics in Rome, to accompany Robert Parsons on the
first Jesuit mission to minister to the English Catholics. Campion
knew full well that this was his death warrant.

Campion reached Dover on 24 June 1580, Parsons having gone
on ahead. The authorities were on the alert, but Campion escaped
arrest and was taken by a Catholic, Thomas Jay, to a house in
Chancery Lane, where he waited ten days for Parsons. London was
too dangerous a place for the two Jesuits to stay for any length of
time and they agreed to separate. A Catholic of the name of Pound
suggested that Campion should write an account of the reasons why
they had come to England, which could be published if they were
arrested. Campion wrote a letter to the Privy Council explaining

that he and Parsons had come to England solely to preach and to minister to the Catholics, and that they were forbidden to have anything to do with politics. Pound was to keep this letter secret until an arrest took place; but Pound could not keep his tongue quiet: news of the letter spread, copies were circulated, and one reached the Bishop of Winchester, who passed it on to the government. As a result, the anti-Catholic laws were more rigorously enforced and a search was begun for Campion.

Campion now travelled from one Catholic house to another, largely in Lancashire. He preached to the families, heard confession, gave advice and encouragement, celebrated Mass and gave the Communion. In 1581 he wrote and Parsons arranged for the secret printing of a pamphlet setting out ten reasons (hence its name, *Decem Rationes*) why the Roman Church and not the Anglican, was the true Church. On 27 June everyone who went to the service in St. Mary's, Oxford, found a copy of the pamphlet in his place.

Campion's chances of escape were now nil. On 17 July he was taken at the house of a Mr. Yate at Lyford in Berkshire, through the treachery of a scoundrel named Eliot, who was suspected of murder and was trying to save his skin by betraying the secrets of the Catholics. Eliot arrived at Lyford on Sunday, 16 July. He met the cook, a friend of his, who took him upstairs where Campion was celebrating Mass. Eliot sat through the service, then sent to the local magistrate to come and arrest Campion. A first search failed to find him, but the next day a second search revealed him and two other priests hidden in a secret chamber above the gatehouse.

Campion was taken to London and put in the Tower. He was then examined in front of the Queen, who offered him a pardon and advancement, if he would attend Anglican services. Campion refused. The government then set out to find some political charge against Campion and invented a plot which, they said, had been hatched at Rheims to murder the Queen. Campion denied all knowledge of it. He was racked three times, and at the last time he seems, on his own admission, to have given away the names of some of the houses where he had stayed. His trial was a mockery of justice. The rack had so broken him that he could not raise his right hand to plead 'not guilty' (14 November 1581). On 1 December he was dragged on a hurdle through the rain and slush to Tyburn, where he was hanged before an enormous crowd. With unwonted humanity, the executioners waited until he was dead before carrying out the rest of the sentence.

Campion was the noblest of all the Catholic martyrs. A scholar, a gentleman, a priest, a man of genuine holiness, he was also a lovable, courageous and honourable Englishman. He had none of that passionate longing for martyrdom which sustained Robert Southwell in similar circumstances. Campion's was a simpler and perhaps a nobler attitude. He saw quite clearly that if the Catholic faith was to survive in England, then English priests must be sent from abroad to save it. He saw as clearly that he must be one of those priests. He never doubted what his fate would be, but he seems hardly to have bothered about that. Nor was he ever anxious to blame the government: he was concerned only with showing that it was for religion and for nothing else that he was being put to death. In the light of his pure religious faith, the natural and necessary political anxieties of his opponents appear almost mean and shabby.

R. Simpson, *Edmund Campion*, 1866.
C. Hollis, 'Edmund Campion, S.J.', *The Great Tudors.*
E. Waugh, *Edmund Campion*, 1947.

FATHER JOHN GERARD (1564–1637), Jesuit, was born on 4 October 1564 and died in Rome at the English College on 27 July 1637. He was the second son of Sir Thomas Gerard of Bryn in Lancashire and of his wife, Elizabeth Port, of Etwall in Derbyshire. He was educated first at Oxford, where he matriculated in 1575, and then in the English College at Douai (1577) and at Rheims (1578). It is possible that he did not go to Oxford till 1579, to Exeter College, whence he left for the Jesuit college of Clermont in Paris (1580–1). In the latter year he met Father Parsons at Rouen, but he was in England again in 1582. In 1583 he tried to leave England without a licence; he was arrested and put into the Marshalsea (5 March), where he remained until he was released at Easter 1584. At the end of May 1586 he left England and on 5 August he arrived at the English College in Rome. He was ordained priest in 1588, entered the Society of Jesus and was at once sent back to England on missionary work.

Gerard was extremely active in ministering to the Catholics,

bringing back to the Roman Church relapsed Catholics, and converting Protestants to Catholicism. The government made every
effort to capture him, but it was not until 1594 that he was arrested.
He was then shut up in the Counter, the Clink and the Tower. In the
Tower he was 'put to the manacles', that is, he was left suspended in
mid-air by his hands with his arms fastened above his head. This
excruciating torture he bore with the greatest courage and stead-
fastly refused to answer the questions put to him.

On 4 October 1597 he made a dramatic escape by swinging
himself along a rope over the ditch of the Tower. This would have
been a remarkable feat for a young athlete in the best of training, but
for a man on his thirty-third birthday who was all but crippled in his
hands as a result of torture, the whole episode (the planning and
contemplation of it must have been nerve-racking) can be called
almost superhuman.

From 1597 to 1606 Gerard continued his missionary work,
moving from house to house, usually living in secret, sometimes
renting a house of his own. Nothing more clearly illustrates the
limitations of police work in the sixteenth century than the failure of
the government to recapture Gerard, in spite of its great efforts.
When the Gunpowder Plot was discovered, Gerard was assumed to
be implicated, although the probability is that he knew nothing
about it. The hue and cry after him was intensified, so that at last he
made up his mind to leave the country. On 3 May 1606 he crossed to
Belgium in company with the Ambassadors of Spain and the Low
Countries. He spent six weeks at St. Omer and then went to Tivoli
for a rest. In 1607 he was appointed English Penitentiary at St.
Peter's: in 1609 he was sent to Flanders to help found the first
novitiate of the English Province at Louvain. In 1614 he became the
first Rector of the new Jesuit college of philosophy and theology at
Liège. In 1622 he went to Rome to obtain Papal support for the new
Institute of Religious Women founded by Mary Ward. On returning
to the Low Countries he was made Rector of the house of the English
Jesuits at Ghent (1622–7). For the last ten years of his life (1627–37)
he was confessor to the English College at Rome, where he died on
27 July 1637.

On 27 August 1601 an agent of Robert Cecil wrote a description
of Gerard: 'of stature tall, high shouldered, especially when his cope
is on his back, black haired, and of complexion swarth, hawk nosed,

high templed, and for the most part attired costly and defencibly in buff leather garnished with gold or silver lace, satin doublet, and velvet hose of all colours with clocks corresponding, and rapiers and daggers gilt or silvered'. Topcliffe, the notorious torturer, recorded in his own spelling, unorthodox even for his century, that Gerard was 'Kewryoos in spetche If he do now contynewe his custome And in his spetche he flourrethe & smyles much and a falteringe or Lispinge, or doublinge of his Tonge in his speeche'.

Gerard's *Autobiography*, written originally in Latin, is a vivid and at times exciting account of the kind of life endured by a Catholic priest in the days of Elizabeth I. It reveals Gerard as a man of invincible courage, of untiring energy and unquestioning faith.

John Gerard, *The Autobiography of an Elizabethan*, translated by Philip Caraman, 1951.

THOMAS CARTWRIGHT (1535–1603), Puritan divine, was born at Royston in Hertfordshire or at Whaddon in Cambridgeshire, and he came of yeoman stock. In 1547 he matriculated as a sizar of Clare Hall, Cambridge. In 1550 he went as a scholar to St. John's College, which was closely identified with the new religious views of the Reformation. On the accession of Mary, Cartwright left the University and went to study law. When Elizabeth came to the throne, Cartwright returned to Cambridge as a Fellow of St. John's, then of Trinity; then he went back to St. John's as Lady Margaret Professor of Divinity (1569). Two years before, he had been elected a University Preacher: his sermons were so effective that 'the Sextone was faigne to take down the Windows' of St. Mary's, so great was the crowd that came to hear. But it was in his lectures delivered in 1570 on church government that Cartwright raised the issue which involved him in a long struggle with the Vice-Chancellor, Whitgift. Cartwright's view was that God had revealed His will in the Scriptures only. The Scriptures laid down a rule for church government. That rule was not episcopacy as set up by Elizabeth in the English Church, but Presbyterianism as conceived by Cartwright and his followers upon the model of the Calvinist Church at Geneva. Under Elizabeth's system the Church was ruled by bishops appointed by the Crown. Cartwright held that ministers must be chosen by the people.

Cartwright was now deprived of his professorship; he left Cambridge and went to Geneva, but at the urgent request of many friends he returned to Cambridge in 1572, only to find himself again in trouble with Whitgift. Cartwright went abroad again to Heidelberg, Antwerp and Middelburg. He fell ill in Holland and in 1585 he came back to England after Leicester and Burghley had pleaded for his return.

Cartwright was now appointed by the Earl of Leicester to be master of the hospital which he had founded in Warwick. He supported, and may have helped to compose, the *Book of Discipline* drawn up in the mid-1580s to justify the imposition on the Church of England of a system of church organization based on Calvin's Geneva. He attended various of the assemblies held in the late 1580s as part of a clandestine attempt to create a sort of Presbyterian system alongside the legally constituted hierarchy. In consequence, he was arrested in 1590, but there was no conclusive evidence to charge him on and his powerful friends protected him again. He went to the Channel Islands where he remained until 1598. His last years were spent in Warwick where he 'grew rich and had great maintenance to live upon and was honoured as a patriarch by many'. But in 1603 he was in London in connection with the Millennary Petition. He was to have taken part in the Hampton Court Conference, but he died on 27 December 1603.

Cartwright was 'unquestionably the most notable Puritan of his generation, and perhaps the most learned and cultured man the sect ever produced' (*Dictionary of English Church History*). Hooker's *Ecclesiastical Polity* was directed against him by name, as also were some of Archbishop Whitgift's writings.

A.F.S.Pearson, *Thomas Cartwright and Elizabethan Puritanism*, 1925.

W.Haller, *The Rise of Puritanism*, 1938, 1957.

V.J.K.Brook, *Whitgift and the English Church*, 1957.

Knappen, *Tudor Puritanism*, Chicago, 1939.

C.Morris, *Political Thought in England: Tyndale to Hooker*, pp.161-4, 1953.

P.Collinson, *The Elizabethan puritan movement*, 1967.

P.Lake, *Moderate puritans and the Elizabethan Church*, 1982.

HENRY BARROW or BARROWE (*c.*1550–1593), Separatist, was the third son of Thomas Barrow and his wife, Mary Bures of Shipdam in Norfolk. He was related to Francis Bacon and distantly connected with Lord Burghley. Bacon records that Henry Barrow was a 'gentleman of a good house'. Nothing at all is known of his early life until 1566, when he was at Clare College, Cambridge. He took his B.A. degree in 1569 or 1570. At the University he was, according to Bacon, a 'vain and libertine youth', an accusation which Barrow himself admitted. In 1576 he became a member of Gray's Inn, but he was never called to the Bar. In 1580 or 1581, 'walking in London one Lord's Day with one of his companions, he heard a preacher very loud as they passed by the church. Upon which Mr. Barrow said unto his consort, "Let us go in and hear what this man saith that is thus earnest". "Tush," saith the other, "What! shall we go to hear a man talk?"' But they went in, and Barrow was so much impressed by what he heard that he wholly changed the course of his life. Giving up the law, he turned to the study of the Bible and devoted himself thereafter to religion.

He soon came under the influence of John Greenwood, who had been ordained, but who had come to deny the scriptural authority of the English church and of episcopal government. Through Greenwood Barrow read the writings of Robert Browne, but he never met the founder of the Brownists. Barrow was now a Puritan, but by 1589 he had become a 'congregationalist', one who regarded each congregation as a Church in itself. Barrow has come to be known as one of the founders of the Separatists and thus of modern Nonconformity. To Barrow separatism meant that sinners must be separated from the saints and the Church must consist only of the saints; that the Church must be separated from the State; that each congregation must be to some degree separated from central control. Barrow held that a man's conscience was the final court of appeal, but he believed firmly in non-resistance, and that rebellion would be 'most unlawful and damnable by the Word of God'.

On 7 October 1586 Greenwood was arrested by the orders of Aylmer, Bishop of London. He was put in the Clink, where on 19 November Barrow visited him. Aylmer was on the lookout for him and Barrow found himself arrested. Between 19 November 1586 and March 1589, Barrow was examined five times, and at the most important examination, when Burghley was present, Barrow alienated Burghley's sympathy by his intemperate language. Finally on 11 March 1593 both Greenwood and Barrow were charged with circulating seditious books; they were convicted on the 23rd and were to be executed the next day. The execution was stayed only when the two victims were 'ready to be bound to the cart'; on the 31st they went to the place of execution and were actually tied by their necks to the tree when a reprieve arrived. But the stay was only temporary, and both men were hanged on 6 April 1593. While Barrow was in prison he wrote many pamphlets and treatises, but there is no evidence that he was the author of the Mar-Prelate tracts.

F. J. Powicke, *Henry Barrow and the Exiled Church of Amsterdam*, 1900.

C. Morris, *Political Thought in England, Tyndale to Hooker*, 1953.

ROBERT BROWNE (*c.*1550–1633), founder of the Brownists or Puritan Separatists, from whom are sprung the modern Congregational Nonconformists, was born in about 1550 at Tolethorpe Hall, near Stamford, in Rutland. He was the third son of Anthony Browne and his wife, Dorothy Boteler, and he was remotely connected with Lord Burghley, who protected him more than once on the grounds of kinship. Browne went up to Corpus Christi College, Cambridge, in 1570 and took his B.A. in 1572.

His period at Cambridge coincided with the time when Cartwright was advocating a Presbyterian system for the Church and Browne came much under his influence. On leaving Cambridge Browne turned to teaching (1572–5) in Northamptonshire, but he came to be depressed by the 'woful and lamentable state of the Church', gave up teaching and after a short time spent at his home, he returned to Cambridge and took to preaching, probably in 1579.

Browne was now a Congregationalist — he held that Christ was the only true Head of the Church, and next under Christ came, not the Crown or the Bishops, but the Church collectively. For a time he compromised over the power of the Bishops, perhaps because his views were not fully settled. He grew more and more difficult and at last he went to Norwich, where he thought people were more 'forward'. Here he set up independent congregations (or conventicles), with the result that he was arrested and was for a short time in prison (1581). He was freed at the request of Burghley and returned to Norwich, where he organized the first Congregational Church and took it overseas to Middelburg in Zeeland (1581). The next two years were years of misery for all concerned. Browne was intolerant and difficult, but so also was his one-time friend, Harrison, who roused the Congregation against its founder. Browne left Holland in 1583 for Scotland, but he found a very cool reception there, came back to England and submitted to the Anglican Church (1585). The next year he became Master of St. Olave's school, Southwark, but he behaved outrageously, ministering to Separatist congregations and yet also attending orthodox services.

In 1591 Browne was ordained deacon and priest in the Anglican Church and Burghley presented him with the living of Achurch-cum-Thorpe Waterville in Northamptonshire. In 1610 his wife died, but two years later he married again. The marriage was an unhappy one, and Browne was sued for restoration of conjugal rights in 1623. He now let the parsonage fall into decay and he separated from his wife altogether. Between 1617 and 1627 he was suspended from clerical office, but suddenly one day he returned to full ministration. This led to many quarrels with his churchwardens and with the parishioners. In 1630 he assaulted a constable who was his godson and he went to gaol for a short time. After his release he lived for two years in Northampton and he died in October 1633 and was buried in the churchyard of St. Giles's.

Browne was an unstable and not very courageous man, nor was he very clear-minded in his views. Cartwright had always held that in reforming the Church it was necessary to 'tarry for the Magistrate', and by a Magistrate he meant a Sovereign or a Lay Ruler. It was because Browne came to despair of the Magistrate's ever doing anything that he wrote his book, *Reformation without Tarrying for Any*, 1582. He then put his trust in the Christian Congregation, but experience made him despair just as much of the Congregation. Browne had two objectives in view. The first was to 'Separate': he began by wanting to separate the Church from the State and then each Congregation from the whole Church. His second object was to 'Reform' the Church. Here he began by wanting to get rid of all relics of Popery (vestments and ritual, etc.): then he went further and wanted to have only what he called a 'gathered Church'. This was really one aspect of Separatism, because Browne wanted to separate the sheep from the goats, the saints from the sinners, the inwardly converted from the the outwardly conforming. (C. Morris, *Political Thought in England*, p. 165.) To achieve all this Browne began to emphasize the duty and powers of the Magistrates, so that he appeared in his own day, as he still appears to us to-day, inconsistent and unreliable.

F. J. Powicke, *Robert Browne, Pioneer of Modern Congregationalism*, 1910.
C. Morris, *Political Thought in England, Tyndale to Hooker*, 1953.

THOMAS TALLIS (c. 1505-1585), composer, was born probably in Leicestershire, although neither the place nor the date of his birth is certain. He is first known to history as one of the musicians who were pensioned in 1540 when Waltham Abbey in Essex was dissolved. He was either a chorister or organist there. Between 1540 and 1542 he held a musical post at Canterbury and was then made one of the gentlemen of the Chapel Royal. Until his death he served the next three rulers of England, latterly as chief organist. Mary considered him her principal composer, and he was, until his death, the doyen of Elizabeth's Chapel Royal.

He received various rewards from grateful sovereigns, and bought property in Greenwich. He married a woman called Joan in 1552 — her maiden name is not known. In his later years he was associated with his much younger and subsequently more famous contemporary, William Byrd, who worked with him in the Chapel and also published with him in 1575 a collection of motets, *Cantiones quae ab arqumento sacrae vocantur*. Byrd and Tallis were jointly granted by the Queen in the same year the monopoly of printing music, which was surprisingly worth almost nothing because so little music was printed at that time.

As a composer, Tallis's first works were pieces of Latin church music, composed for Catholic ritual in the reigns of Henry VIII and Mary I. Five antiphons of his survive, and three masses, all in different styles. One of his masses was probably written to be performed before Philip II in St Paul's Cathedral at Christmas 1554, containing the Introit 'Puer natus est nobis', which was doubtless intended to be prophetic as well as seasonal.

Tallis's Latin church music did not cease with the accession of Elizabeth I, although he had to confine himself to composing shorter pieces. It was probably to celebrate Elizabeth I's fortieth birthday in 1573 (although conceivably for Mary I's in 1556) that Tallis composed what some consider his greatest work, the Motet 'Spem in alium', written for forty voices.

Tallis was adaptable and responded to the new demand for English church music which resulted from the English Reformation. He has been called 'the father of English cathedral music'. He used a great variety of styles, both simple and grand, in his settings of the English Service, while abiding by Cranmer's famous insistence on lucidity. He introduced polyphonic English psalms where before there had only been plainsong. The hymn tune 'Tallis', based on the ninth of his works written for Parker's Psalter of 1567 is still used, while Vaughan Williams' 'Fantasia on a Theme of Tallis' is also drawn from this collection. He composed many memorable English anthems.

Tallis also composed a certain number of keyboard works, with a religious theme but for recreational purposes. He wrote for organ and virginals. He himself was an organist while both Mary I and Elizabeth I were virginal players, the former better than the latter.

Tallis was one of the great composers of his century, although it is generally agreed that his achievement is overshadowed by that of his pupil, Byrd. He developed very considerably as a musician, responding to the challenges presented by the religious changes of his age, although his compositions still kept the restrained, undemonstrative, medieval air which is their great charm.

P. Doe, *Tallis*, 1976.

WILLIAM BYRD (1543–1623), composer, was born probably in Lincolnshire. Of his early life we know almost nothing, although it is likely that he studied under Tallis and hence probable that he was a boy chorister in the Chapel Royal. On 27 February 1563, at the age of twenty or thereabouts, he was made organist at Lincoln Cathedral. In 1568 he married Juliana Birley in London. Two years later he was sworn as a gentleman of the Chapel Royal in succession to the respected composer Robert Parsons, who had drowned in the River Trent. Byrd severed all links with Lincoln finally in 1572 and for the rest of his life was a full-time servant of the royal music in London.

In 1575 he and Tallis were granted a licence from the Queen

which gave them the monopoly to print music for twenty-one years. Under this licence they published in the same year a collection of their own pieces entitled *Cantiones Sacrae*.

Byrd prospered in royal service. He lived at first at Harlington in Middlesex and then in 1593 removed to Stondon Massey in Essex. Here he seems to have lived with a second wife, Ellen. He engaged in a number of law-suits, especially with the Shelley family over his claims to Stondon Place, a manor house.

Byrd was notable as a Catholic who suffered little real harm as a result of his nonconformity and who continued in the service of both Elizabeth I and James I despite his well-known religious views. Government records show Byrd, his wives and their servants involved in recusancy and other illegal activities connected with the practice of the Catholic Faith. The Jesuit, William Weston, describes a secret meeting in 1586 when he was introduced to Byrd, 'the most celebrated musician and organist of the English nation'. Among Byrd's patrons were a number of Catholic or crypto-Catholic noblemen: the Earl of Worcester, Lord Petre, Lord Northampton and Lord Lumley. As a valuable royal employee, as a brilliant musician, and as a generally peaceful, undemonstrative Catholic, Byrd was allowed, in practice, toleration by the Crown.

Byrd was the great composer of his age. His superlative skill is shown by the extraordinary range of his compositions. He took what was largely a medieval art form and left it recognisably modern. He excelled in all forms of music, both secular and sacred, for voice and for instruments.

Among his finest work is his Latin church music. He composed three masses, published secretly, as were all Catholic books of the period. His sacred songs, published as *Cantiones Sacrae* in 1575 (with Tallis), 1589 and 1591, were shorter pieces, motets for small choral groups. In 1603 and 1607 he printed the *Gradualia*, dedicated to Lord Northampton, songs addressed to the Virgin and the Saints and intended for Catholic use. His Latin church music adapted itself to the new Counter-Reformation requirements set out in the Council of Trent, which had condemned the use in Masses of popular secular songs. He in his turn influenced the Catholic tradition on the Continent.

By virtue of his official position, Byrd was required to compose church music in English. Thus, the greatest early composer for the

Anglican liturgy was a Roman Catholic. He composed a short and a great Service, and two other evening Services, works which according to an authoritative critic are 'unsurpassed'. He also wrote over sixty English religious anthems.

Madrigals were not Byrd's strongest suit, but his output was, as usual, considerable, both of secular and religious works. He has been described as the creator of a new form of music in the Art-song, written for solo voice with instrumental accompaniment, where he generally preferred the viol. He composed about fifty such songs, some of which were used on the stage. In writing canons and rounds he showed himself an ingenious contrapuntalist.

Byrd also wrote for instruments alone. Chamber music for strings was encouraged by technical developments in the manufacture of viols and later of violins. But it was in keyboard music that he excelled. In the years 1560 to 1620 about 600 pieces for the virginal were written in England, a quarter of them by Byrd. For the only time in her musical history England led the way here, with Byrd in the vanguard, beating a path for all subsequent keyboard writers to follow. He almost invented keyboard music.

Byrd was one of the greatest Englishmen of his age, respected at home and, as John Baldwin said as early as 1591, 'far to strange countries abroad his skill doth shine'.

E. Fellowes, *William Byrd*, 1948.

CHRISTOPHER MARLOWE (1564–93), playwright, was the son of a prosperous Canterbury shoemaker. He was educated at the King's School, Canterbury and at Corpus Christi College, Cambridge, where he stayed for seven years (1580-87) and graduated both B.A. and M.A. It is possible that at first he intended to follow a career in the church, but he probably took up writing before he left Cambridge.

At Cambridge he was not an unruly student and certainly profited from the classical elements in his education. But even before he went down from university, he seems to have been involved in one dangerous escapade, for it is likely (although not certain) that he was employed by the Privy Council to spy on the Catholic seminary at Rheims. His whole short life was to be peppered with dangerous and disreputable activities of this sort.

From Cambridge he went, as an aspiring writer, to London. It seems likely that his classical translations date from this early period, when his university education was still fresh in his mind. He translated Ovid's 'Amores' as *All Ovid's Elegies*, a work which was burnt on the orders of the Archbishop of Canterbury because of its salacious content. Less controversial was his translation of Lucan's first book of *Pharsalia*, published in 1600 after Marlowe's death.

Marlowe made his name, however, not as a poet but as a playwright, and he did so very quickly on coming to London. His first play was *Dido, Queen of Carthage*, based on the Aeneid, perhaps commenced while he was still at Cambridge, and in part also the work of Thomas Nashe. His next work, almost certainly dating from 1587, was a great London stage hit, *Tamburlaine the Great*. At an early performance of this work, an actor accidentally killed a pregnant woman and her child in the audience when he fired a loaded 'calyver' at the Governor of Babylon tied to a stake and missed. This incident gives a good taste of what Marlowe's plays were like: full of energy and what we might call 'special effects'. So popular was *Tamburlaine* that Marlowe rushed out *Part Two*, where he stretched the factual, biographical basis of the play beyond breaking point. The problem was that he had told Tamburlaine's life-story fully in Part One and now had to rely on imagination.

In 1589 Marlowe wrote *The Famous Tragedy of the Rich Jew of Malta*, another very popular play which gave Shakespeare the idea for the *Merchant of Venice*. There then followed two history plays based on more recent events. First, in 1591 *The Massacre at Paris*, which dealt with the St. Bartholomew's Day Massacre in Paris; and next year, *The Troublesome Reign of Richard II*, based — like much of Shakespeare's work — on Holinshed's chronicles. Perhaps his greatest was *The Tragical History of Dr Faustus*, which is dated 1588-9 by some authorities or 1592 by others. The play was based on a recent German work and its tale of demoniacal magic has since exerted a powerful influence on a variety of European artists.

In addition to this prodigious output of plays and translations, Marlowe found time to compose a number of poems, most notably 'Come live with me and be my love', which has remained popular ever since, and an epic, *Hero and Leander*.

Marlowe led a troubled, violent life as a London playwright. In 1589 he was imprisoned briefly in Newgate Goal for his part in the death of an inn-keeper's son in a street brawl. In 1592 he was bound over to keep the peace in the sum of twenty pounds. In the same year he was deported from the Netherlands for attempting to pass forged gold coins. In 1593 he was in trouble with the Privy Council for being an atheist. It is likely that he and a number of other intellectuals in the circle of Sir Walter Ralegh were free-thinkers, and after Marlowe's death accusations of this sort were made by his former friends. Whether the author of *Dr. Faustus* also dabbled himself in the black arts is unclear. It seems highly probable that he was a homosexual.

Marlowe's death might have fitted well into one of his own plays. We only have his killer's side of the story, of course. According to this, Marlowe and two dubious associates, a slimy Catholic-baiter and spy called Robert Poley and one Ingram Frizer, spent 30 May 1593 at Eleanor Bull's tavern in Deptford Strand. After a convivial lunch, followed by a convivial supper, a quarrel developed over the bill. Marlowe was lying on a bed, with his two friends sitting on the bed's edge, their backs towards him. Marlowe drew a dagger from the back of Frizer's belt and cut his face slightly. In the struggle which followed, Frizer killed Marlowe. The coroner's jury returned a verdict of self-defence, and Frizer escaped unpunished.

Marlowe was under thirty when he died and some of his admirers have claimed that, had he lived, he would have written plays which might have matched those of Shakespeare. He was a pioneer: the first great English playwright for the Elizabethan stage, and Shakespeare benefited from his path-finding work. But,

> Marlowe was happy in his buskined Muse,
> Alas, unhappy in his life and end.

F. Boas, *Christopher Marlowe,* 1964.
A. L. Rowse, *Christopher Marlowe,* 1940.
M. Puirier, *Christopher Marlowe,* 1951.

EDMUND SPENSER (1552–99), poet, was born in London, the son of a merchant. He was educated at the Merchant Taylors' School under Richard Mulcaster. At the age of 17 he contributed a number of verse translations from Dutch, French and Latin, to an anti-Catholic work by Jan van der Noot entitled *A Theatre for*

Worldlings. He went up to Pembroke Hall, Cambridge, in 1569 and took his B.A. in 1573 and M.A. in 1576. He may have visited Ireland or Lancashire on going down, but certainly by 1578 was Secretary to Dr John Young, Bishop of Rochester, who was also Master of his Cambridge college.

In 1579 he obtained a place in the Earl of Leicester's household, where he became acquainted with Sir Philip Sidney. In that year he published his first major work, *The Shepherd's Calendar,* which he dedicated to Sidney. This was a poem of twelve eclogues, one for each month, and each written in a different metre. A number of shepherds conduct philosophical and aesthetic discussions in the poem, which idealizes the pastoral, rural life. One of the eclogues was dedicated to the praise of Eliza or Queen Elizabeth. This work was a success and established Spenser's reputation as the great poet of his age. At about this time he married Machabyas Chylde.

In 1580 Spenser went to Ireland as the Secretary to the Governor, Lord Grey de Wilton. For the next eighteen years, Spenser held a series of offices in Ireland. In 1582 he became Deputy to Ludowick Bryskett, clerk in Dublin to the Council of Munster. In Ireland, Spenser bought and was granted land, becoming one of the 'undertakers', or colonizers, of Munster. From his Irish experiences grew a work which he published in 1596, *A View of the Present State of Ireland.* In this book, written as a dialogue, he advocated taking drastic steps to solve the Irish Question, spending money and sending troops to make Ireland a true English colony. Within a short time of writing the book, Spenser's diagnosis was to be proved correct.

While working as an Irish civil servant, or colonial administrator, Spenser was writing poetry at a furious rate, returning every so often to London to see his compositions through the press. His greatest work was the *Faerie Queen,* published in two stages in 1589 and 1596. This is an epic poem of six books, although the original plan was for twelve. It is allegorical almost to a fault, each character representing an historical figure or an abstract concept, or both. The Faerie Queen herself is Elizabeth I or the personification of glory. A representation of the Anglican Church (Redcrosse Knight of Holiness) also features in the First Book, while in Book Five the defeat of the Spanish Armada and the execution of Mary, Queen of Scots are dealt with, along with the work of Lord Grey de Wilton in Ireland.

It is unlikely that this poem is much read these days, except for examination purposes, but in Elizabeth's reign it was widely popular. It earnt from the Queen a richly deserved pension of fifty pounds a year: Elizabeth was a ruler who recognised talent, and also flattery, when she saw it.

Spenser found time for other verse compositions. In 1591 he completed *Colin Clout's Come Home Again,* in which rural and urban life were contrasted. This great classical theme was one of Spenser's obsessions. In 1591 he published a number of shorter verses, including *Prosopopoia or Mother Hubbard's Tale,* which referred to Lord Burghley in unflattering terms. In 1595 he printed a number of love poems, *Amoretti and Epithalamion,* inspired by his second wife, Elizabeth Boyle, whom he married in about 1594, his first wife having died.

After seeing the second part of *The Faerie Queen* through the press, Spenser returned to Ireland, but was soon caught up there in the tragic events of the great rebellion of 1598. His castle at Kilcolman, County Cork, was destroyed and Spenser was forced to flee first to Cork and then, destitute, to London. Along with all his possessions, he had lost a number of newly composed poems when his castle was burned down by the rebels.

Within a few months he was dead, and buried at the expense of the Earl of Essex in Westminster Abbey. A later monument describes him as 'the prince of poets in his time', a claim which none would challenge. Dryden claimed that 'no man was ever born with so great a genius' and C. S. Lewis says that Pope imitated him as if he were an ancient. Within the classical tradition, says Lewis, he is as secure as Milton, but 'his world has ended and his fame may end with it'.

C. S. Lewis, *English Literature in the Sixteenth Century,* 1954
H. Shire, *A Preface to Spenser,* 1978.
A. C. Judson, *The Life of Edmund Spenser,* 1945.

JOHN CABOT, explorer, the dates of whose birth and death are unknown, was probably a Genoese by birth who became in 1476 a naturalized Venetian. He married a Venetian and had three sons, Ludovico, Sebastiano and Sancio. The names of all three appear in the letters patent issued by Henry VII in 1496, but Sebastiano is the only son of whom anything further is known. While in Venice,

Cabot had been a merchant engaged in the spice trade and had voyaged to the Levant and Black Sea. He also supposedly travelled to Mecca in disguise.

The facts of John Cabot's life have been greatly disputed and even now we have to rely on deductions and guess-work. Exactly when Cabot came to England is unclear, but it was probably in 1494 or 1495 that he arrived in Bristol. He had a scheme, which he managed to sell both to the Bristol merchants and to the King himself; it was to sail west and discover a new sea-route to Asia, and hence to the spice islands. This was, of course, what Columbus had attempted to do in 1492 when he arrived instead in the West Indies. Columbus's brother had come to England in 1488 or 1489 in an attempt to secure financial support from Henry VII, but had failed and eventually received the backing of Spain. Cabot seems to have conceived his idea independently of Columbus, although after the latter's voyage of discovery, the two explorers may have met. Cabot rightly considered that Columbus had been a failure and he felt that the reason was that he had aimed too far South. Having failed to interest the Portuguese in his schemes, Cabot came to Bristol. Here there was an entrepreneurial desire to make a killing and to wrest the spice trade from Southampton, but there was also some indigenous atlantic experience. It seems possible that before Cabot arrived in the port, Bristol sailors had reached the 'Isle of Brasil' (which may be Newfoundland).

Bristol merchants were willing to back Cabot, and when the King himself came to the city, he too gave the explorer his backing. On 5 March 1496 Henry VII issued letters patent giving Cabot and his heirs a monopoly of trade in the new lands and to the Bristol merchants the privilege of being the only port from which this trade could operate. It is probable (though not certain) that Cabot undertook his first voyage in 1496, following the granting of his letters patent. The voyage was unsuccessful. The following year, Cabot was more fortunate. On 20 May 1497 Cabot in the *Matthew* of Bristol set sail, the first English ship to cross the Atlantic. (Is it possible that the ship's real name was *Mattea*, for that was the name of Cabot's wife, and he may well have called the ship after her?) The ship was 50 tons and was manned with a crew of some 18 or 20 men. On 24 June he sighted land and made a landfall on the Island of St. John — he gave it this name because he found it on St. John the Baptist's Day. It is not possible to say for certain exactly where the landfall was, but it could have been anywhere from Maine to Labrador, most probably Newfoundland. He went ashore and formally took possession of the land, in the presence of perhaps a dozen men. He set up a cross, the banner of Henry VII, the banner of the Pope and of St. Mark, the patron saint of Venice. The little party did not advance more than a bowshot from the shore. They saw no inhabitants, but they found traces of them — a track, a burnt out fire, felled trees, snares for game, a carved stick like a netting-needle. Then, 'being in doubt, he returned to his ship'. This was the only landing he made, though he cruised along the coast for a time before turning for home. The passage home took fifteen days, with a fair wind and good weather. He made a landfall in Brittany and came home round Land's End — a course which was taken against his better judgement at the demand of others in the ship. He was back in Bristol by 6 August and he had an interview with Henry VII on the 10th. He became a well-known and popular figure: the King gave him a gratuity of £10 and a pension of £20; he came to be known as 'the great Admiral' and was followed in the streets by crowds of admirers; at Court he moved about splendidly dressed in silks and he gave lectures on the voyage and demonstrations of his instruments.

The third voyage of 1498 was to be a fully equipped expedition. Cabot's plan was to return to the place he had discovered, follow the coast down to the tropics and there carry on a lucrative trade with the mainland and with Cipango. The King provided one fully equipped ship, the Bristol and London merchants provided four other ships and the cargoes. These ships were provisioned for one year. It is said that the King promised a body of convicts to carry out the hard labour of planting a colony, but the evidence for this is far from convincing.

The fleet set sail from Bristol in early May 1498. Next to nothing is known about the voyage. One ship was damaged in a storm and had to put into an Irish port. It was probably Cabot's ship: if so, he must have sailed again after repairs. No direct news of Cabot and his other four ships has ever been heard from that day to this. It is most improbable that all five ships were lost; there are some reasons for thinking that some of the ships did in fact return. It may be deduced that Cabot did reach the coast of America and did follow it down into the tropics, perhaps entering the Caribbean. Whether he arrived home himself can not now be known: it is true that his pension was still being paid in 1499, but there is no proof that Cabot received it — probably it was paid to his wife.

Cabot was a remarkable man, for he had an original mind and considerable intellectual powers. He had read and understood Marco Polo and was thus able to refute the Spanish claim to have reached Asia. He had studied cartography and he knew how to make the best use of maps and globes. He could state a case clearly and persuasively, as is shown by the way in which he won Henry VII's approval for his schemes. He could win popular support and admiration. His reputation has suffered, because no trustworthy records have survived of all his doings.

J. A. Williamson, *The voyages of John and Sebastian Cabot*, Historical Association pamphlet, 1937.
J. A. Williamson, *The Cabot voyages and Bristol discovery under Henry VII*, Hakluyt Society, 1962.
D. B. Quinn, *England and the Discovery of America*, 1974.

SEBASTIAN CABOT (1484?–1557?), cosmographer and cartographer, was born almost for certain in or near Venice not later than 1484, the second son of John Cabot. He was brought to Bristol probably in the early 1490s by his father and he died almost for certain in 1557. There is great difficulty in ascertaining the true facts of his life, very largely because of his own character. We know nothing about his early life, except that the voyages and discoveries before 1500 which have been attributed to him are certainly those of his father, John Cabot. J. A. Williamson says of him that he was 'a vain egoist, fond of giving vent to mysterious utterances containing a maximum of self-praise and a minimum of hard fact'. We know now that Sebastian was not guilty of deliberately perverting the truth, but he was guilty of suppressing the truth, where his father's voyages were concerned. 'It can not be denied that he shewed a strange want of generosity on the point'. 'In other matters he undoubtedly lied freely and frequently.' There is no evidence that he accompanied John on his voyages. What is certain is that he went to Spain in 1512 and returned to England in 1548.

Sebastian was really not a sailor or a leader of men. When in

1505 Henry VII paid him a pension of £10 charged on the customs of Bristol, it was paid, not for any explorations, but for 'diligent service and attendance ... in and about our town and port of Bristol'. He must have known all about the voyages which the Bristol merchants sent out in 1501 and 1502, and it seems certain that he did himself lead an expedition in about 1508 or 1509, before Henry VII died, to discover the north-west passage. Sebastian had seized on the truth that 'the transatlantic land was a separate continent altogether distinct from Asia', and he had learned this from his father's voyage of 1498. When Sebastian sailed in 1508 or 1509, he took two ships with him, partly at the King's expense, and he went to Labrador (as we know it and not Greenland, so called because a *labrador*, a ploughman or landowner, from the Azores first told the King of England of the country). Between 61° and 64° he found a strait going west: he went through it for some 10° of longitude, then it seemed to turn south and to open out. Sebastian felt sure that he had turned the limit of the New Found Land and was now in the Pacific. The sea was thick with floating ice and his men mutinied, so that perforce he returned home. Modern discovery corroborates his story, and he may have found Hudson Strait. He may have gone as far north as 67° and as far south as 25°.

Sebastian was certainly in England in 1512, when he was paid 20s. for making a map of Gascony and Guienne for the Marquis of Dorset's invasion of France. He accompanied Dorset's expedition and then transferred his services to Spain. He lived at Seville from 1512 to 1515; then we lose track of him until 1518, when he was appointed Pilot Major to Charles V. Ferdinand of Spain died in 1516; therefore it is possible that Sebastian came back to England for 1516 and 1517.

There is a story that he went on a voyage with Thomas Spert, who was master of the *Harry Grâce á Dieu*, in 1516, but this is totally unsubstantiated. In 1521 Henry VIII planned an expedition to the west and proposed to put Sebastian in command of it. Sebastian did in fact pay a visit to England in that year, but the necessary subscriptions were not forthcoming and the voyage never took place.

For thirty-five years Sebastian was in the service of Spain; then suddenly he came back to England. He had tried to come back in 1538, but Henry VIII was not prepared to pay higher wages than those paid by the Emperor and no more was heard of the proposal.

With the accession of Edward VI the government on 9 October 1547 made out a warrant for £100 to bring Sebastian once again to England. He arrived in 1548. The next year Protector Somerset gave him a pension of £166 13s. 4d., payable quarterly. Charles V did his best to get Sebastian back to Spain, but the English government answered that Sebastian had no wish to go and as he was an English subject (he had almost certainly been born in Venice) he could not be compelled to go. Sebastian was always ready to claim to be an English or a Venetian subject as best suited his book at the moment. It has been said that he was appointed Grand Pilot of England, but the office and title did not then exist. It is said that he became governor of the Low Countries' Merchant Adventurers, which is wholly untrue, as it is also untrue that he was involved in the struggle with the Hansa. What is true is that he became the first governor of the newly formed Merchant Adventurers of England (1551), who sent out Willoughby's expedition of 1553. Sebastian drew up the ordinances for this and he was called 'the chiefest setter forth of this journey or voyage'.

The last picture we have of him is in 1556 when the Merchant Adventurers sent out their third voyage, which included a pinnace named the *Serchthrift* commanded by Stephen Borough:

> The 27th, being Monday, the right worshipful Sebastian Cabota came aboard our pinnace at Gravesend, accompanied with divers gentlemen and gentlewomen who ... went on shore ... and the good old gentleman Master Cabota gave to the poor most liberal alms, wishing them to pray for the good fortune and prosperous success of the *Serchthrift* our pinnace. And then at the sign of the Christopher, he and his friends banqueted and made me (Stephen Borough) and them that were in the company great cheer: and for very joy that he had to see the towardness of our intended discovery, he entered into the dance himself amongst the rest of the young and lusty company.'

There is no doubt that he died in 1557.

Sebastian Cabot was a 'man of good education and of a subtle and reflective mind', but he was a restless, vain creature, always thinking that his worth was not being properly appreciated. He was undoubtedly a considerable geographer, intensely interested in the shape of the world, and one of the leading authorities on the scientific side of navigation and the making of maps. He gave a most necessary and most valuable stimulus to English sailors when he returned to England in 1549. He himself made one of the finest maps of his time, his 'mappemonde', drawn on parchment and illuminated with gold and colours. The original has perished and of the drafts made from it only one now exists, in the Bibliotheque Nationale in Paris. The search for the north-west passage was originated by Sebastian Cabot. A portrait of him hangs in the ducal palace in Venice. The only relic which Bristol possesses is the Dun Cow, the rib of a whale, said to have been given to Bristol as a proof of the discovery of Newfoundland by Cabot, and preserved now in the chapel under the N. W. Tower of St. Mary Redcliff.

SIR HUGH WILLOUGHBY (d. 1554), navigator, was the son of Sir Henry Willoughby of Middleton, who was made a knight-banneret at the battle of Stoke in 1487 and died in 1528. The date of Hugh's birth is unknown. He first saw military service in Hertford's expedition to Scotland in 1544, when he was knighted at Leith on 11 May. From 1548-9 he was captain of Lowther Castle on the border. When Somerset fell from power, Willoughby lost a valuable patron: it may be either this or the suggestion of friends, among whom Sebastian Cabot would be one, which made him turn his thoughts to the sea.

By the middle of the sixteenth century the manufacture of woollen cloth in England had outstripped home consumption, and the Continental markets, especially after the crash of Antwerp in 1551, were also shrinking. There was great need to find new markets, and the Far East seemed to be the most promising area. No doubt an additional, but subsidiary, attraction was the certainty of a valuable return cargo of pepper and spices. (Foster, *England's Quest of Eastern Trade*, pp. 5-6). The difficulty was how to get there without infringing the Spanish and Portuguese monopolies. In 1553 was formed in London a company of 200 shareholders with a capital of 240 shares of £25 each to open up trade with Cathay by sailing along the North-Eastern shores of Europe by the so-called North-East Passage. The company was given a charter by Edward VI, and Sebastian Cabot became its first Governor.

The first expedition sent out by the company consisted of only three ships, of which the largest was the *Bona Esperanza*, 160 tons, commanded by Sir Hugh Willoughby as Captain-General, with Richard Chancellor in the *Edward Bonaventure* as Pilot-General. The third ship was the *Bona Confidentia*. The fleet set sail from Ratcliffe on 10 May 1553. In August, after passing the Lofoten Islands, Chancellor was separated from the other two ships by a storm and he therefore made straight for the rendezvous at Vardo. Willoughby and his ships never arrived there. For weeks they wandered about in ice and fog: they probably sighted the coast of Novaia Zemlia: in September they reached the bay of Arzina on the coast of Lapland. Here they spent the winter, but although they were provisioned for eighteen months, the arctic cold and possibly also scurvy caused them all to perish miserably (1554).

In the spring some Russian fishermen found the two ships and the frozen corpses, together with Willoughby's will and journal which prove that the party was alive in January 1554. The vessels were recovered and, manned with new crews, were brought home. The journal was printed by Hakluyt, and there is a manuscript copy of it in the Cottonian MSS (Otho E viii 10), but neither the original of it nor of the will can now be traced.

It was said that Willoughby's corpse was brought home for burial, but there is no proof of this at all. A tradition holds that his clothes were sent home and were used in painting the portrait preserved at Wollaton House as the only known authentic portrait of Willoughby: but this cannot be true, because the clothes belong to the seventeenth century. (C. R. Beard, *Connoisseur*, July 1931).

R. Hakluyt, *Principal Navigations*.
W. Foster, *England's Quest for Eastern Trade*, 1933.

RICHARD CHANCELLOR (*d.*1556), navigator; almost nothing is known of his early life and nothing of his family, except that he had two sons. We know that he was brought up in the household of Henry Sidney, father of Sir Philip, and that Henry Sidney had a very high opinion of him. What information we have about his later life comes from Hakluyt.

Chancellor is said to have sailed with 'Roger Bodenham with the great Barke Aucher' on a journey to Candia and Chio, but he first comes into prominence in 1553, when he was appointed Pilot-

General in the *Edward Bonaventure* in the 1553 expedition to Russia, led by Sir Hugh Willoughby. Chancellor was separated from Willoughby in a storm off the Lofoten Islands and therefore made for the rendezvous at Vardo. When, after a week of waiting, Willoughby had not turned up, Chancellor went on by himself and entered the White Sea (hitherto unknown to Western Europe) and anchored at the small port of Nenoksa, near the mouth of the river Dwina. He learned from the natives that he was in Russia, where-upon he journeyed to Moscow — a long and difficult journey overland — and there had an interview with the Tsar, Ivan IV, who received him with great kindness and welcomed the plan to establish trading relations between England and Russia. 'Your country merchants ... shall have their free mart with all free liberties through my whole dominions.' Elated with his success, Chancellor returned to his ship and sailed home (1554). He wrote an account of the Russian Court and of the habits of the Russian peoples which was printed by Hakluyt and is the first such account to be given to the English people. His achievement was considerable, for he had found an all-sea route to Russia, a most valuable market for English goods and for equally valuable goods from Russia — furs, hides, tallow, wax, flax and hemp. In addition, it looked as if Moscow might well prove a valuable half-way house to the Far East, for Moscow is, in fact, farther East than Aleppo. (Foster, *England's Quest of Eastern Trade.*)

The promoters of this first enterprise now followed up Chancellor's success by obtaining a new charter from Mary Tudor to form the Muscovy Company, by which the Company obtained a monopoly in the area and trade which it sought to develop. In 1555 Chancellor sailed again in the *Edward Bonaventure* with another vessel accompanying him. One notable feature of this expedition was that it carried several merchants who were to remain in Russia to act as factors and to organize a regular trade. The great business acumen of the Company is shewn by its instructions to these agents to find out the best routes from Russia to Cathay.

Chancellor reached Moscow in October 1555. He was received again with much consideration by the Tsar, he was able to establish good relations and to obtain valuable trading rights, including exemption from customs dues. That the interest in this new trade was as great on the Tsar's side as on the Company's was shewn by the

Tsar's sending home with Chancellor a special envoy, Ossip Grigorjevitsch Nepeja.

The return journey began in July 1556 and it proved a fearful disaster. Of the four ships which now formed the fleet, two were lost on the Norwegian coast: a third was forced to winter in Trondheim and did not reach England until 1557. The *Edward Bonaventure*, with Chancellor and Nepeja on board, after four months reached the Scottish coast, but the ship was wrecked in Pitsligo Bay, Aberdeenshire, in November. Chancellor and Nepeja tried to land in a ship's boat, but this was quickly swamped. Nepeja and a few others made the shore, but Chancellor was never seen again.

Besides being a seaman Chancellor was also a mathematician who could hold his own with John Dee. He could also make and improve the instruments for navigation. In 1553 he collaborated with Dee in compiling a new table of ephmeerides or planetary movements.

E. G. R. Taylor, *Tudor Geography*, 1930.

SIR HUMPHREY GILBERT (1539?-1583), soldier, navigator, explorer, is generally thought to have been born in 1539, but it is possible that his birth was earlier. He died at sea in 1583. He was the second son of Otho Gilbert of Greenway on the river Dart and of Katherine, daughter of Sir Philip Champernoun of Modbury in Kent. Otho died in 1547 and his widow married Walter Ralegh of Fardell and Hayes in Devonshire, by whom she had three children, one of them a boy named Walter; thus Humphrey Gilbert was the half-brother of Sir Walter Ralegh. The difference in age between them was probably thirteen years.

Humphrey was educated at Eton and Oxford: at the University he is said to have studied navigation and the art of war. His earlier education must have been thorough and along classical lines, for his writings display an intimate knowledge of Greek and Latin philosophers and poets, and it is probable that he could speak both French and Spanish. After Oxford, he was attached to the household of the Princess Elizabeth, and later, for a short time, he resided in one of the Inns of Chancery.

He first saw military service under Ambrose Dudley, Earl of Warwick, at the siege of Newhaven (i.e. Le Havre in Normandy) in 1562-3, during the religious civil wars in France: he was wounded

Sir Humphrey Gilbert
(Artist: Unknown entraver)

on 5 June 1563 — not on 26 September, as the *D.N.B.* states — by which date peace had been made.

In July 1566 he served in Ireland under Sir Henry Sidney in his campaign against Shane O'Neill. After four months, on 12 October he was sent back to England with despatches for the Queen.

Gilbert was in Ireland again in July 1569, for he wrote to Cecil for leave to return to England 'for the recovery of my eyes'. Before that leave was granted, Gilbert had made a name for himself by his so-called 'pacification' of Munster. To our modern way of thinking his treatment of Munster, of which province he was put in complete control, was revolting and uncivilized. Gilbert himself describes his ruthless methods of wholesale slaughter in a letter to Cecil without any apology for them. Sir Henry Sidney wrote, highly praising Gilbert's services, for which he had knighted him on 1 January 1570. The difference in standards between the sixteenth and the twentieth centuries may be judged by the following quotation: 'His manner was that the heads of all those (of what sort soever they were) which were killed in the day should be cut off from their bodies and brought to the place where he encamped at night, and should be laid on the ground by each side of the way leading into his own tent, so that none could come into his tent for any cause but commonly he must pass through a line of heads, which he used *ad terrorem*, the dead feeling nothing the more pains thereby; and yet did it bring greater terror to the people, when they saw the heads of their dead fathers, brothers, children, kinsfolk and friends, lie on the ground before their faces when they came to speak with the said Colonel.' (Thomas Churchyard, *General Rehearsal of Wars*, 1579.) Gilbert left behind him with the Irish a reputation second only to that of Oliver Cromwell.

If Gilbert had all the acquisitiveness of his times — that he had is proved by his petition in 1572 for the grant of all the south-east coast of Ireland — in his defence it may be said that out of his expenses in Ireland for nine months of £3,315 7s. he received repayment of only £600.

In 1570 Sir Humphrey married Anne Ager of Ottenden in Kent, a wealthy heiress, by whom he had five sons and one daughter. The next year (1571) he was returned as M.P. for Plymouth alongside Sir John Hawkins. It may be a proof of his loyalty to his Queen or of his independent and combative mind that he at once fell foul of the

House of Commons in general and of Peter Wentworth in particular, who called him 'a flatterer, a lyer and a naughtie man', for having defended the Queen's prerogative in the unpopular question of royal licences.

The year 1572 was an unfortunate one for Gilbert. He was sent to the Netherlands in command of 1,500 English volunteers to help the Zeelanders in their rebellion against Spain — probably Elizabeth's real purpose was to get possession of Flushing. The campaign was a failure, and Gilbert came back to England disgusted with the quality of the troops which he had been given and with the Zeelanders' commander, t'Zaarets.

From 1573 to 1578 Gilbert lived at Limehouse, retired from public employment and devoted his time to writing. He polished up his old 'Discourse' on the North-West Passage, which his friend Gascoigne, the poet, published in 1576. He also had an idea of going to help John Oxenham, who had been cut off in the Panama isthmus with captured treasure, for he was now developing a plan for breaking up the Spanish empire. He sent to the government schemes for wrecking Spanish maritime power by seizing her Newfoundland fishing fleet, attacking the treasure fleet on its way to Europe and occupying the islands of Hispaniola and Cuba as permanent bases for this purpose. He embodied these ideas in another 'Discourse' entitled *How her Majesty might annoy the King of Spain*, but the government was anxious at all costs to avoid war with Spain and Gilbert's approach was ignored (1577).

The rest of Gilbert's life was devoted to his plans for planting an English colony in North America. Other people were thinking along the same lines; men such as Richard Hakluyt the elder, who was to help Gilbert with advice and had been collecting information for some years. On 11 June 1578 Gilbert obtained from the Queen a patent which authorized him to search for and to occupy with English settlers lands 'not actually possessed of any Christian prince or people'. The patent was valid for six years and he was to hold all the land he discovered from the Crown. He was already beginning to collect ships: he had as his chief partner Henry Knollys, son of Sir Francis Knollys, the treasurer of the household, but he turned for his main support to his own family. He sold some of his wife's property and he raised subscriptions from his brothers Sir John and Adrian Gilbert. He also brought in Walter Ralegh and his elder brother

Carew. Five of Katherine Champernoun's sons were involved in the expedition besides some Champernoun and Carew cousins.

The fleet was to consist of ten ships, gathered together at Plymouth. Unhappily, during the delays in fitting them out quarrels broke out between Knollys and Gilbert: eventually Knollys deserted with three of the ships and sailed off into the Channel and Bay of Biscay, where he took to piracy. On 19 November 1578 Gilbert at last set sail with seven ships. He himself commanded the *Anne Ager* (named after Gilbert's wife), 250 tons, with the title of Admiral of the Fleet: the *Hope of Greenway*, 160 tons, was commanded by Carew Ralegh, the Vice-Admiral: Miles Morgan commanded the *Red Lion*, 110 tons: the *Falcon* of 100 tons was under the command of Walter Ralegh, she being the Queen's ship: the *Galleon* of 40 tons under Richard Veal, the *Swallow* of 40 tons under John Verney and the *Squirrel* of 10 tons carrying eight men completed the squadron.

The destination of the fleet is unknown, for the secret was well-kept, so that not even Mendoza, the Spanish Ambassador, knew. When we remember to what dimensions the expansion of England overseas was to attain, the sailing of Humphrey Gilbert on the first attempt to plant Englishmen overseas is a notable event. In fact, the voyage was a failure from the very start. What evidence we have suggests that the plan was to cross the Atlantic by way of the Canaries to the West Indies and then to work up the coast of North America. The ships were heavily armed in order to repel attacks by Spanish ships. The voyage was to be one of reconnaissance to prepare for a later expedition for colonizing.

The fleet scattered after leaving Plymouth, probably owing to bad weather, and it never reassembled. Gilbert put into an Irish port where he took in more supplies, but he failed to find the rest of his fleet when he again put to sea; therefore he returned to port, where he fell in with the *Hope of Greenway*, which had sprung a leak; Miles Morgan had slipped away to join Knollys in his piracy: later his ship, *Red Lion*, was lost at sea. Walter Ralegh with one or two other ships besides the *Falcon* set out on the course which had been planned, and made for the West Indies, but when he found he was short of food and had lost his right bearings, he turned for home near the Cape Verde Islands. Here he met and fought some Spanish ships which handled Ralegh's vessels very roughly. He reached Dartmouth in May 1579 in a battered condition, almost at the same moment as

Gilbert returned to Plymouth. Both Gilbert and Ralegh wanted to try again in the summer of 1579, but they encountered difficulties with the government, which disapproved of piracy too near home and therefore forbade the expedition, although there is no evidence that either Gilbert or Ralegh indulged in piracy, whatever Knollys and some of Gilbert's men had done.

The last four years of Gilbert's life were given to almost feverish activity to accomplish his American schemes. In 1580 he sent out that Simon Fernandez who had accompanied Ralegh in the *Falcon* in 1578 to reconnoitre the American coast. In three months Fernandez returned with a great deal of first-hand information. There was need for hurry, since Gilbert's patent expired at the end of 1584. Unfortunately, of all his old ships only the tiny *Squirrel* survived, and unfortunately also Gilbert was short of ready money. He therefore set about raising money by every device he could think of. One of the chief methods he employed was to sell in advance tracts of the lands he had not yet discovered. For example, Dr. John Dee purchased all the land north of parallel 50°. By dint of skilful advertising many other purchasers were found. Gilbert represented that a small investment might turn a simple English gentleman into a feudal lord of huge estates. The prospect of finding gold and jewels was held out, the possibility of finding new markets for raw materials and for manufactured goods was exploited. Especially did Gilbert seek to persuade the loyal Catholic gentry that they might create overseas a new state in which they could still serve their Queen and could at the same time preserve their Catholic religion. Between June 1582 and February 1583 Gilbert got rid of nearly nine million acres of land, all on paper, of which most went to the Catholic investors, led by Sir George Peckham and Sir Thomas Gerrard. These latter intended to send out an expedition on their own in 1582 to explore the territories and then to follow that up with a large colonizing expedition in 1583. Thanks, however, to the warnings of Catholic priests and the intriguing of the Spanish Ambassador, Mendoza, most of the Catholics backed out, so that these two expeditions never took place. Gilbert made an agreement with the Southampton merchants that they should have a monopoly of trade with the new colonies in return for financial help here and now. Even so, money was scarce, and the expedition was delayed month after month.

In February 1583 the Queen created a difficulty. She had observed that Gilbert was 'a man noted of not good hap at sea' and she suggested that he should not accompany the venture in person. Elizabeth seems always to have liked Gilbert and she did not now forbid him to go, nor was she angry when he went ahead with his plans. Indeed, she sent Gilbert a message through Ralegh that 'she wished great good hap and safety to your ships as if she herself were there in person' together with a jewel of 'an anchor guided by a lady'.

Gilbert set sail on 11 June for Newfoundland. The fleet consisted of *Delight*, 120 tons, in which Gilbert sailed as Admiral: the *Bark Ralegh*, 200 tons: the *Golden Hind*, 40 tons: the *Swallow*, 40 tons: the *Squirrel*, about 10 tons. On the 13th the *Bark Ralegh* turned for home and went into Plymouth, probably owing to a shortage of victuals brought about by the numerous delays before sailing when the victuals were consumed in harbour. In a fog on 20 July *Swallow* and *Squirrel* lost touch with the rest of the fleet and did not recover it until they arrived at Newfoundland, when Gilbert found the *Swallow* in Conception Bay and on 3 August he met with the *Squirrel* in the harbour of St. John's. Gilbert went ashore on the 4th (Sunday) and on the 5th he formally annexed the harbour and two hundred leagues every way in the name of the Queen and took possession of the land for himself and his heirs. He spent a fortnight prospecting and made up his mind that he would plant a colony here. One ship he sent home with all the sick, nor did he leave any garrison at St. John's when he sailed on 10 August for America. His stay at St. John's had discovered two things: that a great mistake had been made in recruiting the crews from pirates and prisoners, and that Gilbert was quite incapable of dealing with the lawlessness and discontent which immediately broke out. The discontent grew in the ships, especially after the *Delight* had run aground and was wrecked either on Sable Island or near Cape Breton. On 31 August, therefore, Gilbert turned back, having accomplished none of his main objectives. He himself was sailing in the *Squirrel* and he insisted on remaining in her in spite of heavy seas, although his friends tried to persuade him to go aboard the *Golden Hind*. On 9 September the *Squirrel* disappeared and was never seen again. The last sight that men had of Gilbert was sitting in the stern of the *Squirrel* with a book in his hand; whenever he came within hearing distance of the

Golden Hind he was heard to say, 'we are as near to Heaven by sea as by land'.

It is not easy to assess the character of Sir Humphrey Gilbert. Probably the eulogies which have been showered upon him are as far from the truth as is most undiscriminating praise. That he was genuinely pious, patriotic and brave is not to be denied. He was said in his own day to be afraid of the sea, but the manner of his death gives that the lie. There are too many examples of his ungovernable temper for us not to feel he was an obstinate, jealous and self-opinionated man. He was a bad leader, unable to win the respect or the affection of his followers, incapable of dealing with mutiny and insubordination. According to Clark, the master of the *Delight*, the loss of that ship and most of its men was due entirely to Gilbert's refusal to take the advice of a better navigator than himself. When Gilbert asked him which course to take, Clark advised west-south-west, whereupon Gilbert at once commanded him to sail west-north-west. Clark explained that *Delight* would be on the sands before daylight; Gilbert accused Clark of being out of his reckoning and ordered him in the Queen's name to sail as Gilbert had said. Clark obeyed and *Delight* was on the sands by seven o'clock in the morning. (Clark's narrative is printed in W. S. Gosling's *Life*). As a man of action, Gilbert was a failure, except perhaps in Ireland, and one may doubt what value his temporary success there ever had.

But as a man of intellect and imagination Gilbert must rank high. His was an original and creative mind, bold, far-seeing and extremely modern. His whole conception of overseas expansion was new, far ahead of the ideas of his time. And as a writer his reputation should be higher than it is. Among his works there is a 'Discourse' entitled *The Erection of* [Queen Elizabeth's] *Academy in London for Education of her Majesty's Wards and others the youths of nobility and gentlemen*. Broadly it was a plea for a kind of university in London. How modern was Gilbert's mind may be seen in the rules which he suggested for the library of this academy: he laid down almost all the rules which are now generally accepted as necessary for a librarian to observe: he suggested that a copy of every book published should be placed in the library, as is now done, for example, in the British Museum: he anticipated the future law of copyright. Gilbert was a typical product of a brilliant but undisciplined age.

D. B. Quinn, *Sir Humphrey Gilbert*, 1940.

W. G. Gosling, *The Life of Sir Humphrey Gilbert*.

Edward Hayes, (captain and owner of the *Golden Hind*), *A Report of the Voyage . . . by Sir Humphrey Gilbert*, printed in Hakluyt's *Voyages*, 1599, more easily accessible in E. J. Payne's, *Voyages of Elizabethan Seamen*.

THOMAS CAVENDISH [Hakluyt always used the form **CANDISH**] (1560–1592), circumnavigator, was born at Trimley St. Martin in Suffolk in 1560. He died at sea in 1592. Having wasted not only the savings of his minority, but also a large fortune in extravagant living at Court, Cavendish turned to piracy to rebuild his ruined finances. His first voyage was made in a ship of his own which he contributed to Ralegh's expedition of 1585, and which sailed under the command of Sir Richard Grenville in the first attempt to found the colony of Virginia in North America.

The next year Grenville planned an expedition of his own, modelled on the lines of the immensely successful expedition of Drake in 1577–80. Two accounts of Cavendish's voyage exist: one is signed N. H. and was written under the eye of Cavendish on board the *Desire*: the other was partly written by Francis Pretty on board the *Hugh Gallant* before she was sunk in the Pacific owing to a shortage of crews to sail her home. Pretty's account seems to suggest that Cavendish bore the whole expense of the expedition, but there are grounds for thinking that the Lord Chamberlain, Lord Hunsdon, may have been his patron.

The expedition left Plymouth in July. It consisted of three ships under the command of Cavendish, who was only twenty-six years old: the *Desire*, his flagship, 140 tons, the *Contest*, 60 tons, and the *Hugh Gallant*, 40 tons. The crews totalled 123 and the ships were victualled for two years. The first landfall was at Sierra Leone in August, where eleven days were spent in procuring provisions and water. A call was paid at one of the Cape Verde Islands; then the fleet sailed on to Brazil. Three weeks were spent here near the island of San Sebastiano, 120 miles south-west of Rio de Janeiro. Cavendish put to sea again on 23 November and in mid-December he arrived at a Patagonian harbour which he named Port Desire after his ship. Here they stayed over Christmas, studying the habits and manners and arts of the Patagonians. Sailing was resumed on

28 December and on 3 January 1587 the expedition reached the opening of the Straits of Magellan. After losing an anchor in a great storm which lasted for three days, Cavendish entered the straits on 6 January. The next day they saw a party of twenty-three starving Spaniards, the remnants of 400 who had been left by Sarmiento in 1584 to defend the narrows. Cavendish took off one Spaniard, Hernando: all the rest perished.

The passage of the straits took forty-nine days. On the way through they saw the hull of a small barque which they took to be the *John Thomas*, abandoned there by Drake nine years before. On the whole Cavendish had good luck with the weather, but for a month 'we fed almost altogether on mussels and limpets and birds, or such as we could get on shore, seeking for them every day as the fowls of the air do' (Pretty).

On 24 February the fleet entered the Pacific and sailed up the coast of Chile as far as Quintero Bay, just north of Valparaiso. Here the Spaniard Hernando was put ashore to talk with three mounted Spaniards: suddenly he leaped up behind one of the horsemen and galloped away — a piece of singularly bad luck for Cavendish, for he would certainly warn the whole seaboard. One day a watering-party was attacked by 200 Spaniards and twelve men were killed, although the Spanish lost twenty-five (1 April 1587). Cavendish's main object now was to plunder as much as he could, but on the whole he did not have much success: the Spanish had learned a lot since Drake's attacks and they had organized a system of swift ships which carried the news of the English arrival ahead of the fleet. They also had many more men posted along the coastline, but their ships were not yet armed. Cavendish experienced a good deal of stiff fighting and although he captured a few ships and burned a few towns, none gave him plunder enough to compensate for the loss of some thirty men, a loss which forced him to abandon the *Hugh Gallant* as he had not enough crews to sail three vessels.

With *Desire* and *Content* Cavendish went on to Costa Rica (1 July). He captured and burned a ship from which he took a French pilot, but the Spaniards were well aware of his movements: he had a little before this taken a ship carrying letters to the Viceroy to warn him of Cavendish's approach. The letters were revealed by a Spaniard who by the command of Cavendish was 'tormented with his thumbs in a wrench'. Off the west coast of Mexico he learned that the *Santa Anna* of 700 tons was expected with a rich cargo from Manila and that her landfall would be at Cape St. Lucas, the most southerly point of California, 'very like the Needles at the Isle of Wight' (Pretty). For three weeks *Desire* and *Content* hung about the point: at last on 4 November they sighted the *Santa Anna*. She carried no heavy guns and therefore, in spite of a gallant resistance which lasted some six hours, she was compelled to surrender. Cavendish took his prize into a near-by harbour, where he put the Spaniards ashore with a supply of food. The treasure in gold *pesos* amounted to 22,000, but out of a total of 600 tons of merchandise Cavendish could only transfer to his two ships forty tons for each, so heavily laden were they already. The rest of the cargo and the *Santa Anna* herself were burned. Cavendish also took off the prize-ship two Japanese boys and three young native boys from Manila, and also Nicholas Roderigo, a Portuguese from China, from whom he probably got the large map of China to which Hakluyt referred at length in his book. Cavendish also obtained a Spanish pilot for the Philippines.

On 19 November the *Desire* and *Content* set sail for England, but the *Content* belied her name. There had been something like a mutiny among her crew, who were dissatisfied with their share of the plunder from the *Santa Anna*. She was slow in following *Desire* out of harbour and 'so we lost her company and never saw her after' (Pretty). Was she perhaps trying to go home independently by way of the North-West Passage? She was never heard of again.

On 3 January 1588 Cavendish sighted the Ladrone Islands and on the 14th he was in the Philippines. He was by no means strong enough to attack Manila: indeed, Roderigo revealed to him that the Spanish pilot was trying to urge the Spanish in Manila to attack him. Cavendish at once hanged the pilot from the yard-arm. His course is a little disputed, but it is fairly certain that he sailed through the narrows between Java and Bali (1 March) and arrived at a safe haven near the western end of the south coast of Java, probably Wijnkoopers Bay.

In the middle of March he set sail for the Cape of Good Hope which he sighted on 16 May (the *D.N.B.* says 19 March which is manifestly impossible). On 8 June *Desire* called at St. Helena, and Cavendish became the first Englishman to have visited that island, which was occupied by the Portuguese. The ship was here cleaned and revictualled and then set out for home. Early in September Cavendish entered the English Channel: his track must have crossed that of Medina Sidonia, who brought the defeated Armada into Santander three days after Cavendish entered Plymouth (9 September, not the 10th, as the *D.N.B.* records).

Thus at the age of 28 Cavendish became the second Englishman to circumnavigate the globe. In a letter to Lord Hunsdon he claims that he had burnt and sunk nineteen ships; had burned and plundered all the towns on the Spanish littoral that he had touched at; had captured a galleon which was 'one of the richest of merchandise that ever passed those seas', had obtained intelligence concerning China 'such as hath not been heard of in these parts'; had ascertained that trade might be freely had in the Moluccas; and finally, had discovered the island of St. Helena (Foster, *England's Quest of Eastern Trade*). This was a wonderful achievement, the more so for so young and inexperienced a commander, one which might put him on the same pedestal as Drake. Yet it must be admitted that Cavendish lacked what Dr. J. A. Williamson calls 'the artist's touch by which Drake made things go easily'. Cavendish's third voyage was to reveal deeper and more fatal flaws in his character.

The third voyage, 1591: there can be no doubt that, at any rate after the taking of the *Santa Anna*, Cavendish had done well enough out of his expedition to wish to renew the voyage. Men like Robert Parke were already pressing the Chinese market for the English cloth trade as a result of Cavendish's enterprise (Foster, *ib.*). In August 1591 Cavendish joined with John Davis in an expedition to China and the South Sea. They sailed from Plymouth in August. Davis had been persuaded to go by a promise that he should explore the North-West Passage from the Pacific side. Cavendish commanded a ship which had been known as the *Leicester*, but was now named the *Galleon*. Davis commanded Cavendish's old ship *Desire*; the two other vessels were the *Dainty* and the *Roebuck*, to which was added a small ship known as the *Black Pinnace*. On 29 November the fleet reached the coast of Brazil and took the town of Santos, hoping to obtain food: not much was forthcoming. It was not until 24 January 1592 that Cavendish set out again on his voyage. This was too late in the season, the weather was unusually severe, and during a storm Cavendish was separated from the rest of his fleet. He had forgotten to appoint a rendezvous, but Davis expected that Cavendish would make for Port Desire, which eventually he did. It was as late as 18 March when Cavendish rejoined Davis, who had picked up the *Roebuck* in a poor state. The *Dainty* had given up and returned home. In the meantime Cavendish had quarrelled with the officers of the *Galleon* and he now left that ship and went aboard the *Desire*, violently criticizing all in the *Galleon*, it seems without any reason for doing so. Indeed, there is ground for thinking that Cavendish had gone to pieces and that his mind was probably unhinged.

On 20 March they sailed for the Straits of Magellan, which they reached on 8 April. The weather was so bad that by the 21st they were only half way through and had to take refuge in a small cove, where they remained until 15 May, short of food and suffering much from the cold. And another grave danger began to appear: perhaps the capital for the voyage had been insufficient, for now the gear was rotten and the sails old and there were no spares to make good the losses. Davis advised that the ships should press on — but he was anxious to discover the North-West Passage. The men, too, were anxious to go ahead, since they were in search of plunder and spoil. Cavendish by now had lost all capacity for leadership, and against the advice of all he proposed to turn back and try to reach the East Indies by way of the Cape. Davis dissuaded him, arguing that the ships were in bad condition, the crews were short-handed and the provisions almost finished. Cavendish thereupon left the *Desire* and went once more aboard the *Galleon* and gave orders to sail for Santos in Brazil. On the night of 20 May 1592 he suddenly altered the course of his own vessel and deserted the others.

Cavendish soon fell in with the *Roebuck* and the two ships made for the Brazilian coast. An attack by a Portuguese force cost him twenty-five men, and he lost another twenty-five when he attempted to land at Espirito Santo. As a result the *Roebuck* left Cavendish and sailed for England. Cavendish tried vainly to persuade his men to tackle once more the Straits of Magellan, but they refused, and he reluctantly agreed to make for St. Helena and there refit. The *Galleon* got within two leagues of the island, but she was driven away by contrary winds. Cavendish then made for Ascension Island, but he missed the way and turned for the Cape Verde Islands. The last record that we have of Thomas Cavendish is his last letter written to his executor, Sir Tristram Gorges, in which he reports the death of his cousin, John Locke, and his own imminent death. That the *Galleon* must have arrived at long last in some English port is proved by the fact that this letter reached its destination, but Cavendish died within a few days of Locke, but not before in his letter he had stigmatized Davis as 'that villain that hath been the death of me and the decay of this whole action, whose only treachery in running from me hath been an utter ruin of all'. This was the last and most bitter criticism of the many which he made of his friends, and it was of all the least justified.

The end of Cavendish was at the beginning: he who in his youth had squandered his wealth now, at the end of his short life, squandered the splendid reputation he had won by his voyage of circumnavigation. He stands for posterity as a typical Elizabethan, one of that galaxy of brilliant stars which illuminate the Elizabethan firmament, but whose heat too often consumes their splendour. Thomas Cavendish shines in the same constellation as Robert Devereux, Earl of Essex, and Sir Walter Ralegh.

The accounts of his voyages are easily accessible, together with his
    last letter, in E. J. Payne's *Voyages of Elizabethan Seamen*, 1900.
J. A. Williamson, *The Age of Drake*, 1946.
W. Foster, *England's Quest of Eastern Trade*, 1933.

ANTHONY JENKINSON (*d.*1611), merchant, traveller and navigator: the date of his birth is unknown; he died in 1611. Practically nothing at all is known of his early life. It was the custom in his day for a boy who wanted to follow a career in trade to be sent to the Levant, and Jenkinson seems to have left England for the East in 1546. According to his own account, he travelled through Flanders, Germany, over the Alps into Italy, through Piedmont into France; he visited Spain and Portugal, and travelled thence to the Levant via all the principal islands: Malta, Sicily, Candia, Rhodes and Syria; he went all over the Holy Land; he was also in North Africa; and all this he accomplished between 1546 and 1553. (The list of his travels is printed in Delmar Morgan's *Early Voyages and Travels to Russia and Persia*, Hakluyt Society, vol. ii, pp. 341-3.)

In 1553 Jenkinson was in Aleppo, where he witnessed the entry of Suleiman the Magnificent on 4 November. He was granted an interview with that monarch and obtained from him a safe-conduct, which was in reality a guarantee of free trade in all Turkish ports. It is not known for certain what was the purpose Jenkinson was pursuing, but almost certainly the merchants in England were preparing a plan for developing trade between England and the Levant in order to secure a regular supply of spices. Nor is it known whether Jenkinson followed up the privileges he had obtained from the Sultan. If he did, he gave up the hope of cashing in on Eastern trade by this method and turned his attention to developing the promising results which flowed from Chancellor's contacts with Moscow.

The first journey, 1557. In 1557 Jenkinson was admitted a member of the Mercers' Company, the same year in which the Russian Ambassador Nepeja arrived in London after his shipwreck in Scotland. In April 1557 the Muscovy Company fitted out a fleet of four vessels to trade with Russia and explore the possibilities of reaching Cathay by land and it appointed Jenkinson — 'a man well travelled whom we mind to use in further travelling' — as Captain-General of the fleet and as the Company's Agent at a salary of £40 a year for three years. The appointment was made, because Jenkinson was a skilful navigator who understood surveying as far as the science was known in the sixteenth century. His observations for latitude showed wide errors, but they were wonderfully accurate, if we consider how crude were the instruments available to him.

The ships set sail from Gravesend on 12 May 1557, and Nepeja sailed with Jenkinson in the flag-ship, *Noble Primrose*. The Lofoten Islands were reached on 27 June, the North Cape on 2 July; the fleet then passed what Jenkinson called Lappia (Lapland) and Sviatoi Ness, named by Borough Cape Gallant. It entered the White Sea and anchored safely at St. Nicholas Road on 12 July having covered 2,250 miles from London. Jenkinson and Nepeja then landed, went by boat up the Dwina river as far as Kholmogori and Vologhda and thence by land to Moscow, where they arrived on 6 December.

They were kindly received by the Tsar, Ivan the Terrible, with whom they dined on Christmas Day. They spent nearly five months at Moscow, and it was not until 23 April 1558 that the next stage of the journey was begun.

On that day Jenkinson, with letters of recommendation from the Tsar, set out from Moscow for Cathay, taking with him Richard and Robert Johnson — Richard had been with Chancellor on the

1553 voyage and with Borough in the *Serchthrift* in 1556 — and an interpreter. Their first objective was down the Volga to Astrakhan at the head of the Caspian Sea, the farthest outpost of the Russian domains. They found the city in a ghastly condition, for after it had suffered from famine the plague attacked it, so that the Englishmen were met with thousands of corpses lying about in the streets (14 July). Jenkinson here picked up what he called a 'wench' named Aura Soltana, whom he sent to England as a present to the new Queen, Elizabeth I. Jenkinson now bought a boat and set sail from Astrakhan, the first Englishman to enter and navigate the Caspian Sea (10 August 1558). He explored the delta of the Volga and the north coast of the Caspian, and charted the northern shores. (His map of these parts was published in 1562.) During this time Jenkinson was exceedingly ill, and he and his party were all but captured by robbers, who boarded the boat under the pretence of searching for infidels. Only hard swearing by the interpreter saved the four Englishmen. On 3 September they reached the Mangishlak peninsula, where they landed, and set out on the 14th overland for Vezir.

Jenkinson now found himself in a land infested with robbers and marauders, wild tribesmen with whom it was impossible to have any dealings. In the end Jenkinson was glad to pay their many exactions and to be rid of them. The caravan with which he was travelling numbered 1,000 camels. After five days, travelling, they reached the domains of Timur Sultan, brother of Hakjim, the Khan of Khiva. His subjects stopped and plundered the caravan, but Jenkinson rode off to Timur and made his complaints so forcibly that he was given a horse worth half the value of the stolen goods and excellent entertainment. He stayed in Vezir until 14 October, when he moved on to Urgendj. Here he spent six weeks, but he found that it was impossible to trade owing to the wild marauders of those parts; therefore he set out for Bokhara, which he reached on 23 December, having had to repel an attack on the way.

At Bokhara Jenkinson was well received and on the 26th he was granted an interview with Abdullah Khan, to whom he presented the letters he had brought from the Tsar of Russia. Abdullah was much interested in the arquebuses which the Englishmen carried, and 'did himself practise the use thereof'. He also bought some of the travellers' goods, but before he had paid for them he set out on a military expedition and his servants refused to honour his debts, so that Jenkinson had to take what he could get.

So great was the anarchy and confusion of the country that it soon became clear to Jenkinson that it was impossible to pass from Bokhara to Cathay, which put an end to establishing trade with Cathay by this route. Nor did the inhabitants of Bokhara want the English exports. The only thing to do was to go back by the way he had come. On 8 March 1559 Jenkinson left Bokhara with a caravan of 600 camels for the Caspian, where he arrived on 23 April. He found his ship, but it was now without anchor, cable or sail. The travellers set about spinning a cable out of hemp and making a sail out of some cloth, and they were preparing to manufacture an anchor out of a wooden cartwheel, when a barque from Astrakhan arrived with a spare anchor. The three Englishmen, together with six ambassadors who were bound for Russia and twenty-five liberated Russian slaves, set sail and arrived at Astrakhan on 28 May. To his great disappointment, Jenkinson had learned that English cloth could not compete with a similar article imported via the Levant and Syria: he had also discovered that the Caspian area was unsuited to trade owing to its few harbours, its shortage of ships, the frequent ice, and the poverty of the people. Therefore on 10 June he left Astrakhan, went up the Volga for six weeks to Kazan, which he left on 7 August and arrived at Moscow on 2 September, having been on his travels for one year, five months and nine days since he last left that city. He stayed in Moscow until 17 February 1560, when he set out for home via the White Sea, arriving in London probably some time in the autumn, after 'a journey so miserable, dangerous and chargeable with losses, charges and expenses as my pen is not able to express the same'.

It had been and still remains a memorable journey. In spite of the robbers and their exactions, the voyage shewed a satisfactory financial profit. Jenkinson had proved conclusively that further attempts to trade in Central Asia would be a waste of time and money, a verdict 'which was accepted as final and centuries passed before Bokhara saw another English visitor'. (Foster, *England's Quest of Eastern Trade*, p. 22.) But there seemed to be a chance that trade might be built up by exploiting the hatred which existed between the Persian Shiah Mohammedans and the Turkish Sunni Mohammedans, who were frequently at war. English goods might be injected through the north. It might also be possible to persuade the Asian merchants to carry their goods for Syria and Europe to the Persian markets and there to exchange them for English goods: or the Russia Company might secure privileges to pass through Persia and seek the Asian goods themselves. It was Jenkinson who persuaded the Company to send a second expedition to explore these possibilities. Hence the second journey, 1561.

The second journey, 1561. The instructions given to Jenkinson by the Company were to obtain from the Tsar leave to carry its trade through Russia into Persia, for which it was prepared to pay a reasonable tariff. He was then to go on to Persia and there to ask of the Shah — the Great Sophi, as he was known in England — permission to trade freely in Persia, and also for a guarantee 'for free passage also for us at all times to pass, as often as we will, with our goods and merchandise into any part of India, or other countries thereunto adjoining, and in like manner to return through his dominions into Russia or elsewhere'. (Delmar Morgan, *ib*., i, 117.) Jenkinson was also to carry letters from Queen Elizabeth to the Tsar and to the Shah.

Jenkinson sailed from Gravesend in the *Swallow* on 14 May and he arrived at Kholmogori on 26 July. From there he went overland to Moscow, where he arrived on 20 August, having taken only thirteen days over a journey which usually took five weeks by water. He found the Tsar was celebrating his second marriage, and there was considerable delay before an interview could be arranged. So little success did he achieve when at last he met the Tsar that he made up his mind to return to England. He sold the Company's cloth and other goods, received his passport and paid for the post-horses for the return journey; he was on the point of leaving when Nepeja called on him and persuaded him to cancel his arrangements and wait for a time further. Within three days Jenkinson received the permission to travel through Russia into Persia: he was promised letters of recommendation to the foreign princes through whose countries he would have to pass: he was also entrusted by the Tsar with some secret and very important political commissions: and the Tsar, to shew his gratitude, gave to the Company wider privileges than it had ever had before. On 15 March Jenkinson dined with the Tsar and also with the Persian Ambassador, who travelled with him when he left Moscow on 27 April 1562.

Astrakhan was reached on 10 June. The Persian ambassador here parted from Jenkinson, who remained in the city until 15 July, when he sailed into the Caspian. The voyage was beset with dangers from pirates and in one specially severe storm Jenkinson lost an anchor and his ship became very leaky, but he survived these perils and arrived at Derbend on 1 August. Derbend belonged to Persia and Jenkinson was the first Englishman to visit it. From Derbend he moved on to Shabran in the province of Shirvan under the rule of Abdullah Khan. Jenkinson set out to interview Abdullah at Shemakha and he was there entertained at a gigantic feast, 'with divers kinds of meats to the number of 140', which were followed by 'a banquet of fruits of sundry kinds with other banquetting meats to the number of 150 dishes'. Abdullah promised him a bodyguard to carry him safely to the Shah at Kazvin and early in October Jenkinson started for the Persian capital.

The ruling Shah was Shah Tahmasp (Jenkinson calls him Shaw Thamas) with whom Jenkinson had an interview on 20 November, when he presented 'the Queen's Majesty's letters' and also the presents which he had brought for the Great Sophi. The Shah asked in what language the letters were written: 'I answered in the Latin, Italian and Hebrew; well, said he, we have none within our realm that understand those tongues'. The Shah asked whether Jenkinson was a '*Gower*, that is to say an unbeliever, or a Muslim, that is of Mahomet's law'. Jenkinson answered that he was a Christian. 'What is that said he unto the King of the Georgians' son (who being a Christian was fled unto the said Sophi) and he answered that a Christian was he that believeth in *Jesus Christus*, affirming him to be the Son of God and the greatest prophet: Doest thou believe so said the Sophi unto me: Yea, that I do, said I: Oh, thou unbeliever, said he, we have no need to have friendship with the unbelievers, and so willed me to depart.' Jenkinson took his leave, but he was followed by a man with a basin full of sand which he 'sifted all the way that I had gone within the said palace, even from the said Sophi's sight unto the court gate'. At one moment it looked as if the Shah would put Jenkinson to death, but Abdullah Khan intervened on his behalf and 'the said Sophi changed his determined purpose and on the 20th day of March 1562 he sent me a rich garment of cloth of gold and so dismissed me without any harm'.

While he was at Kazvin, Jenkinson got into touch with some

Indian merchants and arranged with them that, if he succeeded in establishing a permanent trade in Persia, they would supply him with as much spice as he was ready to take. On his way home he called again on Abdullah Khan, who gave him most valuable concessions to buy and sell freely in Shirvan exempt from all customs dues.

Meantime the King of Georgia was being attacked by both Turks and Persians and he sent to Jenkinson to ask him to arrange with the Tsar to send him help. Jenkinson urged the King to send an embassy to the Tsar to make his request in person. He also sent one of his companions, Edward Clarke, to try to penetrate into Georgia from Arrash, the centre of the silk industry, and to get permission from the Georgian king for the Company to trade freely in his kingdom, but Clarke found that this was impossible without jeopardizing the good relations with Abdullah Khan. This was a striking example of the way in which Jenkinson lost no opportunity of furthering the trading interests of the Company.

On his arrival at Moscow Jenkinson had another interview with the Tsar who gave him even more valuable privileges for the Company than he had before, in return for the commissions which Jenkinson had carried out for the Tsar in buying for him jewels and silks and fulfilling the secret political negotiations which he had entrusted to him (August 1563).

Jenkinson spent the winter in Moscow (1563/4) and he organized a second expedition to Persia on which Cheinie and Alcock set out probably in May 1564. On 9 July 1564 Jenkinson embarked for England in the *Swallow* and he arrived in London on 28 September, after an absence of over three years. His second journey is no less remarkable than the first and was of great value to the Company, for he had for the first time opened up the possibilities of trade with Persia. He had also established a reputation as a trustworthy and successful political agent.

Jenkinson, as a result of his own wide experience, was now convinced that it would prove perfectly possible to navigate the Polar sea and open the passage from West to East, provided that the right time of year was chosen and proper planning preceded the expedition. In May 1565 he wrote a petition to the Queen, urging her to finance such an exploit and offering himself to lead the expedition. The thrifty Elizabeth was not prepared to risk money on such a scheme and nothing came of Jenkinson's proposal.

In the autumn of 1565 Jenkinson was despatched by the government on a highly responsible mission. The English Channel at this time swarmed with English adventurers who were indistinguishable from mere pirates. They attacked Spanish and French ships, and the complaints of these foreign governments at last alarmed Elizabeth to such an extent that she made up her mind to put an end to their depredations. On 17 September 1565 Jenkinson sailed from Queensborough in command of the *Ayde*, 200 tons, with the Queen's commission to stop the pirates. But he had also a more serious order: he was to prevent Bothwell, husband of Mary, Queen of Scots, and other Scottish lords from landing in Scotland: therefore he at once sailed for the Firth of Forth. Arriving at Berwick, he heard that Bothwell had already landed; therefore Jenkinson turned his attention to the pirates. A certain Charles Wilson had been employed by the governor of Berwick to watch out for Bothwell, but he missed him. Wilson was in reality a pirate, and although he held Bedford's licence, Jenkinson captured him. Thereupon Bedford wrote furiously to the Privy Council, describing Jenkinson as 'that vile man' and asserting that 'never was any so abused by a villain as (Wilson) had been by Jenkinson'. There is no record of how the episode ended (1565).

The third journey, 1566. A few months later the Russia Company sent Jenkinson on a mission to Russia to safeguard its interests against an Italian merchant, Barberini, who had extracted from the Queen letters of recommendation to the Tsar and who, in the opinion of the Company, was infringing its rights granted by the Tsar. Jenkinson sailed from London on 4 May 1566 in the *Harry*, and he arrived at Moscow on 23 August: he had an audience with the Tsar on 1 September, when he delivered the Queen's letters and the normal presents. He was wholly successful in securing a complete monopoly of trade for his Company (1567) (Delmar Morgan, *ib.*, i, 48 seqq).

The fourth journey, 1571–2. The Tsar seems to have been a mercurial creature. In 1571, in a temper against Elizabeth, he annulled the privileges he had granted to the Company: at once the Company sent Jenkinson to Russia to deal with the crisis; so in the summer of 1571 Jenkinson was again in Russia. He arrived at St. Nicholas on 26 July to hear that the Tsar was furious with him and was threatening to cut off his head. With immense bravery Jenkinson set out for Moscow. He reached Kholmogori (1 August 1571), where he found the plague raging. A messenger of his was all but burnt for trying to force the cordon drawn round the city. He remained at Kholmogori until 18 January, ignored by the Tsar, destitute of money and ill-treated by the inhabitants. But at last the plague ended and Jenkinson was ordered to go to Moscow, where he arrived on 3 February. It was not until 23 March that the Tsar admitted him to an interview and explained the reasons for his discontent. Jenkinson attributed everything to the incompetence of the Russian Ambassador in England and to the bad behaviour of the Company's agents in Russia. On 13 May 1572 Jenkinson saw the Tsar again and was well received. The Tsar went out of his way to compliment Jenkinson and he then restored the privileges to the Company. Jenkinson left Russia on 23 July and arrived in England on 10 September. This was the last journey that Jenkinson undertook. For fifteen years he had devoted himself to fostering good relations between England and Russia and he had been entirely successful. 'And thus, being weary and growing old, I am content to take my rest in mine own house, chiefly comforting myself in that my service hath been honourably accepted and rewarded of her Majesty and the rest by whom I have been employed.'

Between 1572 and 1578 Jenkinson moved from London to live at Sywell in Northamptonshire. He was married probably in 1568 and he had twin daughters who died in infancy. A son who was born in 1580 also died as a baby, but there was another son who survived and gave to Jenkinson three grandchildren. He took much interest in the voyages of Frobisher. In 1577 he was sent on a mission to treat with the King of Denmark on the right of the English to navigate the northern seas. He sat on the commission which reported on the ore brought back by Frobisher in 1578. About 1600 he moved to Ashton in Northamptonshire and he died at Tighe in Rutland in 1611. From Anthony Jenkinson was descended Robert Jenkinson, second Lord Liverpool, who was Prime Minister in 1812 to 1827.

If Jenkinson is to be remembered as a traveller and trader and a diplomat, he ought not to be forgotten as a geographer. The vaguest and most inaccurate ideas prevailed in England and Europe about the East. The early voyages of Englishmen to the White Sea dispelled some of the erroneous notions; Jenkinson's travels greatly extended

Western European geographical knowledge. He was the first man to describe from personal observation the eastern parts of Russia, the first to descend the Volga since it had become a Russian river, the first to navigate the Caspian Sea and to realize that it was a landlocked sea, the first to describe accurately the countries which lay along its coasts. Some of his descriptions of lands farther afield, especially of the rivers, were far wide of the mark, as when he tried to explain what he took to be the underground flow of the Oxus. His influence on geography was not always beneficial: his vivid descriptions were published in all the best collections of travels and his map was included by Ortelius in his famous atlas: thus Jenkinson's errors were perpetuated. All the same, he bridges the gap between Marco Polo in the thirteenth century and the English and Russian travellers of the eighteenth century. Jenkinson's map, which was published in 1562, has been attributed to William Borough, but there are good grounds for thinking that it was chiefly the work of Jenkinson. Borough may have done the drawing.

Delmar Morgan, *Early Voyages and Travels to Russia and Persia*, 1886.
W. Foster, *England's Quest of Eastern Trade*, 1933.

THE HAWKINS FAMILY [the family spelt the name **HAW-KYNS**], lived in Plymouth, and for three generations it was one of the most famous names in England. Between 1524 and 1622 three members played a leading part in local politics in Plymouth, in national politics in London, in overseas trade and naval warfare, or in all four at one and the same time. To some extent the Hawkins family was the creator of Plymouth, not only as the leading city in the south-west, but as the leading port for the new trade with the Americas.

M. Lewis, *The Hawkins Dynasty*, 1969.

WILLIAM HAWKINS ([the first] (*d.* 1553?), merchant, politician and sailor, was born between 1490 and 1500, the son of John Hawkins of Tavistock and Joan, daughter of William Amydas of Launceston. He married Joan Trelawny and they had two sons,

William and John, and one daughter. William Hawkins died in 1553 or 1554.

Hawkins was a man of much importance in Plymouth. He became Treasurer to the Corporation in 1524, he was Mayor in 1532 and again in 1538, and he sat in the 1539, 1547 and 1553 Parliaments as Member for Plymouth. But it was as a trader that he is chiefly to be remembered. He began as an exporter of cloth and tin to western Europe, importing salt and wine from France, sugar and pepper from Portugal, soap from Spain and fish from the Banks of the 'newfoundlands'. Between 1530 and 1532 he sent several expeditions to Guinea and Brazil to develop the new Atlantic trade, especially in dyewood (Brazil means dyewood) for the English clothiers. On one voyage an Indian chief was brought back who was introduced to Henry VIII. The 1540 voyage proved how lucrative was this trade — the exports taken on the voyage were valued at £23 15s. 0d., the home-coming cargo of 'one dosen olyfantes tethe' and 92 tons of Brazil wood at £615.

William Hawkins was a quarrelsome man, tough, resolute and uncompromising, very able, loyal to the government, but always looking after his own interests. He was more than once fined, but he never paid the fines: he was in prison once, but we now know he was in the right. He laid the foundations of the new trade with the New World. And he was the father of the great Sir John Hawkins.

WILLIAM HAWKINS [the second] (*c.*1519–1589), merchant, ship-owner and sailor, was born about 1519. He was the elder son of William Hawkins (the first) and brother of Sir John Hawkins.

The second William is a less national and heroic figure than his brother John, a less romantic figure than his nephew Richard, but in his own way he was a man of great local importance and he was often on the fringe of national and international events. In 1553 he was made a freeman of Plymouth; in 1558 he became a Privy Councillor of the borough; he was three times Mayor of Plymouth, in 1567–8, in 1578–9 and in 1587–8. He built the new conduit which improved the water supply of Plymouth (1568–9), and in 1573 he and John farmed the town mills which were worked by power provided by the sea-tides.

It was through his ships and his trading ventures, usually carried out in conjunction with John, that he was brought into touch with the world of national politics. During the war against France in Mary's reign the Hawkins ships went privateering in the Channel, generally with profitable results. When the revolt of the Netherlands broke out, William repeated these tactics with the same success, to judge by the stream of complaints which poured in from France and Spain. Plymouth became the headquarters and William and John the mainspring of the unofficial war which went on between English and Spanish ships for two decades before the Armada set sail. It was William who organized the Protestant ships in the western Channel in co-operation with the Huguenots farther east towards Cowes in the Isle of Wight. It was William who had the chief hand in seizing the Spanish treasure at Plymouth in 1568. It was William who, when he heard (a false story) that John had been killed by the Spanish in the Indies, wrote to Cecil and requested that some of that treasure should be handed over to him, William, as compensation.

In 1582 he led an expedition, at the age of 62, to Brazil, and took with him his nephew Richard.

William Hawkins was Mayor of Plymouth in the year of the Armada. He did not fight in the English fleet, but he helped to fit out seven ships from Plymouth to join the fleet, he collected reinforcements for the fleet, and he subscribed £25 towards the expense of defence.

He died on 7 October 1589 and was buried in the church of St. Nicholas, Deptford.

J. A. Williamson, *Hawkins of Plymouth*, 1949.

SIR JOHN HAWKINS ['Achines' the Spanish called him] (1532–1595), merchant, ship-owner, ship-builder, naval commander, naval administrator, was born at Plymouth in 1532 and died at sea on 12 November 1595. He was the second son of William Hawkins (the first): he was twice married, first to Katherine Gonson, daughter of Benjamin Gonson, Treasurer of the Navy (1559), and secondly to Margaret Vaughan. By his first marriage he had one son, Richard, later Sir Richard Hawkins.

When he was about twenty he killed a barber of Plymouth named White, but he was judged by the coroner to have struck White 'because he could not avoid him'. John was about twenty-one when his father died, leaving his brother William head of the family. John and William went into partnership and worked together until probably 1560, when the business was wound up. After that the two brothers worked separately, but each invested in the ventures of the other. John certainly spent a good deal of time at sea, voyaging principally to the Canary Islands: as certainly he was by 1560 a wealthy man, for when the partnership was broken, his share of the capital was £10,000 — a very large sum in those days. He was also a man of importance, for in 1556 he became a freeman of Plymouth. In the course of his travels to the Canaries he had learned the possibilities of trading slaves between the Guinea coast of Africa and the Spanish possessions in the West Indies. In 1559 or 1560 he left Plymouth and went to live in London, there the more conveniently to further this new opening in trade.

The Slave-trading Voyages

The first slave-trading voyage, 1562. A syndicate was formed which included John's father-in-law, Benjamin Gonson, and Sir William Wynter, Surveyor of the Navy and Master of the Ordnance. This was intended to be a comparatively small expedition to gain experience. Hawkins sailed from Plymouth in October with the *Salomon,* the *Swallow* and the *Jonas,* and possibly with a fourth vessel. He picked up a pilot at Teneriffe and made for the Guinea coast. Here he secured about 400 Negro slaves and chartered a Portuguese ship in which to transport the slaves. A Spanish friend had already ascertained that his presence and his cargo would be welcome in Hispaniola, although officially the Indies were forbidden to trade with foreigners. In April 1563 Hawkins arrived at the small ports on the north coast of the island — San Domingo was too public a place for him to sell his goods there. At Isabella, Puerto de Plata and Monte Christi he disposed of his English merchandise and his slaves, either in exchange for a little gold, a little sugar and a large lading of hides, or else for bills drawn upon Seville, since coined money was scarce in the Indies. He paid the normal customs dues in slaves, chartered a vessel from a Spaniard named Martinez, put Thomas Hampton in command of it and sent him off to Seville with part of the new cargo. He sent the Portuguese ship to Seville under its Portuguese captain and crew. From these actions it is possible to think that Hawkins felt assured that all he had done would be acceptable to the Spanish authorities in Spain and the Portuguese in Portugal. At Seville Hampton's cargo was seized by the Spanish; the Portuguese captain sailed his ship, not to Seville, but to Lisbon, where the cargo was impounded by the Portuguese Guinea traders. Hawkins arrived at Plymouth in August 1563, bringing with him by far the more important results of his trading with the Indies. When he heard what had happened at Seville, he went straight to London to enlist the sympathies of the government on his side against Spain.

On this first voyage Hawkins had, deliberately and openly, broken the three great rules governing trade in the Spanish Indies. He had gone there without a licence to do so: he had traded without a licence: he had carried goods which had not previously been declared at Seville. He must have known the rules perfectly well. It is evident that Hawkins expected to get preferential treatment and that he was making this voyage into a test case. We do not know why he should have expected this, but it is possible that the answer lies in a curious episode when Queen Mary was on the throne. Hawkins was in Plymouth when the negotiations for the Spanish marriage were going on: some of the Spanish emissaries travelled through Plymouth and used the services of Hawkins and his brother. When Philip came to England in 1555 to marry Mary, one Spanish record avers that he knighted Hawkins. This is possibly not true, as we know that Hawkins was knighted during the fight against the Armada. But we also know that Hawkins often spoke of Philip II as 'my old master': the word servant in that context meant something more than merely subject. Is it not likely that Hawkins had done some special service for Philip II which led him to think that Philip would give him privileged treatment in trading with the Spanish West Indies? If so, John Hawkins got his answer: he reckoned that he lost in Seville and Lisbon £20,000. Even so, the voyage paid a handsome dividend.

The second slave-trading voyage, 1564. This was a much more important business than the first, for it had political as well as trading objectives.

The syndicate for the first voyage was now joined by three Privy Councillors, Cecil himself had much to do with supervising the expedition, and the Queen herself chartered to the leaders the largest vessel — it was the *Jesus of Lubeck* of 700 tons, but in a wholly rotten condition, (illustration in Williamson, *ib.*, p.68) — and ordered that the fleet should sail under her own royal standard as well as the Cross of St. George. Probably what she hoped for was, first, to find out the exact position in Florida where a French colony had just been planted to the danger of the Spanish in the New World, and to rebuild the dying alliance with Spain against France. If Spain would allow England to trade freely with the West Indies, England would do what Spain appeared incapable of doing, protect the West Indian possessions, and she would thereby strengthen her own economy by the increase in trade, and her defences against the French and Mary Stuart.

Hawkins at the age of 32 sailed from Plymouth on 18 October 1564, in command of a fleet consisting of the royal ship, the *Jesus*, and three Plymouth vessels, the property of Hawkins, the *Saloman*, 130 tons, the *Tiger*, 50, and the *Swallow*, 30 (not the same as the ship on the first voyage). The total tonnage was 910: the total of the crews was 150, of which 80 sailed in the *Jesus*. Hawkins took only one man to every six tons, a great reduction on the normal, which resulted in his losing from disease not more than a dozen seamen. The orders he issued to the ships were 'Serve God daily (i.e. daily prayers), love one another (i.e. no quarrelling), preserve your victuals (i.e. no wasting), beware of fire and keep good fellowship (i.e. sail close together)'.

After being delayed for five days at Ferrol by contrary winds he went to Teneriffe and thence to Sierra Leone to pick up slaves. He reached San Domingo on 9 March, Margarita on the 16th and he called at Barburata in Venezuela. In all these places the Spanish wanted to trade, but the law was against them: therefore Hawkins had to go through the collusive farce of making a show of force so that the Spaniards could plead afterwards that they had been compelled to trade. Twice also, so treacherous were some of the Spanish governors, Hawkins had to make a real demonstration of force, notably at Rio de la Hacha, where Hawkins landed an armed force, 'standing in doubt of their courtesy'. But he was able to sell all his goods, including the slaves, for which he was paid in gold and silver in lump and also in worked precious metals. At Curacao he took on board a large cargo of hides, which commanded a high price in England, to the value of £2,000.

When he arrived in Florida, he found the French settlement under

Laudonnière in the direst want. He offered them a passage home, but Laudonnière refused it. He sold the *Tiger* to the French, and accepted payment in the form of a bill which he was never able to cash. Hawkins also gave them victuals. Laudonnière's gratitude took the form of a tribute that Hawkins 'has won the reputation of a good and charitable man, deserving to be esteemed as much of us all as if he had saved all our lives'.

Hawkins arrived home at Padstow on 20 September 1565. Details of the profits made on this voyage are missing, but the Spanish Ambassador reported to Philip II that the dividend was 60 per cent. The Queen was certainly satisfied, for she granted a coat of arms to Hawkins — sable, on a point wavy a lion passant or; in chief three bezants; for a crest, a demi-moor proper bound in a cord.

The third voyage, 1567. Of the three voyages this one was by far the largest in size and organization, in its objectives the most hazardous, in its commercial and financial results a failure, and in its political results momentous: it is hardly too much to say that it marks the end of one epoch and the opening of another.

The Queen was once again a shareholder, this time contributing two ships. The syndicate was large and impressive and the whole affair was both an important joint-stock company trading for financial profits and also an act of state, part and parcel of the foreign policy of the government. Cecil, says Williamson, played almost the part of managing director.

The total ships were the *Jesus of Lubeck*, 700 tons and even more rotten than in 1564, in spite of £500 worth of repairs, and the *Minion*, 300 tons, built in 1536, and said to be 'spent and rotten'. The brothers Hawkins contributed four ships — the *William and John*, 150, the *Swallow*, 100, the *Judith*, 50, the *Angel*, 33. The total tonnage was 1333, the total personnel was 408, or one man to 3 ¼ tons, a higher proportion than Hawkins approved of. Among the officers were Hampton and Francis Drake; also a nephew of John Hawkins, a young man named either Paul Hawkins or Horsewell. Drake began the voyage in command of the *Jesus*, but he transferred later to another ship.

Before Hawkins sailed from Plymouth he had proof that he could not expect anything but hostility from Spain during his voyage. A Flemish admiral, de Wachen, entered Plymouth harbour, went into the Cattewater, where lay Hawkins' ships, refused to dip his flags and tried to get as near as he could to the royal ships. Hawkins at once opened fire: the episode was eventually peaceably disposed of. But the omen was clear.

On 2 October 1567 Hawkins set sail with his six ships and 400 men. About seventy of those men were to return. In Sierra Leone he was invited by the king to join in an attack on the town of Conga. Hawkins agreed and after some fairly stiff fighting he was able to sail westwards on 7 February 1568, with a cargo of nearly 500 Negroes. As an offset he had lost eight or nine men killed, with a largish number of wounded.

He arrived at San Domingo at the end of March and went on to Margarita, where he spent nine days and had a friendly reception from the governor. From there he sailed for Barburata in Venezuela. Here, contrary to all expectations, Hawkins was able to spend two months and to trade very profitably. From Barburata he set out for Rio de la Hacha. Here he met with organized opposition and was forced to take the town by direct assault. All the population and all the wealth of the town had been moved inland as soon as Hawkins appeared. But the booty was betrayed by a renegade Negro slave, and Hawkins had it all put aboard his ships. Then he had an interview with the governor, Castellanos, who gave in and paid 4000 gold *pesos* belonging to Philip II for sixty slaves and 1000 *pesos* of his own for another twenty, after which trade was opened to everybody. One of Hawkins' gunners, Job Hortop, was much interested in the wild life which he met with, and on this voyage he studied the habits of alligators, catching one with a dog as live bait on a hook and chain (Williamson, *ib.*, p. 128).

The next port of call was Santa Marta, small but able to trade. The farce of a collusive landing in force had to be used here, after which Hawkins was able to sell more than 100 slaves and some English goods and to revictual the fleet.

From Santa Marta to Cartagena: here it became clear that a landing was impossible, for the place was strongly fortified. Since leaving England Hawkins had increased his fleet from the original six to ten vessels. At Cartagena he reduced it to eight and set out on the homeward voyage not intending to land anywhere else in the West Indies. It was July and he was anxious to get the *Jesus* clear of the Caribbean (Williamson, *ib.*, p. 131). The *Jesus* was in such a parlous state that most commanders would have abandoned her.

Hawkins did not. Nothing more clearly testifies to Hawkins as a loyal servant of the Queen than his dealing with the problem of the *Jesus*. She was the Queen's ship: if she were to be abandoned during the voyage, the loss would fall wholly on the Queen. If she had to be abandoned or repaired after returning home, the loss fell on the syndicate. (After the second voyage she had cost them £500.) As the Queen's servant Hawkins took a risk. It was essential to repair the *Jesus* and San Juan de Ulua was the only place to do it.

On 15 September Hawkins sighted San Juan. He was flying only the royal standard, but the colours were so faded that the Spanish officials mistook the flags for Spanish flags and assumed that the ships were the Spanish plate fleet. The anchorage was very small. An island of 240 yards lay parallel to the main coast and about five hundred yards from it, rising some three feet above the highest water level. On the island were some guns which commanded the port. If he was to be safe from treachery, Hawkins must get possession of the island. By good luck he did, because the port officials thought the fleet was the plate fleet and let it in without opposition. Hawkins arranged for victuals and for the payment for them: he sent word to Mexico to announce his arrival and to make clear that his intentions were peaceful (16 September). The real plate fleet was not expected before the end of the month. Hawkins had time to repair his ship and be gone. Next morning the plate fleet arrived. To prevent it from entering its own harbour would be an act of war. To let it enter was to run grave risks. Hawkins decided he must let the fleet in. An amicable arrangement was come to with the new governor, Don Martin Enriquez, and hostages were exchanged. But Enriquez from the beginning was planning treachery. The wind was unfavourable for an entry until 21 September. When the fleet was inside, there were twenty-eight ships in a much confined space. Enriquez plotted to transfer the pick of the Spanish crews on to a merchantman which could then be manhandled alongside the *Minion*. The English gunners on the island were to be surprised and knocked out and the guns turned on the English ships. Hawkins spotted the treachery and twice sent to Enriquez to protest against the movements which he saw taking place. The Viceroy arrested the English messenger the second time and blew the trumpets to launch his attack.

The ensuing battle lasted from ten in the morning to four in the afternoon. The Spaniards easily overran the English gunners on the island, but Hawkins got the *Minion* cleared from her anchors and withdrew from the island. It took longer for the *Jesus* to be hauled clear, but that too was accomplished. Hawkins then concentrated the fire of these two ships on the two Spanish fighting ships. He brought his guns to bear at point-blank range, sank the Spanish Admiral, and the vice-flagship was set on fire and burnt out. One merchantman also was destroyed. The Spanish sank the *Angel* and captured the *Swallow* and the Portuguese caravel. The *Grace of God* lost her mainmast and had to be abandoned. The *Judith*, commanded by Drake, got clear. The Spanish then tried to dislodge the English by means of fireships which caused a panic in the *Minion*'s men, who cast her off from the *Jesus*. As she began to move, the men on the *Jesus* made a rush to get aboard the *Minion*: Hawkins was the last to leave the *Jesus*.

The *Minion* did not go more than a quarter of a mile, but she was out of range of the island guns. With her was the *Judith*. Next morning the *Judith* was gone, and no one has ever to this day discovered why Drake left Hawkins alone. Hawkins had no food and the *Minion* was leaking. It is not possible to know precisely what his casualties amounted to, but he seems to have left San Juan with about 200 men. After a fortnight he landed all the men who wanted to risk their lives rather on land than on sea. He sailed for home on 16 October: on 31 December he entered the port of Vigo, where he bought victuals, but 'our men with excess of fresh meat grew into miserable diseases and died, a great part of them'. He picked up twelve new men from an English ship and set sail on 20 January 1569. He reached Mount's Bay on 25 January, sent a message to his brother at Plymouth and got from him a new crew to bring the *Minion* home.

The voyage had been a disaster, but it was not a financial failure. The records in the Admiralty Court shew that Hawkins transferred nearly all the treasure from the *Jesus* to the *Minion* and brought it safely to England.

Hawkins and the Ridolfi Plot.   Hawkins was left with a burning fury against Spain for the treachery at San Juan, the more inflamed by the treatment meted out (in Mexico and in Spain) to those of his crews who had been taken prisoners. He was determined to have his revenge for the treachery and to get the prisoners released.

In February 1570 a letter reached Cecil from George Fitzwilliam, one of Hawkins' imprisoned crews at Seville, asking for the government's help to get them released. Hawkins at once had several interviews with the Spanish Ambassador, Don Guereau de Spes. At this moment Fitzwilliam was released. Hawkins sent him to Madrid to interview Philip II (April 1571). Cecil was well aware that Spain was backing the Ridolfi plot for an invasion of England by Alva, the murder of Elizabeth and the enthronement of Mary, Queen of Scots, in her place. But he did not know the details. John Hawkins helped to unravel the plot.

Hawkins succeeded in gulling the foolish de Spes into believing that he was an ardent Catholic, that he wanted to see Mary, Queen of Scots, on the throne of England and that at the moment of invasion by the Spanish navy he would desert with all his ships to the side of Spain. All this was done with Cecil's knowledge and approval; de Spes and Philip were completely hoodwinked. Philip gave Hawkins a patent of Spanish nobility and a pardon for his offences in the West Indies, with a promise to pay for the upkeep of sixteen ships and 1,600 men for two months. Having concerted with Philip the exact plans for the invasion, Hawkins at once passed them on to Cecil, who was now able to bring together all the pieces in the puzzle — the part Alva was to play, the complicity of Mary Stuart's ambassador, the Bishop of Ross, the treachery of the Duke of Norfolk. Ross confessed all, Norfolk was executed and de Spes turned out of the country. Hawkins, the tough naval commander, was now revealed as the subtle diplomatist.

Hawkins and the New Navy. In 1571 Hawkins became M.P. for Plymouth. In 1573 he was all but murdered. He was riding along the Strand, when suddenly a man named Peter Burchett stabbed him, mistaking him for Sir Christopher Hatton, not because of any physical resemblance between Hawkins and Hatton, but probably because both always had a liking for specially fine clothes. The wound was severe, but Hawkins recovered and suffered no ill effects afterwards. In 1577 he succeeded his father-in-law, Sir Benjamin Gonson, as Treasurer of the Navy. For the next ten years Hawkins was taken up with reforming both the administration of the Navy and also the building of the ships themselves.

The men who formed the Navy Board belonged to a generation

which had seen service only in home waters. The only theatre of fighting which they could imagine was the Channel and the North Sea. For such fighting they believed in the old-fashioned ship, the floating castle, of which the *Jesus of Lubeck* was well known to Hawkins. These carracks rose out of the water and were made very unwieldy by the top-heavy castles which were built at the bow and stern in order to repel the enemy, if they were able to board the ship. Hawkins had seen at San Juan de Ulua how unserviceable and dangerous such a ship could be. Further, Hawkins had no intention of confining the war against Spain to the Channel and the North Sea: he intended to fight in the Atlantic, at the Azores, on the Coast of Spain and in the West Indies. For such warfare a new kind of ship was needed. Between 1570 and 1587 the design of the new ships was considerably modified. The evidence that this was wholly the work of Hawkins is not conclusive and some credit may have to be given to Wynter and the rest of the Navy Board. But it is difficult not to feel that the drive towards such a reform must have come from the experienced Hawkins. What Hawkins wanted was ships that could sail much nearer the wind than the old 'round ship', so that they could choose their own range for fighting. Therefore the length of the keel was increased and the ship was what we should call today streamlined. The proportions of the ships built at the Deptford yard were usually three or three and a half times their breadth in the length on keel, or four times their breadth over the whole length of the ship. This gave speed and manoeuvrability, which was increased by cutting down the towering upper works on deck. These were only needed for close fighting, but Hawkins's plan was to increase the armament of the ships and to fight at long range. The ships, therefore, rolled less in heavy weather and greater use could be made of the gun-ports on the lower decks. The enemy was never to be allowed to board, therefore the guns in the upper works were unnecessary.

The ships were more heavily armed — an improvement which was probably the work of Wynter, but of which Hawkins highly approved. A typical example of this new sort of ship is the *Revenge*, which was built in 1575. She was of 450 tons, 92 feet long, 32 feet broad, carrying forty-six guns in all. She remained the model for all English ships for the next three hundred years.

In what may be called the interior economy of the ships Hawkins was a pioneer. He refused to crowd the ships with men. The normal ratio was one man to every one and a half tons, but Hawkins preferred one man to two tons. This reform made the seaworthiness of a fleet greater, since victuals and drink lasted longer. Victuals for one man for four months occupied one ton of stowage: guns, ammunition, etc. had to be allowed for: thus to reduce the number of men to one man for every two tons added fifty per cent. to the time a fleet could stay at sea.

Hawkins also increased the pay of the men from 6s. 8d. to 10s. per month. He was greatly interested in hygiene. In 1586 he introduced into his own ships apples and pears and he kept live pigs and sheep on board. On his last voyage in 1595 he experimented with 'lasting victuals, a new kind of victuals for sea service devised by Mr Hugh Platte, 4 barrels at £4. 10s the barrel'. On this voyage he also took with him 927 'Brasill Beds', probably hammocks copied from a pattern used by the Indians in Guiana, which was looked on as part of Brazil — hence the name 'Brasill beds'.

Hawkins and the Two Bargains. In 1577/8, just after he had become Treasurer of the Navy, Hawkins made a report to Burghley on the corruption which he found rampant in the dockyards. The Queen was being made to pay £9,000 for materials and not £4,000 worth was used in her service. The difference went 'for Sir William Wynter's commodity'. Similarly she was paying for good timber for repairs to her ships, but the repairs were being carried out in rotten timber, while the good was used for other people's private ships. As a result of this report a new system was instituted in 1597 in the First Bargain.

This Bargain comprised two agreements: one between the Queen and Hawkins, by which Hawkins undertook to provide at his own expense all the ropes, cables, hawsers and other gear, for which he was to be paid £1,200 p.a. without having to render detailed accounts, but his work was to be supervised and a report sent in to Burghley: another between the Queen and Pett and Baker, the master-shipwrights, who undertook a regular routine of inspection and repairs of the ships at their own expense, for which they were paid £1,000 p.a. and their work was also to be supervised.

Hawkins saw that war was imminent. He wanted to save the Queen £4,000 which was being wasted by dishonest contractors; to make her unsound ships into sound ships; and to fit the fleet for trans-oceanic service. Naturally enough those who lost by the new system never stopped accusing Hawkins of robbing the Queen and of ruining the ships, but an enquiry in 1583 into the state of the navy exonerated Hawkins.

The Second Bargain was struck in 1585. By it the agreement between the Queen and the master-shipwrights was ended. Hawkins now undertook to do all the repairs to ships afloat or grounded, pay all the wages involved in administering this work, to find all the materials, victuals and lodgings involved. For this he was to receive £4,000 p.a. In addition he undertook to do all the heavy repairs and to find all the materials, wages, etc. For this he was to be paid £1,714 2s. 2d. p.a. Hawkins thus became responsible for the upkeep of the whole Royal Navy, but the armaments were not included. Again he was relentlessly pursued by those who lost their illegal profits by his reforms. The justification for his policy and the integrity of his character were revealed in the efficient state of the fleet when it sailed against the Armada.

Hawkins as a strategist. It is a mistake to regard Hawkins solely as an active naval commander and an administrator in business and commerce or of the Royal Navy. He was also a man whose 'wide-ranging mind' (Williamson) included within its purview the strategical conduct of the war. Hawkins held that Philip II depended on his American treasure to save him from bankruptcy. Therefore, if sea-power were brought to bear on the Atlantic trade routes, Philip would be ruined, England would be safe. Hawkins rejected all idea of military invasions, because England had no army and military adventures were expensive for a country which had no money to spare. He therefore relied on purely naval warfare, which might be made to a large extent to pay for itself.

Hawkins and the Spanish Armada. When the Armada set sail from Spain, Hawkins could not at once leave the Navy Board, and it was June before he joined the fleet at Plymouth. Here he took command of the *Victory*, one of his new ships. He ranked third in seniority below Howard and Drake, and he was a member of the war council which Howard consulted 'on every question of moment'. When the fleet moved out towards Ushant, Hawkins was in command of the in-shore squadron towards the Scilly Isles. He took part in all the engagements with the Armada as it sailed up the Channel, and on Friday, 26 July he was knighted by Howard on board the *Ark Royal*. The fight between Portland and the Isle of Wight had revealed weaknesses in the organization of the English fleet, which was now formed into four squadrons, one of which was under the command of Hawkins. By the time the English fleet left contact with the Armada and abandoned it to destruction by wind and wave Hawkins's policy as Treasurer of the Navy had been fully justified: not one of the English ships had fallen out of the fight owing to damage by the sea or by the enemy.

Hawkins's post-Armada voyages. After the defeat of the Armada Hawkins had a year's leave in order to deal with the naval accounts. In 1591 his wife died, but he soon married again; his new wife was called Margaret Vaughan. In 1592 he founded an almshouse at Chatham, known as Sir John Hawkins' Hospital, and it survives today.

Hawkins made two voyages after the Armada. In 1590 he organized an expedition in two squadrons: one squadron of six of the Queen's galleons under Frobisher sailed for the Azores, victualled for four months, while a second squadron of six under Hawkins, victualled for six months, sailed for the Spanish coast. When Philip heard of it, he cancelled all sailings from the West Indies, so that Frobisher and Hawkins could take only a few prizes, which paid for some of the expenses of the fleets.

In 1595 Hawkins and Drake sailed in a fleet which was put under the joint command of both. This was a joint-stock company in which the Queen took shares. Its purpose was to land a force at Nombre de Dios, march across the isthmus and capture Panama. But in August news came which caused them to change their objective — that the flagship of the plate fleet was lying damaged in San Juan de Puerto Rico. Hawkins and Drake sailed from Plymouth on 28 August with the intention of capturing the treasure and bringing it straight home. The voyage was a disaster. The joint command was a great mistake: Hawkins and Drake were men of wholly different character and they never succeeded in establishing a unity of command by which alone the voyage could succeed. They quarrelled, they wasted time and opportunities, and Spain meanwhile was taking counter-measures. One of the English ships, the small *Francis*, was taken by the Spanish, revealing that Puerto Rico was the destination of the fleet. Spanish reinforcements sailed at once for Puerto Rico. The game was up. On 31 October Hawkins fell ill and he died on 12 November 1595. He was buried at sea.

Character of Hawkins. Modern research has discredited the hostile views about Hawkins which appear in J.K.Laughton's article in the *D.N.B.* The nineteenth-century historians were writing just at the time when public opinion loathed the idea of slaves and slavery. If Hawkins was capable of trafficking in slaves, he was capable of any other sort of dishonesty and cruelty. But in fact in dealing in slaves Hawkins was only doing what public opinion of his own day approved. He was a product of the Tudor age, a man of diversified abilities. He was a consummate seaman, a bold and skilful navigator, a first-class businessman, an original designer of ships and of strategy, in a corrupt age an uncorrupt administrator of the Navy, a politician and diplomatist who could outwit a foreign ambassador, single-minded in his devotion to the Queen. He was also a man of fashion, well educated, able to write clearly technical memoranda for Burghley, finely dressed, one who moved as easily in the company of Kings and courtiers as he did with sailors and contractors. He could command strict discipline among his crews, yet at the same time command their affection and respect. In religion he was, to begin with, an orthodox Catholic, but as the years went by and the fierceness of the war increased, he became gradually more and more Protestant, so that his letters towards the end have a Puritan ring about them. Like most people of his time, at any rate in the later years, and like Oliver Cromwell after him, he identified the enemies of his country with the enemies of God. There is a steadiness about him, a determination to order things carefully and methodically, leaving nothing to chance, which contrasts strongly with the haphazard way in which Drake left everything to the inspiration of the moment. Drake was a genius whose exploits have won for him immortal fame, but it is doubtful whether he contributed more to the defeat of Spain and the salvation of England than his less famous, but not less devoted patriot, Sir John Hawkins.

J.A. Williamson, *Hawkins of Plymouth*, 1949.

M. Lewis, 'Fresh Light on San Juan de Ulua', in *Mariner's Mirror*, July 1937.

I.A. Wright, *Caribbean Documents*.

Raynor Unwin, *The Defeat of John Hawkins*, 1960.

SIR RICHARD HAWKINS (1560–1622), merchant and naval commander, was the only child of Sir John Hawkins and his first wife, Katherine Gonson. Nothing is known of his early life, which must have been spent mainly among ships and commerce, until he appears in history as Vice-Admiral in command of a ship in the voyage made by his uncle, William Hawkins (the second) in 1582–3. In his *Observations*, which were written between 1602 and 1603 and which were being printed at the moment of his death in 1622, Richard records, 'In anno 1582, in the island of Margarita, I was at the dredging of pearl oysters, after the manner we dredge oysters in England; and with mine own hands I opened many and took out the pearls, some greater, some less, and in good quantity'. It was on this voyage that one of the captains reported his ship, *Bark Bonner*, to be leaking so badly that he advised she should be abandoned. A council of captains agreed, but Richard opposed them and undertook to sail the ship home with a crew of volunteers, on condition that they were paid one third of her value as salvage. The *Bark Bonner*'s captain was shamed into sailing her home himself.

Richard next appears in command of the galliot *Duck*, 20 tons, in Drake's expedition to the West Indies, 1585–6. All that is known of him on this voyage is that he suffered from a severe attack of fever, but he learned a valuable lesson from this experience, as also from his father's interest in hygiene. Of the Cape Verde Islands he wrote, 'in two times that I have been in them, either cost us the one half of our people with fevers and fluxes of sundry kinds'. When he himself came to lead an expedition (1593), he refused to land at the Cape Verde Islands.

It is likely enough that Richard accompanied Drake on his 1587 raid on the Armada ports in Spain, but there is no evidence that he did. In that year he sold some guns to Plymouth for its defence. He fought in the English fleet against the Armada in 1588 in command of the Queen's *Swallow*, 350 tons. Two of his private merchant-men were used as fireships at Calais.

When his father, John Hawkins, sailed for the Spanish coast in

1590, Richard went with him, and we owe it to Richard that we know that the rate of mortality on that voyage during six months at sea was much below the average on previous voyages, a sure tribute to John Hawkins' foresight and understanding.

In 1592, according to Richard, there was afoot a project to capture Nombre de Dios and Panama. This plan came to nothing, but it spurred Richard on to build up an enterprise which was to eclipse all previous transatlantic expeditions. He had immediately after the defeat of the Armada (1588) laid down a galleon of his own of about 350 tons. His object was to make a complete survey of eastern Asia, where he was ambitious to plant an English trading empire. He planned to sail through the Straits of Magellan, pay his overhead expenses by plundering the treasure towns of Peru, refit in California and then cross the Pacific to eastern Asia. Hawkins described his ship as 'pleasing to the eye, profitable for stowage, good of sail and well conditioned'. His mother, on being asked to christen the ship, gave it the name of *Repentance,* since for those seeking the port of Heaven repentance was the best ship. Later Queen Elizabeth insisted on the name being changed to *Dainty.* In April 1593 Richard sailed the *Dainty* from the Thames to Plymouth. Late in May he was ready to go, but a gale destroyed *Dainty*'s mainmast, so that he did not get away until 12 June 1593. He was away ten years and never again saw his father.

He followed the normal course across the Atlantic, but he avoided the Atlantic islands after his experience in 1585. Presently he arrived at land which he took to be the Atlantic coast of *Terra Australis Incognita,* but it was in fact the Falkland Islands. He got through the Straits of Magellan in forty-six days (Drake had passed through them in sixteen days), and he intended to sail north until he was above Callao before attacking any Spanish towns. But his men were mutinous and compelled him to attack at once and win treasure. Richard does not seem to have had the complete control over his men which was one of the great gifts his father possessed. Richard gave in and attacked Valparaiso. Some gold was taken, but the news of his arrival in Spanish waters quickly spread. The Viceroy of Peru sent out six ships and 2,000 men against *Dainty* and her 75. The first encounter was lucky but ominous. Richard soon found that the Spanish had devised a new and faster ship for the defence of their towns than they had had in the pre-Armada days. They were heavily armed, much more heavily than *Dainty*. They were more nimble to manoeuvre and could easily take the weather gauge from Richard's ship. Thanks to good luck with the weather Richard escaped at the first meeting. The men were still out of hand and insisted on chasing worthless prizes. At the Bay of Atacames the Spaniards fell in with the English again. The result was a foregone conclusion. After a fearful battering at close range for three days on end *Dainty* was sinking and there were only twenty out of her seventy-five men left unhurt. Hawkins still fought on, but when nineteen of his men were killed and forty wounded, there was nothing for it but to surrender, which Hawkins did on condition that the men were sent back to England (22 June 1594). Hawkins himself was severely wounded and he was taken as a prisoner for Peru. Here he lived for three years, loved by everybody. His men were sent to Spain and after three years were released. It is likely enough that while he was in Peru he conformed to the Catholic religion, but this was not a genuine conversion: once he got back to England he was soon hunting down Catholics. After three years in Peru he was transferred to Spain: he tried to escape and was caught and was imprisoned in Madrid. He was promised release if he would pay a ransom of £3,000. He had the money at home, but it was in the hands of his stepmother and she refused to remit any of it. Eventually the ransom was paid, perhaps through the good offices of Robert Cecil, and Richard Hawkins was freed in 1602.

On the accession of James I Hawkins was knighted and made Vice-Admiral of Devon. He was Mayor of Plymouth (1603–4) and was one of the Members of Parliament for the town. In 1622 he took part in a bungled expedition against the Barbary pirates and on his return he suddenly died. His widow, Judith, survived him for seven years.

A great deal of new evidence on Richard Hawkins became available after the article in the *D.N.B.* was written. This is summarized in J. A. Williamson's *Hawkins of Plymouth* (1949). The documents are printed by the Hakluyt Society, edited by Miss Wright. The *Observations of Sir Richard Hawkins* have been edited and published by J. A. Williamson (1933).

SIR FRANCIS DRAKE (1543?–1596), navigator and naval captain, was born at Crowndale near Tavistock in Devon, probably in 1543. His father, Edmund Drake, had been a sailor, then a yeoman farmer and a staunch Protestant. After the rising in the south-west in 1549 the family escaped to Gillingham in Kent, where Edmund became a preacher to the sailors and naval workmen at the new naval station on the Medway, later to become Chatham. Francis was thus brought up among ships and sailors and he learned to become a fanatical Protestant.

The first transatlantic voyage Drake made was in 1566. At the age of twenty-four he joined a small expedition, financed by his cousin John Hawkins, under the command of Captain John Lovell, which went to the Spanish Main. At Rio de la Hacha the governor tricked Lovell into landing ninety Negroes whom Lovell himself had stolen from Portuguese ships, and then the governor refused to pay for them. Nevertheless, the expedition made a fair profit.

In 1567 Hawkins sailed on his third slave-trading voyage and took Drake with him in the *Jesus of Lubeck*. Drake does not appear to the best advantage, for after the battle was over he sailed home in the *Judith* and left Hawkins to fend for himself. Hawkins accused him of deserting him, but the facts of the case are not now fully known and the quarrel was soon made up.

Drake now set himself to destroy the Spanish monopoly in the New World and to defend English Protestantism against Philip II. He early saw that Philip's strength depended on the treasure which he drew from Mexico and Peru. Drake also realized that the key to this treasure-house was the Isthmus of Panama, the only line of communication between the Peruvian port of Lima on the Pacific side and Nombre de Dios on the Atlantic side. If he could get control of Panama and Nombre de Dios, the supply of Peruvian silver would dry up and the flow of Mexican gold could be seriously interfered with.

Drake's next three voyages were all directed to this main objective. That of 1570–1 was only a voyage of reconnaissance to discover the exact route of the treasure-train from Panama to Nombre de Dios. The voyage of 1572 aimed at the capture of Nombre de Dios and of the treasure-train. The town was easily taken, but Drake was wounded and carried off by his men before any of the treasure in Nombre de Dios could be collected. The attack on the train, after a first failure, was a complete success and when Drake arrived home at Plymouth on Sunday, 9 August 1573, the whole congregation turned out of the church to greet him — 'few or none remained with the preacher'.

Drake arrived just at the moment when the Queen was trying to patch up a reconciliation with Philip of Spain. The danger was that Philip might demand as one of his terms the return of all Drake's plunder and the execution of Drake as a pirate. Somebody warned Drake to disappear, which he did so successfully that we know nothing about him for the next two years. Then in 1575 he turned up in Ireland serving with Essex's army. In 1576 he returned to England, bringing with him Thomas Doughty, a friend of Leicester and soon to be an acquaintance of Burghley, perhaps even his spy in Drake's next voyage, the voyage of circumnavigation of 1577 to 1580. This voyage was undoubtedly intended to carry the unofficial war into the Pacific Ocean and to the west coast of the Spanish-American colonies, whatever other reasons were made public, such as the shipping of currants from Alexandria. Drake had the Queen's secret permission to engage in piracy on Spanish ships. Another motive for the expedition was to seek the Pacific end of the North-West Passage.

The expedition consisted of the *Pelican*, 120 tons and 18 guns, the *Elizabeth*, 80 + 16, the *Marigold*, 30 + 16, the *Benedict* (a pinnace), the *Swan*, 50 + 5, a store ship, and in all about 160 men who set sail from Plymouth in December 1577. In the Atlantic Drake captured a Portuguese ship which he put in the charge of Doughty, a well-educated, but a crooked and unreliable man. Soon Drake was aware that Doughty was stirring up trouble in his ship; Drake therefore moved him to the *Pelican*, but there Doughty began to preach mutiny to the crew, whereupon Drake sent him as a prisoner to the *Swan*. Then came strange weather, fogs and calms alternating with gales. In accordance with the views of the times, Drake and many others were persuaded that Doughty was using magic to ruin the voyage. When Drake announced that the expedition was going to raid the Spanish coast, the gentlemen-adventurers grew discontented, having believed that they were going on a voyage of discovery and in search of trade. The safety of the whole expedition was at stake. Drake took stern measures. When they arrived at Port St. Julian, where Magellan many years before had executed the leaders of a mutiny, Drake set up a jury to try Doughty. He was found guilty of having betrayed the plan of the expedition to Burghley and of stirring up mutiny among the crews. He was sentenced to death: then, in the, to us, strange manner of the times, Drake and Doughty dined together and received the Sacrament and Doughty was then beheaded. The whole trial may have been very irregular, but there is no doubt that the sentence was just and saved the lives of many who would have perished, if mutiny had prevailed.

Some weeks later Drake dealt with the sailors and the gentlemen. At a Sunday service he preached the sermon himself. He openly attacked all in the fleet, the sailors for being mutinous, the gentlemen for shirking their share of the work. 'My masters, I must have it left. I must have the gentleman to haul and draw with the mariner, and the mariner with the gentleman. I would know him that would refuse to set his hand to a rope.' Then, after this direct challenge, came the unexpected compliment, 'but I know there is not any such here'. He then dismissed all the captains and masters from their posts, and he told the men that any of them could go home who wanted to and he would provide a ship for the purpose, but absolute loyalty and obedience he would have from those who stayed. Not a man volunteered to leave him. The mutiny was quashed, peace restored, the officers reinstated. The whole episode illustrates Drake's character, his sternness where sternness was vital, his lack of rancour against the chief villain, his capacity for softening straight talk with a tactful compliment. By such means did he win the hearts of his followers.

On 21 August 1578 the *Pelican* (now renamed the *Golden Hind* in honour of Sir Christopher Hatton, a principal shareholder in the expedition, whose cognizance was a golden hind), the *Elizabeth* and the *Marigold* entered the Straits of Magellan. Luck must have been with him, for Drake got through in the record time of 16 days. At once the weather deteriorated for several weeks; the *Marigold* lost touch and was never seen again; John Winter in the *Elizabeth* took refuge in the Straits and then returned home. We now know that he did not desert Drake, that he intended to try to meet him in the Pacific, but his men refused and compelled him to go back to England.

When the weather improved Drake turned north to plunder the Spanish colonies. At Valdivia he took a ship heavily laden with gold and on the way up the coast he took many more. At Callao he heard that a great treasure-ship had just sailed for Panama. This was the

Sir Francis Drake
(Artist: Studio of Nicholas Hilliard)

so-called *Cacafuego* (Spitfire, or something less decent). He easily overtook and overpowered it, ransacked it, set it free and gave its captain a safe-conduct, in case he fell in with Winter. Going on northwards Drake reached Nicaragua and took on board provisions at Guatalco. He then made for California and reached latitude 38°, where in a now unknown harbour he refitted and in July 1579 set out for home. But before he went he took possession of California in the Queen's name, called it New Albion, and set up a brass plate announcing the annexation.

On the way home he called at the Moluccas and made a treaty

with the Sultan of Ternate, promising to the English a monopoly of the spice trade — a promise which influenced the founding of the East India Company in 1600. After being almost wrecked on a submerged reef, the *Golden Hind* reached Java and then turned for home. Drake arrived at Plymouth in September 1580. He had been away almost three years and he brought back with him treasure which paid a dividend of 1,400 per cent. on the initial outlay of the expedition.

Elizabeth was delighted with the financial success of the voyage, especially as it was at the expense of Spain. She brought the *Golden Hind* to London, where crowds came to see the ship. She herself in April 1581 went on board with the French Ambassador who, at the Queen's command, knighted Drake, whose reputation was now at its height. In 1584 it was clear that war with Spain was likely, and Elizabeth was ready to get in the first blow. A strong expedition was fitted out to attack the Spanish possessions in the West Indies, and Drake was put in command. This was an official voyage, and Drake sailed as the Queen's Admiral (1585). He had with him two of the Queen's ships and 27 other ships belonging to private investors in the venture. These carried 2,300 men, who included twelve companies of soldiers for service on land. Martin Frobisher went as second-in-command, Walsingham's step-son, Christopher Carleill, went as a soldier. The purpose of the expedition was to do the maximum amount of damage to Philip II's source of strength, the wealth from his colonial possessions. The treasure-fleet was to be captured, if possible: the towns on the Spanish Main were to be destroyed, and perhaps even a garrison might be left in one of them as a permanent threat to the Peruvian and Mexican treasure.

Drake sailed from Plymouth in September 1585, and he was home again late in July 1586. In that time, although he lost three hundred men from fever while he crossed the Atlantic, he sacked Santo Domingo in Hispaniola but succeeded in extracting only a small sum as ransom. His next objective was Cartagena, the most important of the towns on the Main. The attack was completely successful, Drake dismantled the defences and carried off the guns. He was paid £30,000 as a ransom and took much more by way of pillage, and he left the town derelict. This would have been the place to garrison, but Drake rightly came to the conclusion that it would have been too difficult to reinforce it. He was most anxious to go on and capture Panama, but sickness broke out again among his men and he had to give up the idea. He set out for home through the Florida channel and would certainly have attacked Havana in Cuba, the point at which the plate fleets assembled on their way home to Spain, but his fighting strength was so much reduced by death and sickness that again he had to abandon the idea. But he captured the Spanish settlement at St. Augustine on the mainland of Florida and took all the guns and money. It is reckoned that, all told, Drake brought away 240 Spanish guns and thereby may have seriously weakened the armament of the Armada, for Spain could not herself manufacture guns and had to pay high prices for them in Italy or even to smuggle them out of England. On his way home he called in at Virginia and found Ralph Lane and his colonists in great distress; therefore he gave them a passage home.

The expedition did not pay for its expenses, but Drake had greatly damaged the Spanish. Had the Queen followed up this voyage with another swift attack under Drake on Panama, perhaps the Spanish invasion of England would not have been possible. But she did not, and the Spanish American colonies were able to recover, as Drake was home again. It was clear to all that only a direct attack on the Spanish ports and shipping would, at best prevent, at worst delay the sailing of the Armada.

Of Drake's exploits, the voyage of circumnavigation was probably the most remarkable — it put England and Drake on the map. The attacks on the Spanish Main in 1585 were immensely valuable, but they were incomplete, through no fault of Drake's. The 'singeing of His Catholic Majesty's Beard' (1587), was probably the most audacious and the most valuable of all the deeds that Drake did for England. The audaciousness is testified to by the opinions of the Spanish; the value, by the time it gave England to meet the Armada. Everybody knew that 1587 was the advertised date for the sailing of the Armada. Drake compelled Philip to postpone the sailing until 1588.

Drake's orders in 1587 were to 'impeach' and 'distress' the King of Spain's ships inside his ports. Twenty-seven ships, including four of the Queen's, and about 2,200 men sailed from Plymouth in April 1587, in so great a hurry that the victualling was not completed: Drake was afraid that the Queen might change her mind, as in fact she did, but too late — Drake was gone. He reached Cadiz on the

19th and at once sailed into the harbour and wrought immense havoc among the 80 ships he found there. His Vice-Admiral, Borough, was so outraged at such dangerous and unorthodox methods, taken without first summoning a council of war, that he took his ship out of Cadiz and refused to co-operate. The Spanish losses were at least 24 ships and may have been 37.

The larger part of the Armada was in Lisbon, but Drake knew that that was too strong a port to be captured. He therefore sailed to Cape St. Vincent in order to cut off supplies to that harbour. An attack on Lagos found that place too strong to be taken, but at Sagres Drake personally led the attack and captured the fort, which gave him a harbour near St. Vincent. Here again Borough refused to join in such unorthodox warfare and Drake made him a prisoner in the *Golden Hind*, Borough's ship. An attempt to lure the Spanish Admiral, Santa Cruz, out of Lisbon by taunts and insults failed, whereupon Drake went back to St. Vincent. Here he captured a whole year's supply of staves for making barrels, so that when the Armada sailed the casks were made of unseasoned wood and leaked badly. He also destroyed the tunny fisheries on which the Armada depended for its supply of fish.

Hearing of the approach of a plate ship, Drake sailed for the Azores, where he fell in at exactly the right moment with the *San Felipe*, which he easily overpowered, and he brought back to England her cargo, which was valuable enough to pay the costs of his expedition twice over. He arrived at Plymouth on 26 June 1587. More valuable than the wealth and the papers which he had captured giving the secrets of the Indian trade was the delay he had imposed on the sailing of the Armada. Furthermore, he had now achieved such a moral ascendancy over the Spanish that they not only regarded him as the Devil, but they were convinced that he used a magic mirror which enabled him to watch the movements of men and ships in any part of the world. When the Armada sailed in 1588, it sailed with an inferiority complex. (J. S. Corbett, *Papers Relating to the Spanish War, 1585–7*, Navy Record Society, vol. xi, for the most interesting account.)

Undoubtedly Drake was now the greatest seaman in the world, and one would expect him to have commanded the English fleet against the Armada. But in the sixteenth century by convention a commander of a national fleet had to be a grandee: and there was a sounder reason than mere convention: the great seamen like Drake, Hawkins, Frobisher, were men of the same social standing and would not necessarily be ready to take orders from one of their own class, whereas all would obey an outstanding member of the aristocracy. For this reason the Lord High Admiral, Howard of Effingham, was put in command of the English fleet, and Drake accepted the appointment cheerfully and loyally.

Had Howard and Drake had their way, they would have sought out the Armada in Spain and fought it in Spanish waters rather than allow it to reach the Channel. The Queen disapproved; she feared the Armada might give the English fleet the slip and arrive in the Channel unopposed. The difficulty in victualling the ships and the vagaries of the wind also made it hazardous for the English to sail too far from the Channel. Between the first sailing of the Armada on 18 May 1588 and its arrival off the Lizard on 19 July, Howard three times put out to sea to search for the Armada and three times was driven back by the wind. Drake was the most vehement supporter of the offensive and he was perfectly right, but he could not get his own way. That Drake was in favour of finishing a game of bowls on Plymouth Hoe before attacking the Spanish is so out of keeping with his impetuous character that the story must be rejected, but it may live on as a proof of Drake's unshakable confidence in the outcome of the battle.

The Armada was off Plymouth on the 20th and the English fleet was caught inside the harbour. Howard got the ships warped out during the night and was to windward of the Spanish in the early morning of the 21st. The Spanish fleet sailed, not in crescent formation, rather in that of an arrow-head or fish-tail (or, as one foreign historian called it, an 'eagle'). The English were in one unit in close-hauled line ahead, while the Spanish were in three divisions, each line abreast. Medina Sidonia's instructions were not to engage the English, unless it became necessary, or to land on the coast, though he might capture an English harbour, if that proved possible: his main purpose was to carry the Armada up the Channel in order to make contact with Parma in the Netherlands and to transport his army across the water to invade England. Howard could not know this, and he rightly feared a landing or an attack on one of the Channel ports. The fighting on the 21st achieved little more than 'we put them to leeward, kept the weather of them and distressed two of their best ships' (Howard). During the night Drake was to lead the English line and keep a light at his stern for the others to follow. Suddenly Drake put out his light and disappeared in the darkness: thus the English lost touch with the enemy. He was for long accused of having gone off in order to capture a Spanish ship (he did in fact capture the *Nuestra Senora del Rosario*, but he fell in with her the next day accidentally), but we now know that he saw some ships sailing to the windward and he thought they were Spanish ships trying to get the weather gauge of the English. He went to investigate and found they were neutral merchantmen.

The next engagement took place on the 23rd between Portland and the Isle of Wight. Drake played a leading part in this. The wind had been NNE, to the advantage of the Spaniards, but it suddenly shifted to SSW Drake got to the windward of the Armada, flung himself at them, cut off Recalde and then joined Howard in attacking Sidonia. The Spanish fleet was soundly beaten, but the English gunpowder ran out and Howard had to break off the action.

Howard decided that the formation in which they had been fighting was too loose and uncontrolled. He reorganized his fleet into four squadrons: Frobisher was in command of the left, next to him was Hawkins, then Howard, with Drake in charge of the right. On the 25th Hawkins and Drake tried to drive the Spanish vanguard (*i.e.* the right rear ships) on to the Owers sandbanks and caused great havoc among them: unfortunately Howard and Frobisher were not so successful with the rearguard (*i.e.* the Spanish left rear ships) and the Armada was able to make its way on up the Channel. (The pace was very slow, not more than two miles an hour.) When the Armada reached Calais, Sidonia heard that Parma could not be ready for him for a week. He was compelled to anchor in the dangerous roadstead of Gravelines in bad weather. Lord Henry Seymour now left his watching of the Narrows and joined Howard. It was decided to dislodge the Armada by the use of fireships, and Drake was the first to offer some of his own ships for the purpose. Panic seized the Spanish, they cut their cables and fled in the utmost confusion. The English attacked at once, but the old-fashioned Howard broke out of the fleet in order to capture a galleass stranded on the French coast. Thus Drake led the attack, drew up to short range and poured his fire into Sidonia's ship, then turned NE to prevent the Armada from reforming, while Hawkins dealt with the rest of the ships. The defection of Howard was felt at this point, for alone Drake could not prevent some ships from re-forming, but the bulk of the Armada was scattered to leeward along the French coast. A running fight ensued, but just at the moment when the English were about to destroy the Armada, a storm blew up from the West and the English had to break off the action. But the Armada was in fact defeated and when the wind shifted to the South the fleet had to crawl North, with its ships unworkable as a result of the last fighting and of the damage done in the confusion caused by the fireships. The English were now short of powder and short of food and therefore they turned for home, leaving the Armada to its fate on the Scottish and Irish coasts.

For once, Elizabeth was ready to follow up the victory with a view to preventing a second Armada. She wanted to intercept the Spanish treasure-fleet, as being the cheapest and most profitable method of warfare. Hawkins urged a permanent squadron cruising off the Azores. Drake argued for capturing Lisbon and putting Don Antonio, the claimant, on to the Portuguese throne. He was allowed to have his way, but his star was waning and he was never again to know the resounding successes which had been his up to the defeat of the Armada.

The Lisbon expedition of 1589 was a failure. The preparations for the voyage were drawn out and consumed valuable time. There was confusion over the purpose of the expedition: Drake understood its main purpose to be an attack on Lisbon and underestimated the difficulties of such a scheme. The Queen was more concerned to destroy the remnants of the Armada which were gathered in the ports of Northern Spain — a less spectacular but probably sounder purpose. In the event, the fleet failed to achieve either goal. The soldiers were under the command of Sir John Norris, and he never fully co-operated with Drake. The attack on Corunna in Northern Spain wasted time and had no valuable results: the land battle at El Burgo was an arid victory: by the time the expedition reached Lisbon, which had been totally unprepared and must have fallen, if Drake had been allowed to go there first of all, it had put its defences in order and was ready for an attack. Drake realized this and strongly opposed Norris's plan that the fleet should land the army at Peniche, that the army should then march 50 miles to Lisbon and raise the country in favour of Don Antonio, and Drake should take the fleet round by sea, enter the Tagus and be prepared to re-embark the army after it had taken Lisbon. Drake disliked being separated from the army; he argued rightly that, even if the wind were fair for the fleet to sail up the Tagus, it might change at any moment and leave the ships unable to get to sea again. And if the army by any chance came to grief, it might well need the help of the fleet before either of them reached Lisbon, or worse still after the fleet was in the Tagus and before the army was in Lisbon. Norris insisted on his plan: Drake hung about Cascaes until he got news that Norris was at Lisbon: he at once made plans for forcing the harbour and was on the point of entering when he got fresh news that Norris was in retreat. Drake took the fleet to Cascaes and found the army there, in desperate straits. Norris had lost many men on the march to Lisbon and of those left, a third were unfit for duty. The army's only artillery were the guns on the ships, and these he had left behind; therefore he could not breach the walls of Lisbon. He had no transport and he found no enthusiasm in Portugal for Don Antonio. Drake's judgment had been vindicated in every respect.

It was necessary for the expedition to pay for itself. Drake therefore set off for the Azores in hopes of capturing a treasure ship. But a terrific storm broke up his fleet and he only just got back into Plymouth after a complete failure. He was court-martialled, but acquitted, but for the next five years he was in disgrace with the Queen. He retired to live at his Devon home of Buckland Abbey. Old age was settling down on all the great figures of the last thirty years, including in some respects the Queen herself. Spain was gradually rebuilding her energies, her morale and her ships, so that Philip was in a position twice again to threaten invasion: only bad weather destroyed his hopes. He and his commanders learned much about strengthening the defences of their overseas possessions, although some historians doubt this. At last, in 1595, Elizabeth agreed to an expedition to intercept the treasure-fleet and she gave the joint command of it to Drake and Hawkins. It was a fatal mistake — fatal to divide the command, fatal to share it between two men who were so wholly opposite in character and abilities, and fatal to organize the expedition so that in effect there were two fleets, one under Drake and one under Hawkins. They sailed from Plymouth in August 1595. Quarrels broke out at once. Drake had too many men for too few victuals and Hawkins declined to help him. When they reached the West Indies, the plan was to try to capture Panama, strategically a sound plan. Unluckily the Spanish captured an English ship and thus learnt that Puerto Rico was to be the objective, because Drake had heard of a disabled treasure-ship in that harbour. The new and speedy methods of the Spanish soon carried the news to the governor. Hawkins now died and Drake was in sole command (1595). The attack on Puerto Rico failed, and Drake made his way towards Nombre de Dios, which he easily captured. But the march to the town of Panama ended in disaster and Drake never again 'carried mirth nor joy in his face'. He died at Porto Bello of dysentry on 28 January 1596 and was buried at sea.

Drake was a genius with all the merits and all the faults which go with genius. His intellect was brilliant and bold, his courage invincible, his patriotism deep and fiery. His Protestantism was genuine and even fanatical. He was a great commander of men and he had all the attributes of a leader. He could be kind and generous, as he usually was, courteous to his enemies and yet ruthless in attaining his purpose. He was also overbearing and hasty, extremely difficult to work with, irritable and not above using the normal methods of his times — he employed torture in order to extract information from some prisoners, as any other commander would have done. His real greatness is to be seen in his original views on naval warfare, according to J. Corbett. He was one of the greatest of all naval tacticians. He was the first to recognize that the ship was the fighting unit and not the soldiers on board: that manoeuvring and shooting were more important than boarding. He alone insisted on target practice, he alone recognized how much greater must be the supply of gunpowder to meet modern conditions of naval warfare. He was always for the offensive, never for the defensive, because he understood and preached that the destruction of the enemy's fleet was the first duty of the navy. And he was probably the first commander to understand and to put into practice the combined use of sea and land operations. More modern interpretations of Drake's importance are less enthusiastic than Corbett's. K. R. Andrews describes him as a 'great corsair' but not a 'great admiral'.

J. Corbett, *Drake and the Tudor Navy*, 1917.
J. A. Williamson, *The Age of Drake*, 1946.

J. A. Williamson, *Sir Francis Drake*, 1951.

M. Lewis, *The Spanish Armada*, 1960.

G. Mattingley, *The Defeat of the Spanish Armada*, 1959.

K. R. Andrews, *Drake's Voyages*, 1967.

H. P. Kraus, *Sir Francis Drake*, 1970.

K. R. Andrews, *The Last voyage of Drake and Hawkins*, Hakluyt Society, 1972.

M. F. Keeler, *Sir Francis Drake's West Indian Voyage 1585–6*, Hakluyt Society, 1981.

SIR MARTIN FROBISHER (1539–1594), navigator, was born in 1539 in the West Riding of Yorkshire. He was the son of Bernard Frobisher and his wife, a daughter of Sir John York, Master of the Mint and a well-known merchant adventurer in London. The family was in origin Welsh, but it had migrated from Chirk to Yorkshire in the middle of the fourteenth century. By the time Martin was born, the family was one of the most important in the county. There are known to be over fifty variants in the spelling of the family name in the sixteenth century.

In 1542 Martin's father died, and the boy was sent by his mother to live with her father, Sir John York, who soon noticed that the boy was 'of great spirit and bold courage and natural hardiness of body'. Therefore Martin was sent to sea as a member of the 1553 expedition to the Guinea coast under the command of Thomas Wyndham. This voyage was disastrous in its loss of life — but Martin came home safely — yet it was triumphant in its financial profits. Therefore in 1554 John Lok led a second expedition to the Guinea coast and Martin went with it. One of the native chiefs demanded a hostage before he would trade: it would seem that, at his own request, Martin was left as the hostage in the Castle of 'Mayne' (Mina). He later fell into the hands of the Portuguese and was imprisoned, but after a while he was released and returned home. In 1559 Martin was on a voyage to the Barbary coast.

Between 1559 and 1576 (from twenty years of age up to thirty-seven) Frobisher was employed as a pirate, but he also had an interest in the coal trade. As a pirate he took many prizes, usually holding a commission from some Protestant Frenchman, such as the Prince de Condé, or from the Protestant William of Orange. He was arrested by the English government at least five times and was imprisoned for a short while, but he was never brought to trial on a criminal charge. Likely enough Elizabeth and the Council found him a useful, if unofficial, servant, and certainly Frobisher's name was both well known to and well hated by Philip II of Spain.

During this period three curious and not wholly explained episodes took place. In 1572 Frobisher was involved in a scheme planned by the Earl of Desmond to escape from London, where he was prisoner. It looks as if Frobisher agreed at first to help Desmond, but the plot was revealed, and it is not impossible that Frobisher gave it away to the government.

In 1573 Philip II approached certain Englishmen, among whom Frobisher was one, about a service which he believed they were ready to do for him — perhaps the capture of Flushing. The evidence is too incomplete to know what were Frobisher's intentions. On the whole, it is at least possible that he played with the idea of collaborating with Spain. There is no evidence that he did in fact do so.

In 1575 Frobisher may have been implicated in the nefarious plans of Thomas Stucley, that adventurer in Ireland. It seems that Frobisher's wife got wind of this and intervened ... 'some jarre happened between Furbisher and her', but we do not know the ultimate result. At this point Frobisher seems to have abandoned piracy and turned to the search for the North-West Passage. For more than fifteen years he had been examining the possibilities, consulting with Portuguese travellers and with English cosmographers such as Hakluyt, Gilbert and Dee. Now, thanks mostly to the driving enthusiasm and the financial backing given by Michael Lok, Frobisher embarked on the first of the three voyages he was to make into Arctic waters. He set sail on 7 June 1576. His fleet consisted of a newly built ship, the *Gabriel*, 15 to 20 tons, under the command of Christopher Hall: the *Michael*, 20 to 25 tons, commanded by Owen Griffyn: and a pinnace of 7 to 10 tons. Frobisher was its admiral and pilot; the crew consisted of 35 men and boys. In 1558 a Venetian named Zeno had published a map of the Arctic regions which was mostly either inaccurate or frankly fictitious. Frobisher knew this map and was thereby misled. Sailing up the North Sea, passing the Shetlands and the Faroes, he sighted Cape Farewell, the southern point of Greenland. This he took to be Friesland (or the Faroes) as depicted on the Zeno map. He then lost company with the *Michael*, which deserted him and returned home. Then the pinnace was lost, and Frobisher was left with only the *Gabriel* and eighteen men. Hemmed in by 'monstrous great ilands of ise which lay dryving all alongst the coast', enveloped in thick fog, his ship all but in pieces, Frobisher showed what a consummate seaman and man of courage he was, being 'determined rather to make a sacrifice onto God of his lyfe than to return home without the discovery of Kathay ...' After a time of extreme danger and hardship the ice was 'consumed and gone' and the *Gabriel* was able to sail on northwards. On 11 August the ship entered the 'strait', which they named Frobisher's Strait, believing themselves to be in the North-West Passage which would lead them to Cathay. They thought the land on their right was Asia, that on their left America. After exchanging gifts with the Eskimos, five men were put ashore, none of whom was ever seen again. An Eskimo woman called Ookijoxy Ninoo told an American in 1862 that oral tradition related that the abandoned Englishmen tried to sail home in a makeshift boat, but perished in the attempt. Annoyed by the loss of his five men and in the hope of being able to ransom them back, Frobisher himself kidnapped an Eskimo, by lifting him bodily, kayak and all, out of the water and into the *Gabriel*. Frobisher took the Eskimo home with him, where he died. Frobisher arrived at Harwich on 2 October 1576. One of his men had brought with him a piece of black pyrites. The English goldsmiths denied that it contained any gold at all, but an Italian assayer insisted that there was gold in the stone. Thus was formed the Cathay Company with Michael Lok as its Governor. All the liabilities of the first voyage were transferred to the new Company, which expected to pay for the expenses of the first voyage out of the profits from gold from the second voyage.

The second voyage was on a bigger scale: the Queen lent a ship of 200 tons (the *Ayde*), supplies were for seven months and condemned criminals were to be taken and left in Friesland to make friends with the natives. The object of the expedition was not primarily to find the North-West Passage, but to bring home as much of the pyrites as possible. Our knowledge of this voyage is drawn from two vivid accounts written by George Best, Frobisher's lieutenant on the *Ayde* or *Aid*, and by Dionyse Settle, a gentleman who accompanied Frobisher. The fleet sailed on 27 May 1577, and it returned to

England at Milford Haven on 23 September, bringing with it some 200 tons of worthless pyrites and a native man, woman and child, all three of whom died within a month of reaching England. There was so much wrangling over the value of the ore that a third expedition was planned to bring back 2,000 tons of the pyrites and to establish a colony of 120 in the Arctic regions.

This third expedition consisted of fifteen ships. They left England on 31 May 1578 and returned in October. The most notable event was that Frobisher entered what now is known as Hudson Strait, but which he called 'Mistaken Strait', because it proved not to be the one he was looking for. Historically the most interesting result of the voyage was that a box of nails was discovered, which has now been accepted as proving that there was a European trade with Greenland prior to the Frobisher voyages. There is every reason for believing that Michael Lok was pretty well ruined by his investments in these voyages. Frobisher also lost *pari passu*. But he lost no time in recovering his losses.

In 1578 he took part in the expedition under Sir William Winter which was sent to put down the rebellion of Fitzmaurice and Desmond in Ireland. When this work was completed, Frobisher seems to have returned to his old game of piracy, if we are to judge by the frequent complaints which poured in from the Netherlands to the Council. That he was by 1582 again in funds may be seen from his subscribing £300 towards an expedition to the East Indies and Cathay by the Southern route. Frobisher was to have commanded it in conjunction with Fenton, but the two never got on well together and Frobisher withdrew — fortunately, as the voyage under Fenton was a failure. In 1585 Frobisher went as Vice-Admiral under Drake on the 1585 expedition to the Spanish West Indies, which brought home spoils worth £60,000. Frobisher was then in 1587 put in command of the Channel Fleet to guard the Channel against the Spanish invasion. He spent his time 'capturing everything which savoured of the Spaniard'. When the Armada did come in 1588, Frobisher was in command of the *Triumph* and fought under Howard in the battle up the Channel, in which he distinguished himself perhaps more signally than any other commander. When the fleet was reorganized into four squadrons, Frobisher was in command of one of them and for his splendid work he was knighted by Howard.

After the defeat of the Armada Frobisher was an outspoken supporter of Hawkins's theory that Spain ought to be ruined by England's cutting off her treasure from the Indies. Between 1589 and 1592 he went on three expeditions to the Azores and captured many valuable prizes, especially in 1592 the *Madre de Dios*, which was worth £150,000. Two years later, in 1594, he went in command of a small squadron which the Queen sent to help the French Huguenots, but he was wounded at the storming of the fort at Crozon, near Brest, and died from the wound in Plymouth.

Frobisher was a rough diamond in some ways, but his reputation as an impossibly bad-tempered and impetuous man probably derives from the abuse which Michael Lok poured out on him. He was as brave as a lion, a consummate seaman, much loved by his men and always very popular with the Queen. He was immensely strong physically and was noted for his feats of strength, and it should be remembered in his favour that he wanted to treat the natives in the Arctic regions with kindness.

V. Stefansson, *The Three Voyages of Martin Frobisher*, 1938.
W. McFee, *Sir Martin Frobisher*, 1928.
S. E. Morison, *The Great Explorers*, 1978.

SIR RICHARD GRENVILLE (1542–1591), naval commander, was born on 15 June 1542, and he died probably on 12 September 1591. He was the son of Roger Grenville and his wife, Thomasine Cole of Slade in Devon. His father died on Sunday, 19 July 1545, when his ship *Mary Rose*, the second largest of Henry VIII's ships, capsized. His mother married again, to Thomas Arundell of Clifton, and it is probable that Richard spent most of his early days at Clifton, that house to which Theodore Palaeologus, last descendant of the Byzantine emperors, retired, who lies buried in the church at Landulph.

At the age of seventeen (1559) Richard entered the Inner Temple to acquire a sound, general training with enough law to enable him to run his family estates. In 1562 he, Nicholas Specott, and their servants, were involved in an affray in the Strand with Sir Edward Unton, Fulke Greville, Robert Bannester and their servants. Grenville ran Bannester through with his sword, left him dead in the street and fled. He was later pardoned, on what grounds is not known. In that same year he seems to have been returned as M.P. for Dunheved (Launceston), although he was still a minor, but it is possible that this may have been a different Richard Grenville. Not later than 1565 he married Mary, the daughter of Sir John St. Leger. He had two boys, Bernard and John, the former of whom was father of that Sir Bevil Grenville who became famous during the Civil Wars, in which he supported Charles I.

In 1566 Grenville went abroad to fight in the wars in Hungary against the Turks. He was home in 1568 and the next year he went to Ireland with Sir Warham St. Leger to arrange for the lands which had been mortgaged to St. Leger by the Earl of Desmond. Grenville's intention was to settle the lands in Munster as one form of investment, but the outbreak of the Fitzmaurice rebellion ruined his plans and his lands, so that he had to give up the proposition, though he was to return to it twenty years later.

Dr. A. L. Rowse has emphasized that Grenville came from an old established family, was an aristocrat and well aware of it, whereas the Drakes and Hawkins were new men. This may explain the curious episode in 1572, when information was laid against Grenville 'as a gentleman who belonged to the Earl of Arundel'. This was the year in which Cecil had defeated his opponents, that aristocratic faction, led by the Earl of Arundel and the Duke of Norfolk, which resented the new man's political monopoly of power. Norfolk had been executed and the accusation brought against Grenville was that he had said he 'feared the said Earl would prove himself a coward, for if he had not been one never a Cicil in England could have chopped off the Duke's head'. It is surprising to find 'this alignment of the forward-looking, undeviatingly Protestant Grenville with the conservative and Catholic earl' (Rowse, *Sir Richard Grenville's Place in English History*, p. 82).

Grenville was M.P. for Cornwall in the 1571 Parliament: he was returned to the 1572 Parliament as Member for Launceston, and he did a certain amount of work in committees. But at this time he was mainly taken up with preparations for his South-Sea project. His plan was to sail through the Straits of Magellan into the South Sea, take possession of Terra Australis and find the western outlet of the imagined Straits of Anian, which would provide the most direct North-West Passage for England to Cathay. This was the first English attempt to break the Spanish monopoly of the Pacific by

Neptuni proles, qui magni Martis alumnus
GRENVILVS patrias sanguine tinxit aquas

Sir Richard Grenville
(Artist: Unknown)

way of the Straits of Magellan, rather than by way of Baccalaos
(Labrador), the route approved by Humphrey Gilbert. Grenville
obtained his Letters Patent from the Queen in 1574 and by June he
had leave to sail. But at that moment the government began a policy

of appeasement towards Spain, and as a result Grenville was forbidden to go on his expedition. Three years later (1577) Drake set out
on his voyage of circumnavigation, which was in reality a con-
tinuation of Grenville's plans.

Forbidden to sail the seas, Grenville turned his attention to local
affairs and family interests. As Sheriff of Cornwall (1576–7) he was
engaged in putting into practice in Cornwall the government's anti-
Catholic policy. He arrested Father Mayne at the home of the
Tregian family and he put a stop to the activities of other Cornish
Catholic families — for which work he was knighted in 1577. It was
at this time also that he went in for large building changes in the
family home at Buckland Abbey near Plymouth.

In 1585 Grenville sailed from Plymouth in command of Ralegh's
first expedition to plant a colony in North America. He landed a
hundred men on the coast of what is now North Carolina, left Ralph
Lane in charge and returned home, on the way capturing a Spanish
ship, the *Santa Maria*, with a cargo of gold, silver, pearls, ginger and
sugar, the sale of which more than paid for the expedition.
Grenville's conduct on the voyage to Roanoke, where the colony was
planted, was violently attacked by Lane, who accused him of
'intolerable pride and unsatiable ambition'. In truth, it was
Grenville's firm leadership which enabled the colony to be planted at
all.

The next year (1586) Grenville took three ships to Roanoke with
supplies for the colonists. Meantime Drake, on his way home from
plundering the Spanish Main, had arrived at Roanoke. Finding the
colonists short of food and discontented with their lot, he gave them
a passage home. When Grenville arrived there in July, the colonists
were gone. He left fifteen men to hold the fort and set out home
again. There was sickness among his crews, many died and he called
at Newfoundland in order to rest and feed his men. Then he made
for the Azores in order to capture some prizes to pay for the
expedition, in which he was not so successful as in 1585.

The struggle between England and Spain was nearing the crisis.
All 1587 Grenville was engaged in strengthening the defences of the
west country, but he was also busy planning and building a third
expedition to Roanoke. News that the Spanish Armada was about
to sail put an end to his hopes and plans; he was ordered to send his
ships to join Drake's squadron off Plymouth. For a moment there

was a chance that Grenville might have gone in command of an expedition 'to singe the King of Spain's beard', but it was doubtful whether Grenville and Drake could get on well enough together. At the moment when the Armada arrived, we have no information of what Grenville was doing. Apparently he did not serve at sea against the Armada; probably he was in command of the land forces in Cornwall.

When the danger was passed, Ralegh and Grenville were commissioned to keep watch at sea on the approaches to Ireland, in case the Spanish fleet returned. When the need for this precaution disappeared, Ralegh and Grenville turned their attention to Ireland. Grenville bought land in Munster, took over to Ireland some settlers from western England and set seriously to work to make a plantation in Munster to provide an estate for his younger son. He spent two years there and then was suddenly summoned to England by the government, whose plan was now to maintain a squadron at the Azores to waylay the Spanish treasure fleet. After his failure in the Lisbon expedition of 1589 Drake was in eclipse. Grenville was to be Vice-Admiral of the fleet under Lord Thomas Howard (1591). It is not possible here to retell the story of Grenville's last fight in the *Revenge*: that has been done superbly by Sir Walter Ralegh. It must suffice to record that the English fleet was caught unawares at Flores by the main Spanish fleet under Don Alonso de Bazan. After the strategic retreat (fully justifiable) by Lord Thomas with his five ships, Grenville, who had ninety-five men sick ashore, was left alone to face the fifty-three Spanish ships. Even if one allows that he ought to have tried to get away, it is extremely doubtful whether he could have done so. At any rate, it was not within the make-up of Grenville to fly, 'out of the greatness of his mind he could not be persuaded' (Ralegh). Between 3.0 p.m. on 9 September to the morning of the 10th, *Revenge* beat off the attacks of and so much damaged fifteen Spanish galleons that they were 'far more willing to hearken to a composition than hastily to make any more assaults'. There could be only one end, and it came: surrender by the crew, not by Grenville (he wanted to blow up the ship); the death of Grenville; and then, a little later, a gigantic cyclone in which some sixteen ships of Bazan were destroyed, and down went also *Revenge*. The inhabitants of the Azores were fully convinced that as Grenville was a devil, all the devils rose from the bottom of the sea to avenge his death.

Grenville may well stand as the personification of the robuster side of Elizabethan England. Less intellectual than Ralegh, he was as tough as, but less rough than Frobisher: as competent as Hawkins, he was more boisterous: as brave as Drake, he was even more explosive. Unscrupulous in pursuit of his own interests, he was a loyal and honest servant of the Queen, but high-handed in carrying out his duties, as he showed in his method of arresting Mayne. The stories which have grown up round all these famous men reveal their character to us — Drake finishing his game of bowls on Plymouth Hoe, Ralegh spreading his cloak in a plashy place; Essex at Cadiz flinging his hat upon the waves; Grenville at dinner biting his glass and crunching the splinters in his mouth till the blood ran out. That last legend is the most revealing of them all. It is not the veracity of the story which signifies: it is that men should find it easy to believe such things of such heroes.

A. L. Rowse, *Sir Richard Grenville of the Revenge*, 1937.
A. L. Rowse: *Sir Richard Grenville's Place in English History*, The Ralegh Lecture, British Academy, 1957.
Sir Walter Ralegh, *A Report of the Truth of the Fight about the Isles of Açores*. Arber's *English Reprints*, 1871.

CHARLES HOWARD, LORD HOWARD OF EFFINGHAM, EARL OF NOTTINGHAM (1536–1624), Lord Admiral of

England, commander of the English fleet against the Armada, was the son of William Howard, first Lord Howard of Effingham, who was the eldest son of Thomas Howard, second Duke of Norfolk. Charles probably served at sea with his father (1554–7), and therefore he was not destitute of naval experience when later he became Lord Admiral. He became very popular at Court, where he resided for twelve years, a favourite of the Queen, whose cousin he was through Anne Boleyn. He saw military service under the Earl of Warwick, when he played a minor part in putting down the rising in the north in 1569. The next year he was given command of the naval squadron which escorted the young Queen of Spain down the Channel, when she moved from Flanders to Spain. In 1573 his father died, and he became Lord Howard of Effingham. In 1575 he was made a Knight of the Garter.

The turning-point in his career came in 1585, when he was made

Lord Admiral. He was now 50 years old. The office combined in his one person responsibilities which to-day are divided between a Cabinet Minister, First Lord of the Admiralty, First Sea Lord and Chief of the Naval Staff, Second, Third and Fourth Sea Lords, Commander-in-Chief of the whole fleet always, and of the main fleet in wartime. His appointment might be called quasi-hereditary, for his father, two uncles and a great-grandfather had held the office before him.

In 1586 he was one of the commission set up to try Mary, Queen of Scots. He was not, in fact, present at the trial, but William Davison, the Queen's Secretary, declared that it was Howard who urged the Queen to sign the death warrant.

In 1587 he was appointed 'lieutenant-general, commander-in-chief and governor of the whole fleet and army at sea fitted against the Spaniards and their allies'. Later generations have wondered why Drake was not put in command. Howard's appointment caused no surprise to his contemporaries. Drake was a finer seaman, but to have elevated Drake to the top would have aroused jealousies among the other seamen. In the sixteenth century rank was of the highest importance and men of rank expected to command: men of lesser degree expected to serve under them. To have put 'gentlemen' to serve under Drake might well have led to a refusal to obey his orders. There was no need to run this risk. In Howard of Effingham the Queen could call on a man of the highest birth, of long experience, of unfailing commonsense, and one who recognized his limitations and was ready to take advice from others, but who never shovelled off the final responsibility. He and Drake worked together in perfect amity and with complete success.

In 1588, Howard took command in the *Ark*, 800 tons, a ship originally built by Ralegh and known variously as *Ark, Ark Ralegh, Ark Royal*. He joined Drake at Plymouth on 23 May, leaving the defence of the Downs to Sir Edward Seymour. At Plymouth Howard set up a Council of War which he regularly consulted all through the campaign. He then tackled three urgent problems. First, he backed up Drake's incessant plea to the Government that the right strategy was for the English fleet to search out and destroy the Armada before ever it entered English waters. The Queen shilly-shallied, and it was not until 7 July that the fleet was allowed to set sail for Corunna. On the 9th the wind changed and the fleet was

Charles Howard, Lord of Effingham, Earl of Nottingham
(Artist: Unknown)

forced to return to Plymouth, for Howard dared not run the risk of being by-passed by the Armada.

There was a second reason for turning back, which was the second problem facing Howard — there were not enough victuals. He had already written to Burghley pointing out the dangers which would arise, if the victuals ran short at the time of service. 'We shall now be victualled, beginning the 20th of this April unto the 18th of May, and the advertisement that giveth the largest time for the coming of the Spanish forces is the midst of May, being the 15th. Then have we three days' victual. If it be fit to be so, it passeth my reason'. This is the letter of a man who knows his business and is not afraid to pursue it.

The Queen's reluctance to allow the fleet to search out the enemy aroused in Howard's mind the fear that there was treachery about and that the Queen was being hoodwinked. On 23 June he wrote to Walsingham, 'Let her Majesty trust no more to Judas kisses; for let her assure herself there is no trust to French King nor Duke of Parma'. And that same day he wrote to the Queen herself, 'For the love of Jesus Christ, Madam, awake thoroughly and see the villainous treasons round about you ... and draw your forces round about you, like a mighty prince, to defend you. Truly, Madam, if you do so, there is no cause to fear. If you do not, there will be danger'. This is not the letter of a mere courtier and favourite.

Howard was a courageous man, but he was also a prudent one, and his conduct of the earlier stages of the fights against the Armada was sound and sensible. Ralegh wrote in his *History of the World* (book 5, ch. 1, sect. 6) that Howard was 'better advised than a great many malignant fools were that found fault with his demeanour'. Of course, he made mistakes, and one mistake in particular has rightly earned him much condemnation. On the night of Sunday, 28 July, the English launched eight fireships against the Armada. Panic ensued and the formation of the Spanish fleet was broken. At dawn on the 29th Howard saw the Spanish *capitana, San Lorenzo*, stranded on the shore of Calais. At once he led his whole squadron to capture the prize. At the very moment when Drake, Hawkins and Frobisher were seizing the first opportunity of attacking the now demoralized Armada, the Lord Admiral and all his ships were out of the fight. The truth is that Howard was to a large extent a mediaevally-minded man. War was still to him something of a stately ceremony. He had not grasped what Drake and his companions understood, that war was now an entirely new thing: the enemy must be annihilated by a concerted attack. Howard was content to 'pluck their feathers by little and little'. The *San Lorenzo* was a splendid feather.

Even before the fleet returned home to England, disease had begun to ravage the crews. Their conditions grew worse as soon as demobilization began. One of the noblest traits in Howard's character was his unfailing interest in his men and his unremitting attempts to alleviate their distress — notably in his protests against the callous treatment by the Government, which even refused to supply Howard with pay for the men. It was typical of Howard, Hawkins and Drake that in 1590 they co-operated in establishing the naval charity, 'The Chest at Chatham', which was later incorporated in the Greenwich Hospital. The actual chest is preserved in the Royal Naval College at Greenwich.

Howard continued as Lord Admiral, but he took active part in only one of the post-Armada expeditions — that of 1596, when he was joint commander with the Earl of Essex in the expedition against Cadiz. The Spanish fleet was totally defeated, but Essex landed in too great haste, which allowed many of the ships to escape. It was Howard who decided that the English fleet must return home and not carry the war to the other ports along the coast. This decision infuriated Essex, and the quarrel was exacerbated in 1597 when Howard was made Earl of Nottingham and in virtue of his office as Lord Admiral now took precedence over Essex.

As long as Elizabeth survived, Howard retained her confidence and affection; it was to Howard, according to one story, that on her deathbed she nominated James VI as her successor. The new King treated Howard with as much respect and confidence as had the old Queen. There was no commission on which he did not sit: in 1605 he went to Spain to negotiate the treaty of peace; in 1613 he commanded the squadron which escorted the Princess Elizabeth to Flushing for her marriage to the Elector Palatine.

The office of Lord Admiral was for life, and Howard clung to it far too long. He held it for thirty-four years, and thirty-one of them were after 1588. Corruption set in among the offices for which Howard was responsible, and he did nothing to cure the evil. In 1619, at long last, he was bought out by the Duke of Buckingham and retired with a pension of £1,000 a year. He died on 14 December 1624, at the age of eighty-eight.

There is no evidence at all that Howard was ever a 'papist', a good deal of evidence that he was a staunch 'protestant'.

M. Lewis, *The Spanish Armada*, 1960.

J. K. Laughton, *From Howard to Nelson*, 1899.

J. Corbett, *The Successors of Drake*, 1900.

R. W. Kenny, *Elizabeth's Admiral*, 1970.

G. Mattingley, *The defeat of the Spanish Armada*, 1959.

EDWARD FENTON (*d.*1603), soldier and sailor, came of a Nottinghamshire family. The date of his birth is unknown: he died in 1603. The first record of him shows that he sacrificed his patrimony to a preference for a military career. He held a command in Ireland under Sir Henry Sidney in the suppressing of Shane O'Neill's rebellion in 1566. In 1577 he was in command of the *Gabriel* in Frobisher's second voyage in search of the North-West passage and of Cathay: he seems to have performed a very small part in this expedition. In May 1578 he sailed as Lieutenant-General and second in command (in the *Judith*) of Frobisher's third voyage to Meta Incognita. He was home again by October. The next year he was again employed in Ireland. By far the most important event in his life was when he was made commander of the Earl of Leicester's expedition in 1582–3, which was intended to develop trade by way of the Cape of Good Hope, the Moluccas and China, and so home.

The voyage was a signal failure, partly and inevitably because it started too late in the year, partly owing to the most unusual weather experienced in the Channel, very largely because Fenton was entirely the wrong man to command such an expedition. By profession he was a soldier, but other soldiers have proved good commanders at sea: even so, the appointment bred great jealousy among the section of the crew which had lately been serving with Drake. The commission under which he sailed gave him powers which went to his head; he behaved frequently in the most high-handed way. He himself had planned first to make himself king of St. Helena, and from there to raid the Portuguese carracks. This ran counter to the ideas of the group of merchants who sailed with him:

they only wanted peaceful trade. It is true that Fenton was circumscribed by a Council whose majority decisions were binding. But it is revealing that Fenton should have described an illness in his ship as 'only the scurvy' and that he should have quarrelled with everybody.

The expedition consisted of the *Leicester*, 400 tons, the *Edward Bonaventure*, 250 or 300, with two other small vessels of 50 and 10 tons. It left Southampton in May 1582, reached Sierra Leone in August, and then, there being no hope of reaching the Cape so late in the year, made it way towards Brazil. Fenton himself intended to go through the Magellan Straits, but he heard that these were now guarded by some Spanish ships. He therefore went to St. Vincent on the coast of Brazil, where the governor at first refused to deal with the English: later he allowed them to buy victuals and some sugar. A sudden attack by three Spanish warships resulted in a fierce fight in which one Spanish ship was sunk. Fenton was by now despairing of any financial success and decided to sail for home, which was reached in May 1583.

Our chief source of information for this voyage is the most interesting diary kept by one of the chaplains, Richard Madox, a very remarkable young man, well-read, familiar with the most up-to-date methods of navigation. He took with him an *Ephemerides*, that is, a book of astronomical tables, and 'a very perfect instrument', probably an astrolabe. He also seems to have known something about coastal survey. Madox was a man of intelligence and shrewdness, of perfect integrity, one who behaved courageously and sensibly in difficult circumstances.

In 1588 Fenton commanded the *Mary Rose*, 600 tons, against the Spanish Armada. He died in 1603.

E.G.R.Taylor, *The Troublesome Voyage of Captain Edward Fenton 1582–1583*. The Hakluyt Society, 1959.

GEORGE CLIFFORD, 3rd EARL OF CUMBERLAND (1558–1605), naval commander, was the eldest son of Henry, second Earl of Cumberland, whom he succeeded in the earldom in 1569/70. His mother was Lady Eleanor Brandon, daughter of Charles Brandon, Duke of Suffolk, and Mary Tudor, daughter of Henry VII, Dowager Queen of France, who had married Louis XII.

In 1571 Cumberland entered Trinity College, Cambridge. He

George Clifford, 3rd Earl of Cumberland
(Artist: Unknown, after Hilliard)

remained there until 1574; he took his M.A. in 1576, having chiefly studied mathematics. His tutor was John Whitgift, later to be Archbishop of Canterbury. From Cambridge Cumberland moved to Oxford in order to study geography, a subject in which he was expert and 'took great delight'. In 1577 he married his cousin, Lady Margaret Russell.

Cumberland's naval life opened in 1586. Between that date and 1598, he fitted out at his own expense twelve expeditions — 1586, 1588, 1589, 1591, 1592, 1593, 1594, 1595, 1597, 1598. As well as commanding the *Elizabeth Bonaventure* (600 tons) against the Armada in 1588, he may have taken part in the Cadiz expedition of 1596. Of these expeditions the twelfth and last voyage was the most considerable, consisting of twenty ships. Cumberland took command of the *Malice Scourge*, led his fleet to Porto Rico and captured San Juan. The intention was to plant an English settlement there, but illness compelled him to abandon the attempt and the whole episode proved an expensive failure. Indeed, none of his voyages paid him a satisfactory dividend. At the start of his active life he was a very wealthy man, but when he died he was more than £1,000 in debt. Much of his money was wasted on mere gambling, dicing, betting and other forms of extravagant living, but his expeditions ruined him.

Cumberland was a man of action, his courage was invincible, his vitality enormous, and he was prepared to spend himself in order to share the burdens of storms, illness and shortage of food. He was a skilful and much beloved commander, and it would seem that he undertook his unsuccessful voyages principally in order to damage Spain and to benefit his own country. He was in high favour with the Queen, whose glove he wore in his hat, but he was an unfaithful husband and was separated from his wife for many years, although at the end he sought for and obtained her forgiveness.

G. C. Williamson, *George, Third Earl of Cumberland*, 1920.

GEORGE FENNER (*d*.1618), naval commander, came of a Sussex family which had many connections with the sea. George was the most notable seaman of them all, but his cousin Thomas had almost as fine a record as George, and William was a worthy third in the trio. Thomas was with Drake in the Indies voyage of 1585 and took a leading part in the highly successful attack on Cartagena. He was present at Drake's attack on the Spanish Armada in Cadiz in 1587 and he played a distinguished part in the series of fights in the Channel against the Armada in 1588. William accompanied Drake and Norris in the Corunna expedition of 1589 and he died of his wounds on the voyage home.

Little is known of the early years of George's life, and even later, when he had become famous, there are many gaps in our knowledge of his life. He may have made a voyage to the Gold Coast, but nothing is known of it. He seems never to have accompanied Drake on any of his voyages. He comes into prominence first in 1566. John Hawkins was fitting out an expedition, but at the last moment the Queen refused to let him sail. In the last days of October 1566 George Fenner set sail from Plymouth with exactly the same number of ships as Hawkins had fitted out. Were there two voyages being prepared at the same moment, or did Fenner take over Hawkins' ships, men and stores? He was allowed to sail only after giving a bond that he would not injure the privileges of the King of Spain in the Indies. His first port of call was at Santiago in the Cape Verde Islands. During the night the Spanish attacked him, and Fenner and his ships barely escaped by cutting their cables. A few days later, cruising alone in his *The Castle of Comfort* off the Azores while he was following a Spanish ship with the purpose, Fenner said, of 'borrowing a cable', he was set upon by three Portuguese ships, a galleon of 400 tons and two caravels. Fenner, by dint of splendid gunnery, beat off three separate attacks before night fell. At dawn the Portuguese were still in contact with him and had been reinforced by two more ships, making the odds five to one. Once again, by superb gunnery Fenner not only beat off the enemy, but he so badly mauled them that they withdrew and Fenner escaped, returning home to Plymouth.

For the next twelve years all that is known of Fenner's life is that he was a privateer who was continually complaining to the Privy Council against Spain or answering complaints from Spain and France. The Council seems to have ignored all the complaints impartially.

In 1587 George in the *Leicester* (400 tons, 160 men) with Thomas Fenner in the *Nonpareil* (500 tons, 250 men) patrolled the north coast of France on the look-out for the Spanish Armada. When in 1588 the Armada came, George took a distinguished part in the fighting up the Channel and at Gravelines, and then up the North Sea to the Firth of Forth. In 1591 with Howard of Effingham he was in the *Leicester* once again, patrolling the coast of Brittany. In 1597 he and Howard were together again in the Islands Voyage led by Essex — a failure, but not through any fault of Fenner's. Later in the same year the two were watching out for the 'Invisible' Armada. Fenner was given false information with which he hurried back to Plymouth. He was sent off back to Brest: again he was given false news, again he took it to Plymouth, but his reputation was so high that he was not blamed. When at last real news came that five Spanish galleys had arrived, the government turned at once to George. 'Tarry not, good George, but do the best you can.' Howard was in the Channel, Fenner pursued westwards, but the galleys were two days ahead of him and he had no hope of catching them.

The article in the *D.N.B.* suggests that Fenner died perhaps in 1600. But there is one more record of him, for he became the first Brother or pensioner in Sutton's Hospital in the Charterhouse, where he died on 26 October 1618.

George Fenner was 'one of the greatest English seamen even of the days of Elizabeth' (G. S. Davies). His fight against the Portuguese was the first example of the power of modern gunnery, to be followed later by Grenville in the *Revenge* at the Azores.

G. S. Davies, 'Master of the Charterhouse', *Cornhill Magazine*, 1920.
J. Corbett, *Drake and the Tudor Navy (passim)*, 1900.
J. Corbett, *The Successors of Drake (passim)*, 1917.

SIR JAMES LANCASTER (1554/55–1618), mercantile captain, was the son of James Lancaster of Basingstoke, husbandman. In 1571 he became an apprentice in the Skinners' Company, being 'prentice to Blasse from the feast of John the Baptist for ten years'. He was sworn a Freeman of the Company on 10 March 1579, on payment of 3s. 4d. His early life was spent in Portugal.

When the Armada set sail, Lancaster commanded the *Edward Bonaventure*, 250 tons, in the English fleet under Drake, but no details of his service seem to be known.

In 1591 he again commanded the *Edward Bonaventure* in the first English voyage to the East Indies. The general of the expedition was George Raymond in the *Penelope*. The fleet set sail on 10 April, much too late in the year, so that it did not arrive at Table Bay until the end of July, the first visit of any English ships to that port. There was so much sickness on board that a month was spent here, but so many died that the *Merchant Royal* was sent home with 50 men and the rest of the crews were split between the other two ships. The story of the voyage is one of disaster on disaster. The *Penelope* was lost off Cape Corrientes (12 September 1591). On the 16th the *Edward Bonaventure*'s mainmast was struck by lightning and four men were killed. She sailed on to Mozambique and the Comoro Islands, where she lost a third of her crew in a surprise attack by natives. At the end of November Lancaster reached Zanzibar and stayed there till mid-February 1592. His plan was to make for Cape Comorin and lie in wait for the shipping plying between Goa and the Portuguese eastern settlements. The ship lost her course, victuals ran short and Lancaster's attempts to make Sokotra, the Laccadives and the Nicobar Islands all failed. In June he reached Sumatra and then made for Penang in order to prey on Portuguese shipping. He lay there till the beginning of September, but his crew suffered much sickness and was reduced to 34, of which only 22 were fit for work. He succeeded in taking a Portuguese ship filled with pepper and another filled with rice, and then one from Goa with a varied cargo. He moved away to the Nicobar Islands to take in supplies and then to Ceylon, but his men now insisted on going home. Lancaster was 'very sick, more like to die than to live', and in no condition to enforce his own wishes. In April 1593 they reached St. Helena, where provisions and nineteen days' rest restored the crew, but as their morale rose their discipline fell, they got out of hand and made for England. Foul winds delayed their passage, provisions again ran short and in desperation Lancaster made for Trinidad. No supplies were available here, but in June he reached Mona and was provisioned by some French ships. He then set sail for Newfoundland to make contact with the fishing fleets, but the wind drove him back to the West Indies and he was again at Mona in November. Lancaster and his second in command, Barker, landed in order to get supplies, leaving six sailors on board. These men cut the cable and sailed off to San Domingo, where they surrendered the ship to the Spaniards.

For a month Lancaster and his party of eighteen were marooned with only vegetables to eat. Then twelve were taken off by two French ships, and Lancaster was one of them. They remained off San Domingo until April 1594; then Lancaster and Barker got a passage home in another French ship commanded by Jean Lenoir which reached Dieppe on 19 May. On the 24th Lancaster reached Rye in

Sussex after having been away for three years. It is usually said that the voyage was financially a great success. There is not the slightest evidence that this was so. What Lancaster had succeeded in doing was to penetrate into the Indian Ocean as far as the Malay peninsula without any opposition from the Portuguese. Out of the 198 men who set sail only twenty-five returned to England.

Within five months Lancaster was at sea again with three ships financed by London merchants. Lancaster commanded the *Consent*, 240 tons, Barker commanded the *Solomon*, 170 tons, and a third ship went with them, the *Virgin*, 60 tons. The objectives of the expedition were to raid the Portuguese possessions in Brazil (Pernambuco) and to capture Spanish and Portuguese shipping throughout the voyage. This expedition was a great success and paid a high dividend. Pernambuco was reached on 18 April 1595, and the town was taken and held until all the merchandise in the warehouses had been transferred to Lancaster's ships. The booty was far too great for his ships to accommodate all of it. At that moment by good chance Jean Lenoir turned up and joined his ships to Lancaster's. An arrangement was made with some Dutch ships to carry the rest of the spoils home, and Lancaster was just about to sail when he heard that the Portuguese were building a redoubt at the mouth of the harbour. Lancaster was for ignoring it, but his companions thought it necessary to capture it. Lancaster was too ill to lead the attack himself, which he entrusted to Cotton, Barker and Lenoir with some three hundred men. He gave them strict orders never to go beyond the range of the English guns. The redoubt was easily taken; then the force began to chase the enemy and soon found itself faced with a superior force far out of range of the English ships. Cotton, Barker and Lenoir were killed and some thirty-five men. Lancaster set sail at once and reached England in July 1595 after a most profitable expedition.

For four years nothing is heard of Lancaster except that in 1598 he was one of the managers of Cumberland's twelfth expedition. Then in 1601 Lancaster was selected to lead the first expedition sent out by the new East India Company.

It is not possible here to give a detailed account of this long and dangerous voyage. It was an aggressive expedition planned with the object of spoiling the Portuguese, and it was much helped by the friendly co-operation of the Dutch, who hated the Portuguese quite as much as did the English (*Mariner's Mirror*, xviii, 4, October, 1932). Five ships were employed: Lancaster was 'General of the Voyage' and commanded the *Red Dragon* (this was Cumberland's old *Malice Scourge*, 600 tons). His crew numbered 202 men and the guns forty. In all 480 men set sail, of whom more than 180 died before the ships started back for England and at least half of the 480 never returned home.

The fleet sailed from Tor Bay on 20 April 1601. By September it had reached Saldanha Bay, but all the crews were suffering from scurvy, 'the plague of the sea and the spoil of mariners' (Sir Richard Hawkins). Lancaster's crew was in much better shape than the others because he had taken bottled lime juice with him as an experiment — the first sailor to do this. By 29 October 107 men had died. By Christmas Day eighteen more were lost. Discontent grew among the men, and five men stole a boat and tried to desert, but they were caught. The fleet reached Sumatra in June 1602, and here Lancaster had a most satisfactory interview with the nonagenarian King of Achin, Alauddin, who was delighted with the presents given to him and with the letters which Queen Elizabeth had sent him. Commercial privileges were easily granted to the East India Company, but very little pepper was to be had. However, on 3 October a rich carrack was captured and the cargo was transferred to Lancaster's ships; the carrack was then returned to the Portuguese, who much appreciated this 'courtesy'.

Lancaster then sailed for Priaman, where he found the *Susan* ready to return to England with a large cargo of pepper and cloves. Sending her home independently, Lancaster moved on to Bantam, a thousand miles from Achin. The king here was a boy of nine years old, trading privileges were granted; in five weeks the ships were laden with a huge cargo; and the first 'factory' of the East India Company was settled at Bantam.

The return journey was made with the utmost difficulty: bad storms, contrary winds, leaky ships, rudders lost and the ever-present fear of mutiny justified Lancaster's description of the voyage on his return to England in September 1603, when he gave thanks that he had been 'delivered from infinite perils and dangers in this long and tedious navigation'.

Lancaster was knighted in 1603 and gave his time and attention to organizing the affairs of the East India Company He was also

interested in the search for the North-west Passage, and Baffin gave
the name of Lancaster to one of the sounds in the north-west (1616).
Lancaster died on 6 June 1618, a wealthy man. He left most of his
money to charities (he was never married and therefore had no
claimants), some of which are administered today by the Skinners'
Company.

Sir William Foster, *The Voyages of Sir James Lancaster*, Hakluyt
Society, 1940.

JOHN NEWBERY (*d*.1584), traveller. Virtually nothing is
known of the early life of this very interesting, intrepid and
important man. There is a slight possibility that he was related to
Ralph Newbery, who published Hakluyt's *Principal Navigations*: he
may also have been in his early years in Holland and have learned
Dutch. (Foster, *England's Quest of Eastern Trade*, pp. 79 and 94.)
He first appears in history in 1579 as a 'citizen and merchant of
London', 'desirous to see the world'. He made three remarkable
journeys which give him the right to a place in any dictionary of
biographies: his only failure is not to have found a place in *D.N.B.*

The first voyage, 1579. Newbery left London in March and
travelled overland to Marseilles. Thence he sailed to Tripoli in
Syria; from there he took ship to Jaffa and then went on to
Jerusalem, where he visited 'the monuments of those countries'. The
return journey to England was made via Jaffa, Tripoli, Marseilles,
Paris to London. Newbery had been away for eight months.

The second voyage, 1580. Newbery left England on 19 September
in an English ship bound for Tripoli. He arrived there in January
1581, and went northwards to Aleppo. Here he dressed himself as a
Mohammedan trader, provided himself with a Greek servant and on
19 March set out for the Portuguese port of Hormuz at the southern
end of the Persian Gulf. The next day he was at Bir, where he took a
boat down the Euphrates to Fallujah and thence by land to Baghdad
(15 April 1581). After staying there for nine days he went by boat
down the Tigris to Basra (May). Here he changed boats and went
down the Persian Gulf to the island of Kishm. On the way the party
was all but taken and made into slaves. From Kishm Newbery
crossed over to Hormuz, (22 June). At Hormuz he took a house and
stayed there for six weeks. The Portuguese at that time had no

objections to the English visitor, but the Venetian merchants were very jealous of him. One of them, Michael Stropene, seduced Newbery's Greek servant 'to understand my secret purposes'.

On 1 August 1581 Newbery left Hormuz and made up his mind to go home by land through Persia. He knew a little Arabic, but he had no European companion, only a servant, this time a Persian Jew. On this journey he carried with him a small stock of cloves as merchandise. On 6 September he reached Shiraz, where he spent sixteen days, and Isfahan on 4 October, where he stayed three days. He then travelled north to Kashen (12 October) and he spent more than three weeks in this important trading centre. His next move was north-west to Tabriz, where he arrived on 23 November. He left Tabriz on 1 December 1581 for Julfa, arriving eventually at Erzerum on 21 December. Here he spent Christmas and arrived at Erzingan on 3 January 1582 and Constantinople on 9 March.

Most people would have taken ship for Venice and then have travelled to England overland, but that was too easy for Newbery. He decided to go straight across Europe northwards to Dantzig on the Baltic Sea and then home by ship along the northern European coast. On 4 April 1582 he sailed into the Black Sea, where he encountered a violent storm. On 25 April he reached Reni at the mouth of the river Pruth, where he was fascinated by the methods of making caviare. On 1 May he left for Jassy, then on to Kaminietz on the Russo-Polish frontier. We know next to nothing about his journey from there to Dantzig, but we do know that he picked up a boat at Dantzig and reached London on 31 August 1582. His journey had taken all but two years. By the end of it he was the first Englishman to have travelled down the valley of the Euphrates; probably the first, certainly the second, if not the first, to set eyes on the famous depot of Hormuz; the first to cross southern Persia and to visit Shiraz and Isfahan; the first to reach Constantinople from Persia via Asia Minor: the first to sail on the Black Sea and to travel through the Danubian countries to Poland and the Baltic.

The third voyage, 1583. In the autumn of 1582 a plan was formed by the New Turkey Company (later the Levant Company) for reaching Cathay by way of Hormuz and India. Newbery was selected to lead the party and to carry letters from the Queen to the Great Mogul and to the Emperor of China. No one was better fitted for the post, for Newbery could speak Arabic, he was already on good terms with the governor of Hormuz, and his courage and business ability had been fully proved. The Hakluyts were involved in the plan and Newbery had been in correspondence with the younger Hakluyt, for he had written to him from Aleppo as 'Right wellbeloved and my assured good friend'. Hakluyt had given him a note from the writings of a Portuguese pilot, Fernando Fernandez, and a letter from Thomas Stevens to his father, containing valuable information about sailing by the Portuguese route round the Cape. Stevens was a Jesuit, which proved valuable later, for otherwise 'we might have rotten in prison' (Taylor, *Tudor Geography, 1485–1583*, p. 136). Newbery was also to find a second copy of *The Geography of Abulfeda*. He failed to find one in Syria, but he wrote hoping for success in Baghdad or Persia. Hakluyt did get a copy, probably not from Newbery.

Newbery was to lead a party of six to Baghdad: there, two were to stay with part of the stock-in-trade: the four were to go on to Basra, and there two were to stay to trade: Newbery and Ralph Fitch were then to take £300 or £400 worth of stock and 'so to go for the Indies'. There also accompanied the party a gem-polisher named William Leeds, and a painter of the name of James Story, who went at his own expense for the fun of it.

The party sailed from London in the *Tiger* on 13 February 1583 — ('Her husband's to Aleppo gone, master of the *Tiger*', Macbeth, 1.iii), but a storm drove the ship into Falmouth, and it was 11 March before they got away again. They arrived at Tripoli in Syria at the end of April, stayed there for a fortnight and then went on to Aleppo. At the end of May they set out for Baghdad, travelling to Bir on camels, by boat down the Euphrates to Felujah, then on camels by night because of the heat to Baghdad, where two of the party remained. On 6 August the rest reached Basra, where two more remained with some of the stock: Newbery and Fitch set off with £400 in goods and money, accompanied by Leeds and Story.

In mid-August they embarked at Basra for Hormuz, where they arrived on 5 September. Unluckily, there was a new Governor who knew not Newbery, and he had the party arrested and thrown into prison. This was the work of Michael Stropene, who denounced them as spies, and the Governor sent the four travellers off to Goa to be dealt with by the Viceroy (29 November 1583). Here they were interrogated to see whether they were heretics, but nothing was proved against them, and they were released on bail. It was here that Thomas Stevens came to the rescue by helping to find the surety. Story had been taken up by the Jesuits, who persuaded him to paint their church and to join their order as a probationer, and he was free as air: Newbery, Fitch and Leeds were freed on condition they did not leave Portuguese territory. They now hired a house and began to trade and felt pretty confident that all was now well. After a few months they asked that their bail should be cancelled and the money returned to them. To their surprise the Viceroy threatened them that they 'should be better sifted before it were long and that they had further matter against' them. The three of them, therefore, turned their money into jewels, left their shop open with all the goods displayed for sale and slipped away (April 1584).

Newbery led his companions into south India to Bijapur, the capital of the kingdom of that name. They moved on to Golconda, famous for its diamond mines, in order to investigate the possibilities of trading in precious metals and stones, since Leeds was an expert in these things. We know nothing of what transpired there: the next matter of interest is that they came to Agra to the Court of the great Emperor Akbar, but finding he was away at Fatehpur Sikri, they travelled twenty miles and obtained an interview with Akbar and presented Queen Elizabeth's letter. We have to deduce a personal meeting from Fitch's account of the Emperor's dress and Court, but he does not specifically state that they met the Mogul in person.

In September 1584 the trio separated: Leeds remained as an expert on jewels to the Emperor: Fitch went on down the Ganges and Newbery set off home to England to plan fresh travels. On 28 September the three parted company. Newbery on his way home met a lonely death, nobody knows where or how. He deserves a memorial.

There is no life of Newbery in the *D.N.B.* The above account owes everything to W. Foster's *England's Quest of Eastern Trade*, 1933, supplemented by E. G. R. Taylor's *Tudor Geography 1485–1583, 1930.*

RALPH FITCH (1550?–1611), traveller, was born probably in 1550. Little is known of his family or of his early life. Just before he started on his first journey in 1583 he made a will which shews him to have been a bachelor and in which he mentions a brother Thomas and a sister and niece both named Frances. He describes himself in that will as 'citizen and leatherseller of London', by which he means that he was a member of the Leathersellers' Company. Some details of his connection with the Leathersellers' Company are preserved in its records and have been printed by Sir William Foster in his *England's Quest of Eastern Trade*. But it was not until he joined Newbery's third expedition in 1583 that Fitch became important. His part in that journey will be found described in the article on NEWBERY up to the time when they parted company on 28 September 1584.

When Newbery and Fitch parted company at Fatehpur Sikri, Fitch took boat with 180 other passengers down the river Jumna to Allahabad, then down the Ganges to Benares, Patna and Tanda, a trip which took five months, during which Fitch studied with interest the search for alluvial gold at Patna and the trade in cottons, sugar and opium. From Tanda he moved northwards to Kutch Bihar, no doubt to investigate the trade from China which arrived in India via Tibet. This diversion occupied some two months or more, after which he came south again down the Ganges to Hugli, where was a Portuguese trading centre which was wholly independent of the Viceroy of Goa and which welcomed the English traveller and merchant. (For Fitch's experiences at Goa see under NEWBERY, *third voyage*.) Fitch stayed here until 28 November 1586, but he moved about visiting Kachua, Sripur and Sonargaon in Eastern Bengal. Newbery had promised 'if it pleased God, to meet me in Bengala within two years with a ship out of England'. The two years were up and there was no sign of Newbery. Fitch, therefore, embarked at Sripur in a small Portuguese ship which took him to Bassein, where he became the first Englishman to enter Burma. From Bassein he went by inland navigation of the Irrawadi delta to Syriam and thus to Pegu. Fitch made many sketches of Burmese life and he wrote a colourful description of the city and of the royal Court, including the methods used for capturing wild elephants.

From Pegu Fitch moved to Chiengmai in the Siamese Shan states, a journey of more than two hundred miles which took him twenty-five days. Here he investigated the trade from China and he found Chiengmai 'a very fair and great town, with fair houses of stone, well peopled'. This must have been late in 1587, for on 10 January

1588 he sailed from Pegu for Malacca, which he reached on 8 February. Here he remained for seven weeks, studying the trade with China and the Malayan Archipelago, until 29 March, when he set out for Martaban and back to Pegu, where he stayed until 17 September, when he took boat again for Bassein and thence to Bengal, which he reached in November 1588.

Fitch's account of his travels at this point becomes very obscure. It seems that on 3 February 1589, he shipped for Cochin on the Malabar coast in a crowded ship. The voyage was much delayed by many calms and it was made very uncomfortable by the heat and by the overcrowding, but eventually the ship arrived at Colombo in Ceylon, where five days were spent. Fitch arrived at Cochin only to find that the last boat of the season for Europe had sailed only two days before. For eight months he languished at Cochin, but at last on 2 November he secured a passage to Goa. It was a dangerous business to revisit the Viceroyalty of Goa, but Fitch took the risk and he spent three days in the city, probably in disguise. From Goa he went to Chaul, and here once again he was delayed, this time for three weeks, when he got a boat for Hormuz. Hormuz was as dangerous for him as was Goa, and he had to remain there for fifty days before he could book a passage for Basra. Somehow he managed to avoid being recognized and he got away safely.

Undaunted by his adventures, Fitch scorned to go from Basra to Aleppo by the direct route. Instead he went up the Tigris as far as Mosul, then to Mardin, Urfa and Bir. 'From Bir', he records, 'I went to Aleppo, where I stayed certain months for company, and then I went to Tripolis, where, finding English shipping, I came with a prosperous voyage to London, where, by God's assistance, I safely arrived the 29th April, 1591, having been eight years out of my native country'.

When he got home, he found that his family had given him up for dead and had already divided his estate. He set about writing an account of his journeys, but he had little skill in writing and he relied to a great extent for his descriptions of places on Thomas Hickock's English translation of Cesare Federici's *Viaggio* (published 1588). Hakluyt published Fitch's account in the second edition of his *Principal Navigations* and Purchas also used it in his *Pilgrimes*. In 1592 Fitch became a member of the newly incorporated 'Governor and Company of Merchants of the Levant'.

In August 1596 Fitch was again in Aleppo trading. His fellow-merchants made him consul, a post which he had already refused in London and which he now accepted very reluctantly. The appointment was cancelled in March 1597 by the Company, not out of dissatisfaction with Fitch, but on the grounds that the merchants in Aleppo had no right to make the appointment. Hakluyt records that Fitch was living in London in 1599. He was more than once consulted by the East India Company. In October 1611 he made a second will which was signed on 3 October and proved on the 15th, which shews that Fitch died on some day between the 3rd and the 15th. Fitch must be accounted one of the greatest of the merchant adventurers.

R Hakluyt, *Principal Navigations.*
S. Purchas, *Purchas His Pilgrimes.*
W. Foster, *England's Quest of Eastern Trade*, 1933.

DR. JOHN DEE (1527–1608), mathematician, astrologer, alchemist, was the son of Roland Dee and his wife Joanna, daughter of William Wild, and he came of a Welsh family which claimed to trace its descent back to Roderick the Great, Prince of Wales. John was educated at Chelmsford Grammar School, and in 1542 he went to St. John's College, Cambridge. He took his B.A. in 1544, became a fellow in 1545, and when in 1546 Henry VIII founded Trinity College, Dee was made one of its original fellows. In this capacity he was responsible for producing several classical plays. In one of them a man and his basket were carried up to Jupiter's palace, 'whereat was great wondering and many vain reports spread abroad of the means how that was effected'. It was thus that Dee first acquired a reputation as a conjuror and magician which was to stick to him for the rest of his life.

In 1547 Dee went to the Low Countries and brought back to England the first astronomer's staff and ring made of brass which had been designed by Gemma Frisius, Cosmographer to the Emperor Charles V, and two globes constructed by Mercator. These instruments Dee gave to Trinity College when he left Cambridge the following year to go to Louvain. Before he left, he took his M.A. degree. Dee was generally referred to as 'Doctor Dee', but where he acquired the degree is unclear; perhaps, it has been suggested, from the University of Prague as a Doctor of Medicine.

At Louvain Dee began to form a number of friendships which lasted all through his life. He was taught by all the great geographers of the time, either in person or by correspondence, by Gemma Frisius, Mercator, Pedro Nunez, Ortelius, Finaeus, and all these men became his intimate friends. Later, Dee himself became the technical instructor of all the great English seamen — Chancellor, the Boroughs, Jenkinson, Frobisher, Gilbert, Ralegh, and probably also Drake. He was the friend of Stow, Camden and especially of Richard Hakluyt the elder and the younger. He was always popular with Queen Elizabeth, and he counted among his acquaintances the Emperors Maximilian II and Rudolph, Henry II of France, and had many other friends throughout Europe.

Dee remained at Louvain until 1550, in which year he moved to Paris and there he gave by invitation a series of lectures on Euclid, the first on that subject ever to be delivered. It is likely that Dee's approach to Euclid was based rather on magic than on mathematics; Dee, according to his biographer P. J. French, was presenting himself to the Parisians as an 'Agrippan magus'. He was listened to by enormous audiences, so large that many had to listen through the windows. On his return in 1551 to England he was introduced by Sir John Cheke (Edward VI's tutor) to Cecil and by Cecil to the King, who gave him an annuity of 100 crowns, which was later exchanged for the living of Upton-on-Severn.

In 1555 he was accused of trying to take Queen Mary's life by poison or by magic, and he was for a time in prison, but eventually he was acquitted by Star Chamber of treason, but he was sent to Bonner to be examined on a charge of heresy. At last, by the special favour of Philip and Mary, Dee was given his full liberty. The originality of Dee's mind is revealed by his petition to Mary to establish a royal library and to ensure the preservation of manuscripts and of historical monuments — a petition which unhappily failed.

When Elizabeth came to the throne, Dee was taken into royal favour, partly because he selected a fit day for the coronation by means of an astrological calculation. Unfortunately for Dee the royal favour did not go beyond the promise of many lucrative preferments which were never fulfilled. In 1562 Dee went to

Antwerp to arrange for the printing of some of his writings, and he wrote to Cecil that he had bought a book called *Steganographia*, by John Trithemius, a treatise on writing in cipher, obviously a subject which would much interest Cecil. This book was also probably in part a work of Cabbalistic angel-magic, concerned with the summoning and employment of demons. The next year Dee was in Venice and probably at this time he visited the island of St. Helena.

These were busy years for Dee. In 1563 he was in Hungary and met the Emperor Maximilian II. They were also years of renewed disappointment, for in 1564 he was promised the Deanery of Gloucester, but it went to somebody else, and he only narrowly missed the Provostship of Eton College. In 1571 he was in Lorraine; on his return he explained the appearance of a new star (1572). More than once he was summoned to an interview with the Queen; more than once the Queen visited Dee at his own house. On one occasion she listened for three days to his discourses on a new comet which had terrified the court, and once he was hastily summoned to cope with a crisis of the greatest importance — a wax figure of the Queen had been found in Lincoln's Inn Fields with a pin driven into the breast. In between his travels he settled at Mortlake, where he lived from about 1570 to 1583. Here he collected around him what has been described as Elizabethan England's greatest library, especially strong in the scientific subjects.

In 1584-5 Dee was employed by the government to make calculations to show the effects on England of adopting the Gregorian calendar. He made the most exact investigations and discovered that eleven days and not ten would have to be omitted. He was prepared to compromise on ten in order to get uniformity with foreign countries, but the Church, led by Grindal, would have nothing to do with such a Papistical innovation.

At about this time Dee took to experiments in alchemy, involving gazing into a crystal, summoning spirits and recording their answers given through a medium. His interest in alchemy was part of his wider devotion to the writings of Hermes Trismegistus, the great source of Renaissance magical philosophy. Dee fell in with a scoundrel of the name of Kelly, who exploited Dee shamelessly. In 1583 the Bohemian Laski met Dee and Kelly and promised to finance them in his own country. Dee and Kelly left England on 21 September, and the mob at Mortlake broke into his house and destroyed much of his books, furniture and instruments, looking upon him as a magician. The visit to Bohemia was a failure; Dee then had an interview with the Emperor Rudolph, but Rudolph soon saw through the impostures. A similar failure attended Dee's interview with the King of Poland in 1585, and he had to leave the country as a result of protests from the Bishop of Piacenza, apostolic nuncio at the Emperor's court. In 1586 the Emperor of Russia made a handsome offer to Dee, but Dee refused it.

One of Dee's interests was a search for the philosopher's stone. He is said to have transmuted into gold a piece of metal cut from a warming-pan and to have sent to Queen Elizabeth the piece of gold together with the pan with a hole in it which exactly fitted the piece of gold. At last Kelly carried the seances with spirits too far (1587) when he declared that the angels had announced that he and Dee must have their two wives in common. Dee actually consented to this, but the arrangement not unnaturally caused violent quarrels and Kelly parted from Dee. But they kept up a correspondence for some time.

Dee's finances had fallen into chaos and he made many attempts to secure some preferment, especially the Deanery of Gloucester. At last, in 1595, he was appointed Warden of Manchester College: it is hardly surprising to hear that he got on very ill with his staff. When James I came to the throne, Dee unsuccessfully petitioned him that he might be tried and cleared of the charge of being a sorcerer (1604). Being in bad health, Dee resigned from Manchester College (1604). He was now desperately poor and had to sell his books from time to time to keep body and soul together. What his family life can have been like it is impossible to imagine. He was twice married: the first time in 1565 to Katherine Constable, the widow of a London grocer, who died in 1574: the second time to Jane, daughter of Bartholomew Fromond, in 1577, by whom he had one son and ten other children. He died in December 1608, and was buried in Mortlake church.

Dee was a prolific writer and one of the first English Diarists. Seventy-nine works by him are known, few of which were ever printed. (A list appears in the D.N.B.) He is said to have invented the phrase 'The British Empire'. Aubrey describes him as having 'a very fair clear rosy complexion; a long beard as white as milk; he was tall and slender; a very handsome man ... He wore a gown like an artist's gown, with hanging sleeves and a slit; a mighty good man he was.'

It is easy to dismiss Dee as a crank or charlatan, but he gained an international reputation in his own day. He was an expert in the sixteenth-century sciences of magic, astrology, alchemy, as well as the more mundane fields of mathematics, geography and history: a true Renaissance man.

C.F. Smith, *John Dee, 1527–1608*, 1909.

J.O. Halliwell, *The Private Diary of John Dee*, Camden Society, 1842.

E.G.R. Taylor, *Tudor Geography*, 1485–1583, 1930.

A. Ponsonby, *English Diaries*, 1923.

P.J. French, *John Dee*, 1972.

RICHARD HAKLUYT (1552/53–1616), author of *The Principal Navigations*, was born probably in 1552 or 1553. His family had been perhaps in origin Dutch, but it had been settled for centuries in Herefordshire. Richard was left an orphan and was looked after by his cousin, Richard Hakluyt the Elder, a member of the Middle Temple, well known to the Queen's statesmen, Burghley and Walsingham especially, as also to the businessmen of the City of London. His main interests were literary and intellectual and he was a friend of Ortelius and Mercator, the cosmographers, and of Dr. John Dee, the mathematician. It was at his guardian's house one day that young Richard saw lying on a table a map of the world. Richard the Elder explained the map and the developments which were taking place in geography: from that moment Richard the Younger made up his mind to devote himself to the study of geography.

Richard was educated first at Westminster School and then in 1570 he went up to Christ Church, Oxford, with a school scholarship and an exhibition from the Skinners' Company. He took his B.A. in 1574 and his M.A. in 1577. He devoted all the spare time he could find from his university curriculum to reading the travels and voyages recorded in Greek, Latin, Italian, French and Portuguese books (Spanish he seems not to have learned for a long time), and after he had taken his degrees he gave lectures on these subjects at Oxford. At some point he took holy orders and in the course of his life he held a number of preferments. In 1583 he was chaplain to Sir

Edward Stafford, brother-in-law of Lord Howard of Effingham and English Ambassador in Paris. In 1586 he was prebendary of Bristol and in 1590 he became rector of Wetheringsett in Suffolk, where most of the work on the second edition of *The Principal Navigations* was done. In 1602 he was prebendary of Westminster and in 1603 Archdeacon. He was also chaplain of the Savoy and in 1612 he held the living of Gedney in Lincolnshire. He was twice married and left one son who did him little credit. He died on 23 November 1616 and was buried in Westminster Abbey.

Hakluyt's fame rests on his books and on one book in particular. In some ways Hakluyt was a practical man rather than a man of letters, a researcher and an editor rather than an original writer. In the making of his books he had before him a very clear objective — to urge the expansion of England overseas. His earliest piece of writing was an essay (1579–80) entitled *A Discourse on the Strait of Magellan*. His object was to demonstrate how easily England could plant a self-supporting colony there which would control the gateway into the Pacific. He also urged that an expedition should be sent to search for the North-East Passage in order to open a market for English woollens and a short route to the Spice Islands. Hence the voyage by Pet and Jackman in 1580. This essay was never printed.

Hakluyt's first printed work was his *Divers Voyages to America* of 1582. This was a collection of all the documents bearing on Queen Elizabeth's title to newly discovered lands and the voyages so far made to America. The book established his place as a cosmographer and probably produced the offer of the chaplaincy to Sir Edward Stafford in Paris.

The six years in Paris revealed Hakluyt's unquenchable energy. He was tutor to Lady Sheffield's illegitimate son by the Earl of Leicester (she had since married Sir Edward Stafford): he acted as a Queen's messenger between Paris and London; he was engaged by Walsingham to discover what the French were doing in Canada, and to achieve this he would be off to St. Malo to interview sea captains who knew well the St. Lawrence and the Banks: he had an English translation made of Cartier's discoveries in Canada and he consulted Mercator on the North-West Passage. And all the time he was collecting more material for a manuscript which he wrote in 1584 entitled *A Discourse on Western Planting*. This was never printed until 1877, but copies were sent to the Queen, Walsingham and Leicester, all of whom treated it like a confidential diplomatic document. This pamphlet once again illustrated the practical side of Hakluyt, for he urged every argument for planting colonies overseas, to break the Spanish monopoly, to reinforce the naval power of England and to spread the Gospel, and he maintained that effective occupation conferred on the Queen a right to own such territories.

The defeat of the Spanish Armada roused the spirit of the English and not least the patriotism of Hakluyt. He made up his mind to produce a volume of documents devoted entirely to the exploits of the English seamen. The first edition of *The Principal Navigations* appeared in one folio volume in 1589. It was dedicated to Sir Francis Walsingham and it confined itself to voyages planned for discovery, colonization and the opening up of new trade routes. The second edition was published ten years later in three volumes, dedicated to the Lord High Admiral, Howard of Effingham. In this edition Hakluyt greatly extended the field of his researches. He set out to illustrate the whole history of English navigation, which he called 'the very walls of this our islands'. He went back to 'the learned, witty, and profound Geoffrey Chaucer'; he drew upon the antiquarians of his own day, on Camden; he included stories of warlike raids, sea fights, and especially the defeat of the Armada. Nor did he neglect foreign sources: Spain, Portugal and the Netherlands.

Professor Walter Raleigh has called Hakluyt 'the silent man, seated in the dark corner, who is content to listen and remember . . .' But Hakluyt was not content with sitting in a corner. He was up and about travelling hundreds of miles to interview some sea captain of whom by chance he had heard. He examined the records in the Tower; he talked with Don Antonio, the Portuguese Pretender; he met 'five or six of his best captains and pilots, one of whom had been born in East India'; he was in Bristol interviewing the master and master's mate of the ship *Toby*, who could give him information about Florida; he talked with Captain Muffett, an English gentleman who had been a prisoner in Spain. Friends from overseas gave him gifts of silver ore and stuffed animals. Mr. Pryhouse of Guernsey explained to him the French plans in Canada. Hakluyt was one of the greatest ransackers and pillagers of other men's memories that ever lived and we are his fortunate heirs. For down it all goes into his book, the factual information which may help later sailors:

deep-sea soundings and sailing orders; the strange sights of birds and beasts, the crocodiles and the origin of crocodile tears; the wonderful anatomy of the camel, exactly suited to its work and its surroundings; the fearful noise of whales which terrified Anthony Jenkinson; even the smells do not escape him — the soap from Benin which smelt like 'beaten violets'. Then back to the practical side of things — the best exports to take to Russia, a full description of the currency in use there. And how proud he is of the Elizabethan English people: 'What English ships did heretofore ever anchor in the mighty river of the Plate, pass and repass the impassable (in former opinion) Strait of Magellan, range along the coast of Chile, Peru, and all the backside of Nova Hispania, further than any Christian ever passed, traverse the mighty breadth of the South Seas, land upon the Luzones in despite of the enemy, enter into alliance, amity, and traffic with the princes of the Moluccas and the Isle of Java, double the famous Cape of Bona Speranza, arrive at the Isle of Santa Helena, and last of all return home most richly laden with the commodities of China, as the subjects of this now flourishing monarchy have done?' It is said that when Hakluyt died, he left enough material for a fourth volume, some of which Purchas used later in his *Pilgrimes* with less skill as an editor. What Hooker's *Ecclesiastical Polity* was to the beginnings of the Anglican Church; what Foxe's *Book of Martyrs* was to the foundations of the Protestant tradition, that Hakluyt's *Principal Navigations* was to those men who were laying the foundations of English sea power and of England's new Empire overseas.

Richard Hakluyt, *The Principal Navigations, Voyages, Traffiques and Discoveries of the English Nation*, Hakluyt Society, 1903-5.
E. G. R. Taylor, *Late Tudor and Early Stuart Geography, 1583-1650,* 1934.
Professor Walter Raleigh, *The English Voyages of the Sixteenth Century*, section II, being the introduction to the Hakluyt Society's edition of *The Principal Navigations*, 1926.
Sir Keith Feiling, *In Christ Church Hall,* 1960.
G. B. Parks, *Richard Hakluyt and the English voyages,* 1928.

WILLIAM SHAKESPEARE (1564-1616), poet and dramatist: modern research has greatly increased the evidence for the life of

Shakespeare and reasonable deductions from that evidence have further enlarged our knowledge. The following account assumes the truth of both evidence and deductions, but references are given to books which discuss fully the problems involved.

William Shakespeare was baptized in Holy Trinity church at Stratford-upon-Avon on 26 April 1564. It was usual to hurry children to baptism, because the rate of mortality among babies was so high in the sixteenth century: by convention Shakespeare's birthday is now celebrated on 23 April, but there is no evidence to justify the choice of that date or of the room now shewn to the public as the birthplace. (M. M. Reese, *Shakespeare, his world and his work*, p. 9, Chambers and Williams, *A Short Life of Shakespeare*, pp. 11 and 133.) He was the third child in the family of eight and the eldest of four sons born to John Shakespeare and Mary Arden. John was a well-to-do yeoman, a glover and curer of soft skins for gloves, at Stratford-upon-Avon, himself a native of Snitterfield who came to Stratford halfway through the sixteenth century. He became a man of much importance: he bought two houses in 1556, two more in 1575 and by 1590 he owned two contiguous houses in Henley Street. Between 1557 and 1568 he held all the chief municipal offices and reached that of Bailiff. Later he fell on evil days and declined in importance, but all the same in 1596 he was granted a coat of arms. He died in September 1601. There is no evidence to prove that the Shakespeares were either Protestant or Catholic 'recusants', but we know that William became godfather to William Walker in 1608 (and godfathers had to be sound Anglicans) and remembered him in his will ('to my godson William Walker xxs in gold'). The significance of this is discussed in a chapter entitled 'William Shakespeare, Anglican' in T. W. Baldwin's *William Shakespeare's Petty School*, 1943. (M. M. Reese, *ib*, pp. 16 *ff*.)

William's mother was Mary Arden, the youngest of eight daughters of Robert Arden of Wilmcote. She was connected with the Ardens of Park Hall; she married John in 1557 or 1558 and outlived him by seven years.

Of William's education we know nothing for certain, but the probability is that he went to the King's New School in Stratford, but there are no lists existing of these early years. Certainly at some time or other he acquired a knowledge of the usual subjects taught in the grammar schools of his day. Ben Jonson's famous tag, 'Small

Latin and less Greek' means no more than that. Judged by Jonson's own high standard of scholarship, Shakespeare was no scholar, but he was as well educated as any other boy of his standing: he learned and loved Ovid, but he does seem to have disliked the formal education of his time and it is noteworthy that the only people for whom he shews in his writings no sympathy are the schoolmasters. (M. M. Reese, *ib.* pp. 10, 389 *ff.*) It is possible, however, that he himself was a teacher in the years before he took to the theatre.

In 1582 Shakespeare was granted a licence by the Bishop of Worcester to marry Anne Whateley of Temple Grafton. Here lies a problem which has never been solved. Certain it is that William Shakespeare married 'Anne Hathwey of Stratford', though nobody knows when or where. Who then was Anne Whateley? Was she merely a clerical error in the licence? Yet, if it is easy to write Whateley for Hathwey, it is more than difficult to write Temple Grafton for Stratford. (Chambers and Williams, *Short Life of Shakespeare*, pp. 16–17, 140-2.)

Anne Hathaway of Shottery was 26 when she married Shakespeare, eight years older than her husband, and she was already pregnant. A daughter Susanna was baptized on 26 May 1583, and on 2 February 1585 were baptized the twins, Hamnet and Judith. There is no convincing evidence that the marriage was an unhappy one, but if we may judge from the frequent allusions throughout his plays, Shakespeare seems to have held strongly that wedlock must be sanctioned by the Church. (M. M. Reese, *ib.*, pp. 28-31.)

By 1592 Shakespeare was in London. We do not know why he left Stratford. The legend, as now presented, that he made Stratford too hot to hold him by poaching Sir Thomas Lucy's deer in Charlecote Park will not stand up to detailed examination, even if there may be a grain of truth in the episode (M. M. Reese, *ib.* pp. 31-4.) The fact remains that Shakespeare was in London by 1592, and he was a professional actor with one, but we know not which, of the 'Companies' of actors. It is possible that he may have begun his theatrical life with Alleyn's Company, if the story is true that he started his career by holding gentlemen's horses at the playhouse door, for the only theatres to be reached by horseback were The Theatre and The Curtain, both of which were in the hands of Alleyn in 1590–1. By 1592 Shakespeare was successful enough to arouse the jealousy and anger of Greene, who attacked him as 'an upstart

Crow, beautified with our feathers'. It is possible that Shakespeare was writing plays for more than one Company between 1592 and 1594, but by 1594 he was a full member of the Lord Chamberlain's Men, with whom he was to spend the rest of his professional life.

Shakespeare was living in London in St. Helen's, Bishopsgate, and the probability is that he had his wife and family with him. In 1596 one of the twins, Hamnet, died and Shakespeare may well have thought that he would move his family to Stratford to avoid the dangers to health in London. Certainly the next year he bought New Place, the best house in Stratford, to provide a home for his wife and daughters. He himself moved from Bishopsgate to Bankside. At this time he was closely associated with Francis Langley, owner of the new Swan theatre in Paris Garden in Southwark, and it is possible that his Company was then playing at the Swan. Shakespeare and Langley became involved in a violent quarrel with the notorious Justice of the Peace, William Gardiner, a Puritan who was opposed to play-acting, and Shakespeare was bound over to keep the peace. (Hotson, *Shakespeare versus Shallow*.) From 1596 onwards Shakespeare visited Stratford more frequently and for longer periods, nor was New Place the only property he bought. It is clear that Shakespeare was making a good deal of money and he gradually became the largest property holder in Stratford.

In 1601 his father died and left Shakespeare the houses in Henley Street, which he let. He bought 107 acres of land and a cottage and garden in Chapel Lane. In 1605 he bought for £440 a thirty-two year lease of tithes in Stratford and nearby villages, and for the last ten years of his life Shakespeare was the outstanding citizen in Stratford.

He was in London in 1612, 1613 and 1614, and at some point he moved his London lodgings to Silver Street in Cripplegate. In 1613 he bought the gatehouse of the Blackfriars Priory for £140 as an investment. In that year his last play, *Henry VIII*, was produced at the Globe Theatre in June. Tradition has it that he himself spoke the Prologue, so that he would have been present at the fire which destroyed the Globe during that first performance. There is no one moment when Shakespeare retired from the theatre: rather he spent more and more time at Stratford and gradually gave up his theatrical work in London.

In 1608 Shakespeare's mother died. The year before his daughter,

Susanna, had married Dr. John Hall, but unhappily there was only one child, a daughter. He made his will in either 1615 or 1616, and that will has become famous for the clause in it by which he left to his wife Anne 'my second-best bed with furniture' — the only mention of his wife in his will. This is no proof of a lack of affection on Shakespeare's part: rather it suggests that he knew that in his happy and united family he could take it for granted that Anne would be properly looked after at New Place to the end of her life. The greater part of his estate went to Susanna, for it is clear that Shakespeare wanted most of his property to pass undivided and to remain within the family. Wealthy widows did not long remain widows in the sixteenth century. Their new husbands saw that they took their wealth with them.

Shakespeare died (tradition has it) on his birthday, 23 April 1616. He lies buried in the chancel in front of the altar in Holy Trinity Church, Stratford-upon-Avon.

Lack of space forbids any discussion here of the many problems which surround the dates of composition of the plays.

The generally accepted chronology of his plays is as follows: 1590–1, 2 Henry VI and 3 Henry VI; 1591–2, 1 Henry VI; 1592–3, Richard III and The Comedy of Errors; 1593–4, Titus Andronicus and The Taming of the Shrew; 1594–5, Two Gentlemen of Verona, Love's Labour's Lost and Romeo and Juliet; 1595–6, Richard II and A Midsummer Night's Dream; 1596–7, King John and The Merchant of Venice; 1597–8, 1 Henry IV and 2 Henry IV; 1598–9, Much ado about Nothing and Henry V; 1599–1600, Julius Caesar, As You Like It and Twelfth Night; 1600–1, Hamlet and The Merry Wives of Windsor; 1601–2, Troilus and Cressida; 1602–3, All's Well That Ends Well; 1604–5, Measure for Measure and Othello; 1605–6, King Lear and Macbeth; 1606–7, Antony and Cleopatra; 1607–8, Coriolanus and Timon of Athens; 1608–9, Pericles; 1609–10, Cymbeline; 1610–11, The Winter's Tale; 1611–12, The Tempest; 1612–13, Henry VIII, perhaps part of The Two Noble Kinsmen.

Shakespeare also wrote the poems Venus and Adonis (1592–3); The Rape of Lucrece (1593–4); The Sonnets (1595–9); The Phoenix and The Turtle (1600).

Equally, it is not possible here to discuss the problem of the Sonnets, which were published by a piratical printer in 1609. Who was the 'Mr. W.H.' to whom the sonnets were dedicated? Was it

Shakespeare's patron, the Earl of Southampton? Was it William Herbert, son and heir of the Earl of Pembroke? Was it the printer, William Hall? Who was the Dark Lady?

Many thorny problems surround the dates when the plays were published. By the end of Elizabeth's reign fifteen Shakespearean texts had appeared, of which six, (perhaps seven) were 'bad' quartos: of eight the original texts were 'good' quartos. Not much more printing was done before the issue of the First Folio in 1623 by Heminges and Condell, which covered eighteen of the nineteen plays already issued in quarto. *Pericles* was omitted. The Second Folio was printed in 1632, the Third Folio in 1663 (a second issue of 1664 included *Pericles* and one or two plays not by Shakespeare). The Fourth Folio was printed in 1685. It is one of the tragedies of English literature that not a single manuscript of Shakespeare's work remains to us. The only handwriting of his which we possess is to be found in six signatures (to one are appended the words 'by me'), three of which are on his will. It is possible that in the manuscript play, *Sir Thomas More*, one page is in the handwriting of Shakespeare.

Shakespeare's tremendous success arose from the fact that he combined in himself three roles — he was a poet, a playwright and an actor: up to his time the theatre had never known such a trinity in unity. Shakespeare created the theatre as we understand that word. But Shakespeare was first and foremost a poet, before he was a playwright or an actor. We know nothing about his ability as an actor, but he understood the professional needs of the theatre, because he lived with, acted with and wrote for actors — not actresses, because feminine parts were then played by boys. His dramatic work was at first conditioned by the literary conventions of his times — the classical imagery, the use of the soliloquy, the affectations of speech which appear, notably, in the verbal agility in punning. He was also governed by the general views of his time on the nature and purpose of Man, the supernatural, etc. What raises Shakespeare far above all his contemporaries is his ability to emancipate himself from these conventions and yet to transmute them by his own genius to his own use. Shakespeare was a poet who for his living had to write plays. Because he was a poet, and one of the greatest, he could not but produce dramatic poetry: his triumph was that he gave to the theatre poetic drama — every dramatic thought, every dramatic situation was to be presented in the imagery of poetry. (Spurgeon, *Shakespeare's Imagery*: H. Morris, *Elizabethan Literature*, pp. 205 *sqq.*)

Two other points have to be remembered: Shakespeare was never an entirely free agent, for he had to provide suitable parts for the actors in the Company, and also he had to provide the right sort of play for the audience which was going to hear it. A play which would score a success at The Theatre in Finsbury Fields might offend the public at the Globe on the South Bank: a royal command to perform in front of the Queen or a private performance at a nobleman's house would demand a totally different sort of play. (Milton Holmes, *Shakespeare's Public.*)

What sort of a man was this William Shakespeare? 'Without a single dissentient voice his contemporaries testify to his sweetness, gentleness, honesty and "civil demeanour": no famous man has had so little evil spoken of him'. (M. M. R. *ib.*, pp. 381, *seqq.*) And, indeed, the width of his sympathy with every sort of human being (except schoolmasters) stands out in all his writings. To him evil is detestable, but the evil doer is an object of compassion, except where the criminal has given himself over to evil, as in Iago. Nothing is more moving in Shakespeare's plays than the defence by Costard of Sir Nathaniel in *Love's Labour's Lost* (Act. V, sc. ii, 569) — and Sir Nathaniel was a schoolmaster. Shakespeare is the most merciful of all the great men. Ben Jonson called him 'my gentle Shakespeare' and 'my beloved author'; 'I lov'd the man, and do honour his memory (on this side Idolatry) as much as any. He was indeed honest and of an open and free nature: had an excellent Phantasy: brave notions and gentle expressions.' In his last years Shakespeare became the best known figure and the most popular in Stratford, so that he was welcome in many homes and welcomed many to his own New Place. Down the centuries and across the continents his name glows ever brighter, so that perhaps Carlyle's claim is no empty boast, 'he is the grandest thing we have yet done'.

There is no authentic portrait of Shakespeare. On the chancel wall in the Stratford church stands a bust, the work of Gheerart Janssen, commissioned and completed a few years after Shakespeare's death, but it is to be hoped that this dull and heavy work reinforces Shakespeare's own verdict, 'there's no art To find the mind's construction in the face'. In the First Folio there was printed a drawing by Martin Droeshout, a Dutch engraver, but as he was only fifteen years old when Shakespeare died he must have copied another picture. The painting now at Stratford was copied from the engraving.

E.K. Chambers & C. Williams, *A Short Life of Shakespeare*, 1933.

M.M. Reese, *Shakespeare, His World and his Work*, 1953.

Lamborn & Harrison, *Shakespeare, The Man & His Stage*, 1924.

Milton Holmes, *Shakespeare's Public*, 1960.

Granville-Barker & G.B. Harrison, *A Companion to Shakespeare Studies*, 1934.

Ivor Brown, *Shakespeare*, 1949.

M.C. Bradbrook, *Shakespeare: the Poet in his World*, 1978.

S. Schoenbaum, *William Shakespeare*, 1977.

HANS HOLBEIN [the younger] (1497–1543), was born at Augsburg in 1497, the son of Hans Holbein the Elder, a painter. He died in London in 1543. We are concerned here only with his life and work in England. He came to England on a first visit from Basle in 1526, driven out by the effects of the Reformation which were making painting there less and less profitable. His friend Erasmus gave him a letter of introduction to Sir Thomas More. During the eighteen months he spent in England he devoted himself wholly to portraiture. There survive of his paintings at this time his 'Archbishop Warham' 1527 (Louvre); 'Sir Thomas More' 1527 (Frick Gallery, New York); 'John and Thomas Godsalve' 1528 (Dresden); 'Niklaus Kratzer' 1528 (Louvre). His greatest work was a group of Sir Thomas More and his family. The original has not survived, but there is at Basle a drawing for the picture and at Windsor drawings for seven of the heads.

In 1528 he went back to Basle, but he returned to England in 1532 and spent the rest of his life here. The first circle from whom he found patrons was that of the merchants of the Hansa steelyard in London, and in 1532 and 1533 he painted many of these prosperous gentlemen in their flat velvet hats. Of these portraits the most famous is 'The Ambassadors', now in the National Gallery. By the end of 1533 he was working for Henry VIII and his courtiers. The portrait of Thomas Cromwell, 1533 (Frick Gallery) was the first in this series; in 1536 he painted Jane Seymour (Vienna), after which he was officially employed by the King. In 1537 he was commissioned to paint a fresco on the wall of the Privy Chamber in the Palace of Whitehall of Henry VIII and Jane Seymour with Henry VII and his wife, Elizabeth of York. The original was destroyed in the fire of 1698, but part of the cartoon for the painting survived and is now in the National Portrait Gallery, London. Only one other portrait of Henry VIII is accepted as indubitably by Holbein, in the Thyssen collection at Lugano. The well-known portraits of Henry VIII at Rome, Belvoir, Liverpool, Warwick and Castle Howard are not now generally accepted as being by Holbein. There is at Windsor a grisaille miniature on vellum, 'Solomon and the Queen of Sheba', in which Solomon is personified by Henry VIII. During these years Holbein was also used by the King to travel abroad and paint portraits of possible wives for Henry. Examples of these are the 'Anne, Duchess of Milan' 1538 (National Gallery) and the 'Anne of Cleves' 1539 (Louvre).

Much of his time was occupied in painting the courtiers. Of this work Windsor Castle possesses the splendid collection of drawings which, in spite of damage and attempts at restorations by later and lesser artists, still reveal to us the men and women of the sixteenth century.

Holbein was perhaps the greatest of all portrait painters certainly he was the greatest of all painters in miniature. He also illustrated books and painted religious subjects, made designs for buildings and for glass, and drew also settings for jewels which appear in many of his portraits.

Hans Reinhardt, *Holbein.*
K. T. Parker, *The Drawings of Holbein at Windsor Castle.*

NICHOLAS HILLIARD (*c.* 1547–1619), miniaturist, 'is the central artistic figure of the Elizabethan age, the only English painter whose work reflects ... the world of Shakespeare's earlier plays' (Waterhouse). The art of painting in miniature was known in the sixteenth century as 'limning'; Hilliard at some unknown date was appointed limner and goldsmith — for he was also a worker in gold and in jewels — to Queen Elizabeth I. Hilliard's right to make small portraits of the Queen in limning probably dates from before 1572. It is possible that he made a miniature of Lady Arabella Stuart for the Duke of Parma at the time when the Catholics were proposing that these two should marry, but the miniature does not now exist. It was Hilliard who designed and executed Queen Elizabeth's second Great Seal, in 1584. He was friends with Sir Philip Sidney and Sir Christopher Hatton, and from time to time he received large grants of money. All the same, he was frequently in financial difficulties. James I carried on Elizabeth's patronage, but in 1617 Hilliard was imprisoned in Ludgate for debt, and he died two years later. His character is best revealed in his *Treatise concerning the Arte of Limning*, which he published in 1600, where he appears as a gentle, kindly, artistic gentleman, devoted to his art and a great admirer of the English race: 'Rare beauties are . . . more commonly found in this isle of England than elsewhere.' Hilliard interprets the English of the sixteenth century with complete understanding and sympathy. He must be looked on as one of the leaders of the English Renaissance.

E. Waterhouse, *Painting in Britain, 1530–1790.*
C. Winter, *Elizabethan Miniatures*, 1943.
M. Edmond, *Hilliard and Oliver*, 1983.

CAPTAIN JOHN DAVIS or DAVYS (1543–1605), navigator and explorer, was born in 1543 at Sandridge Barton, near Dartmouth in Devon, and he died at sea in 1605. He was born the son of a yeoman farmer, and little is known of his early days. The first mention of him occurs in the diary of John Dee, the magician, in 1579, and again in 1583. Dee met Davis to discuss expeditions to discover Northern routes to the Indies. In 1584 Adrian Gilbert organized an expedition to find the North-West Passage to China sailed in 1585 under the command of John Davis. The voyage was financed mainly by London merchants and those in the west country, especially by William Sanderson, who became a close friend and unfailing supporter of Davis in all his northern voyages. Davis must by this time have been an experienced seaman and a competent surveyor for on this voyage he 'platted' the exact position of islands, rocks and harbours 'with lines and scales thereunto convenient'.

This first voyage lasted from June 1585 to the end of September. Davis reached the east coast of Greenland and went up Cumberland Gulf in Baffin Island, naming the prominent places after his friends and places at home — Mount Ralegh, Cape Walsingham, Gilbert Sound, Totnes Road, Exeter Sound.

His second expedition was subscribed chiefly by west country-men. It sailed from Dartmouth on 7 May 1586, Davis taking with him the *Mermaid* and the *Moonshine*. He sailed in the same direction as on the previous voyage, reaching Baffin Island and then turning South. He met many Eskimos who were very friendly, but who proved great thieves and skilful wrestlers. Davis soon sent the *Mermaid* home and went on himself in the *Moonshine* westwards to Labrador, where he caught an immense amount of cod, which he salted and took home. In October he joined up with the *Sunshine*, which he had previously sent to explore the east coast of Greenland. Both ships were back in the Thames in October. The profits from this voyage were small, and a bale of cloth was lost, which so seriously disturbed the west country merchants that they declined to take shares in the next expedition.

The third voyage (May to September 1587) consisted of three ships, the *Elizabeth* from Dartmouth, the *Sunshine* and a small pinnace of about 20 tons. Davis elected to sail in the pinnace, the *Ellen*, as it was handier for dealing with ice. He intended to explore in this small vessel, while the other two ships were to go to the cod fishing grounds. The fleet arrived in Gilbert Sound in June 1587. The two fishing ships separated from the *Ellen* in September and Davis sailed north along the Greenland coast as far as latitude 72 degrees 46 minutes. He named the most northerly point in Green-land that he reached Sanderson's Hope, then he turned west and then south to rejoin the fishing ships, but they had broken their promise and had gone back to England sixteen days after leaving Davis.

Davis had failed to find the North-West Passage, but that was not his fault, as years later, in 1616, William Baffin explained. The voyage had been a very daring one, demanding extreme skill and high seamanship. Davis had to meet a good deal of criticism, to answer which he produced in 1595 his *World's Hydrographical Description*. His own account of this voyage became a guide to later navigators, and there is no doubt that it was thanks to what Davis had accomplished that Hudson was able to reach Hudson Strait. Davis also produced his *Traverse Book* (1587), which became the model for all future log books. Davis had also now to reconcile his discoveries with the previous work of Frobisher and with the old

Zeno map of the Arctic regions published in 1558. He made a large scale map to show his voyages, but this has been lost. He also delineated his results on the Molyneux globe which is now in the Middle Temple Library (for full description, see A. H. Markham, *The Voyages and Works of John Davis*, pp. xxxiii, *f.*). His voyages are also recorded on what Shakespeare called 'the new map' of the world prepared by Edward Wright, the first map to be drawn on the projection discovered by him but erroneously attributed to Mercator.

Davis's next employment was with Cumberland's squadron off the Azores in 1589. He was captain of the *Desire* in Cavendish's expedition to the South Sea in 1591, a voyage he undertook because he was eager to sail round America and because Cavendish promised him a bark to explore for the North-West Passage on the Pacific side of America. The voyage was a disaster: Davis and Cavendish lost touch with each other in bad weather, and Cavendish, who died on the way home, accused Davis of deliberately deserting him — a false accusation, for Davis three times tried to break into the Pacific through the Straits of Magellan and three times was driven back by storms. He then went to the rendezvous at Port Desire on the east coast of Patagonia, but Cavendish was not there, and Davis was compelled to sail home (June 1593). Out of the 76 men who started out with him only 15 got home. On this voyage Davis discovered the Falkland Islands. The claim to have done this was made by Sir Richard Hawkins, but he arrived there only in 1594.

In 1594 Davis produced his *Seaman's Secrets*, a practical guide for sailors, providing from his own experience all the scientific knowledge necessary for successful navigation. He had also invented the backstaff, an improvement on the old cross-staff, an instrument for calculating the altitude of the heavenly bodies.

In 1596 and 1597 Davis was probably with Essex at Cadiz and the Azores. 1598 saw him in service with the Dutch on a voyage to the East Indies — a disastrous voyage, the only account of which was written by Davis and published later by Purchas in his *Pilgrimes*. The Dutch historian, de Jonge, falsely accused Davis of being an English spy and ruining the voyage, whereas in fact Davis did yeoman service as chief pilot.

In 1600 Davis again joined a Dutch expedition, and then in 1601 he was Pilot Major on the *Red Dragon*, Lancaster's ship in the first expedition sent out by the East India Company. He was home in 1603 and the next year he sailed with Sir Edward Michelbourne in the second venture of the East India Company. He went in the *Tiger* from Cowes in December 1604. The fleet fell in with some Japanese pirates near Bantam who accepted English hospitality and then treacherously attacked the crews. Davis was murdered and died on 29 or 30 December 1605.

John Davis was one of the greatest of English seamen. Not such a notable fighting sailor, strategist and tactician as Drake, not such an able administrator as Hawkins, not such a glamorous figure as Grenville, he was yet as tough and enduring an explorer as Frobisher, as great a seaman and as beloved by his men as were Drake and Hawkins, and he possessed an inventive genius and a scientific knowledge which none of his predecessors could claim. And he, a Puritan, had something else, too — a mystic and fanatical faith in the destiny of the English people: 'There is no doubt but that we of England are this saved people, by the eternal and infallible presence of the Lord predestinated to be sent unto these Gentiles in the sea, to those Islands and famous Kingdoms, there to preach the peace of the Lord: for are not we only set upon Mount Zion to give light to the rest of the world? Have not we the true handmaid of the Lord to rule us, unto whom the eternal majesty of God hath revealed his truth and supreme power of Excellency? ... It is only we, therefore, that must be these shining messengers of the Lord, and none but we.' (Hakluyt, *Principal Navigations*, Hakluyt Society, 1905, xii, 32, n.1.)

Capt. A.H.Markham, R.N., *The Voyages and Works of John Davis*, Hakluyt Society, 1880.

Walter Raleigh, *The English Voyages of the Sixteenth Century*, 1926.

S.E. Morison, *The Great Explorers*, 1978.

GLOSSARY

Anabaptist. A comprehensive word to cover various sects on the Continent which denied the validity of infant baptism. They were hated and persecuted by both Catholics and Protestants in the sixteenth century, because they took literally the New Testament on communism, pacifism, etc.

Anti-Clericalism. Hostility felt by the laity for the clergy.

Attainder. The usual method adopted by the Tudors for getting rid of inconvenient or unwanted persons: an Act of Parliament which authorized execution without any trial. The heirs of an attainted noble lost the title and possessions.

Austin Friars. An older English form of the word 'Augustinian'.

Auto-da-Fe (act of faith). The ceremony under the Spanish Inquisition at which heretics underwent the sentences passed on them: used specially to mean the burning of convicted heretics.

Benevolence. The free or so-called free gifts made by the wealthier people to the Crown: made illegal by Richard III, reappeared under Henry VII and Henry VIII, not used by Elizabeth, unless perhaps in 1568 at the expense of the clergy.

Calvinism. That form of Protestantism set up by Calvin at Geneva, denying Free Will, asserting Predestination, rejecting Bishops and Transubstantiation: the sort of Church which Presbyterians wanted in England, because (they claimed) it alone had scriptural warrant.

Convocation. The general assembly of the clergy of England.

Council, General. Assemblies of the clergy of the Catholic Church throughout the world, whose decisions were regarded as binding on all Christians.

Council of Trent. A meeting of the General Council at Trent in 1545 to 1563 to counter the growth of Protestantism and to make reforms in the Catholic Church. It launched the Counter-Reformation against Protestantism.

Court of Arches. The Archbishop's court held at the church of St. Mary-le-Bow (*i.e.*, St. Mary of the Arches, *de arcubus*), so called because the church was built on arches or 'bows' above the marshy ground: heard appeals from diocesan courts and grew into a court of first instance.

Courts of Audience. Archiepiscopal courts of appeal.

Court of Augmentations. Established by Act of Parliament in 1536 to

467

administer the transfer of ecclesiastical lands to the Crown at the dissolution of the monasteries.

Court of Chancery. A court of law presided over by the Lord Chancellor, which dispensed a form of law that came to be known as Equity.

Court of Star Chamber. The King's Council sitting as a court in the old starred chamber and exercising the old judicial authority of the Council. It did not arise out of any Act of Parliament. It greatly increased in activity and importance under Wolsey. Most of the cases dealt with were between private individuals, only occasionally on Crown matters. (Elton, *Tudor Constitution,* pp. 158 ff.)

Court of Wards. Established by statute by Henry VIII in 1540 to safeguard the Crown's financial interests in the royal wards and the administration of their lands, their marriages, etc. (Hurstfield, *The Queen's Wards.*)

Erastian. The subordination of the Church to the State: derived from Thomas Erastus (1524–1583), a German who was not himself an Erastian. (Figgis, *The Divine Right of Kings.*)

Golden Rose. An ornament in the shape of a rose of gold and jewels, blessed by the Pope on the 4th Sunday in Lent and then presented by him as a mark of special favour to an individual or a community.

Hanaper. The financial department of Chancery responsible for collecting the fees due to the Crown upon the issue of any writs or letters patent.

Humanist. In the sixteenth century anyone who studied Greek and Latin literature in the original and who held the cultural and educational ideals associated with the movement we call the Renaissance.

The Index (*index librorum prohibitorum*). The list of books prohibited by the Papacy which members of the Catholic Church were and are forbidden to read or to possess. Started by Paul IV in 1557.

King de Facto. The actually ruling king.

King de Jure. The legal king by lineal descent, though not necessarily the ruling king.

Knight Banneret. Degree of knighthood superior to that of knight-bachelor, distinguishable by the square banner he carried in place of the pointed pennon. Awarded for bravery in the field. Ranked before all other knights except those of the Garter. Now extinct.

Legatus a Latere. A papal plenipotentiary whose commands could be resisted only by appeal to the Pope: usually appointed for a particular and temporary purpose. Wolsey was appointed with Campeggio in 1518 to preach a crusade and was continued in office with wide powers.

Letters of Marque. Authority issued by a ruler or a claimant to a throne (*e.g.,* Don Antonio of Portugal) to a shipmaster to prey upon the merchant shipping of the king's enemies. Often issued in times of peace to enable the holder to recover what he had lost in some previous attack, either from the same attacker or from any of his countrymen.

Lord High Steward. In the sixteenth century purely a ceremonial office. Originally a household official who ordered the King's meals.

Lutheranism. That form of Protestantism evolved by Martin Luther of which the chief characteristic was that a man is justified by faith alone and not by good works.

Master of the Rolls. Originally the keeper of the rolls of Chancery, the administrative records of that office. By Tudor times the work was more legal than administrative.

Misprision of Treason. Knowing that treason is being plotted and not revealing it: having some hand, but only an indirect one, in treason.

Pentateuch. The five books of Moses — Genesis, Exodus, Leviticus, Numbers, Deuteronomy.

Peter's Pence. A very ancient tax which by the sixteenth century had amounted to £200 paid annually by English bishops to the Pope. The tax was profitable to the bishops, because they collected the sum from their dioceses, but more than was needed, and kept the surplus. Payment to Rome was abolished by Act of Parliament in 1534, when Henry VIII broke with Rome, but Henry took the tax.

Piracy. Unlicensed robbery at sea by men without letters of marque.

Pluralist. An ecclesiastic who held more than one church office or living and thereby increased his income.

Praemunire. A series of Acts passed between 1353 and 1393 to protect the king's rights against foreign, especially papal, interference in ecclesiastical property or jurisdiction. Extended later to protect the lay courts against the ecclesiastical courts.

Prebend (*praebere*, to provide). One who draws an income from a cathedral in return for a limited amount of service (adj. prebendary).

Privateering. Licensed robbery at sea by men carrying letters of marque.

Puritanism. A word which covers three groups of people who wanted the Church to be 'purified': (1) the Presbyterians who wanted to reconstruct the Church on the lines of the Geneva model of Calvin and to do away with bishops and the royal supremacy; (2) the separatists or sectarians, who would abolish any form of national church and allow freedom of worship and organization to individual congregations, electing their own ministers; (3) the moderates, who wanted changes in ritual and worship, but did not worry much about the government of the Church.

Sacramentaries. The name given by Luther to those who held that the bread and wine in the Communion service are the Body and Blood of Christ only in a purely symbolical sense; then used of all who denied the Real Presence.

Seminary. Used especially of the English theological colleges established on the Continent (Douai, Rome) to plant the seed (*semen*) of Roman Catholicism in Englishmen with a view to their returning to England to save and spread Catholicism there.

St. Paul's Cross. A pulpit in the N.E. corner of the Close of St. Paul's Cathedral, which formed a national centre for sermons and disputations usually arranged by the government for purposes of propaganda.

Subsidy. A tax mde by Parliament to increase the sum produced by the Tenth and the Fifteenth: became fixed at 4s. in the £ on the annual value of land, and 2s. 8d. in the £ on the annual value of goods. No one paid on both. Usually under-assessed by local assessors who would not return the true value of their own and their friends' wealth.

Tenth and Fifteenth. The normal Parliamentary taxation on landed property. Towns represented in Parliament paid a tenth, others a fifteenth.

Transubstantiation. The Catholic belief that after the prayer of consecration in the Communion service the bread and the wine cease to be bread and wine except in appearance and become the real body and blood of Christ.

Visitations. Periodical inspections of his diocese by the bishop: metropolitical visitation, inspection of every diocese by the Archbishop of the Province — Canterbury or York.

Warden of the Cinque Ports. The governor of the five ports of Hastings, Romney, Hythe, Dover and Sandwich, to which were added Winchelsea and Rye. Allowed to deduct £500 from their share of any Tenth or Fifteenth levied on Sussex or Kent, a privilege confirmed to them by Elizabeth as a reward for their services against the Armada.

Zwinglianism. That form of Protestantism evolved in Zurich by Zwingli of which the chief characteristic was that he denied any form of corporeal presence in the Eucharist. He regarded the Eucharist as purely symbolic.

INDEX